DEPARTMENT OF PUBLIC INFORMATION

Basic Facts

About the United Nations

**United Nations,
New York, 2004**

341.23

Published by the News and Media Division
United Nations Department of Public Information
New York, NY 10017
www.un.org

Note: Data current as of December 2003, unless otherwise stated

ISBN: 92-1-100936-7
United Nations Publication
Sales No. E.04.I.7
Copyright © 2004 United Nations

CONTENTS

Chapter 3: Economic and Social Development 139

Chapter 4: Human Rights 225

Chapter 5: Humanitarian Action 251

Chapter 6: International Law 265

Charts and maps

UNITED NATIONS WEBSITES

United Nations: *www.un.org*

United Nations system: *www.unsystem.org*

United Nations Programmes and Offices:

International Trade Center (UNCTAD/WTO): *www.intracen.org*

Joint United Nations Programme on HIV/AIDS: *www.unaids.org*

United Nations Children's Fund (UNICEF): *www.unicef.org*

United Nations Conference on Trade and Development (UNCTAD): *www.unctad.org*

United Nations Development Fund for Women (UNIFEM): *www.unifem.org*

United Nations Development Programme (UNDP): *www.undp.org*

United Nations Environment Programme (UNEP): *www.unep.org*

United Nations High Commissioner for Human Rights: *www.unhchr.ch*

United Nations High Commissioner for Refugees (UNHCR): *www.unhcr.ch*

United Nations Human Settlements Programme (UN-HABITAT): *www.unhabitat.org*

United Nations Institute for Disarmament Research (UNIDIR): *www.unidir.org*

United Nations Institute for Training and Research (UNITAR): *www.unitar.org*

United Nations International Research and Training Institute for the Advancement of Women (INSTRAW): *www.un-instraw.org*

United Nations Interregional Crime and Justice Research Institute (UNICRI): *www.unicri.it*

United Nations Office for Project Services (UNOPS): *www.unops.org*

United Nations Office on Drugs and Crime (UNODC): *www.unodc.org*

United Nations Population Fund (UNFPA): *www.unfpa.org*

United Nations Relief and Works Agency for Palestine Refugees in the Near East (UNRWA): *www.unrwa.org*

United Nations Research Institute for Social Development (UNRISD): *www.unrisd.org*

United Nations System Staff College (UNSSC): *www.unssc.org*

United Nations University (UNU): *www.unu.edu*

United Nations Volunteers (UNV): *www.unv.org*

World Food Programme (WFP): *www.wfp.org*

United Nations Regional Commissions:

Economic Commission for Africa (ECA): *www.uneca.org*

Economic Commission for Asia and the Pacific (ESCAP): *www.unescap.org*

Economic Commission for Europe (ECE): *www.unece.org*

Economic Commission for Latin America and the Caribbean (ECLAC):
  www.eclac.org

Economic Commission for Western Asia (ESCWA): *www.escwa.org.lb*

United Nations Specialized Agencies:

Food and Agriculture Organization of the United Nations (FAO): *www.fao.org*

International Civil Aviation Organization (ICAO): *www.icao.org*

International Fund for Agricultural Development (IFAD): *www.ifad.org*

International Labour Organization (ILO): *www.ilo.org*

International Maritime Organization (IMO): *www.imo.org*

International Monetary Fund (IMF): *www.imf.org*

International Telecommunication Union (ITU): *www.itu.int*

United Nations Educational, Scientific and Cultural Organization (UNESCO):
  www.unesco.org

United Nations Industrial Development Organization (UNIDO): *www.unido.org*

Universal Postal Union (UPU): *www.upu.int*

The World Bank Group: *www.worldbank.org*

World Health Organization (WHO): *www.who.int*

World Intellectual Property Organization (WIPO): *www.wipo.int*

World Meteorological Organization (WMO): *www.wmo.ch*

World Tourism Organization (WTO): *www.world-tourism.org*

Related Organizations:

International Atomic Energy Agency (IAEA): *www.iaea.org*

Organization for the Prohibition of Chemical Weapons (OPCW): *www.opcw.org*

Preparatory Committee for the Nuclear-Test-Ban Treaty Organization (CTBTO):
  www.ctbto.org

World Trade Organization (WTO): *www.wto.org*

LIST OF ACRONYMS

CEB	United Nations System Chief Executives Board for Coordination
CTBTO	Preparatory Committee for the Nuclear-Test-Ban Treaty Organization
DDA	Department for Disarmament Affairs
DESA	Department of Economic and Social Affairs
DGACM	Department of General Assembly and Conference Management
DM	Department of Management
DPA	Department of Political Affairs
DPI	Department of Public Information
DPKO	Department of Peacekeeping Operations
ECA	Economic Commission for Africa
ECE	Economic Commission for Europe
ECLAC	Economic Commission for Latin America and the Caribbean
ECOSOC	Economic and Social Council
EOSG	Executive Office of the Secretary-General
ESCAP	Economic and Social Commission for Asia and the Pacific
ESCWA	Economic and Social Commission for Western Asia
FAO	Food and Agriculture Organization of the United Nations
IAEA	International Atomic Energy Agency
IBRD	International Bank for Reconstruction and Development (World Bank)
ICAO	International Civil Aviation Organization
ICJ	International Court of Justice
ICRC	International Committee of the Red Cross
ICSID	International Centre for Settlement of Investment Disputes (World Bank Group)
IDA	International Development Association (World Bank Group)
IFAD	International Fund for Agricultural Development
IFC	International Finance Corporation (World Bank Group)
ILO	International Labour Organization
IMF	International Monetary Fund
IMO	International Maritime Organization
INSTRAW	International Research and Training Institute for the Advancement of Women
ITC	International Trade Centre UNCTAD/WTO
ITU	International Telecommunication Union
MIGA	Multilateral Investment Guarantee Agency (World Bank Group)
NGLS	United Nations Non-Governmental Liaison Service
NGOs	Non-governmental organizations
OCHA	Office for the Coordination of Humanitarian Affairs
OHCHR	Office of the United Nations High Commissioner for Human Rights

OHRLLS	Office of the High Representative for the Least Developed Countries, Landlocked Developing Countries and Small Island Developing States
OIOS	Office of Internal Oversight Services
OLA	Office of Legal Affairs
OPCW	Organization for the Prohibition of Chemical Weapons
PFII	Permanent Forum on Indigenous Issues
UNAIDS	Joint United Nations Programme on HIV/AIDS
UNCTAD	United Nations Conference on Trade and Development
UNDP	United Nations Development Programme
UNEP	United Nations Environment Programme
UNESCO	United Nations Educational, Scientific and Cultural Organization
UNFIP	United Nations Fund for International Partnerships
UNFPA	United Nations Population Fund
UN-HABITAT	United Nations Human Settlements Programme (UNHSP)
UNHCR	Office of the United Nations High Commissioner for Refugees
UNICEF	United Nations Children's Fund
UNICRI	United Nations Interregional Crime and Justice Research Institute
UNIDIR	United Nations Institute for Disarmament Research
UNIDO	United Nations Industrial Development Organization
UNIFEM	United Nations Development Fund for Women
UNITAR	United Nations Institute for Training and Research
UNMOVIC	United Nations Monitoring, Verification and Inspection Commission
UNODC	United Nations Office on Drugs and Crime
UNOG	United Nations Office at Geneva
UNON	United Nations Office at Nairobi
UNOPS	United Nations Office for Project Services
UNOV	United Nations Office at Vienna
UNRISD	United Nations Research Institute for Social Development
UNRWA	United Nations Relief and Works Agency for Palestine Refugees in the Near East
UNSECOORD	Office of the United Nations Security Coordinator
UNSSC	United Nations System Staff College
UNU	United Nations University
UNV	United Nations Volunteers
UPU	Universal Postal Union
WFP	World Food Programme
WHO	World Health Organization
WIPO	World Intellectual Property Organization
WMO	World Meteorological Organization
WTO	World Tourism Organization
WTO	World Trade Organization

The United Nations is the only truly universal body in which the States of the world, and the peoples they represent, can come together to meet the challenges of our time. The principles and purposes of the United Nations Charter are furthered every day, all around the globe, by the United Nations family of organizations and the men and women who serve them. It is the purpose of Basic Facts About the United Nations to promote understanding of this work and its impact on people's lives.

Most people today can expect to live longer than their parents, and a number of countries have made great strides in lifting themselves out of poverty. But many have not. Extreme poverty and deprivation is still widespread. Indeed, dozens of nations, many of them in Africa, grew poorer in the last decade. Some have been devastated by HIV/AIDS or ravaged by war. In many of the poorest countries, health care and education are in decline. Nearly everywhere the environment is deteriorating. The record in advancing women's opportunities, so crucial to human rights and development, is not what it should be. The benefits of globalization have so far passed many by.

In the year 2000, the Member States of the United Nations, in the Millennium Declaration, articulated a vision of development, peace and human rights. They also committed themselves to the Millennium Development Goals, with specific targets to be achieved by 2015. This compact among nations was an unprecedented declaration of aims and a statement of intent to meet them. Bold and urgent steps are now required to match those commitments with action. Poor countries need to make significant reforms. But developed countries must also deliver – especially through increased aid, more systematic debt relief, and levelling the playing field on trade.

Reducing poverty and advancing the cause of peace and human rights is rendered more, not less, urgent by the threat of international terrorism and by other global security concerns. The United Nations has for many years played an important role in international efforts to combat terrorism. These efforts were greatly intensified after the terrorist attacks of 11 September 2001. Terrorism is a global concern. It requires global solutions, which must not only defeat terrorists, but must also address the suffering and hopelessness that they exploit, and advance the human rights that they seek to destroy. Multilateral solutions are also required to prevent the proliferation of weapons of mass destruction, to reduce the flow of small arms and light weapons, and to achieve concrete progress on disarmament. The United Nations is active in efforts to strengthen international cooperation and the rule of law in all these fields.

This work is complemented by the efforts of the United Nations throughout the world to prevent violent conflict, resolve conflicts that have erupted, protect civilians and deliver humanitarian assistance, keep the peace when combatants have reached a truce, and build lasting peace in the aftermath of war. Many reforms have been and are being made to ensure that the United Nations is more effective on the ground when it is called upon to act.

It is the Member States which ultimately decide whether to issue that call. The challenges we face, and some of the crises we have been through, suggest the need to re-examine and update the inter-governmental architecture of the United Nations so that it can truly serve the global interest in the new millennium. But this alone will not suffice. Equally crucial is a broadly shared appreciation of the intimate connection between the national interest of every State and the global interest.

We are one world. We face shared challenges. I hope readers will find that *Basic Facts About the United Nations* demonstrates the magnitude of those challenges, the work the United Nations is doing to meet them, and the areas where still greater efforts are required.

Kofi A. Annan
Secretary-General

PART ONE

Chapter 1
The United Nations Organization

The name "United Nations", coined by United States President Franklin D. Roosevelt, was first used in the "Declaration by United Nations" of 1 January 1942, during the Second World War, when representatives of 26 nations pledged their governments to continue fighting together against the Axis Powers.

States first established international organizations to cooperate on specific matters. The International Telecommunication Union was founded in 1865 as the International Telegraph Union, and the Universal Postal Union was established in 1874. Both are now United Nations specialized agencies.

In 1899, the first International Peace Conference was held in The Hague to elaborate instruments for settling crises peacefully, preventing wars and codifying rules of warfare. It adopted the Convention for the Pacific Settlement of International Disputes and established the Permanent Court of Arbitration, which began work in 1902.

The forerunner of the United Nations was the League of Nations, an organization conceived in similar circumstances during the First World War, and established in 1919 under the Treaty of Versailles "to promote international cooperation and to achieve peace and security."

The International Labour Organization was also created under the Treaty of Versailles as an affiliated agency of the League. The League of Nations ceased its activities after failing to prevent the Second World War.

In 1945, representatives of 50 countries met in San Francisco at the United Nations Conference on International Organization to draw up the United Nations Charter. Those delegates deliberated on the basis of proposals worked out by the representatives of China, the Soviet Union, the United Kingdom and the United States at Dumbarton Oaks, United States, in August-October 1944. The Charter was signed on 26 June 1945 by the representatives of the 50 countries. Poland, which was not represented at the Conference, signed it later and became one of the original 51 member states.

The United Nations officially came into existence on 24 October 1945, when the Charter had been ratified by China, France, the Soviet Union, the United Kingdom, the United States and a majority of other signatories. **United Nations Day** is celebrated on 24 October each year.

United Nations Charter

(www.un.org/aboutun/charter)

The Charter is the constituting instrument of the Organization, setting out the rights and obligations of member states, and establishing the United Nations organs and procedures. An international treaty, the Charter codifies the major principles of international relations — from the sovereign equality of states to prohibition of the use of

Amendments to the United Nations Charter

The Charter may be amended by a vote of two thirds of the members of the General Assembly and ratification by two thirds of the members of the United Nations, including the five permanent members of the Security Council. So far, four Charter Articles have been amended, one of them twice:

- In 1965, the membership of the Security Council was increased from 11 to 15 (Article 23) and the number of affirmative votes needed for a decision was increased from seven to nine, including the concurring vote of the five permanent members for all matters of substance rather than procedure (Article 27).

- In 1965, the membership of the Economic and Social Council was increased from 18 to 27, and in 1973, was increased to 54 (Article 61).

- In 1968, the number of votes required in the Security Council to convene a General Conference to review the Charter was increased from seven to nine (Article 109).

force in international relations in any manner inconsistent with the purposes of the United Nations.

Preamble to the Charter

The Preamble to the Charter expresses the ideals and common aims of all the peoples whose governments joined together to form the United Nations:

"WE THE PEOPLES OF THE UNITED NATIONS DETERMINED to save succeeding generations from the scourge of war, which twice in our lifetime has brought untold sorrow to mankind, and to reaffirm faith in fundamental human rights, in the dignity and worth of the human person, in the equal rights of men and women and of nations large and small, and to establish conditions under which justice and respect for the obligations arising from treaties and other sources of international law can be maintained, and to promote social progress and better standards of life in larger freedom,

"AND FOR THESE ENDS to practice tolerance and live together in peace with one another as good neighbours, and to unite our strength to maintain international peace and security, and to ensure, by the acceptance of principles and the institution of methods, that armed force shall not be used, save in the common interest, and to employ international machinery for the promotion of the economic and social advancement of all peoples,

4

"HAVE RESOLVED TO COMBINE OUR EFFORTS TO ACCOMPLISH THESE AIMS. Accordingly, our respective Governments, through representatives assembled in the city of San Francisco, who have exhibited their full powers found to be in good and due form, have agreed to the present Charter of the United Nations and do hereby establish an international organization to be known as the United Nations."

Purposes and principles

The *purposes* of the United Nations, as set forth in the Charter, are:

- to maintain international peace and security;
- to develop friendly relations among nations based on respect for the principle of equal rights and self-determination of peoples;
- to cooperate in solving international economic, social, cultural and humanitarian problems and in promoting respect for human rights and fundamental freedoms;
- to be a centre for harmonizing the actions of nations in attaining these common ends.

The United Nations acts in accordance with the following *principles*:

- it is based on the sovereign equality of all its members;
- tall members are to fulfil in good faith their Charter obligations;
- they are to settle their international disputes by peaceful means and without endangering international peace and security and justice;
- they are to refrain from the threat or use of force against any other state;
- they are to give the United Nations every assistance in any action it takes in accordance with the Charter;
- nothing in the Charter is to authorize the United Nations to intervene in matters which are essentially within the domestic jurisdiction of any state.

Membership

Membership of the United Nations is open to all peace-loving nations which accept the obligations of the Charter and are willing and able to carry out these obligations.

The General Assembly admits new member states on the recommendation of the Security Council. The Charter provides for the suspension or expulsion of a member for violation of the principles of the Charter, but no such action has ever been taken.

Official languages

Under the Charter, the official languages of the United Nations are Chinese, English, French, Russian and Spanish. Arabic was later added as an official language of the General Assembly, the Security Council and the Economic and Social Council.

Structure of the Organization

The Charter established six principal organs of the United Nations: the General Assembly, the Security Council, the Economic and Social Council, the Trusteeship Council, the International Court of Justice, and the Secretariat. The United Nations family, however, is much larger, encompassing 15 agencies and several programmes and bodies.

General Assembly
(www.un.org/ga)

The General Assembly is the main deliberative organ. It is composed of representatives of all member states, each of which has one vote. Decisions on important questions, such as those on peace and security, admission of new members and budgetary matters, require a two-thirds majority. Decisions on other questions are by simple majority.

Functions and powers

Under the Charter, the functions and powers of the General Assembly include:

- to consider and make recommendations on the principles of cooperation in the maintenance of international peace and security, including the principles governing disarmament and arms regulation;

- to discuss any question relating to international peace and security and, except where a dispute or situation is being discussed by the Security Council, to make recommendations on it;*

- to discuss and, with the same exception, make recommendations on any question within the scope of the Charter or affecting the powers and functions of any organ of the United Nations;

---

* Under the "Uniting for peace" resolution, adopted by the General Assembly in November 1950, the Assembly may take action if the Security Council, because of lack of unanimity of its permanent members, fails to act where there appears to be a threat to international peace, breach of the peace or act of aggression. The Assembly is empowered to consider the matter immediately with a view to making recommendations to members for collective measures, including, in case of a breach of the peace or act of aggression, the use of armed forces when necessary to maintain or restore international peace and security.

- to initiate studies and make recommendations to promote international political cooperation, the development and codification of international law, the realization of human rights and fundamental freedoms for all, and international collaboration in the economic, social, cultural, educational and health fields;

- to make recommendations for the peaceful settlement of any situation, regardless of origin, which might impair friendly relations among nations;

- to receive and consider reports from the Security Council and other United Nations organs;

- to consider and approve the United Nations budget and to apportion the contributions among members;

- to elect the non-permanent members of the Security Council, the members of the Economic and Social Council and additional members of the Trusteeship Council (when necessary); to elect jointly with the Security Council the Judges of the International Court of Justice; and, on the recommendation of the Security Council, to appoint the Secretary-General.

Sessions

The General Assembly's regular session usually begins each year in September. Beginning with its fifty-eighth regular session (2003-2004), the Assembly will open on Tuesday of the third week in September, counting from the first week that contains at least one working day. The election of the President of the Assembly, as well as its 21 Vice-Presidents and the Chairpersons of its six main committees, will take place at least three months before the start of the regular session. To ensure equitable geographical representation, the presidency of the Assembly rotates each year among five groups of states: African, Asian, Eastern European, Latin American and the Caribbean, and Western European and other states.

In addition, the Assembly may meet in special sessions at the request of the Security Council, of a majority of member states, or of one member if the majority of members concur. Emergency special sessions may be called within 24 hours of a request by the Security Council on the vote of any nine Council members, or by a majority of the United Nations members, or by one member if the majority of members concur.

At the beginning of each regular session, the Assembly holds a general debate, often addressed by heads of state and government, in which member states express their views on the most pressing international issues. Most questions are then discussed in its six main committees:

- **First Committee** (Disarmament and International Security);
- **Second Committee** (Economic and Financial);

7

- **Third Committee** (Social, Humanitarian and Cultural);
- **Fourth Committee** (Special Political and Decolonization);
- **Fifth Committee** (Administrative and Budgetary);
- **Sixth Committee** (Legal).

Some issues are considered directly in plenary meetings while others are allocated to one of the six main committees. Resolutions and decisions, including those recommended by the committees, are adopted in plenary meetings — usually before the recess of the regular session in December. They may be adopted with or without a vote.

The Assembly generally adopts its resolutions and decisions by a majority of members present and voting. Important questions, including recommendations on international peace and security, the election of members to some principal organs and budgetary matters, are decided by a two-thirds majority. Voting may be conducted as a recorded vote, a show-of-hands or a roll-call vote.

While the decisions of the Assembly have no legally binding force for governments, they carry the weight of world opinion, as well as the moral authority of the world community.

The work of the United Nations year-round derives largely from the mandates given by the General Assembly — that is to say, the will of the majority of the members as expressed in resolutions and decisions adopted by the Assembly. That work is carried out:

- by committees and other bodies established by the Assembly to study and report on specific issues, such as disarmament, peacekeeping, development and human rights;
- in international conferences called for by the Assembly; and
- by the Secretariat of the United Nations — the Secretary-General and his staff of international civil servants.

Security Council
(*www.un.org/Docs/sc*)

The Security Council has primary responsibility, under the Charter, for the maintenance of international peace and security.

The Council has 15 members: five permanent — China, France, the Russian Federation, the United Kingdom and the United States — and 10 members elected by the General Assembly for two-year terms.

Each member has one vote. Decisions on procedural matters are made by an affirmative vote of at least 9 of the 15 members. Decisions on substantive matters require nine votes and the absence of a negative vote by any of the five permanent members.

All five permanent members have exercised the right of veto at one time or another. If a permanent member does not fully agree with a proposed resolution but does not wish to cast its veto, it may choose to abstain — thus allowing the resolution to be adopted if it obtains the required number of nine votes in favour.

Under Article 25 of the Charter, all members of the United Nations agree to accept and carry out the decisions of the Security Council. While other organs of the United Nations make recommendations to member states, the Council alone has the power to take decisions which member states are obligated under the Charter to implement.

Functions and powers

Under the Charter, the functions and powers of the Security Council include the following:

- to maintain international peace and security in accordance with the principles and purposes of the United Nations;
- to formulate plans for establishing a system to regulate armaments;
- to call upon the parties to a dispute to settle it by peaceful means;
- to investigate any dispute or situation which might lead to international friction, and to recommend methods of adjusting such disputes or the terms of settlement;
- to determine the existence of a threat to the peace or act of aggression and to recommend what action should be taken;
- to call upon the parties concerned to comply with such provisional measures as it deems necessary or desirable to prevent an aggravation of the situation;
- to call on members of the United Nations to take measures not involving the use of armed force — such as sanctions — to give effect to the Council's decisions;
- to resort to or authorize the use of force to maintain or restore international peace and security;
- to encourage the peaceful settlement of local disputes through regional arrangements and to use such regional arrangements for enforcement action under its authority;
- to recommend to the General Assembly the appointment of the Secretary-General and, together with the Assembly, to elect the Judges of the International Court of Justice;
- to request the International Court of Justice to give an advisory opinion on any legal question;

- to recommend to the General Assembly the admission of new members to the United Nations.

The Security Council is so organized as to be able to function continuously, and a representative of each of its members must be present at all times at United Nations Headquarters. The Council may meet elsewhere: in 1972 it held a session in Addis Ababa, Ethiopia; in 1973 it met in Panama City, Panama; and in 1990 it met in Geneva, Switzerland.

When a complaint concerning a threat to peace is brought before it, the Council's first action is usually to recommend that the parties try to reach agreement by peaceful means. The Council may set forth principles for a peaceful settlement. In some cases, the Council itself undertakes investigation and mediation. It may dispatch a mission, appoint special envoys or request the Secretary-General to use his good offices.

When a dispute leads to hostilities, the Council's first concern is to bring them to an end as soon as possible. The Council may issue ceasefire directives that can be instrumental in preventing an escalation of the conflict.

The Council may also dispatch military observers or a peacekeeping force to help reduce tensions, keep opposing forces apart, and create conditions of calm in which peaceful settlements may be sought. Under Chapter VII of the Charter, the Council may decide on enforcement measures, including economic sanctions, arms embargoes, financial sanctions, travel bans or collective military action.

The sanctions instrument is an important tool available to the Security Council in seeking to promote international peace and security. Each of the sanctions regimes currently in existence features "smart" or targeted sanctions — arms embargoes, financial sanctions and travel bans — designed to eliminate or minimize unintended effects by focusing on those responsible for the policies condemned by the international community, while leaving other parts of the population and international trade relations unaffected (see Chapter 2).

After the 1991 Gulf war, the Council established the United Nations Special Commission (UNSCOM) to verify, together with the International Atomic Energy Agency (IAEA), the elimination of Iraq's weapons of mass destruction. UNSCOM's responsibilities were taken over in 1999 by the United Nations Monitoring, Verification and Inspection Commission (UNMOVIC).

The Council has established two international criminal tribunals to prosecute crimes against humanity in the former Yugoslavia and in Rwanda. The tribunals are subsidiary organs of the Council. Following the terrorist attacks on the United States on 11 September 2001, the Council established its Counter-Terrorism Committee, also a subsidiary organ.

Since 1993, a working group of the General Assembly has been considering Security Council reform, including the issue of equitable representation and expansion of membership.

Economic and Social Council
(*www.un.org/esa/coordination/ecosoc*)

The Charter established the Economic and Social Council as the principal organ to coordinate the economic, social and related work of the United Nations and the specialized agencies and institutions — known as the United Nations family of organizations. The Council has 54 members, who serve for three-year terms. Voting in the Council is by simple majority; each member has one vote.

Functions and powers

The functions and powers of the Economic and Social Council are:

- to serve as the central forum for discussing international economic and social issues, and for formulating policy recommendations addressed to member states and the United Nations system;
- to make or initiate studies and reports and make recommendations on international economic, social, cultural, educational, health and related matters;
- to promote respect for, and observance of, human rights and fundamental freedoms;
- to assist in preparing and organizing major international conferences in the economic, social and related fields and promote a coordinated follow-up to these conferences;
- to coordinate the activities of the specialized agencies, through consultations with and recommendations to them, and through recommendations to the General Assembly.

Through its discussion of international economic and social issues and its policy recommendations, ECOSOC plays a key role in fostering international cooperation for development and in setting the priorities for action.

Sessions

The Council generally holds several short sessions and many preparatory meetings, round tables and panel discussions with the members of civil society throughout the year, to deal with the organization of its work. It also holds a four-week substantive session in July, alternating between New York and Geneva. That session includes a high-level segment, attended by Ministers and other high officials, to discuss major economic, social and humanitarian issues. The year-round work of the Council is carried out in its subsidiary and related bodies.

Subsidiary and related bodies

The Council's subsidiary machinery includes:

- Nine functional commissions, which are deliberative bodies whose role is to consider and make recommendations on issues in their areas of responsibility and expertise: Statistical Commission, Commission on Population and Development, Commission for Social Development, Commission on Human Rights, Commission on the Status of Women, Commission on Narcotic Drugs, Commission on Crime Prevention and Criminal Justice, Commission on Science and Technology for Development, and Commission on Sustainable Development.

- Five Regional Commissions: Economic Commission for Africa (Addis Ababa, Ethiopia), Economic and Social Commission for Asia and the Pacific (Bangkok, Thailand), Economic Commission for Europe (Geneva, Switzerland), Economic Commission for Latin America and the Caribbean (Santiago, Chile), and Economic and Social Commission for Western Asia (Beirut, Lebanon).

- Six standing committees and expert bodies: Committee for Programme and Coordination, Commission on Human Settlements, Committee on Non-Governmental Organizations, Committee on Negotiations with Intergovernmental Agencies, Committee on Energy and Natural Resources, and Committee on Public Administration.

- A number of expert bodies on subjects such as development planning, natural resources, economic, social and cultural rights, and the Permanent Forum on Indigenous Issues.

The Council also cooperates with and to a certain extent coordinates the work of United Nations programmes (such as UNDP, UNEP, UNICEF, UN-HABITAT and UNFPA) and the specialized agencies (such as FAO, WHO, ILO and UNESCO), all of which report to the Council and make recommendations for its substantive sessions.

Relations with non-governmental organizations

Under the Charter, the Economic and Social Council consults with non-governmental organizations (NGOs) concerned with matters within its competence. Over 2,100 NGOs have consultative status with the Council. The Council recognizes that these organizations should have the opportunity to express their views, and that they possess special experience or technical knowledge of value to its work.

The Council classifies NGOs into three categories: category I organizations are those concerned with most of the Council's activities; category II organizations have special competence in specific areas; and organizations that can occasionally contribute to the Council are placed on a roster for ad hoc consultations.

NGOs with consultative status may send observers to meetings of the Council and its subsidiary bodies and may submit written statements relevant to its work. They may also consult with the United Nations Secretariat on matters of mutual concern.

Over the years, the relationship between the United Nations and affiliated NGOs has developed significantly. Increasingly, NGOs are seen as partners who are consulted on policy and programme matters and seen as valuable links to civil society. NGOs around the world, in increasing numbers, are working daily with the United Nations community to help achieve the objectives of the Charter.

Trusteeship Council
(www.un.org/documents/tc)

The Trusteeship Council was established by the Charter in 1945 to provide international supervision for 11 Trust Territories placed under the administration of 7 member states, and ensure that adequate steps were taken to prepare the Territories for self-government or independence. The Charter authorized the Trusteeship Council to examine and discuss reports from the Administering Authority on the political, economic, social and educational advancement of the peoples of Trust Territories; to examine petitions from the Territories; and to undertake special missions to the Territories.

By 1994, all Trust Territories had attained self-government or independence, either as separate states or by joining neighbouring independent countries. The last to do so was the Trust Territory of the Pacific Islands (Palau), which became the 185th member state.

Its work completed, the Trusteeship Council — its membership reduced now to the five permanent members of the Security Council (China, France, the Russian Federation, the United Kingdom and the United States) — has amended its rules of procedure to meet as and where occasion may require.

International Court of Justice
(www.icj-cij.org)

Located at The Hague, in the Netherlands, the International Court of Justice is the principal judicial organ of the United Nations. It settles legal disputes between states and gives advisory opinions to the United Nations and its specialized agencies. Its Statute is an integral part of the United Nations Charter.

The Court is open to all states that are parties to its Statute, which include all members of the United Nations. Only states may be parties in contentious cases before the Court and submit disputes to it. The Court is not open to private persons and entities or international organizations.

The General Assembly and the Security Council can ask the Court for an advisory opinion on any legal question. Other organs of the United Nations and the specialized agencies, when authorized by the Assembly, can ask for advisory opinions on legal questions within the scope of their activities.

Jurisdiction

The Court's jurisdiction covers all questions that states refer to it, and all matters provided for in the United Nations Charter, or in international treaties and conventions. States may bind themselves in advance to accept the jurisdiction of the Court, either by signing a treaty or convention that provides for referral to the Court or by making a declaration to that effect. Such declarations accepting compulsory jurisdiction often contain reservations excluding certain classes of disputes.

In accordance with its Statute, the Court decides disputes by applying:

- international conventions establishing rules expressly recognized by the contesting states;
- international custom as evidence of a general practice accepted as law;
- the general principles of law recognized by nations; and
- judicial decisions and the teachings of the most qualified scholars of the various nations.

Membership

The Court is composed of 15 Judges elected by the General Assembly and the Security Council, voting independently. They are chosen on the basis of their qualifications, and care is taken to ensure that the principal legal systems of the world are represented in the Court. No two Judges may be from the same country. The Judges serve a nine-year term and may be re-elected. They cannot engage in any other occupation during their term of office.

The Court normally sits in plenary session, but may form smaller units called chambers if the parties so request. Judgments given by chambers are considered as rendered by the full Court. The Court also has a Chamber for Environmental Matters and forms annually a Chamber of Summary Procedure.

Secretariat
(www.un.org/documents/st)

The Secretariat — consisting of international staff working in duty stations around the world — carries out the diverse day-to-day work of the Organization. It services the other principal organs of the United Nations and administers the programmes and policies laid down by them. At its head is the Secretary-General, who is appointed by the General Assembly on the recommendation of the Security Council for a five-year, renewable term.

The duties carried out by the Secretariat are as varied as the problems dealt with by the United Nations. These range from administering peacekeeping operations to mediating international disputes, from surveying economic and social trends to preparing studies on human rights and sustainable development. Secretariat staff also inform the world's communications media about the work of the United Nations; organize international conferences on issues of worldwide concern; and interpret speeches and translate documents into the Organization's official languages.

The Secretariat has a staff of about 7,500 under the regular budget, drawn from some 170 countries. As international civil servants, staff members and the Secretary-General answer to the United Nations alone for their activities, and take an oath not to seek or receive instructions from any government or outside authority. Under the Charter, each member state undertakes to respect the exclusively international character of the responsibilities of the Secretary-General and the staff, and to refrain from seeking to influence them improperly.

The United Nations, while headquartered in New York, maintains a significant presence in Addis Ababa, Bangkok, Beirut, Geneva, Nairobi, Santiago and Vienna, and has offices all over the world.

Secretary-General
(www.un.org/News/ossg/sg)

Equal parts diplomat and advocate, civil servant and CEO, the Secretary-General is a symbol of United Nations ideals and a spokesman for the interests of the world's peoples, in particular the poor and vulnerable. The current Secretary-General, and the seventh occupant of the post, is Mr. Kofi Annan of Ghana, who took office on 1 January 1997 and was subsequently re-elected to a second five-year term (2002-2006).

The Charter describes the Secretary-General as "chief administrative officer" of the Organization, who shall act in that capacity and perform "such other functions as are entrusted" to him or her by the Security Council, General Assembly, Economic and Social Council and other United Nations organs. The Charter also empowers the Secretary-General to "bring to the attention of the Security Council any matter which in his opinion may threaten the maintenance of international peace and security". These guidelines both define the powers of the office and grant it considerable scope for action. The Secretary-General would fail if he did not take careful account of the concerns of member states, but he must also uphold the values and moral authority of the United Nations, and speak and act for peace — even at the risk, from time to time, of challenging or disagreeing with those same member states.

This creative tension accompanies the Secretary-General through day-to-day work, which includes attendance at sessions of United Nations bodies; consultations with world leaders, government officials, representatives of civil society groups, the private sector and others; and worldwide travel intended to keep him in touch with the peoples of member states and informed about the vast array of issues of international concern that are on the Organization's agenda. Each year, the Secretary-General issues a report on the work of the Organization that appraises its activities and outlines future priorities.

One of the most vital roles played by the Secretary-General is the use of his "good offices" — steps taken publicly and in private, drawing upon his independence, impartiality and integrity, to prevent international disputes from arising, escalating or spreading. Since becoming Secretary-General, Mr. Annan has made use of his good offices in a range of situations, including Cyprus, East Timor, Iraq, Libya, the Middle East, Nigeria and Western Sahara.

Each Secretary-General also defines his role within the context of his particular time in office. Mr. Annan's efforts have focused on:

Reform. Shortly after taking office, Mr. Annan presented a sweeping reform package aimed at helping the United Nations to change with the times and adapt to a new era of global affairs.

Reform measures falling under the authority of the Secretary-General have been largely implemented or set in motion. They have been both administrative — such as a rigorous effort to upgrade management practices — as well as organizational, with the emphasis on enabling the United Nations to respond more effectively to the growing demands placed on it, particularly in the areas of development and peacekeeping.

A new post of **Deputy Secretary-General** was created to assist the Secretary-General in the array of responsibilities assigned to his office. The first holder of this position is Ms. Louise Fréchette, who was Canada's Deputy Minister of National Defence before her appointment in 1998.

At the outset of his second term, the Secretary-General put forward another package of reform — "Strengthening of the United Nations: An agenda for further change" — that aimed to realign the work of the Organization with the priorities set out in the Millennium Declaration adopted by member states in September 2000. The package also proposed major changes in the way the Secretariat services member states, and launched an effort by a high-level panel to review and recommend improvements in the Organization's relations with non-governmental organizations, parliamentarians, foundations and members of the private sector.

16

The General Assembly, meanwhile, has continued to consider several questions of institutional change that fall under its authority, including the size and composition of the Security Council, methods of financing the Organization and bringing greater coherence to the wider United Nations system of specialized agencies.

Africa. The Secretary-General has sought to maintain a focus on Africa and to mobilize international support for the continent's efforts to chart a path to peace and higher levels of development. His approach is encapsulated in a 1998 report, "The causes of conflict and the promotion of durable peace and sustainable development in Africa", which contains a comprehensive set of "realistic and achievable" measures designed to reduce political tension and violence within and between African states, and to address such development issues as governance, debt, trade, official development assistance and the spread of diseases such as AIDS. He has also established an Office of the Special Adviser on Africa to promote and coordinate a system-wide response by the United Nations in support of Africa's development — particularly in implementing the New Partnership for Africa's Development (NEPAD).

Peace operations. The 1990s saw an upsurge in United Nations peacekeeping and peacemaking activities and dramatic changes in the nature of conflict itself — primarily a decline in conflicts between states and a rise in the frequency and brutality of conflicts within states. Difficult experiences in responding to these complex humanitarian emergencies have led the Secretary-General to place great emphasis on ensuring that the United Nations, when asked to undertake a peace operation, is fully equipped to do so — militarily, financially and politically.

In addition to measures contained in the Secretary-General's reform plans, three key reports have contributed to this effort. The first, requested by the General Assembly and submitted by the Secretary-General in 1999, examined the atrocities committed against the Bosnian Muslim population in 1995 in the United Nations-designated "safe area" of Srebrenica. The second, commissioned by the Secretary-General and released in 1999, was an independent inquiry, led by former Swedish Prime Minister Ingvar Carlsson, into the actions of the United Nations during the 1994 genocide in Rwanda.

The third, an initiative of the Secretary-General released in 2000, was a comprehensive review of United Nations peace and security activities by a high-level panel appointed by the Secretary-General and chaired by former Algerian Foreign Minister Lakhdar Brahimi. This report, intended to draw conclusions for the future from the other two, contains wide-ranging recommendations for the Secretariat and the member states, particularly those serving on the Security Council. Implementation of many of these proposals has helped improve the Organization's capacity to deploy and manage complex peacekeeping and peace-building operations, even if the full value of these improvements will be realized only over time.

Global Compact. In 1999, at the World Economic Forum in Davos, Switzerland, the Secretary-General proposed a "Global Compact" that would bring private

The United Nations as a catalyst for change

Today's actors on the global stage are not only states, says Secretary-General Kofi Annan in his "Millennium Report", *We the peoples: the role of the United Nations in the 21st century.** The private sector, NGOs and multilateral agencies increasingly work with governments to find consensus solutions to global problems.

The United Nations must strive not to usurp the role of those global actors, but to become a more effective catalyst for change and coordination among them, stimulating collective action at the global level. The Secretary-General recommends action in these areas:

- *Identifying the United Nations core strengths.* The Organization's influence derives not from power but from the values it represents, its role in helping to set and sustain global norms, its ability to stimulate global concern and action, and the trust inspired by its practical work to improve people's lives. The United Nations must build on those strengths and at the same time adapt, so it can both work effectively and enjoy unquestioned legitimacy. And it must expand its relationship with civil society organizations and the private sector.

- *Networking for change.* The United Nations must supplement formal institutions with informal policy networks, bringing together international institutions, civil society, the private sector and governments in pursuit of common goals.

- *Making digital connections.* The United Nations must fully exploit new information technology to become more efficient and to improve its interaction with the rest of the world.

- *Advancing the quiet revolution.* The United Nations needs structural reform and clearer consensus on priorities among member states. To better serve states and people alike, the United Nations "must become more effective, efficient, and accessible to the world's peoples".

The Millennium Report was issued in preparation for the Millennium Summit — the largest-ever gathering of heads of state or government. At the Summit, held at UN Headquarters from 6 to 8 September 2000, world leaders established clear directions for the UN in the new century. The Millennium Declaration, adopted unanimously, set a series of concrete goals and specific targets for the international community to meet the central challenge of ensuring that globalization becomes a positive force for all.

*"Millennium Report", *We the peoples: the role of the United Nations in the 21st century.* United Nations, 2000, ISBN 92-1-100844-1, E.00.I.16. Also available at www.un.org/millennium/sg/report.

corporations together with UN agencies, governments, labour and non-governmental organizations to advance nine universally recognized principles in the areas of human rights, labour and the environment.

The Global Compact has grown rapidly since its official launch in July 2000, when 50 companies pledged their support. As of June 2004, the network of participants included nearly 1,500 companies worldwide, international labour groups and dozens of civil society organizations. The Compact is now rooted in more than 70 countries, most in the developing world. It has inspired dozens of projects and initiatives, including a project to promote business and investment in the world's least developed countries, and an agreement by the International Organization of Employers and the International Confederation of Free Trade Unions to work together in the global fight against HIV/AIDS.

HIV/AIDS. In April 2001, the Secretary-General issued a "Call to Action" to address the HIV/AIDS epidemic — which he described as his "personal priority" — and proposed the establishment of a Global AIDS and Health Fund to serve as a mechanism for some of the increased spending needed to help developing countries confront the crisis. The Fund became operational in 2002.

Budget of the United Nations

The regular budget of the United Nations is approved by the General Assembly for a two-year period. The budget is initially submitted by the Secretary-General and reviewed by the **Advisory Committee on Administrative and Budgetary Questions**, made up of 16 experts who are nominated by their governments and elected by the General Assembly but who serve in their personal capacity. The programmatic aspects are reviewed by the **Committee for Programme and Coordination**, made up of 34 experts who are elected by the General Assembly and who represent the views of their governments.

The budget approved for the biennium 2004-2005 is $3.16 billion — representing zero per cent growth in real terms from the 2002-2003 biennium. The budget covers the costs of United Nations programmes in areas such as political affairs, international justice and law, international cooperation for development, public information, human rights and humanitarian affairs.

The main source of funds for the budget is the contributions of member states. These are assessed on a scale approved by the Assembly on the recommendation of the **Committee on Contributions**, made up of 18 experts who serve in their personal capacity and are selected by the General Assembly on the recommendation of its Administrative and Budgetary (Fifth) Committee.

The fundamental criterion on which the scale of assessments is based is the capacity of countries to pay. This is determined by considering their relative shares of total gross national product, adjusted to take into account a number of factors, including their per capita incomes. The Committee completely reviews the scale of assessments every three years, on the basis of the latest national income statistics, to ensure that assessments are fair and accurate. In 2000, the Assembly fixed a maximum of 22 per cent of the budget for any one contributor.

The overall financial situation of the United Nations has been precarious for several years because of the continuing failure of many member states to pay, in full and on time, their assessed contributions. The United Nations has managed to continue to operate thanks to voluntary contributions from some countries and to its Working Capital Fund (to which member states advance sums in proportion to their assessed contributions), and by borrowing from peacekeeping operations.

Member states' unpaid contributions to the regular budget totalled just under $442 million at the end of 2003. Out of 191 assessed member states, 127 had paid their assessments in full, while the remaining 66 had failed to meet their statutory financial obligations to the Organization.

In addition to the regular budget, member states are assessed for the costs of the international tribunals and, in accordance with a modified version of the basic scale, for the costs of peacekeeping operations.

Peacekeeping costs peaked at $3 billion in 1995, reflecting in particular the expense of operations in Somalia and the former Yugoslavia, but were down to $889 million in 1999. By the end of 2001, the annual cost of United Nations peacekeeping had again risen to just over $3 billion — reflecting major new missions in Kosovo, East Timor (now Timor-Leste), Sierra Leone, the Democratic Republic of the Congo, and Eritrea and Ethiopia. By 1 July 2003, the approved budgets for the following 12 months were just under $2.2 billion.

Outstanding contributions for peacekeeping operations at the end of 2003 totalled nearly $1.1 billion. Shortfalls in the receipt of assessed contributions were met by delaying reimbursements to states that had contributed troops, equipment and logistical support, thus placing an unfair burden on them.

United Nations funds and programmes — such as the United Nations Children's Fund (UNICEF), the United Nations Development Programme (UNDP) and the United Nations High Commissioner for Refugees (UNHCR) — have separate budgets. The bulk of their resources is provided on a voluntary basis by governments, and also by individuals, as in the case of UNICEF. The United Nations specialized agencies also have separate budgets, which are supplemented through voluntary contributions by states.

The United Nations family of organizations

(*www.unsystem.org*)

The United Nations family of organizations (the "United Nations system") consists of the **United Nations Secretariat**, the United Nations **funds and programmes** (such as UNICEF and UNDP), the specialized agencies (such as UNESCO and WHO) and **related organizations**. The funds and programmes are subsidiary bodies of the General Assembly. The specialized agencies are linked to the United Nations through special agreements and report to the Economic and Social Council and/or the General Assembly. The related organizations — including IAEA and the World Trade Organization — address specialized areas and have their own legislative bodies and budgets. Together, the organizations of the UN system address all areas of economic and social endeavour.

United Nations System Chief Executives Board for Coordination (CEB). The CEB — formerly known as the Administrative Committee on Coordination (ACC) — represents the entire UN system. Its members are the Executive Heads of 27 organizations, including the United Nations funds, programmes, specialized agencies and related organizations. Its purpose is to facilitate increased coordination of the UN system in the pursuit of the common goals of member states on a wide range of concerns. Chaired by the Secretary-General, the CEB meets twice a year to consider the substantive and management issues facing the UN system. Its work is carried out, in part, by subsidiary bodies, each of which focuses on a particular aspect of coordination within the system. (See *http://ceb.unsystem.org*)

United Nations Secretariat
(www.un.org/documents/st)

The United Nations Secretariat consists of departments and offices, described below. The **Executive Office of the Secretary-General**, composed of the Secretary-General and his senior advisers, establishes general policies and provides overall guidance to the Organization. The Secretariat has its headquarters in New York and offices in all regions of the world.

Three main centres of activities are in Geneva, Vienna and Nairobi. The **United Nations Office at Geneva (UNOG)**, headed by Director-General Sergei Alexandrovitch Ordzhonikidze (Russian Federation), is a centre for conference diplomacy and a forum for disarmament and human rights. The **United Nations Office at Vienna (UNOV)**, headed by Director-General Antonio Maria Costa (Italy), is the headquarters for activities in the fields of international drug-abuse control, crime prevention and criminal justice, peaceful uses of outer space and international trade law. The **United Nations Office at Nairobi (UNON)**, headed by Director-General Klaus Topfer (Germany), is the headquarters for activities in the fields of environment and human settlements.

Office of Internal Oversight Services (OIOS)
(www.un.org/Depts/oios)

Under-Secretary-General   Mr. Dileep Nair (Singapore)

The Office of Internal Oversight Services provides independent, professional and timely internal audit, including monitoring, inspection and evaluation, as well as management consulting and investigation services. It aims to be an agent of change that promotes responsible administration of resources, a culture of accountability and transparency, and improved programme performance. The Office:

- monitors and evaluates the efficiency and effectiveness of the implementation of programmes and mandates;

- conducts comprehensive internal audits;

The United

| Trusteeship Council | Security Council | General Assembly |

Subsidiary Bodies
Military Staff Committee
Standing Committee and ad hoc bodies
International Criminal Tribunal for the Former
   Yugoslavia
International Criminal Tribunal for Rwanda
UN Monitoring, Verification and Inspection
   Commission (Iraq)
United Nations Compensation Commission
Peacekeeping Operations and Missions

Subsidiary Bodies
Main committees
Other sessional committees
Standing committees and
   ad hoc bodies
Other subsidiary organs

Programmes and Funds

UNCTAD United Nations
Conference on Trade and
Development

   ITC International Trade Centre
   (UNCTAD/WTO)

UNDCP United Nations Drug
Control Programme[1]

UNEP United Nations
Environment Programme

UNICEF United Nations
Children's Fund

UNDP United Nations
Development Programme

   UNIFEM United Nations
   Development Fund for Women

   UNV United Nations
   Volunteers

   UNCDF United Nations
   Capital Development Fund

UNFPA United Nations
Population Fund

UNHCR Office of the United
Nations High Commissioner for
Refugees

WFP World Food Programme

UNRWA[2] United Nations Relief
and Works Agency for Palestine
Refugees in the Near East

UN–HABITAT United
Nations Human Settlements
Programme (UNHSP)

Research and Training Institutes

UNICRI United Nations
Interregional Crime and Justice
Research Institute

UNITAR United Nations
Institute for Training and
Research

UNRISD United Nations
Research Institute for Social
Development

UNIDIR[2] United Nations
Institute for Disarmament
Research

INSTRAW International
Research and Training Institute
for the Advancement of Women

Other UN Entities

OHCHR Office of the
United Nations High
Commissioner for
Human Rights

UNOPS United
Nations Office for
Project Services

UNU United Nations
University

UNSSC United
Nations System Staff
College

UNAIDS Joint United
Nations Programme on
HIV/AIDS

NOTES: Solid lines from a Principal Organ indicate a direct reporting relationship; dashes indicate a non-subsidiary relationship. [1]The UN Drug Control Programme is part of the UN Office on Drugs and Crime. [2]UNRWA and UNIDIR report only to the GA. [3]The World Trade Organization and World Tourism Organization use the same acronym. [4]IAEA reports to the Security Council and the General Assembly (GA). [5]The CTBTO Prep.Com and OPCW report to the GA. [6]Specialized agencies are autonomous organizations working with the UN and each other through the coordinating machinery of the ECOSOC at the intergovernmental level, and through the Chief Executives Board for coordination (CEB) at the inter-secretariat level.

Nations system

Economic and Social Council	International Court of Justice	Secretariat

Functional Commissions

Commissions on:
  Human Rights
  Narcotic Drugs
  Crime Prevention and Criminal Justice
  Science and Technology for Development
  Sustainable Development
  Status of Women
  Population and Development
Commission for Social Development
Statistical Commission

Regional Commissions

Economic Commission for Africa (ECA)
Economic Commission for Europe (ECE)
Economic Commission for Latin America and the Caribbean (ECLAC)
Economic and Social Commission for Asia and the Pacific (ESCAP)
Economic and Social Commission for Western Asia (ESCWA)

Other Bodies

Permanent Forum on Indigenous Issues (PFII)
United Nations Forum on Forests
Sessional and standing committees
Expert, ad hoc and related bodies

Related Organizations

WTO[3] World Trade Organization
IAEA[4] International Atomic Energy Agency
CTBTO PREP.COM[5] PrepCom for the Nuclear-Test-Ban-Treaty Organization
OPCW[5] Organization for the Prohibition of Chemical Weapons

Specialized Agencies[6]

ILO International Labour Organization
FAO Food and Agriculture Organization of the United Nations
UNESCO United Nations Educational, Scientific and Cultural Organization
WHO World Health Organization

WORLD BANK GROUP

IBRD International Bank for Reconstruction and Development
IDA International Development Association
IFC International Finance Corporation
MIGA Multilateral Investment Guarantee Agency
ICSID International Centre for Settlement of Investment Disputes

IMF International Monetary Fund
ICAO International Civil Aviation Organization
IMO International Maritime Organization
ITU International Telecommunication Union
UPU Universal Postal Union
WMO World Meterological Organization
WIPO World Intellectual Property Organization
IFAD International Fund for Agricultural Development
UNIDO United Nations Industrial Development Organization
WTO[3] World Tourism Organization

Departments and Offices

OSG Office of the Secretary-General
OIOS Office of Internal Oversight Services
OLA Office of Legal Affairs
DPA Department of Political Affairs
DDA Department for Disarmament Affairs
DPKO Department of Peace-keeping Operations
OCHA Office for the Coordination of Humanitarian Affairs
DESA Department of Economic and Social Affairs
DGACM Department for General Assembly and Conference Management
DPI Department of Public Information
DM Department of Management
OHRLLS Office of the High Representative for the Least Developed Countries, Landlocked Developing Countries and Small Island Developing States
UNSECOORD Office of the United Nations Security Coordinator
UNODC United Nations Office on Drugs and Crime

UNOG UN Office at Geneva
UNOV UN Office at Vienna
UNON UN Office at Nairobi

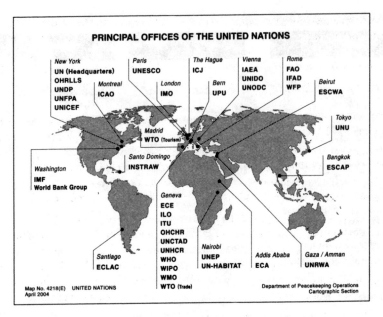

PRINCIPAL OFFICES OF THE UNITED NATIONS

New York
UN (Headquarters)
OHRLLS
UNDP
UNFPA
UNICEF

Montreal
ICAO

Paris
UNESCO

London
IMO

The Hague
ICJ

Bern
UPU

Vienna
IAEA
UNIDO
UNODC

Rome
FAO
IFAD
WFP

Beirut
ESCWA

Madrid
WTO (Tourism)

Tokyo
UNU

Santo Domingo
INSTRAW

Bangkok
ESCAP

Washington
IMF
World Bank Group

Geneva
ECE
ILO
ITU
OHCHR
UNCTAD
UNHCR
WHO
WIPO
WMO
WTO (Trade)

Nairobi
UNEP
UN-HABITAT

Addis Ababa
ECA

Gaza / Amman
UNRWA

Santiago
ECLAC

Map No. 4218(E)   UNITED NATIONS
April 2004

Department of Peacekeeping Operations
Cartographic Section

- conducts inspections of programmes and organizational units;
- investigates reports of mismanagement and misconduct;
- provides consulting services to programme managers to assist them in increasing effectiveness;
- monitors the implementation of recommendations emanating from audits, evaluations, inspections and investigations.

OIOS covers the Secretariat and major peacekeeping and humanitarian operations, and provides assistance to various operational funds and programmes. It has a staff of about 172 and an annual budget of approximately $20 million. Since 1994, the Office has exposed waste and fraud in the Organization totalling $250 million.

The Under-Secretary-General for Internal Oversight Services is appointed by the Secretary-General and approved by the General Assembly for one five-year term without possibility of renewal.

Office of Legal Affairs (OLA)
(http://untreaty.un.org/ola-internet/olahome.html)

Under-Secretary-General
The Legal Counsel

Mr. Nicolas Michel (Switzerland)
(as of 16 August 2004)

The Office of Legal Affairs is the central legal service of the Organization. It provides legal advice to the Secretary-General, Secretariat departments and offices, and principal and subsidiary organs of the United Nations in the field of public and private international law; performs substantive and secretariat functions for legal organs involved in public international law, the law of the sea and international trade law; and performs the functions conferred on the Secretary-General in Article 102 of the Charter of the United Nations and the Statute of the International Court of Justice.

OLA deals with legal questions relating to international peace and security; to the status, privileges and immunities of the United Nations; and to the credentials and representations of member states. It prepares drafts of international conventions, agreements, rules of procedure of United Nations organs and conferences, and other legal instruments. It also provides legal services and advice on issues of international private and administrative law and on United Nations resolutions and regulations.

In addition, the Office provides secretariat services for the General Assembly's Sixth Committee, the International Law Commission, the Commission on International Trade Law, the organs established by the United Nations Convention on the Law of the Sea, the United Nations Administrative Tribunal and other legal bodies. It also discharges the Secretary-General's responsibilities regarding the registration and publication of treaties as the depositary of multilateral conventions.

The head of the Office — the Legal Counsel — represents the Secretary-General at meetings and conferences of a legal nature, as well as in judicial and arbitral proceedings. The Legal Counsel also certifies legal instruments issued on behalf of the United Nations, convenes meetings of the Legal Advisers of the United Nations System, and represents the United Nations at such meetings.

Department of Political Affairs (DPA)
(www.un.org/Depts/dpa)

Under-Secretary-General   Mr. Kieran Prendergast (United Kingdom)

The Department of Political Affairs provides advice and support on all political matters to the Secretary-General in the exercise of his global responsibilities under the Charter related to the maintenance and restoration of peace and security. DPA accordingly:

- monitors, analyses and assesses political developments throughout the world;
- identifies potential or actual conflicts in whose control and resolution the United Nations could play a useful role;
- recommends to the Secretary-General appropriate action in such cases and executes the approved policy;
- assists the Secretary-General in carrying out political activities decided by him, the General Assembly and the Security Council, in the areas of preventive diplomacy, peacemaking, peacekeeping and peace-building;

- advises the Secretary-General on requests for electoral assistance received from member states and coordinates programmes established in response to such requests;
- advises and supports the Secretary-General in the political aspects of his relations with member states;
- services the Security Council and its subsidiary bodies, as well as the Committee on the Exercise of the Inalienable Rights of the Palestinian People and the Special Committee of 24 on decolonization.

The head of the Department — the Under-Secretary-General for Political Affairs — among other things undertakes consultations and negotiations relating to peaceful settlement of disputes, and is the focal point for United Nations peace-building, preventive and electoral assistance activities.

Department for Disarmament Affairs (DDA)
(http://disarmament.un.org)

Under-Secretary-General   Mr. Nobuyasu Abe (Japan)

The Department for Disarmament Affairs promotes the goal of nuclear disarmament and non-proliferation, as well as the strengthening of the disarmament regimes with respect to other weapons of mass destruction, including chemical and biological weapons. It promotes disarmament in the area of conventional weapons, especially with respect to implementation of the 2001 programme of action on illicit trade in small arms — the weapons of choice in contemporary conflicts. This includes arms collection and stockpile management programmes, as well as the disarmament and demobilization of former combatants and their reintegration into civil society. It also advocates restrictions on and eventual disarmament of anti-personnel landmines.

DDA provides substantive and organizational support for norm-setting in the area of disarmament through the work of the General Assembly and its First Committee, the Disarmament Commission, the Conference on Disarmament and other bodies. It fosters preventive disarmament measures, such as dialogue, transparency and confidence-building on military matters, including the United Nations Register of Conventional Arms and standardized reporting on military expenditures. It encourages regional disarmament efforts, including nuclear-weapon-free zones and regional and subregional transparency regimes. It also provides information and supports educational initiatives on UN disarmament efforts.

Department of Peacekeeping Operations (DPKO)
(www.un.org/Depts/dpko)

Under-Secretary-General   Mr. Jean-Marie Guéhenno (France)

The Department of Peacekeeping Operations is responsible for assisting member states and the Secretary-General in their efforts to maintain, achieve and sustain international peace and security. It does this by planning, preparing and conducting United Nations peacekeeping operations, in accordance with mandates provided by the member states. The Department:

- Undertakes contingency planning for possible new peacekeeping operations;
- Develops plans, methodologies and budgets for these operations once they are mandated;
- Secures, through negotiations with member states, the civilian, military and police personnel, the military units, and the equipment and services required to accomplish the mandate;
- Provides logistical and administrative support for the operations once established, and also for political and humanitarian missions;
- Provides political and executive guidance and support to peacekeeping operations;
- Maintains contacts with parties to conflicts and with members of the Security Council on the implementation of Security Council resolutions;
- Analyses emerging policy questions and best practices related to peacekeeping, and formulates policies and procedures on them;
- Coordinates all United Nations activities related to landmines, and develops and supports mine action programmes in peacekeeping and emergency situations.

The head of the Department — the Under-Secretary-General for Peacekeeping Operations — directs peacekeeping operations on behalf of the Secretary-General; formulates policies and guidelines for operations; and advises the Secretary-General on all matters relating to peacekeeping and mine action.

Office for the Coordination of Humanitarian Affairs (OCHA)
(www.reliefweb.int/ocha_ol)

Under-Secretary-General for Humanitarian Affairs   Mr. Jan Egeland (Norway)
Emergency Relief Coordinator

The mandate of the Office for the Coordination of Humanitarian Affairs is to strengthen coordination among the United Nations bodies that provide assistance in response to emergencies. The Office works to secure agreement among the organizations of the Inter-Agency Standing Committee on the division of responsibilities, such as establishing coordination mechanisms, mounting need-assessment missions, preparing consolidated appeals and mobilizing resources.

The core functions of the Emergency Relief Coordinator are:

- policy development and coordination, ensuring that all humanitarian issues, including those which fall between gaps in the mandates of agencies, are addressed;

- advocacy of humanitarian issues with political organs, notably the Security Council;
- coordination of humanitarian emergency response, by ensuring that an appropriate response mechanism is established on the ground; this is done through the Inter-Agency Standing Committee, which is chaired by the Emergency Relief Coordinator.

OCHA has a staff of 375 worldwide and a core regular budget of $20.5 million.

Department of Economic and Social Affairs (DESA)
(*www.un.org/esa/desa*)

Under-Secretary-General   Mr. José Antonio Ocampo (Colombia)

The Department of Economic and Social Affairs has three broad, interlinked areas of work:

- It compiles and analyses a broad range of social, economic and environmental data and information on relevant issues and trends. This analytical information serves to inform the United Nations policy-making processes, as well as a wider audience.

- DESA facilitates negotiations in the General Assembly and in the Economic and Social Council and its subsidiary bodies, providing support to member states and other participants as they build consensus on matters of global concern in the economic, social and related areas.

- It also advises governments, at their request, on ways and means of addressing their development challenges — including the development of national programmes and activities to carry out actions agreed to at the Millennium Summit, the Monterrey International Conference on Financing for Development, the World Summit on Sustainable Development, and other global economic, social and environmental conferences and summits.

DESA works in the areas of sustainable development, gender issues and the advancement of women, development policy analysis, population, statistics, public administration and e-government, and social policy and development. New spheres of work include support for the Permanent Forum on Indigenous Issues, for the United Nations Information and Communications Technologies Task Force, and for the United Nations Forum on Forests. It collaborates closely with NGOs, as well as other representatives of civil society.

Department for General Assembly and Conference Management (DGACM)
(*www.un.org/Depts/DGACM*)

Under-Secretary-General   Mr. Chen Jian (China)

The Department of General Assembly and Conference Management provides technical and secretariat support services to the General Assembly, the Security Council, the Economic and Social Council, their committees and other subsidiary bodies, and to conferences held away from Headquarters. It is responsible for the processing and issuance at Headquarters of all official documents in Arabic, Chinese, English, French, Russian and Spanish and provides interpretation services from and into these languages to intergovernmental meetings. It also produces the official records of the United Nations.

The head of the Department — the Under-Secretary-General for General Assembly and Conference Management — is responsible for the development and coordination of conference-management policies for the United Nations worldwide. He advises the President of the General Assembly on all matters relating to the session and work of the General Assembly and its General and Main Committees.

Department of Public Information (DPI)

Under-Secretary-General   Mr. Shashi Tharoor (India)

DPI's mission is to help fulfil the substantive purposes of the United Nations by strategically communicating information on the Organization's activities and concerns to the public. It does this to encourage public support for the achievement of the aims of the Organization. The Department uses outreach programmes, information campaigns, news and feature services, radio and television programmes, press releases, publications, documentary videos and special events to communicate its messages, and provides library services. In addition to its staff at UN Headquarters, DPI has 57 information centres and services around the world, as well as a regional centre (RUNIC) in Brussels, and information components in eight UN Offices.

The Under-Secretary-General for Communications and Public Information, who is the head of the Department, is responsible for United Nations communications and public information policy. He is charged with ensuring that the Organization provides a coordinated, accurate and transparent flow of information about its responsibilities and its work to the media, civil society and the general public.

The Department consists of three divisions. The Strategic Communications Division develops communication strategies to promote United Nations priorities and coordinates their implementation within the Department and across the UN system. It develops information products to publicize key thematic issues, targeting in particular the global media. It provides programmatic and operational support to the global network of United Nations information centres, as well as communications planning and backstopping to the information component of peace missions.

The News and Media Division is charged with producing and distributing United Nations news and information to the media around the world. It provides logistical support to journalists covering the UN and maintains a constant flow of news in six languages through the UN News Centre on the web. It provides coverage of UN meetings and events — including press releases, live TV feeds, radio programmes and photographs — and produces and distributes radio and video documentary and news programmes about the United Nations. This Division also produces regular UN publications, such as Basic Facts About the United Nations.

The main United Nations library — the Dag Hammarskjöld Library — is part of the Outreach Division, as are the sections of the Department that work with non-governmental organizations and educational institutions and those that market United Nations information products and services. The Outreach Division organizes special events and exhibitions on priority issues, organizes an annual training programme for journalists from developing countries, and develops partnerships with private and public sector organizations to further the aims of the Organization. Conducting guided tours of UN Headquarters, responding to public inquiries, and providing public speakers on UN issues are also responsibilities of this Division. It also produces the Yearbook of the United Nations and the UN Chronicle.

The Office of the Spokesman for the Secretary-General is responsible for planning the Secretary-General's media-related activities and explaining the policies and work of the United Nations to the world's media. The Spokesman briefs journalists on a daily basis on the work of the Secretary-General and on developments throughout the UN system, including the Security Council and other principal organs, along with the tribunals, agencies, funds and programmes. The Spokesman reports directly to the Secretary-General.

Department of Management (DM)

Under-Secretary-General   Ms. Catherine Bertini (United States)

The Department of Management provides strategic policy guidance and management support to all entities of the Secretariat in three management areas: finance, human resources and support services. These fall under the purview of the Offices of Programme Planning, Budget and Accounts; Human Resources Management; and Central Support Services.

The Department is responsible for formulating and implementing improved management policies in the Secretariat; the management and training of staff; programme planning, budgetary, financial and human resources management; and technological innovations. It also provides technical servicing for the General Assembly's Fifth Committee (Administrative and Budgetary), as well as servicing for the Committee for Programme and Coordination.

The head of the Department — the Under-Secretary-General for Management — provides policy guidance, coordination and direction for preparation of the Organization's medium-term plan and biennial budgets. She represents the Secretary-General on matters relating to management and monitors emerging management issues throughout the Secretariat. With authority delegated by the Secretary-General, the Under-Secretary-General also ensures the efficient implementation of the Organization's internal system of justice.

Office of the United Nations Security Coordinator (UNSECOORD)

Assistant Secretary-General
United Nations Security Coordinator*

The Office of the United Nations Security Coordinator acts on behalf of the Secretary-General and the heads of United Nations agencies, programmes and funds, to ensure a coherent response by the United Nations system to any emergency situation. It is responsible for all policy and procedural matters related to security, and, on behalf of the Secretary-General, takes decisions relating to all aspects of evacuation.

The Office formulates detailed recommendations to ensure the safety and security of staff members and eligible family members of the entire United Nations system; coordinates, plans and implements inter-agency security and safety programmes; and acts as the focal point for inter-agency cooperation.

The Office is funded on an inter-agency basis by all the participants in the United Nations System Chief Executives Board for Coordination (CEB).

Office of the High Representative for the Least Developed Countries, Landlocked Developing Countries and Small Island Developing States (OHRLLS)
(http://www.un.org/ohrlls)

Under-Secretary-General   Mr. Anwarul K. Chowdhury (Bangladesh)
High Representative for the
Least Developed Countries,
Landlocked Developing Countries
and Small Island Developing States

The Office of the High Representative for the Least Developed Countries, Landlocked Developing Countries and Small Island Developing States was established by the

---

* On 3 March 2004, the Secretary-General received the report of the Security in Iraq Accountability Panel, which he had established to investigate the security situation in Iraq in the period leading up to the terrorist attack of 19 August 2003 on the UN headquarters at the Canal Hotel in Baghdad. The Panel reported that the standard of security management as regards the Canal Hotel had been "seriously deficient and lacking cohesion" and that "the UN Security Coordinator failed to take remedial action with regard to difficulties being encountered by Office of the UN Security Coordinator (UNSECOORD) staff in Baghdad". Among other actions, the Secretary-General requested and received the resignation of UN Security Coordinator Tun Myat (Myanmar). A new Security Coordinator will be appointed.

General Assembly in December 2001. It aims to help mobilize international support for implementation of the *2001 Brussels Declaration and Programme of Action*, adopted by the least developed countries and their development partners, and to ensure effective coordination, monitoring and review of their implementation.

The key functions of the Office include: assisting the Secretary-General in ensuring the full mobilization and coordination of the United Nations system in the implementation, follow-up and monitoring of the Programme of Action at country, regional and global levels; providing support to the Economic and Social Council and the General Assembly in assessing progress, including the annual review of implementation of the Programme; and supporting, as appropriate, coordinated follow-up on the implementation of the *Global Framework for Transit Transport Cooperation between Landlocked and Transit Developing Countries and the Donor Community*, and the *Barbados Programme of Action for the Sustainable Development of Small Island Developing States*.

Its key functions also include: advocacy work in favour of least developed, landlocked and small island developing states, in partnership with the relevant UN bodies, civil society, the media, academia and foundations; and helping to mobilize international support and resources for implementation of the Programme of Action for Least Developed Countries, as well as for other programmes and initiatives in favour of landlocked developing countries and small island developing states.

The Office of the High Representative convened the first global conference to address the specific needs and problems of landlocked developing countries in Almaty, Kazakhstan, on 28 and 29 August 2003. Held at the ministerial level, the meeting sought to negotiate systemic improvements for these countries through the cooperation of transit nations, donor countries, multilateral agencies and the landlocked countries themselves. Mr. Chowdhury was designated as Secretary-General of the International Ministerial Conference.

Regional commissions

The United Nations regional commissions report to ECOSOC and their secretariats are under the authority of the Secretary-General. Their mandate is to initiate measures that promote the economic development of each region and strengthen the economic relations of the countries in that region, both among themselves and with other countries of the world. They are funded under the regular United Nations budget.

Economic Commission for Africa (ECA)
(*www.uneca.org*)

Set up in 1958, ECA carries out activities encouraging the growth of the economic and social sectors of the continent. It promotes policies and strategies to increase economic cooperation and integration among its 53 member countries, particularly in the production, trade, monetary, infrastructure and institutional fields. ECA focuses on producing information and analysis on economic and social issues; promoting food security and sustainable development; strengthening development management; harnessing the information revolution for development; and promoting regional cooperation and integration. Special attention is paid to improving the condition of women, enhancing their involvement and decision-making in development, and ensuring that women and gender equity are key elements in national development.

Executive Secretary: Mr. K. Y. Amoako (Ghana)
Address: PO Box 3001, Addis Ababa, Ethiopia
Tel: (251-1) 51-7200; Fax: (251-1) 51-0365; Email: *ecainfo@uneca.org*

Economic Commission for Europe (ECE)
(www.unece.org)

Created in 1947, ECE is the forum at which the countries of North America, Europe and central Asia forge the tools of their economic cooperation. It has 55 member countries, including Israel. Priority areas include economic analysis, environment and human settlements, statistics, sustainable energy, trade, industry and enterprise development, timber and transport. The ECE pursues its goals primarily through policy analysis and debates, and development of conventions, regulations and standards. The implementation of these instruments contributes to eliminating obstacles and simplifying procedures for trade in the region and with the rest of the world. Several aim at improving the environment. The Commission contributes to their implementation by providing technical assistance, in particular to countries with economies in transition.

Executive Secretary: Ms. Brigita Schmögnerová (Slovakia)
Address: Palais des Nations, CH-1211 Geneva 10, Switzerland
Tel: (41-22) 917-4444; Fax: (41-22) 917-0505; Email: *info.ece@unece.org*

Economic Commission for Latin America and the Caribbean (ECLAC)
(www.eclac.cl, www.eclac.org)

Established in 1948, ECLAC works to coordinate policies for promoting economic development in the region. It collaborates with its 41 member states and 7 associate members in the research and analysis of regional and national development processes. Its mission includes proposing, evaluating and following up on public policy measures as well as providing assistance in areas of specialized information.

ECLAC — the Spanish acronym is CEPAL — cooperates with national, regional and international organizations on subjects such as: agricultural development; economic and social planning; industrial, technological and entrepreneurial development; international trade, regional integration and cooperation; investment and financing; social development and equity; integration of women in development; natural resources and infrastructure; environment and human settlements; statistics; administrative management; demography and population policies.

Headquartered in Santiago, Chile, ECLAC has a subregional headquarters in Mexico City, for Central America, and another in Port-of-Spain, Trinidad and Tobago, for the Caribbean. It also maintains country offices in Buenos Aires, Brasilia, Montevideo and Bogota, as well as a liaison office in Washington, D.C.

Executive Secretary: Mr. José Luis Machinea (Argentina)
Address: Avenida Dag Hammarskjöld 3477,
Casilla de Correo 179-D, Santiago, Chile
Tel: (56-2) 471-2000, 210-2000; Fax: (56-2) 208-0252; Email: *cepal@eclac.clc*

Economic and Social Commission for Asia and the Pacific (ESCAP)
(www.unescap.org)

ESCAP, established in 1947, has a mandate to address the economic and social issues of the region. It plays a unique role as the only comprehensive intergovernmental forum for all the countries of Asia and the Pacific. Its 53 member states and 9 associate member states represent some 60 per cent of the world's population. ESCAP gives technical support to governments for social and economic development. The assistance comes through direct advisory services to governments, training and sharing of regional experience, and information through meetings, publications and inter-country networks. ESCAP executes programmes and projects to stimulate growth, improve socio-economic conditions and help build the foundations of modern society. Four regional research and training institutions — for agricultural development, agricultural machinery and engineering, statistics, and technology transfer — operate under its auspices. ESCAP also has a Pacific Operation Centre. Current priority areas are poverty reduction, managing globalization and addressing emerging social issues.

Executive Secretary: Mr. Kim Hak-Su (Republic of Korea)
Address: United Nations Building, Rajadamnern Nok Avenue,
Bangkok 10200 Thailand
Tel: (66-2) 288-1234; Fax: (66-2) 288-1000; Email: *escap-registry@un.org*

Economic and Social Commission for Western Asia (ESCWA)
(www.escwa.org.lb)

Established in 1973, ESCWA facilitates concerted action for the economic and social development of the countries of Western Asia by promoting economic cooperation and integration in the region. Comprised of 13 member states, ESCWA serves as the main general economic and social development forum for the region within the United Nations system. Its programmes address such areas as economic development, social development, agriculture, industry, natural resources, the environment, transport, communications and statistics.

Executive Secretary: Ms. Mervat M. Tallawy (Egypt)
Address: PO Box 11-8575, Riad el-Solh Square, Beirut, Lebanon
Tel: (961-1) 98-1301; Fax: (961-1) 98-1510; Email: *unescwa@escwa.org.lb*

International tribunals

International Criminal Tribunal for the Former Yugoslavia (ICTY)
(www.un.org/icty)

Established by the Security Council in 1993, the Tribunal is mandated to prosecute persons responsible for serious violations of international humanitarian law committed in the former Yugoslavia since 1991. It has 16 permanent judges, 27 ad litem judges, of whom it can use up to nine at any given time, and a staff of 1,238 from 84 countries. Its 2002-2003 budget was $223 million.

Since its inception, more than 130 people have been publicly indicted. At the end of 2003, 55 accused were in proceedings before the Tribunal and 20 were at large. Forty-six accused have been tried to date, of whom 25 have been convicted and sentenced, five have been found not guilty or acquitted, and one was recently convicted. The cases of the other 15 accused are currently on appeal.

President: Judge Theodor Meron (United States of America)
Prosecutor: Mrs. Carla Del Ponte (Switzerland)
Registrar: Mr. Hans Holthuis (Netherlands)
Headquarters: Churchillplein 1, 2517 JW, The Hague, Netherlands
Tel: (31-70) 512-5000; Fax: (31-70) 512-8990

International Criminal Tribunal for Rwanda (ICTR)
(www.ictr.org)

Created by the Security Council in 1994, the Tribunal has the mandate to prosecute persons responsible for genocide and other serious violations of international humanitarian law committed in Rwanda during 1994, as well as Rwandan citizens responsible for such violations committed in the territory of neighbouring states. It has three Trial Chambers made up of three judges each, and an Appeals Chamber made up of seven judges — five of whom sit on any given case. It also has a pool of 18 ad litem judges, of whom it can use up to four at any given time, and a staff of 872. Its 2002-2003 budget was $177.7 million.

By December 2003, it had secured the arrest of more than 60 persons. Of these, 16 had been convicted — with eight convictions upheld on appeal or otherwise finalized — and one acquitted (also upheld on appeal). Another 24 were currently being tried. Those convicted include Jean Kambanda, Prime Minister during the genocide — the first head of government to be arrested and subsequently convicted for that genocide.

President: Judge Erik Møse (Norway)
Prosecutor: Mr. Hassan B. Jallow (Gambia)
Registrar: Mr. Adama Dieng (Senegal)
Headquarters: Arusha International Conference Centre, PO Box 6016, Arusha, Tanzania
Tel. (212) 963-2850 or (255-27) 250-4369/4372
Fax (212) 963-2848 or (255-27) 250-4000/4373

United Nations programmes and other bodies

United Nations Conference on Trade and Development (UNCTAD)
(www.unctad.org)

Established in 1964 as a permanent intergovernmental body, the United Nations Conference on Trade and Development is the principal organ of the General Assembly in the field of trade and development. Its mandate is to accelerate trade and economic development, particularly of developing countries.

UNCTAD is the focal point within the United Nations system for development and related issues in the areas of trade, finance, technology, investment and sustainable development. Its main goals are to facilitate the integration of developing countries and economies in transition into the world economy and to promote development through trade and investment. In pursuing its goals, UNCTAD carries out research and policy analysis, intergovernmental deliberations, technical cooperation, and interaction with civil society and the business sector.

UNCTAD's Conference, its highest policy-making body, is composed of 192 member states (including the Holy See) and meets every four years. The tenth Conference was held in 2000 in Bangkok; UNCTAD XI took place in June 2004 in Sao Paolo, Brazil. Its executive body, the Trade and Development Board, meets annually in regular session to review the work of the secretariat.

The annual operational budget is about $45 million, drawn from the United Nations regular budget. Technical cooperation activities, financed from extrabudgetary resources, amount to about $24 million. UNCTAD has a staff of some 400. Its main publications are: the *Trade and Development Report, World Investment Report, Least Developed Countries Report, UNCTAD Handbook of Statistics, E-Commerce and Development Report, Review of Maritime Transport,* and *Economic Development in Africa.*

Secretary-General: Mr. Rubens Ricupero (Brazil)
Headquarters: Palais des Nations, CH-1211 Geneva 10, Switzerland
Tel: (41-22) 907-1234; Fax: (41-22) 907-0043; Email: *info@unctad.org*

International Trade Centre (ITC)
(*www.intracen.org*)

The International Trade Centre (ITC) is the technical cooperation agency of the United Nations Conference on Trade and Development (UNCTAD) and the World Trade Organization (WTO) for operational, enterprise-oriented aspects of trade development. It supports developing and transition economies — and particularly their business sector — in their efforts to realize their full potential for developing exports and improving import operations.

ITC's goals are: to facilitate the integration of developing and transition economy enterprises into the multilateral trading system; to support national efforts to design and implement trade development strategies; to strengthen key trade support services, both public and private; to improve export performance in sectors of critical importance and opportunity; and to foster international competitiveness within the business community as a whole, and the small and medium-sized enterprise (SME) sector in particular.

The Centre's technical programmes include: strategic and operational market research; business advisory services; trade information management; export training capacity development; sector-specific product and market development; trade in services; and international purchasing and supply chain management.

ITC's regular programme is financed in equal parts by WTO and the United Nations. The Centre also implements projects, at the demand of beneficiary countries, with voluntary contributions from donor governments and civil society institutions. Its annual budget is about $33 million; it has a headquarters staff of around 200, as well as several hundred consultants in the field.

Executive Director: Mr. J. Denis Bélisle (Canada)
Headquarters: Palais des Nations, CH-1211 Geneva 10, Switzerland
Tel: (41-22) 730-0111; Fax: (41-22) 733-4439; Email: *itcreg@intracen.org*

United Nations Office on Drugs and Crime (UNODC)
(*www.unodc.org*)

The United Nations Office on Drugs and Crime — formerly called the Office for Drug Control and Crime Prevention (established in 1997) — was created to enhance the United Nations capacity to address the interrelated issues of drug control, crime prevention and terrorism. It consists of a drug programme and a crime programme.

The drug programme is responsible for coordinating and leading United Nations drug control activities. It provides technical advice to member states on drug control matters; statistics on drug abuse, seizures and trends; and helps draft legislation and train judicial officials. The programme also works to educate the world on the dangers of drug abuse and to strengthen international action against production, trafficking and drug-related crime.

The crime programme is responsible for activities in the field of crime prevention and criminal justice. It works with member states to strengthen the rule of law and to promote stable and viable criminal justice systems. It pays special attention to combating transnational organized crime, illicit trafficking in human beings and firearms, financial crimes, corruption and terrorism.

UNODC has some 500 staff members, working at the national, regional and global levels through a network of 22 field offices worldwide, as well as liaison offices in New York and Brussels. Its budget for 2002-2003 was $181.9 million, comprising $166.4 million for the drug programme and $15.5 million for the crime programme. Ninety per cent of resources for the drug programme and 49 per cent for the crime programme are expected to come from voluntary contributions, and the remainder from the United Nations regular budget.

Executive Director: Mr. Antonio Maria Costa (Italy)
Headquarters: Vienna International Centre, Wagramerstrasse 5,
PO Box 500, A-1400 Vienna, Austria
Tel: (43-1) 26060-0; Fax: (43-1) 26060-5866; Email: *unodc@unodc.org*

United Nations Environment Programme (UNEP)
(*www.unep.org*)

The United Nations Environment Programme was founded in 1972. Its mission is to provide leadership and encourage partnerships in caring for the environment by enabling nations and peoples to improve their quality of life without compromising that of future generations.

As the principal United Nations body in the field of the environment, UNEP sets the global environmental agenda, promotes implementation of the environmental dimension of sustainable development in the United Nations system, and serves as an authoritative advocate of the global environment.

UNEP's governing body — the Governing Council — made up of 58 countries, meets annually. Programmes are financed by the Environment Fund, made up of voluntary contributions from governments and supplemented by trust funds and a small allocation from the United Nations regular budget. The Fund's budget for 2003-2004 is $130 million. UNEP has a staff of 605.

Executive Director: Mr. Klaus Toepfer (Germany)
Headquarters: United Nations Avenue, Gigiri, PO Box 30552, Nairobi, Kenya
Tel: (254-20) 621-234; Fax: (254-20) 624-489/490; Email: *cpiinfo@unep.org*

United Nations Development Programme (UNDP)
(www.undp.org)

The United Nations Development Programme (UNDP) is the UN's global development network. It advocates for change and connects countries to knowledge, experience and resources, to help their people build a better life. UNDP is on the ground in 166 countries, working with them on their own solutions to global and national development challenges. As they develop local capacity, they draw on the expertise of UNDP and its wide range of partners.

World leaders have pledged to achieve the Millennium Development Goals, which include the overarching goal of cutting poverty in half by 2015. UNDP's network links and coordinates global and national efforts to reach these goals. Its focus is on helping countries build and share solutions to the challenges of democratic governance, poverty reduction, crisis prevention and recovery, energy and environment, information and communications technology, and HIV/AIDS.

UNDP also administers the UN Capital Development Fund (UNCDF), the UN Development Fund for Women (UNIFEM) and the UN Volunteers (UNV). It is governed by a 36-member Executive Board, representing both developing and developed countries. Among its major publications is the annual *Human Development Report*.

Administrator: Mr. Mark Malloch Brown (United Kingdom)
Headquarters: 1 UN Plaza, New York, NY 10017, USA
Tel: (1-212) 906-5000; Fax: (1-212) 906-5001; Email: *hq@undp.org*

United Nations Development Fund for Women (UNIFEM)
(www.unifem.org)

The United Nations Development Fund for Women promotes women's empowerment and gender equality. It works to ensure the participation of women in all levels of development planning and practice. It also acts as a catalyst within the United Nations system for efforts to link the needs and concerns of women to all critical issues on the national, regional and global agendas.

Since its creation in 1976, UNIFEM has supported projects and initiatives throughout the developing world that promote women's human rights, as well as the political, economic and social empowerment of women. These have ranged from small grass-roots enterprises improving women's working conditions to public education campaigns and the design of new gender-sensitive laws.

UNIFEM works in autonomous association with UNDP. It reports to a Consultative Committee consisting of representatives from all regions and to UNDP's Executive Board. UNIFEM is represented at the regional and country levels by its 14 subregional offices. Its annual budget is around $35 million.

Director: Ms. Noeleen Heyzer (Singapore)
Headquarters: 304 East 45th Street, 15th floor, New York, NY 10017, USA
Tel: (1-212) 906-6400; Fax: (1-212) 906-6705; Email: *unifem@undp.org*

United Nations Volunteers (UNV)
(*www.unv.org*)

The United Nations Volunteers (UNV) programme is the volunteer arm of the UN system, supporting peace, relief and development initiatives in nearly 150 countries. Created by the General Assembly in 1970, it is administered by the UN Development Programme and reports to the Executive Board of UNDP/UNFPA. It works through UNDP country offices to send volunteers and promote the idea of volunteerism. As a volunteer-based programme, UNV is both unique within the United Nations family and in its scale as an international undertaking. It assigns mid-career professionals to sectoral and community-based development projects, humanitarian aid activities, and the promotion of human rights and democracy.

In any given year, more than 5,000 UNV specialists, field workers and national UNVs, short-term business/industry consultants and returning expatriate advisers, comprising close to 160 nationalities, are at work in 140 developing countries. Two thirds are themselves citizens of developing countries and one third come from industrialized countries. More than 30,000 persons have served as UNVs since 1971.

Graduate qualifications and several years' working experience are preconditions for recruitment. Contracts are normally for two years, with shorter assignments for humanitarian, electoral and other missions. UNVs receive a modest monthly living allowance. Funding comes from UNDP, partner UN agencies and donor contributions to the UNV Special Voluntary Fund.

Executive Coordinator a.i.: Mr. Ad de Raad (Netherlands)
Headquarters: Postfach 260 111, D-53153 Bonn, Germany
Tel: (49-228) 815-2000; Fax: (49-228) 815-2001; Email: *information@unv.org*

United Nations Population Fund (UNFPA)
(*www.unfpa.org*)

Established operationally in 1969 at the initiative of the General Assembly, the United Nations Population Fund is the largest internationally funded source of population assistance to developing countries and those with economies in transition. It assists countries, at their request, to improve reproductive health and family planning services on the basis of individual choice, and to formulate population policies in support of efforts towards sustainable development. It is a subsidiary organ of the General Assembly and has the same Executive Board as UNDP.

UNFPA is wholly funded by voluntary contributions, which totalled nearly $261.1 million in 2002, plus $113 million earmarked for specific activities. About 64 per cent of its assistance is used for reproductive health, including safe motherhood, family planning and sexual health, to refine approaches to adolescent reproductive health, reduce maternal disabilities such as obstetric fistula, address HIV/AIDS, and provide assistance in emergencies.

Nearly 20 per cent of UNFPA assistance relates to population and development strategies. It aims to ensure a balance between development and population dynamics by providing information, influencing policy, and building national capacity in population programming. The rest is used for advocacy. UNFPA seeks to mobilize resources and political commitment for population activities relating to agreed international development goals, including those in the Millennium Declaration. The Fund has a staffing level of 972 staff posts.

Executive Director: Ms. Thoraya Ahmed Obaid (Saudi Arabia)
Headquarters: 220 East 42nd Street, New York, NY 10017, USA
Tel: (1-212) 297-5000; Fax: (1-212) 370-0201; Email: *hq@unfpa.org*

Office of the United Nations High Commissioner for Refugees (UNHCR)
(*www.unhcr.ch*)

Created by the General Assembly in 1950, the Office of the United Nations High Commissioner for Refugees is mandated to lead and coordinate international action for the worldwide protection of refugees and the resolution of refugee problems. Since its creation, UNHCR has helped around 50 million refugees, earning two Nobel Peace Prizes in 1954 and in 1981.

UNHCR's most important responsibility, known as "international protection", is to ensure respect for refugees' basic human rights, including their ability to seek asylum and to ensure that no one is returned involuntarily to a country where he or she has reason to fear persecution. UNHCR also promotes international refugee agreements, monitors government compliance with international law and provides material assistance such as food, water, shelter and medical care to fleeing civilians. UNHCR seeks long-term solutions for refugees through voluntary repatriation, integration in countries where they first sought asylum, or resettlement in a third country.

By 2003, with a staff of more than 5,000 people working in 254 offices in 115 countries, the agency was looking after some 20 million people, including refugees, returnees and people displaced within their own countries. Over 700 governmental, intergovernmental and NGO partners work with UNHCR. Of these, 143 are international NGOs and 404 are national NGOs.

The High Commissioner's programmes are approved and supervised by UNHCR's Executive Committee, composed of 64 member countries. Programmes are financed by voluntary contributions, mainly from governments, but also from other groups including private citizens and organizations. UNHCR receives a limited subsidy — only around 2 per cent of the total — from the United Nations regular budget, which is used exclusively for administrative costs. The 2003 budget totalled some $1.18 billion.

High Commissioner: Mr. Ruud Lubbers (Netherlands)
Headquarters: Case Postale 2500, CH-1211 Geneva 2, Switzerland
Tel: (41-22) 739-8111; Fax: (41-22) 739-7314/15/16; Email: *hqpi00@unhcr.ch*

United Nations Children's Fund (UNICEF)
(*www.unicef.org*)

The United Nations Children's Fund was created in 1946 to help overcome the obstacles that poverty, violence, disease and discrimination place in a child's path. Its work is guided by the Convention on the Rights of the Child — the most widely accepted human rights treaty in the world. UNICEF believes that caring for children and protecting their rights are the cornerstones of human progress.

UNICEF is engaged in every facet of child health, from birth through adolescence. It works to ensure that all children are immunized against common childhood diseases, and that children and their mothers are well nourished. It works to prevent the spread of HIV/AIDS among young people, and helps children and families affected by the disease to live with dignity. UNICEF promotes girls' education because it benefits all children. It relieves suffering during emergencies and wherever children are exposed to violence, abuse or exploitation. As part of the Global Movement for Children, UNICEF encourages young people to speak out and participate in the decisions that affect their lives. In all its work, UNICEF encourages the participation of children and young people.

UNICEF is governed by an Executive Board comprising delegates from 36 countries who govern its policies, programmes and finances. There are more than 7,000 UNICEF employees working in 158 countries and territories around the world. UNICEF is funded entirely by voluntary contributions; its total programme expenditures in 2002 were slightly over $1 billion. While its strongest support comes from governments, UNICEF also receives considerable aid from the private sector, and from some 6 million individuals who give through National Committees in the industrialized world.

In 1965, UNICEF was awarded the Nobel Peace Prize. Its major publication, The State of the World's Children, is released annually.

Executive Director: Ms. Carol Bellamy (USA)
Headquarters: UNICEF House, 3 United Nations Plaza, New York, NY 10017, USA
Tel: (1-212) 326-7000; Fax: (1-212) 888-7465; Email: *info@unicef.org*

World Food Programme (WFP)
(*www.wfp.org*)

The World Food Programme is the world's largest humanitarian organization, responsible for delivering around 4 million metric tonnes of food annually. Established in 1963 as the authority on food aid in the UN system, WFP's mandate is to help poor people in developing countries by combating hunger and poverty. It uses food aid to promote economic and social development.

The Programme's global school feeding campaign seeks to ensure that the world's 300 million undernourished children are fed and educated. In emergencies, WFP provides fast, life-sustaining relief to victims of wars and natural and man-made disasters. In 2002, 57 per cent of its resources were used for emergency relief and 26 per cent for protracted relief and recovery efforts. While a large portion of WFP's food supplies are pledged in kind by donor countries, over $300 million is bought by WFP using multilateral and bilateral cash resources. It buys more goods and services from developing countries than any other UN agency or programme — $204 million in 2002 alone.

WFP has a staff of more than 9,000, most of whom work in the field. In 2002, nearly 3.7 million tonnes of food was delivered to 72 million people in 82 countries. In 2003, WFP reached 110 million people with food aid — a record in its 40-year history — made possible by generous contributions towards its $4.3 billion budget. In Iraq, it mounted the largest humanitarian operation ever, while also feeding some 40 million people across Africa in one of the worst food disasters to hit that continent in decades.

WFP is governed by a 36-member Executive Board, half of whom are elected by ECOSOC and half by FAO. It meets four times a year and oversees WFP's humanitarian and food aid activities.

Executive Director: Mr. James T. Morris (USA)
Headquarters: Via C.G. Viola 68, Parco dei Medici, 00148 Rome, Italy
Tel: (39-06) 6513-1; Fax: (39-06) 6513-2840; Email: *wfpinfo@wfp.org*

United Nations Relief and Works Agency for Palestine Refugees in the Near East (UNRWA)
(*www.unrwa.org*)

The United Nations Relief and Works Agency for Palestine Refugees in the Near East was established by the General Assembly in 1949 to carry out relief work for Palestine refugees. In the absence of a solution to the Palestine refugee problem, its mandate has been periodically renewed, most recently until 30 June 2005.

UNRWA initially provided emergency relief to some 750,000 Palestine refugees who had lost their homes and livelihoods as a result of the 1948 Arab-Israeli conflict. It is now the main provider of basic services — education, health, relief and social services — to more than 4.1 million registered Palestine refugees in the Middle East, including some 1.3 million living in 59 refugee camps in Jordan, Lebanon, Syria, the Gaza Strip and the West Bank. Since October 2000, the Agency has also conducted emergency relief operations in the occupied Palestinian territory to mitigate the worst effects of the strife there.

UNRWA's operations are supervised and supported by its headquarters in Gaza and in Amman, Jordan. The Commissioner-General, who reports directly to the General Assembly, is assisted by an Advisory Commission composed of Belgium, Egypt, France, Japan, Jordan, Lebanon, Syria, Turkey, the United Kingdom and the United States.

UNRWA employs over 24,200 area staff, mainly Palestine refugees, while the United Nations covers the costs of more than 100 international staff posts. UNRWA depends almost entirely on voluntary contributions for its regular and emergency operations. Most contributions are in cash, although 7 per cent is in kind — mainly food donations for distribution to needy refugees. The regular budget for 2003 was $344 million.

Commissioner-General: Mr. Peter Hansen (Denmark
Headquarters (Gaza): Gamal Abdul Nasser Street, Gaza City
Tel: (972-8) 677-7333; Fax: (972-8) 677-7555; Email: *unrwa-pio@unrwa.org*
Headquarters (Amman, Jordan):
Bayader Wadi Seer, PO Box 140157, Amman 11814, Jordan
Tel: (962-6) 582-6171/6176; Fax: (962-6) 582-6177; Email: *jorpio@unrwa.org*

Office of the United Nations High Commissioner for Human Rights (OHCHR)
(www.unhchr.ch)

The General Assembly in 1993 established the post of United Nations High Commissioner for Human Rights as the official with principal responsibility for United Nations human rights activities. The High Commissioner is charged with promoting and protecting the enjoyment by all of civil, cultural, economic, political and social rights. The mandate is carried out through the Office of the High Commissioner for Human Rights.

OHCHR acts as the focal point for all human rights activities of the United Nations. It prepares reports and undertakes research at the request of the General Assembly and other policy-making bodies. It cooperates with governments and international, regional and non-governmental organizations for the promotion and protection of human rights. It acts as the secretariat for the meetings of United Nations human rights bodies. OHCHR, which has a staff of some 500, is organized into five branches:

- The Research and Right to Development Branch does research and analysis on human rights issues and develops and oversees the implementation of a strategy for the realization of the right to development.

- The Activities and Programme Branch carries out an extensive programme of technical assistance to countries, provides support to fact-finding bodies (country-specific special rapporteurs, working groups, etc.) that look into alleged violations, and plays a support and training role for human rights field activities.

- The Support Services Branch ensures support for United Nations human rights bodies, like the Commission on Human Rights and the treaty bodies.

- The External Relations Branch publicizes the work of the Office and human rights mechanisms, is responsible for media relations, coordinates partnerships with NGOs and civil society, and follows all resource mobilization and donor relations.

- The newly created Special Procedures Branch provides enhanced support to extra-conventional mechanisms of the Commission on Human Rights — including such thematic mechanisms as special rapporteurs, special representatives and thematic working groups — established with a view to documenting human rights violations worldwide, enhancing the protection of victims of human rights violations and promoting their rights.

High Commissioner: Ms. Louise Arbour (Canada)*
Headquarters: 8-14 Avenue de la Paix, CH-1211 Geneva 10, Switzerland
Tel: (41-22) 917-9000; Fax: (41-22) 917-9010
Email: *InfoDesk@ohchr.org* ["Request for information" in "Subject" field]

United Nations Human Settlements Programme (UN-HABITAT)
(www.unhabitat.org)

The United Nations Human Settlements Programme (UN-HABITAT) — formerly known as the United Nations Centre for Human Settlements — promotes sustainable human settlements development through advocacy, policy formulation, capacity building, knowledge creation and the strengthening of partnerships between governments and civil society.

UN-HABITAT was established in 1978. It is the lead agency for implementing the "Habitat Agenda" and coordinating human settlements development activities within the United Nations family, focusing on two priority areas: adequate shelter for all; and sustainable urban development. UN-HABITAT is also responsible for helping the international community meet the Millennium Development Goal of improving the lives of 100 million slum dwellers by 2020.

The Human Settlements Programme supports and works in partnership with governments, local authorities, NGOs and the private sector. Its technical programmes and

---

* Ms. Arbour's appointment was approved by the General Assembly on 25 February 2004. She took up her post on 1 July, following her retirement from the Supreme Court of Canada. Her predecessor, Mr. Sergio Vieira de Mello (Brazil), was killed in the 19 August 2003 attack on UN headquarters in Baghdad, where he was on assignment as head of the UN mission in Iraq. In the interim, Mr. Bertrand Ramcharan (Guyana) served as Acting High Commissioner.

projects focus on a wide range of issues, including slum upgrading, urban poverty reduction, post-disaster reconstruction, the provision of urban water and sanitation and the mobilization of domestic financial resources for shelter delivery. Most of these programmes are implemented in partnership with other bilateral support agencies.

UN-HABITAT is governed by a 58-member Governing Council which meets every two years. Appropriations of nearly $300 million were approved for the biennium 2002-2003, not including final expenditures for the period. The Programme produces two flagship publications: the Global Report on Human Settlements, a complete review of human settlements conditions worldwide, and the State of the World's Cities.

Executive Director: Mrs. Anna Kajumulo Tibaijuka (Tanzania)
Headquarters: PO Box 30030, 00100 Nairobi GPO, Kenya
Tel: (254-20) 621-234; Fax: (254-20) 624-266/267; Email: *infohabitat@unhabitat.org*

United Nations Office for Project Services (UNOPS)
(*www.unops.org*)

The United Nations Office for Project Services manages project resources to help developing countries and countries with economies in transition in their quest for peace, social stability, economic growth and sustainable development.

At the request of the members of the UN system, UNOPS provides services raging from overall project management to such specific inputs as loan administration, financial management, project supervision, recruitment, procurement and training. It responds flexibly and rapidly to its clients' demands, tailoring its services to their particular needs to attain cost-effective results.

UNOPS is self-financing through fees earned for services rendered. Income for 2002 was $43.8 million; project delivery was valued at $503 million. It had 330 staff, 4,900 national project personnel, 560 international project personnel and experts, and 1,550 international consultants.

Executive Director: Mr. Nigel Fisher (Canada)
Headquarters: 405 Lexington Avenue, New York, NY 10174, USA
Tel: (1-212) 457-4000; Fax: (1-212) 457-4001; Email: *unops.newyork@unops.org*

United Nations University (UNU)
(*www.unu.edu*)

The United Nations University is an international community of scholars engaged in research, postgraduate training and the dissemination of knowledge to further the United Nations aims of peace and progress. The Charter of the University was adopted in 1973; it commenced operations in 1975. The University has 14 Research and Training Centres and Programmes around the world.

UNU is financed entirely by voluntary contributions from governments, agencies, foundations and individual donors. It receives no funds from the United Nations budget: its basic annual income for operating expenses comes from investment income derived from its Endowment Fund. UNU's budget for 2003 was $36.8 million. It has a staff of 247.

UNU is governed by a 24-member Council that meets annually.

Rector: Prof. Hans van Ginkel (Netherlands)
Headquarters: 53-70 Jingumae 5-Chome, Shibuya-ku, Tokyo 150-8925, Japan
Tel: (81-3) 3499-2811; Fax: (81-3) 3499-2828; Email: *mbox@hq.unu.edu*

International Research and Training Institute for the Advancement of Women (INSTRAW)
(*www.un-instraw.org*)

The International Research and Training Institute for the Advancement of Women was established in 1976 on the recommendation of the first World Conference on Women. It has the unique mandate to promote and undertake policy research and training programmes at the international level to contribute to the advancement of women; to enhance their active and equal participation in the development process; to raise awareness of gender issues; and to create networks worldwide for the attainment of gender equality.

Since 1999, the Institute has used new information technologies to produce, manage and disseminate gender knowledge and information on critical issues and trends affecting women and men in their roles in development, through the Gender Awareness Information and Networking System (GAINS). The Institute also carries out research projects on such strategic areas as women and men, building partnerships for gender equality, women and men in the information society, the impact of globalization on women, and gender and peace.

Director: Ms. Carmen Moreno (Mexico)
Headquarters: César Nicolás Penson 102-A, Santo Domingo, Dominican Republic
Tel: (1-809) 685-2111; Fax: (1-809) 685-2117; Email: *comments@un-instraw.org*

United Nations Interregional Crime and Justice Research Institute (UNICRI)
(*www.unicri.it*)

The United Nations Interregional Crime and Justice Research Institute collects, analyses and disseminates information, and carries out training and technical co-operation projects.

Established in 1968, UNICRI promotes and supports analysis, in collaboration with the countries concerned, to establish a reliable base of knowledge and information on organized crime and, in particular, against trafficking in human beings, corruption and terrorism. It seeks to identify strategies for crime prevention and control — as a contribution to socio-economic development and the protection of human rights — and to design practical systems aimed at providing support for policy formulation, implementation and evaluation.

The Institute also designs and carries out training activities at the international and national levels in these fields, and promotes the exchange of information through its international documentation centre on criminology.

UNICRI is funded by voluntary contributions from member states, governmental and non-governmental organizations, and academic institutions.

Director: Mr. Alberto Bradanini (Italy)
Headquarters: Viale Maestri del Lavoro 10, 10127 Turin, Italy
Tel: (39-011) 653-7111; Fax: (39-011) 631-3368; Email: *unicri@unicri.it*

United Nations Institute for Training and Research (UNITAR)
(*www.unitar.org*)

An autonomous United Nations body established in 1965, the United Nations Institute for Training and Research has the mandate to enhance the effectiveness of the United Nations through training and research. UNITAR provides training to assist countries in meeting the challenges of the 21st century; conducts research to explore innovative training and capacity-building approaches; and forms partnerships with other United Nations agencies, governments and NGOs for developing and organizing training and capacity-building programmes that meet countries' needs.

UNITAR is governed by a Board of Trustees (*ad personam*). The Institute is fully self-funded and is sponsored by voluntary contributions from governments, intergovernmental organizations, foundations and other non-governmental sources. Its biennial budget is around $18 million. UNITAR's activities are conducted from its headquarters in Geneva, as well as through its New York office. It has a total staff of 49.

Executive Director: Mr. Marcel Boisard (Switzerland)
Headquarters: International Environment House, Chemin des Anémones 11-13, 1219 Châtelaine, Geneva, Switzerland. By mail: UNITAR, Palais des Nations, CH-1211 Geneva 10, Switzerland
Tel: (41-22) 917-1234; Fax: (41-22) 917-8047; Email: *info@unitar.org*

United Nations Research Institute for Social Development (UNRISD)
(*www.unrisd.org*)

An autonomous United Nations body created in 1963, the United Nations Research Institute for Social Development engages in research on the social dimensions of contemporary problems affecting development. UNRISD provides governments, development agencies, grass-roots organizations and scholars with a better understanding of how development policies and processes of economic and social change affect different social groups.

UNRISD relies wholly on voluntary contributions for financing its activities. In 2002, it received approximately $2.5 million from Denmark, Finland, Mexico, the Netherlands, Norway, Sweden, Switzerland and the United Kingdom. An additional $1.1 million for specific projects was received from a variety of foundations, bilateral donors and United Nations agencies. An 11-member Board approves the annual budget and research programme.

Director: Mr. Thandika Mkandawire (Sweden)
Headquarters: Palais des Nations, CH-1211 Geneva 10, Switzerland
Tel: (41-22) 917-3020; Fax: (41-22) 917-0650; Email: *info@unrisd.org*

United Nations Institute for Disarmament Research (UNIDIR)
(*www.unidir.org*)

Established in 1980, the United Nations Institute for Disarmament Research undertakes independent research on security, disarmament and development at the national, regional and global levels, as interrelated aspects of overall human security.

The Institute organizes expert-level meetings and discussions; hosts an annual fellowship programme focused on regional conflicts; and maintains an online database of research institutes, NGOs and civil society groups concerned with disarmament, security, peace and arms control. It publishes a wide range of books, reports and papers, and the quarterly *Disarmament Forum*, both in hard copy and online.

UNIDIR relies predominantly on voluntary contributions from governments and private funders. Its core staff is supplemented by visiting fellows and research interns.

Director: Dr. Patricia Lewis (United Kingdom, Ireland)
Headquarters: Palais des Nations, CH-1211 Geneva 10, Switzerland
Tel: (41-22) 917-3186 or 917-4263; Fax: (41-22) 917-0176; Email: *unidir@unog.ch*

Specialized agencies and other organizations

International Labour Organization (ILO)
(*www.ilo.org*)

The International Labour Organization is the specialized agency that seeks the promotion of social justice and internationally recognized human and labour rights. Established in 1919, it became the first specialized agency of the United Nations in 1946.

ILO formulates international policies and programmes to help improve working and living conditions; creates international labour standards to serve as guidelines for national authorities in putting these policies into action; carries out an extensive programme of technical cooperation to help governments in making these policies effective; and engages in training, education and research to help advance these efforts.

ILO is unique among world organizations in that workers' and employers' representatives have an equal voice with those of governments in formulating its policies. It is composed of three bodies:

- The International Labour Conference brings together governmental, employer and worker delegates from member countries every year. It sets international labour standards and acts as a forum where social and labour questions of importance to the entire world are discussed.

- The Governing Body meets twice a year and directs ILO operations, prepares the programme and budget and examines cases of non-observance of ILO standards.

- The International Labour Office is the permanent secretariat of the Organization.

Opportunities for study and training are offered at the International Training Centre in Turin, Italy. ILO's International Institute for Labour Studies' means of action include: research networks; social policy forums; courses and seminars; visiting scholar and internship programmes; and publications.

On its fiftieth anniversary, in 1969, ILO was awarded the Nobel Peace Prize.

ILO employs 2,500 officials and experts at its Geneva headquarters and in 49 field offices around the world. It adopted a programme and budget for 2004-2005 of over $529 million.

Director-General: Mr. Juan Somavía (Chile)
Headquarters: 4, route des Morillons, CH-1211 Geneva 22, Switzerland
Tel: (41-22) 799-6111; Fax: (41-22) 798-8685; Email: *ilo@ilo.org*

Food and Agriculture Organization of the United Nations (FAO)
(*www.fao.org*)

The Food and Agriculture Organization of the United Nations is the lead agency for rural development in the United Nations system. It works to alleviate poverty and hunger by promoting agricultural development, improved nutrition and the pursuit of food security — the access of all people at all times to the food they need for an active and healthy life. FAO was founded at a conference in Quebec City on 16 October 1945, a date observed annually as World Food Day.

FAO offers development assistance, provides policy and planning advice to governments, collects, analyses and disseminates information, and acts as an international forum for debate on food and agriculture issues. Special programmes help countries prepare for emergency food crisis and provide relief assistance. On average, FAO has some 2,000 field projects operating at any one time. FAO-assisted projects spend more than $300 million per year from funds provided by donor agencies and governments.

FAO is governed by the Conference of member nations, which meets biennially. The Conference elects a 49-member Council that serves as the governing body between sessions of the Conference.

The regular programme budget for 2002-2003 was $651.8 million. FAO has a staff of 3,700, working at headquarters and in the field.

Director-General: Dr. Jacques Diouf (Senegal)
Headquarters: Viale delle Terme di Caracalla, 00100 Rome, Italy
Tel: (39-06) 5705-1; Fax: (39-06) 5705-3152; Email: *FAO-HQ@fao.org*

United Nations Educational, Scientific and Cultural Organization (UNESCO)
(*www.unesco.org*)

UNESCO was created in 1946 to build lasting world peace based on the intellectual and moral solidarity of humankind. Its areas of work are education, natural sciences, social and human sciences, culture and communication.

Its programmes aim at promoting a culture of peace and human and sustainable development. They focus on: achieving education for all; promoting environmental research through international scientific programmes; supporting the expression of cultural identities; protecting and enhancing the world's natural and cultural heritage; and promoting the free flow of information and press freedom, as well as strengthening the communication capacities of developing countries.

UNESCO maintains a system of 190 National Commissions and is supported by some 5,000 UNESCO Associations, Centres and Clubs. It enjoys official relations with 350 NGOs, and also cooperates with various foundations and international and regional networks.

UNESCO's governing body — the General Conference — is made up of all member states and meets every two years. The Executive Board, consisting of 58 members elected by the Conference, is responsible for supervising the programme adopted by the Conference.

UNESCO has a staff of 2,145. Its regular budget for 2002-2003 was $544 million.

Director-General: Mr. Koïchiro Matsuura (Japan)
Headquarters: 7 Place de Fontenoy, 75352 Paris 07-SP, France
Tel: (33-1) 4568-1000; Fax: (33-1) 4567-1690; Email: *bpi@unesco.org*

World Health Organization (WHO)
(www.who.int)

Established in 1948, the World Health Organization promotes technical cooperation for health among nations, carries out programmes to control and eradicate disease, and strives to improve the quality of life. Its objective is the attainment by all people of the highest possible level of health.

Its strategic directions are:

- reducing excess mortality, morbidity and disability, especially in poor and marginalized populations;
- promoting healthy lifestyles and reducing health risks that arise from environmental, economic, social and behavioural causes;
- developing health systems that are more equitable and effective, respond to people's legitimate demands, and are financially fair;
- developing appropriate health policies and institutional environments, and promoting the health dimension of social, economic, environmental and development policies.

WHO's governing body, the World Health Assembly, is composed of 192 member states (including the Cook Islands) and meets annually. Its decisions and policies are given effect by the Executive Board, composed of 32 government-appointed health experts, which it meets twice a year.

WHO has Regional Offices in Brazzaville, Congo; Washington, D.C., USA; Cairo, Egypt; Copenhagen, Denmark; New Delhi, India; and Manila, Philippines.

WHO has a staff of about 3,500. Its regular budget for 2002-2003 was $935.7 million.

Director-General: Dr. Lee Jong-wook (Republic of Korea)
Headquarters: 20 Avenue Appia, CH-1211 Geneva 27, Switzerland
Tel: (41-22) 791-2111; Fax: (41-22) 791-3111; Email: *inf@who.int*

International Monetary Fund (IMF)
(www.imf.org)

Established at the Bretton Woods Conference in 1944, the International Monetary Fund:

- facilitates international monetary cooperation;
- promotes exchange rate stability and orderly exchange arrangements;
- assists in the establishment of a multilateral system of payments and the elimination of foreign exchange restrictions;

- assists members by temporarily providing financial resources to correct maladjustments in their balance of payments.

The IMF has authority to create and allocate to its members international financial reserves in the form of "Special Drawing Rights (SDRs)". The Fund's financial resources consist primarily of the subscriptions ("quotas") of its 184 member countries, which currently total SDR 212.7 billion, or about $293 billion. Quotas are determined by a formula based upon the relative economic size of the members.

The IMF's main financial role is to provide temporary credits to members experiencing balance-of-payments difficulties. In return, members borrowing from the Fund agree to undertake policy reforms to correct the problems that underlie these difficulties. The amounts that IMF members may borrow are limited in proportion to their quotas. The Fund also offers concessional assistance to low-income member countries.

Its governing body, the Board of Governors, in which all member countries are represented, meets annually. Day-to-day work is conducted by the 24-member Executive Board. The International Monetary and Finance Committee, whose 24 members are on the Board of Governors, advises the Board on matters under its purview.

The IMF has a staff of about 2,650 from 140 countries, headed by a Managing Director who is selected by the Executive Board. Its administrative budget for financial year 2003 was $746.4 million net of estimated reimbursements.

The IMF publishes the World Economic Outlook and the Global Financial Stability Report twice a year, along with a variety of other studies.

Managing Director (As of 7 June 2004): Mr. Rodrigo de Rato y Figaredo (Spain)
Headquarters: 700 19th Street NW, Washington, D.C. 20431, USA
Tel: (1-202) 623-7300; Fax: (1-202) 623-6278; Email: *publicaffairs@imf.org*

The World Bank Group
(*www.worldbank.org*)

The World Bank is a group of five institutions: the International Bank for Reconstruction and Development (established in 1945); the International Finance Corporation (1956); the International Development Association (1960); the Multilateral Investment Guarantee Agency (1988); and the International Centre for Settlement of Investment Disputes (1966).

The common goal of the Bank is to reduce poverty around the world by strengthening the economies of poor nations. Its aim is to improve people's living standards, in line with the Millennium Development Goals, by promoting economic growth and development. The Bank orients its lending activities and capacity-building activities based on two pillars for development: building the climate for investment, jobs and sustainable growth; and investing in poor people and empowering them to participate in development.

The World Bank is owned by its 184 member countries, which constitute its Board of Governors. General operations are delegated to a smaller group, the Board of Executive Directors, with the President of the Bank serving as Chairman of the Board. It has a staff of about 10,000 employees.

In 2003, the World Bank Group provided $18.5 billion for operations in more than 100 developing countries. Among its major publications is the annual World Development Report.

President: Mr. James D. Wolfensohn (USA)
Headquarters: 1818 H Street NW, Washington, D.C. 20433, USA
Tel: (1-202) 473-1000; Fax: (1-202) 477-6391; Email: *pic@worldbank.org*

International Bank for Reconstruction and Development (IBRD)

The articles of IBRD were drawn up in 1944 at the Bretton Woods Conference, and the Bank began operations in 1946. IBRD aims to reduce poverty in middle-income and creditworthy poorer countries by promoting sustainable development through loans, guarantees and non-lending — including analytical and advisory services. IBRD does not maximize profit but has earned a net income each year since 1948.

The Bank raises almost all its money through the sale of AAA-rated bonds and other securities in international capital markets. The amount paid in by countries when they join the Bank constitutes less than 5 per cent of IBRD's funds, but it has been leveraged into some $383 billion in loans since the Bank was established.

In fiscal 2003, the Bank's new loan commitments amounted to $11.2 billion, covering 99 new operations in 37 countries.

International Development Association (IDA)

IDA helps the world's poorest countries reduce poverty by providing credits — loans at zero interest with a 10-year grace period and maturities of 35 to 40 years. Since its establishment in 1960, IDA has provided $142 billion in interest-free credits to the world's 81 poorest countries, home to 2.5 billion people.

The bulk of IDA's resources come from donor government contributions. These contributions come mainly from richer IDA members, but donor countries also include some that are current recipients of IBRD loans. Donors are asked every three years to replenish IDA funds. There have been 13 replenishments since IDA was established. In July 2002, donor representatives ("IDA Deputies") concluded negotiations on the 13th replenishment of IDA and agreed on a framework for the projected programme and its financing needs. That replenishment made possible the commitment of SDR 18 billion (about $23 billion) to poor IDA members over the following three years, beginning on 1 July 2002.

In fiscal 2003, IDA lending totalled $7.3 billion for 141 new operations in 55 countries.

International Finance Corporation (IFC)

IFC is the largest multilateral source of loan and equity financing for private-sector projects in the developing world. It finances and provides advice for private-sector ventures and projects in developing countries, in partnership with private investors. Through its advisory work, IFC also helps governments create conditions that stimulate the flow of both domestic and foreign private savings and investment.

Its focus is to promote economic development by encouraging the growth of productive enterprise and efficient capital markets in member countries. IFC participates in an investment only when it can make a special contribution that complements the role of market investors. It also plays a catalytic role, stimulating and mobilizing private investment in the developing world by demonstrating that investments there can be profitable.

IFC is a separate entity within the World Bank Group and its funds are distinct from those of IBRD. In fiscal 2003, its commitments amounted to $3.9 billion in 204 companies for 64 countries. Its portfolio totalled $23.4 billion, including $6.6 billion in syndicated loans.

Multilateral Investment Guarantee Agency (MIGA)

MIGA helps to encourage foreign investment in developing countries by providing insurance (guarantees) to foreign private investors against loss caused by non-commercial (i.e., political) risks — such as currency transfer, expropriation, war and civil disturbance. It also provides technical assistance to help countries disseminate information on investment opportunities.

MIGA's subscribed capital comes from its 157 member countries. In fiscal 2003, it issued guarantees of some $1.4 billion — part of $12.4 billion in guarantees issued since its establishment in 1988.

MIGA has successfully promoted the flow of capital to developing countries. It has issued more than 650 guarantees, facilitating more than $50 billion in foreign direct investment in 85 developing countries.

International Centre for Settlement of Investment Disputes (ICSID)

ICSID provides facilities for the settlement, by conciliation or arbitration, of investment disputes between governments and private foreign investors. It was established under the 1966 Convention on the Settlement of Investment Disputes between States and Nationals of Other States, which has been ratified by 140 countries as of November 2003. Recourse to the Centre is voluntary, but once the parties have consented to arbitration, neither can unilaterally withdraw its consent.

The Centre is an autonomous organization with close links to the Bank, and all of its members are also members of the Bank. Its Administrative Council, chaired by the World Bank's President, consists of one representative of each country that has ratified the Convention.

International Civil Aviation Organization (ICAO)
(*www.icao.int*)

The International Civil Aviation Organization makes it safer and easier to fly from one country to another. Created in 1944, it sets international standards and regulations necessary for the safety, security, efficiency and regularity of air transport, and serves as the medium for cooperation in all fields of civil aviation among its 188 Contracting States.

ICAO has an Assembly, its sovereign body, comprising delegates from all Contracting States, and a Council of representatives of 36 nations elected by the Assembly. The Assembly meets at least once every three years: it decides ICAO policy and examines any matters not specifically referred to the Council. The Council is the executive body, and carries out Assembly directives.

Its budget for 2003 was $60.5 million. ICAO has a staff of 800.

President of the Council: Dr. Assad Kotaite (Lebanon)
Secretary General: Dr. Taïeb Chérif (Algeria)
Headquarters: 999 University Street, Montreal, Quebec H3C 5H7, Canada
Tel: (1-514) 954-8219; Fax: (1-514) 954-6077; Email: *icaohq@icao.int*

International Maritime Organization (IMO)
(*www.imo.org*)

The International Maritime Organization, which began functioning in 1959, is responsible for improving the safety and security of shipping engaged in international trade and for preventing marine pollution from ships.

IMO provides the machinery for governments to cooperate in formulating regulations and practices relating to technical matters affecting international shipping; to facilitate the adoption of the highest practicable standards of maritime safety and efficiency in navigation; and to protect the marine environment through prevention and control of pollution from ships.

More than 40 conventions and agreements and some 1,000 codes and recommendations have been produced by IMO and implemented globally.

In 1983, IMO established the World Maritime University in Malmö, Sweden, which provides advanced training for administrators, educators and others involved in shipping at the senior level. The IMO International Maritime Law Institute (Valletta, Malta) was established in 1989 to train lawyers in international maritime law. The IMO International Maritime Academy (Trieste, Italy), established in 1989, offers specialized short courses in a variety of maritime disciplines.

IMO's governing body, the Assembly, consists of all 163 member states and meets every two years. It elects the 40-member Council, which is IMO's executive organ and meets twice a year.

IMO's budget for 2004-2005 is £46.2 million. It has a staff of about 300.

Secretary-General: Mr. Efthimios E. Mitropolous (Greece)
Headquarters: 4 Albert Embankment, London SE1 7SR, United Kingdom
Tel: (44-0-207) 735-7611; Fax: (44-0-207) 587-3210; Email: *info@imo.org*

International Telecommunication Union (ITU)
(*www.itu.int*)

The International Telecommunication Union is an international organization within which governments and the private sector coordinate global telecommunication networks and services. Founded in Paris in 1865 as the International Telegraph Union, ITU took its present name in 1934 and became a United Nations specialized agency in 1947.

ITU's mandate covers the following areas:

- a technical area: to promote the development and efficient operation of telecommunication facilities, in order to improve the efficiency of telecommunication services and their availability to the public;

- a policy area: to promote the adoption of a broader approach to the issues of telecommunications in the global information economy and society;

- a development area: to promote and offer technical assistance to developing countries in the field of telecommunications, to promote the mobilization of the human and financial resources needed to develop telecommunications, and to promote the extension of the benefits of new technologies to people everywhere.

ITU is composed of 189 member states and some 719 sector members and associates (scientific and industrial companies, public and private operators, broadcasters, regional and international organizations). Its governing body is the Plenipotentiary Conference, which meets every four years, and which elects the 46-member ITU Council that meets annually.

ITU has a staff of 794. Its budget for 2002-2003 was CHF 342 million.

Secretary-General: Mr. Yoshio Utsumi (Japan)
Headquarters: Place des Nations, CH-1211 Geneva 20, Switzerland
Tel: (41-22) 730-5111; Fax: (41-22) 733-7256; Email: *itumail@itu.int*

Universal Postal Union (UPU)
(*www.upu.int*)

The Universal Postal Union is the specialized institution that regulates international postal services. Established by the Berne Treaty of 1874, it became a United Nations specialized agency in 1948.

The UPU plays a leadership role in promoting the continued revitalization of postal services. With 190 member countries, it is the primary vehicle for cooperation between postal services. It advises, mediates and renders technical assistance. Among its principal objectives are the promotion of universal postal service, growth in mail volumes through the provision of up-to-date postal products and services, and improvement in the quality of postal service for customers. In so doing, the UPU fulfils its basic mission of promoting and developing communication between all the people of the world.

The Universal Postal Congress is the supreme authority of the UPU. Meeting every five years, it examines strategic issues of concern to the postal sector and lays down the general programme of activities. The twenty-third Congress is to take place in Bucharest, Romania, in September 2004.

UPU's budget for 2001-2002 was CHF 71.4 million gross. It has a staff of around 150.

Director-General: Mr. Thomas E. Leavey (USA)
Headquarters: Weltpoststrasse 4, Case Postale 3000, Berne 15, Switzerland
Tel: (41-31) 350-3111; Fax: (41-31) 350-3110; Email: *info@upu.int*

World Meteorological Organization (WMO)
(*www.wmo.ch*)

The World Meteorological Organization, a United Nations specialized agency since 1951, provides authoritative scientific information on atmospheric environment, the earth's freshwater resources and climate issues. It develops weather-forecasting services, including seasonal forecasting, and through international collaboration contributes to tracking of global weather conditions, makes possible the rapid exchange of weather information and promotes activities in operational hydrology.

WMO operates various major programmes on issues including climate, the atmosphere, applied meteorology, the environment and water resources. These programmes provide the basis for better preparation and forewarning of severe weather events such as tropical cyclones, El Niño, floods, droughts and other natural disasters — saving life and property, and improving our understanding of the environment and the climate. WMO has drawn attention to issues of major concern, such as ozone layer depletion, global warming and diminishing water resources.

WMO has 187 members, comprising 181 states and 6 territories, all of which maintain their own meteorological and hydrological services. Its governing body, the World Meteorological Congress, meets every four years. The 37-member Executive Council meets annually.

WMO has a staff of 213. Its budget for 2004-2007 is $253.8 million.

Secretary-General: Michel Jarraud (France)
Headquarters: 7 bis, Avenue de la Paix, CH-1211 Geneva 2, Switzerland
Tel: (41-22) 730-8111; Fax: (41-22) 730-8181; Email: *wmo@ wmo.int*

World Intellectual Property Organization (WIPO)
(*www.wipo.int*)

The World Intellectual Property Organization was established in 1970 and became a United Nations specialized agency in 1974. Its objectives are to promote the protection of intellectual property throughout the world through cooperation among its 179 member states, and to ensure administrative cooperation among the Unions established to afford protection in the field of intellectual property.

The principal Unions so established are:

- the Paris Union, officially the International Union for the Protection of Industrial Property;

- the Berne Union, officially the International Union for the Protection of Literary and Artistic Works.

Intellectual property comprises two main branches: industrial property, chiefly inventions, trademarks, industrial designs and appellations of origin; and copyright, mainly of literary, musical, artistic, photographic and audiovisual works. WIPO administers 23 international treaties, including 16 on industrial property and 6 on copyright.

WIPO's three governing bodies are: the General Assembly, comprised of WIPO member states which are members of the Paris and/or Berne Union, and which meets every two years; the Conference, comprising all member states, which also meets every two years; and the 79-member Coordination Committee, which meets every year.

WIPO's programme and budget are established biennially by its governing bodies. Its 2004-2005 budget is about 639 million Swiss francs. WIPO has some 950 staff members from 90 countries.

Director-General: Dr. Kamil Idris (Sudan)
Headquarters: 34 chemin des Colombettes, PO Box 18, CH-1211 Geneva 20, Switzerland
Tel: (41-22) 338-9111; Fax: (41-22) 733-5428; Email: *publicinf@wipo.int*

International Fund for Agricultural Development (IFAD)
(*www.ifad.org*)

The International Fund for Agricultural Development, a multilateral financial institution established in 1977 following a decision by the 1974 World Food Conference, is mandated to combat hunger and rural poverty in the developing countries.

The Fund mobilizes resources that enable poor rural households to improve nutrition, increase agricultural productivity and generate income. Chronic hunger and malnutrition almost always accompany extreme poverty — 75 per cent of which is in rural areas, and most often among women and indigenous peoples.

IFAD provides direct financing through loans and grants, and mobilizes additional resources for its projects and programmes. Lending terms and conditions vary according to the country's gross national product per capita. IFAD works with many other institutions, including the World Bank, regional development banks, other regional financial agencies and United Nations agencies. Many of these institutions co-finance IFAD projects.

IFAD is financed by voluntary contributions from governments, special contributions, loan repayments and investment income. The annual commitment for new projects and grants is around $450 million. The Fund has some 315 staff members.

Its governing body, the Governing Council, is made up of all 163 member states and meets annually. The Executive Board, consisting of 18 members and 18 alternate members, oversees the Fund's operations and approves loans and grants.

President: Mr. Lennart Båge (Sweden)
Headquarters: Via del Serafico 107, 00142 Rome, Italy
Tel: (39-06) 54-591; Fax: (39-06) 504-3463; Email: *ifad@ifad.org*

United Nations Industrial Development Organization (UNIDO)
(www.unido.org)

The mandate of the United Nations Industrial Development Organization is to promote industrial development and cooperation. Established by the General Assembly in 1966, it became a United Nations specialized agency in 1985.

UNIDO helps to improve the living conditions of people and promote global prosperity by offering tailor-made solutions for the sustainable industrial development of developing countries and countries in transition. It cooperates with governments, business associations and the private industrial sector to build industrial capabilities for meeting the challenges and spreading the benefits of the globalization of industry.

To support its services, UNIDO has engineers, economists and technology and environment specialists in Vienna, as well as professional staff in its network of Investment Promotion Service offices and field offices. Field offices are headed by UNIDO regional and country representatives.

UNIDO's 170 member states meet every two years at the General Conference, which approves the budget and work programme. The Industrial Development Board, comprising 53 member states, makes recommendations relating to the planning and implementation of the programme and budget.

UNIDO has a staff of some 530 at headquarters, 100 at field offices, and employs over 1,800 experts worldwide for short- and long-term assignments. Its budget for 2002-2003 was $133 million. Additional funds are increasingly mobilized from multilateral and bilateral sources.

Director-General: Mr. Carlos Magariños (Argentina)
Headquarters: Vienna International Centre, PO Box 300, A-1400 Vienna, Austria
Tel: (43-1) 26026; Fax: (43-1) 269-2669; Email: *unido@unido.org*

International Atomic Energy Agency (IAEA)
(*www.iaea.org*)

The International Atomic Energy Agency promotes the peaceful uses of nuclear energy for the benefit of humanity and guards against its use for military purposes. It is the world's foremost intergovernmental forum for scientific and technical cooperation in the peaceful uses of nuclear energy, and the international inspectorate for the application of nuclear safeguards and verification measures covering civilian nuclear programmes. The Agency is also at the centre of international efforts to promote international cooperation on nuclear safety and security-related matters.

Established in 1957 as an autonomous agency under the aegis of the United Nations, it has 137 member states. It provides technical assistance to member states in need, focusing on the application of nuclear science and technology to sustainable development, according to priorities set by the states themselves — in areas including food and agricultural production, human health, industry, water management, improvement of the marine environment, generation of electricity and nuclear safety and security.

The IAEA monitors and verifies states' compliance with their non-proliferation obligations pursuant to bilateral agreements and international treaties, meant to ensure that nuclear materials and facilities are not diverted for military purposes. Some 250 inspectors are deployed worldwide to more than 900 installations and other locations covered under the IAEA Safeguards Programme.

The Agency's governing bodies are: the General Conference, in which all member states are represented and which meets annually; and the Board of Governors, with 35 member states, which meets periodically throughout the year. The IAEA has a staff of 2,257. Its regular budget for 2004 is $268.5 million; the target for additional, voluntary contributions is $74.8 million.

Director General: Dr. Mohamed ElBaradei (Egypt)
Headquarters: PO Box 100, Wagramer Strasse 5, A-1400 Vienna, Austria
Tel: (43-1) 2600-0; Fax: (43-1) 2600-7; Email: *Official.Mail@iaea.org*

Preparatory Commission for the Comprehensive
Nuclear-Test-Ban Treaty Organization (CTBTO)
(www.ctbto.org)

The Preparatory Commission for the Comprehensive Nuclear-Test-Ban Treaty Organization was established on 19 November 1996 at a Meeting of States Signatories to the Treaty held in New York. As an international organization financed by the States Signatories, it consists of two organs: a plenary body composed of all the States Signatories — also known as the Preparatory Commission — and the Provisional Technical Secretariat. The main task of the Preparatory Commission is to establish the global verification regime foreseen in the Treaty, so that it will be operational by the time the Treaty enters into force.

The Commission has three subsidiary bodies: Working Group A, on administrative and budgetary matters; Working Group B, on verification issues; and the Advisory Group on financial, budgetary and associated administrative issues. Its budget for 2003 was $88.5 million, of which some 80 per cent was dedicated to establishment of the global verification regime.

Executive Secretary: Mr. Wolfgang Hoffmann (Germany)
Headquarters: Vienna International Centre, PO Box 1200, A-1400 Vienna, Austria
Tel: (43-1) 26030-6200; Fax: (43-1) 26030-5823; Email: *info@ctbto.org*

Organisation for the Prohibition of Chemical Weapons (OPCW)
(www.opcw.org)

The Organisation for the Prohibition of Chemical Weapons monitors the implementation of the Convention on the Prohibition of the Development, Production, Stockpiling and Use of Chemical Weapons and on their Destruction. The Convention, which entered into force on 29 April 1997, is the first multilateral disarmament and non-proliferation agreement that provides for the global elimination of an entire category of weapons of mass destruction, under stringent international verification and within prescribed timelines.

The OPCW is composed of 153 states parties. Since 1997, its inspectors have verified the destruction of over 7,500 tonnes of chemical agents, in nearly 2 million munitions, in five states parties — as well as the destruction or conversion of two thirds of 61 former chemical weapons production facilities in 11 member states. They have conducted 1,400 inspections at military and industrial plants in 55 countries to ensure that chemical weapons are being destroyed, and dual-use chemicals are not misused. OPCW member states are obliged to assist their fellow states parties if they are threatened or attacked with chemical weapons. The OPCW also has a range of international cooperation programmes to facilitate peaceful use of chemistry.

The OPCW Technical Secretariat has a staff of some 500, representing 66 nationalities. Its budget for 2003 was EUR 68.5 million.

Director-General: Mr. Rogelio Pfirter (Argentina)
Headquarters: Johan de Wittlaan 32, 2517 JR, The Hague, Netherlands
Tel: (31-70) 416-3300; Fax: (31-70) 306-3535; Email: *inquiries@opcw.org*

World Tourism Organization (WTO) (OMT)
(www.world-tourism.org)

Established in 1925, the World Tourism Organization is the leading international organization in the field of tourism. It serves as a global forum for tourism policy issues and a practical source of tourism know-how. Its membership includes 148 countries and territories, two observers, and more than 350 affiliate members representing local government, tourism associations and private-sector companies, including airlines, hotel groups and tour operators.

An intergovernmental body entrusted by the United Nations with the promotion and development of tourism, WTO became a specialized agency of the United Nations on 23 December 2003, by General Assembly resolution 58/232. Through tourism, WTO aims to stimulate economic growth and job creation, provide incentives for protecting the environment and heritage of tourist destinations, and promote peace and understanding among nations.

WTO's General Assembly, its supreme body, is made up of full, associate and affiliate members. It meets every two years to approve the budget and the programme of work, and to debate major topics in the tourism sector. The Executive Council is WTO's governing board, composed of 27 full members elected by the Assembly, and a permanent member, Spain; it meets twice a year. The six regional commissions — Africa, the Americas, East Asia and the Pacific, Europe, the Middle East and South Asia — meet at least once a year.

WTO has a staff of 90. Its budget for 2002-2003 was $20,818,000.

Secretary-General: Francesco Frangialli (France)
Headquarters: Capitán Haya 42, 28020 Madrid, Spain
Tel: (34-91) 567-8100; Fax: (34-91) 571-3733; Email: *omt@world-tourism.org*

World Trade Organization (WTO)
(www.wto.org)

The World Trade Organization was established in 1995, replacing the General Agreement on Tariffs and Trade (GATT) as the only international body dealing with the global rules of trade between nations. It is not a specialized agency, but has cooperative arrangements and practices with the United Nations.

The purpose of the WTO is to help trade flow smoothly, in a system based on rules; to impartially settle trade disputes between governments; and to organize trade negotiations. At its heart are some 60 WTO agreements, the legal ground rules for international commerce and trade policy. The principles on which these agreements are based include: non-discrimination (the "most-favoured nation" clause and the national treatment provision), freer trade, encouraging competition, and extra provisions for less developed countries. One of WTO's objectives is to reduce protectionism.

Since its establishment, the WTO has been the forum for successful negotiations to open markets in telecommunications, information technology equipment and financial services. It has been involved in settling more than 200 trade disputes, and continues to oversee implementation of the agreements reached in the 1986-1994 Uruguay Round of world trade talks. In 2001, at Doha, Qatar, the WTO launched a new round of multilateral trade negotiations known as the Doha Development Agenda.

The WTO has 146 member countries. Its governing body, the Ministerial Conference, meets every two years; the General Council carries out the day-to-day work. WTO's budget for 2003 was CHF 155 million. It has a staff of some 550.

Director-General: Dr. Supachai Panitchpakdi (Thailand)
Headquarters: 154 Rue de Lausanne, CH-1211 Geneva 21, Switzerland
Tel: (41-22) 739-5111; Fax: (41-22) 731-4206; Email: *enquiries@wto.org*

Chapter 2
International
Peace and Security

INTERNATIONAL PEACE AND SECURITY

One of the primary purposes of the United Nations is the maintenance of international peace and security. Since its creation, the United Nations has often been called upon to prevent disputes from escalating into war, to persuade opposing parties to use the conference table rather than force of arms, or to help restore peace when armed conflict does break out. Over the decades, the United Nations has helped to end numerous conflicts, often through actions of the Security Council — the primary organ for dealing with issues of international peace and security.

During the 1990s, the end of the cold war led to an entirely new global security environment, one marked by a focus on internal rather than inter-state wars. In the early 21st century, new global threats emerged. The attacks of 11 September 2001 on the United States clearly demonstrated the challenge of international terrorism, while subsequent events heightened concern about the proliferation of nuclear weapons and the dangers from other non-conventional weapons, casting a shadow over people throughout the world.

The organizations of the UN system mobilized immediately in their respective spheres to step up action against terrorism. On 28 September, the Security Council adopted a wide-ranging resolution under the enforcement provisions of the UN Charter to prevent the financing of terrorism, criminalize the collection of funds for such purposes, and immediately freeze terrorist financial assets — establishing a Counter-Terrorism Committee to oversee its implementation.

The UN has also reshaped and enhanced the traditional range of instruments at its command, adapting peacekeeping operations to meet new challenges, increasingly involving regional organizations, and strengthening post-conflict peace-building. Civil conflicts have raised complex issues regarding the response of the international community, including the question of how best to assist civilian victims of war.

To deal with civil conflicts, the Security Council has authorized complex and innovative peacekeeping operations. In El Salvador and Guatemala, in Cambodia and Mozambique, the United Nations played a major role in ending conflict and fostering reconciliation.

Other conflicts, however — in Somalia, Rwanda and the former Yugoslavia — often characterized by ethnic violence, brought new challenges to the United Nations peacemaking role. Confronted with the problems encountered in these conflicts, the Security Council did not establish any new operation from 1995 to 1997. But soon, the essential role of the UN was dramatically reaffirmed, as continuing crises in the Democratic Republic of the Congo, the Central African Republic, East Timor, Kosovo and Sierra Leone led the Council to establish five new missions as the 1990s drew to a close.

Since then, the Council has established the United Nations Mission in Ethiopia and Eritrea (UNMEE) in 2000; the United Nations Mission of Support in East Timor (UNMISET) in 2002; and the United Nations Mission in Liberia (UNMIL) in 2003.

The experience of recent years has also led the United Nations to focus as never before on peace-building — action to support structures that will strengthen and consolidate peace. Experience has shown that the creation of lasting peace can only be achieved by helping countries to foster economic development, social justice, respect for human rights, good governance and the democratic process. No other institution has the multilateral experience, competence, coordinating ability and impartiality that the United Nations brings in support of these tasks. In addition to its peace-building tasks in such missions as those in Timor-Leste and Kosovo, the United Nations has established peace-building support offices in the Central African Republic, Guinea-Bissau, Liberia and Tajikistan.

The **Security Council**, the **General Assembly** and the **Secretary-General** all play major, complementary roles in fostering peace and security. United Nations activities cover the principal areas of *conflict prevention*, *peacemaking*, *peacekeeping*, *enforcement* and *peace-building*. These types of engagement must overlap or take place simultaneously if they are to be effective.

The Security Council

The United Nations Charter — an international treaty — obligates member states to settle their disputes by peaceful means, in such a manner that international peace and security and justice are not endangered. They are to refrain from the threat or use of force against any state, and may bring any dispute before the Security Council.

The Security Council is the United Nations organ with primary responsibility for maintaining peace and security. Under the Charter, member states are obliged to accept and carry out its decisions. Recommendations of other United Nations bodies do not have the mandatory force of Security Council decisions, but can influence situations by expressing the opinion of the international community.

When a dispute is brought to its attention, the Council usually urges the parties to settle it by peaceful means. The Council may make recommendations to the parties for a peaceful settlement, appoint special representatives, ask the Secretary-General to use his good offices, and undertake investigation and mediation.

When a dispute leads to fighting, the Council seeks to bring it to an end as quickly as possible. Often the Council has issued ceasefire directives that have been instrumental in preventing wider hostilities. In support of a peace process, the Council may deploy military observers or a peacekeeping force to an area of conflict.

Under Chapter VII of the Charter, the Council is empowered to take measures to enforce its decisions. It can impose embargoes and sanctions, or authorize the use of force to ensure that mandates are fulfilled.

In some cases, the Council has authorized, under Chapter VII, the use of military force by a coalition of member states or by a regional organization or arrangement. But the Council takes such action only as a last resort, when peaceful means of settling a dispute have been exhausted, and after determining that a threat to the peace, a breach of the peace or an act of aggression exists.

Also under Chapter VII, the Council has established international tribunals to prosecute persons accused of serious violations of international humanitarian and human rights law, including genocide.

The General Assembly

The United Nations Charter (Article 11) empowers the General Assembly to "consider the general principles of cooperation in the maintenance of international peace and security" and "make recommendations ... to the Members or to the Security Council or to both". The Assembly offers a means for finding consensus on difficult issues, providing a forum for the airing of grievances and diplomatic exchanges. To foster the maintenance of peace, it has held special sessions or emergency special sessions on such issues as disarmament, the question of Palestine and the situation in Afghanistan.

The General Assembly considers peace and security issues in its First (Disarmament and International Security) Committee and in its Fourth (Special Political and Decolonization) Committee. Over the years, the Assembly has helped promote peaceful relations among nations by adopting declarations on peace, the peaceful settlement of disputes and international cooperation.

The Assembly in 1980 approved the establishment in San José, Costa Rica, of the **University for Peace**, an international institute for studies, research and dissemination of knowledge on peace-related issues.

The Assembly has designated 21 September each year as the **International Day of Peace**.

Conflict prevention

The main strategies for preventing disputes from escalating into conflict, and for preventing the recurrence of conflict, are preventive diplomacy, preventive deployment and preventive disarmament.

Preventive diplomacy refers to action to prevent disputes from arising, to resolve them before they escalate into conflicts, or to limit the spread of conflicts when they occur. It may take the form of mediation, conciliation or negotiation. Early warning is an essential component of prevention, and the United Nations carefully monitors political and other developments around the world to detect threats to international peace and security, thereby enabling the Security Council and the Secretary-General to carry out preventive action.

Envoys and special representatives of the Secretary-General are engaged in mediation and preventive diplomacy throughout the world. In some trouble spots, the

The question of intervention

Should the international community intervene in a country to stop gross, systematic and widespread violations of human rights? The question was raised in 1998 by Secretary-General Kofi Annan, generating wide debate.

In the wake of genocide, crimes against humanity, and war crimes in Central Africa, the Balkans and elsewhere, the Secretary-General argued that the international community should agree on legitimate and universal principles, within the framework of international law, for protecting civilians against massive and systematic human rights violations.

The legal framework, Mr. Annan said, was provided by universal norms embodied in the Charter, international humanitarian law, human rights law and refugee law. The concept of intervention covers a wide range of actions, including, in some circumstances, the Security Council intervening in internal conflicts by authorizing the creation of "safe corridors" and "safe areas" in conflict zones, imposing sanctions against recalcitrant states, or taking other measures. At the same time, Mr. Annan has warned that such coercive action will have the support of the world's people only if it is fairly and consistently applied.

In the ensuing debate, one group of nations maintained that, in the face of massive human rights violations and crimes against humanity, the responsibility of the international community to prevent violations is paramount. Thus, in the last resort, human rights can be legitimately protected through the use of force authorized by the Security Council.

A second group of nations raised three major questions: Where does humanitarian assistance stop and interference in the internal affairs of states begin? How does one distinguish between humanitarian imperatives and political or economic motivations? Is humanitarian intervention valid only for weak states, or for all states without distinctions? These nations have called for a broad dialogue, and urged that any decision be based on the consensus of member states.

A third group of states argued that the notion of humanitarian intervention has the potential to undermine the Charter, eroding the sovereignty of states and threatening legitimate governments and the stability of the international system. They emphasized that measures to protect human rights should respect the independence, sovereignty and territorial integrity of all countries, with the support of the government and people of the country concerned.

The moral rights and wrongs of this complex issue have continued to be debated, and the principles involved are likely to be tested again when a major humanitarian crisis challenges the international community.

mere presence of a skilled special representative can prevent the escalation of tension. This work is often undertaken in close cooperation with regional organizations.

Complementing preventive diplomacy are preventive deployment and preventive disarmament. *Preventive deployment* — the fielding of peacekeepers to forestall probable conflict — is intended to provide a "thin blue line" to help contain conflicts by building trust where there is tension. To date, the only specific instances are the United Nations missions in the former Yugoslav Republic of Macedonia[1] and in the Central African Republic. Preventive deployment has been considered in other conflicts and remains a valuable option.

Preventive disarmament seeks to reduce the number of small arms in conflict-prone regions. In El Salvador, Mozambique and elsewhere, this has entailed demobilizing combat forces as well as collecting and destroying their weapons as part of an overall peace agreement. Destroying yesterday's weapons prevents their being used in tomorrow's wars.

Peacemaking

Peacemaking refers to the use of diplomatic means to persuade parties in conflict to cease hostilities and to negotiate the peaceful settlement of a dispute. The United Nations provides various means through which conflicts may be contained and resolved, and their root causes addressed. The Security Council may recommend ways to resolve a dispute or request the Secretary-General's mediation. The **Secretary-General** may take diplomatic initiatives to encourage and maintain the momentum of negotiations.

The Secretary-General plays a central role in peacemaking, both personally and by dispatching special envoys or missions for specific tasks, such as negotiation or fact-finding. Under the Charter, the Secretary-General may bring to the attention of the Security Council any matter that might threaten the maintenance of international peace and security.

To help resolve disputes, the Secretary-General may use his "good offices" for mediation or to exercise preventive diplomacy. The impartiality of the Secretary-General is one of the United Nations great assets. In many instances, the Secretary-General has been instrumental in averting a threat to peace or in securing a peace agreement.

---

[1] United Nations action in the former Yugoslav Republic of Macedonia is an example of successful "preventive deployment". Concerned about being drawn into the Yugoslav conflict, the country in 1992 requested the deployment of UN observers. The Security Council agreed and dispatched a peacekeeping contingent to the country's borders with Yugoslavia and Albania. The 1,100-strong **United Nations Preventive Deployment Force (UNPREDEP)** monitored developments in the border areas that might have threatened the country's territory or undermined its stability. The country repeatedly requested the extension of the mission, which stayed until 1999 and stands as a model for future preventive operations.

For example, action by the Secretary-General led, in 1988, to the end of the war between Iran and Iraq, which had raged since 1980. In Afghanistan, mediation by the Secretary-General and his envoy led to the 1988 agreements that resulted in the withdrawal of Soviet troops from the country. Cases such as Cambodia, Central America, Cyprus, the Middle East, Mozambique and Namibia reflect the many different ways the Secretary-General becomes involved as a peacemaker.

Peacekeeping

United Nations peacekeeping operations are a crucial instrument at the disposal of the international community to advance peace and security. The role of peacekeeping was recognized in 1988, when United Nations peacekeeping forces received the Nobel Peace Prize.

While not specifically envisaged in the Charter, the United Nations pioneered peacekeeping in 1948 with the establishment of the United Nations Truce Supervision Organization in the Middle East. Since then, it has established a total of 56 operations — 43 of these since 1988.[2] As of April 2004, there were 14 active peacekeeping operations.

Peacekeeping operations and their deployment are authorized by the Security Council, with the consent of the host governments and usually of the other parties involved. They may include military and police personnel, together with civilian staff. Operations may involve military observer missions, peacekeeping forces, or a combination of both. Military observer missions are made up of unarmed officers, typically to monitor an agreement or a ceasefire. The soldiers in peacekeeping forces have weapons, but in most situations can use them only in self-defence.

The military personnel of peacekeeping operations are voluntarily provided by member states and are financed by the member states, who are assessed under the peacekeeping budget. Troop-contributing states are compensated at a standard rate from that budget.

Peacekeeping operations were expected to cost some $2.2 billion for the fiscal year beginning July 2003 — approximately 0.15 per cent of world military spending. Operations are financed through the peacekeeping budget and include troops from

---

[2] The intervention in Korea in 1950 was not a United Nations peacekeeping operation. In June 1950, the United States and the United Nations Commission on Korea informed the United Nations that the Republic of Korea had been attacked by forces from North Korea. The Security Council recommended that member states furnish the necessary assistance to the Republic of Korea to repel the attack and restore peace and security. In July, the Council recommended that member states providing military forces make them available to a unified command under the United States; 16 nations made troops available. This force, known as the United Nations Command and authorized by the Council to fly the United Nations flag, was not a United Nations peacekeeping operation, but an international force acting under a unified command. The Soviet Union, which had been absent from the Security Council in protest against the Chinese Nationalist government representing China at the United Nations, deemed the Council's decisions illegal on the grounds that two permanent members (the Soviet Union and China) were absent. Fighting continued until July 1953, when an armistice agreement was signed.

many countries. This worldwide "burden-sharing" can offer extraordinary efficiency in human, financial and political terms.

Since 1948, well over 750,000 military, police and civilian personnel from nearly 130 countries have served in peacekeeping operations. Of these, some 1,910 lost their lives in the line of duty (as of June 2004).

Conflicts today are a complex mix. Their roots may be essentially internal, but they are complicated by cross-border involvement, either by states or by economic interests and other non-state actors. Recent conflicts in Africa have shown the deadly mix of civil strife and illegal export of natural resources — primarily diamonds — to fuel arms purchases. In addition, the consequences of conflicts can quickly become international because of illegal arms flows, terrorism, drug trafficking, refugee flows and environmental degradation.

United Nations operations, because of their universality, offer unique advantages as a means to address conflicts. Their universality adds to their legitimacy and limits the implications for the host country's sovereignty. Peacekeepers from outside a conflict can foster discussion among warring parties while focusing global attention upon local concerns — opening doors that would otherwise remain closed for collective peace efforts.

Certain prerequisites for the success of an operation have become increasingly clear. These include a genuine desire on the part of the opposing forces to resolve their differences peacefully, a clear mandate, strong political support by the international community, and the provision of the financial and human resources necessary to achieve the operation's objectives.

This support may require positive engagement by non-state actors. Recent conflicts in Africa have shown how civil strife may be exploited by private interests for financial gain. Yet at the same time, an injection of private capital, if coordinated with international efforts to promote peace, may make an essential contribution to the recovery of a post-conflict economy.

United Nations peacekeeping operations*

- United Nations Truce Supervision Organization (UNTSO, established 1948), in the Middle East (strength: military 153; civilian 205)

- United Nations Military Observer Group in India and Pakistan (UNMOGIP, 1949) (military 44; civilian 65)

- United Nations Peacekeeping Force in Cyprus (UNFICYP, 1964) (military 1,202; civilian police 45; civilian 147)

- United Nations Disengagement Observer Force (UNDOF, 1974), in the Syrian Golan Heights (military 1,029; civilian 129)

- United Nations Interim Force in Lebanon (UNIFIL, 1978) (military 1,994; civilian 407)

- United Nations Mission for the Referendum in Western Sahara (MINURSO, 1991) (military 230; civilian 242)

- United Nations Observer Mission in Georgia (UNOMIG, 1993) (military 118; civilian police 11; civilian 278)

- United Nations Interim Administration Mission in Kosovo (UNMIK, 1999) (military 36; civilian police 3,510; civilian 3,557)

- United Nations Mission in Sierra Leone (UNAMSIL, 1999) (military 11,539; civilian police 116; civilian 831)

- United Nations Observer Mission in the Democratic Republic of the Congo (MONUC, 1999) (military 10,576; civilian police 139; civilian 1,632)

- United Nations Mission in Ethiopia and Eritrea (UNMEE, 2000) (military 4,006; civilian 497)

- United Nations Mission of Support in East Timor (UNMISET, 2002) (military 1,609; civilian police 129; civilian 894)

- United Nations Mission in Liberia (UNMIL, 2003) (military 14,833; civilian police 791; civilian 796)

- United Nations Operation in Côte d'Ivoire (UNOCI, 2004) (military 3,036; civilian police 60; civilian 110) (authorized strength: military 6,240, including 200 observers; civilian police 350; civilians 964)

- United Nations Stabilization Mission in Haiti (MINUSTAH, 2004) (military 240; civilian police 7; civilian 123) (authorized strength: military 6,700; civilian police 1,622; and civilian staff)

- United Nations Operation in Burundi (ONUB, 2004) (authorized strength: military 5,650; civilian police 120)

---

* As of 1 June 2004. For all operations, past and present, see Part Three (Appendices).

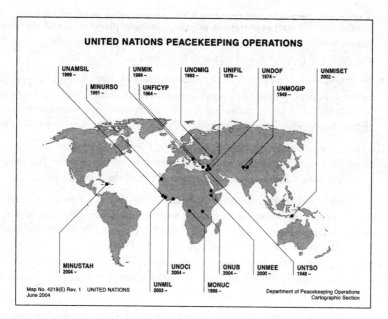

UNITED NATIONS PEACEKEEPING OPERATIONS

| UNAMSIL 1999 – | MINURSO 1991 – | UNMIK 1999 – | UNFICYP 1964 – | UNOMIG 1993 – | UNIFIL 1978 – | UNDOF 1974 – | UNMOGIP 1949 – | UNMISET 2002 – |

| MINUSTAH 2004 – | UNOCI 2004 – | UNMIL 2003 – | ONUB 2004 – | MONUC 1999 – | UNMEE 2000 – | UNTSO 1948 – |

Map No. 4219(E) Rev. 1   UNITED NATIONS
June 2004

Department of Peacekeeping Operations
Cartographic Section

The international community has drawn lessons from past operations and is working to strengthen the United Nations peacekeeping capacity in a number of areas. A blueprint for reform was provided by the Secretary-General's Panel on Peace Operations, chaired by Ambassador Lakhdar Brahimi, which issued its report in 2000.[3]

The Security Council and other bodies are now tackling the major issues at stake, which include: enhancing preparedness; speeding up deployment; strengthening the deterrent capacities of peacekeepers; and ensuring full political and financial support by member states.

Operations can take many forms. They are constantly evolving in the light of changing circumstances. Among the tasks discharged by peacekeeping operations over the years are:

- *Maintenance of ceasefires and separation of forces.* By providing "breathing space", an operation based on a limited agreement between parties can foster an atmosphere conducive to negotiations.

- *Preventive deployment.* Deployed before conflict breaks out, an operation can provide a reassuring presence and a degree of transparency which favours political progress.

- *Protection of humanitarian operations.* In many conflicts, civilian populations have been deliberately targeted as a means to gain political ends. In such situ-

---

[3] Report of the Panel on United Nations Peace Operations, A/55/305-S/2000/809, 21 August 2000. Also available at *www.un.org/peace/reports/peace_operations*.

ations, peacekeepers have been asked to provide protection and support for humanitarian operations. However, such tasks can place peacekeepers in difficult political positions, and can lead to threats to their security.

- *Implementation of a comprehensive peace settlement.* Complex, multi-dimensional operations, deployed on the basis of comprehensive peace agreements, can assist in such diverse tasks as providing humanitarian assistance, monitoring human rights, observing elections and coordinating support for economic reconstruction.

No catalogue of such roles can be exhaustive. Future conflicts are likely to continue to present complex challenges to the international community. An effective response will require courageous and imaginative use of the tools for peace.

Cooperating with regional organizations. In the search for peace, the United Nations has been increasingly cooperating with regional organizations and other actors and mechanisms provided for in Chapter VIII of the Charter. It has worked closely with the Organization of American States in Haiti, the European Union in the former Yugoslavia, the Economic Community of West African States in Liberia and Sierra Leone, and the African Union (AU) in Western Sahara, the Great Lakes region, Sierra Leone and Ethiopia and Eritrea.[4]

United Nations military observers have cooperated with peacekeeping forces of regional organizations in Liberia, Sierra Leone, Georgia and Tajikistan.

In the former Yugoslavia, the United Nations has cooperated with the Council of Europe and the Organization for Security and Cooperation in Europe (OSCE) in the areas of human rights, electoral assistance, peacemaking and economic development. The complex mission in Kosovo brought together the United Nations, the European Union and the OSCE.

Enforcement

Under Chapter VII of the Charter, the Security Council can take enforcement measures to maintain or restore international peace and security. Such measures range from economic sanctions to international military action.

Sanctions

The Council has resorted to mandatory sanctions as an enforcement tool when peace was threatened and diplomatic efforts had failed. In the last decade, sanctions have been

---

[4] The Organization of African Union (OAU), originally established in 1963 to promote unity, solidarity and international cooperation among the newly independent African states, was reconstituted on 10 July 2002 as the African Union (AU). Headquartered in Ethiopia, it has 53 members and is modelled after the European Union (EU).

imposed against Iraq, the former Yugoslavia, Libya, Haiti, Liberia, Rwanda, Somalia, UNITA forces in Angola, Sudan, Sierra Leone, the Federal Republic of Yugoslavia (including Kosovo), Afghanistan, and Ethiopia and Eritrea. The range of sanctions has included comprehensive economic and trade sanctions, or more specific measures such as arms embargoes, travel bans and financial or diplomatic restrictions.

The use of sanctions seeks to apply pressure on a state or entity to comply with the objectives set by the Security Council without resorting to the use of force. Sanctions thus offer the Council an important tool to enforce its decisions. The universal character of the United Nations makes it an especially appropriate body to establish and monitor sanctions.

At the same time, many states and humanitarian organizations have expressed concerns at the possible adverse impact of sanctions on the most vulnerable segments of the civilian population, such as the elderly, the disabled, refugees or mothers with children. Concerns have also been expressed at the negative economic, social and even political impact sanctions can have on the economies of third or neighbouring countries, where trade and economic relations with the sanctioned state are interrupted.

It is increasingly accepted that the design and application of sanctions need to be improved. The negative effects of sanctions can be reduced either by incorporating humanitarian exceptions directly into Security Council resolutions, or by better targeting them. So-called "smart sanctions" — which seek to pressure those in power rather than the population at large, thus reducing humanitarian costs — have been gaining support. Smart sanctions may, for instance, involve freezing the financial assets and blocking the financial transactions of elites or entities whose illicit activities triggered sanctions in the first place.

Authorizing military action

When peacemaking efforts fail, stronger action by member states may be authorized under Chapter VII of the Charter. The Security Council has authorized coalitions of member states to use "all necessary means", including military action, to deal with a conflict — as it did to restore the sovereignty of Kuwait after its invasion by Iraq (1991); to establish a secure environment for humanitarian relief operations in Somalia (1992); to contribute to the protection of civilians at risk in Rwanda (1994); to restore the democratically elected government in Haiti (1994); to protect humanitarian operations in Albania (1997); and to restore peace and security in East Timor (1999).

These actions, though sanctioned by the Security Council, were entirely under the control of the participating states. They were not United Nations peacekeeping operations — which are established by the Security Council and directed by the Secretary-General.

Peace-building

For the United Nations, peace-building refers to efforts to assist countries and regions in their transitions from war to peace, including activities and programmes to support and strengthen these transitions. A peace-building process normally begins with the signing of a peace agreement by former warring parties and a United Nations role in facilitating its implementation. This may include a continued diplomatic role for the UN, to ensure that difficulties are overcome through negotiation rather than resort to arms.

It may also include various types of assistance — such as the deployment of military forces as peacekeepers; the repatriation and reintegration of refugees; the holding of elections; and the disarmament, demobilization and reintegration of soldiers. At the heart of peace-building is the attempt to build a new and legitimate state, one which will have the capacity to peacefully manage disputes, protect its civilians and ensure respect for basic human rights.

Peace-building involves action by a wide array of organizations of the United Nations system, including the World Bank, regional economic and other organizations,

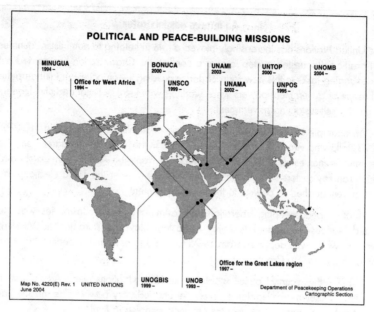

non-governmental organizations (NGOs) and local citizens' groups. Peace-building has played a prominent role in United Nations operations in Cambodia, El Salvador, Guatemala, Mozambique, Liberia, Bosnia and Herzegovina and Sierra Leone, as well as more recently in Kosovo and Timor-Leste (formerly East Timor). A recent example of inter-state peace-building has been the UN Mission in Ethiopia and Eritrea.

Electoral assistance

The United Nations broke new ground in 1989, when it supervised the entire election process that led to the independence of Namibia. Since then, the United Nations, at the request of governments, has assisted with elections in countries such as Nicaragua and Haiti (1990), Angola (1992), Cambodia (1993), El Salvador, South Africa and Mozambique (1994), Eastern Slavonia (Croatia) and Liberia (1997), and the Central African Republic (1998 and 1999). It also observed the 1993 referendum in Eritrea, and organized and conducted the 1999 popular consultation in East Timor and its 2001 and 2002 elections, which led to the independence of East Timor as Timor-Leste.

The degree and type of United Nations involvement depends upon such factors as the requests received from governments, provisions of peace agreements, or mandates from the General Assembly or the Security Council. The United Nations has played a variety of roles, ranging from technical assistance to the actual conduct of the electoral process. In many cases, the UN will coordinate the activities of international observers. Typically, such observers follow the registration of voters, the electoral campaign and the organization of the polls.

Since 1992, the **Electoral Assistance Division** in the Department of Political Affairs, in its role as coordinator of electoral assistance for the UN system, has provided various forms of electoral assistance to more than 85 countries — including advisory services, logistics, training, civic education, computer applications and short-term observation. In recent years, the Division has increasingly been called upon to provide support and guidance for electoral processes as key elements of UN-brokered peace negotiations, or in the context of peacekeeping and peace-building efforts. The United Nations Development Programme (UNDP) provides technical support to the election process, helps countries establish electoral structures, and often coordinates UN electoral assistance in the field. The Office of the United Nations High Commissioner for Human Rights helps to train election officials, establish guidelines for drafting electoral laws and procedures, and set up information activities on human rights and elections.

Building peace through development

A central tool of United Nations action to consolidate peace is development assistance. Many organizations — including UNDP, the United Nations Children's Fund

(UNICEF), the World Food Programme (WFP) and the Office of the United Nations High Commissioner for Refugees (UNHCR) — play roles in the recovery stage, which is crucial for providing opportunities for displaced persons and restoring confidence in national and local institutions.

The United Nations can help repatriate refugees, clear landmines, repair infrastructure, mobilize resources and stimulate economic recovery. While war is the worst enemy of development, a healthy and balanced development is the best form of conflict prevention.

United Nations action for peace
Africa
Southern Africa

At the end of the 1980s, with the cold war waning, the United Nations was able to reap the fruits of many years of efforts aimed at ending wars that had plagued southern Africa. The decline of the apartheid regime in South Africa, whose influence extended to the bordering "frontline" states, and which had supported opposition forces in Angola and Mozambique, was a major factor in these efforts.

In 1988, South Africa agreed to cooperate with the Secretary-General to ensure the independence of **Namibia**. In 1992, the government of **Mozambique** and the Mozambican National Resistance (RENAMO) signed a peace agreement to end a long and debilitating civil war. As part of the agreement, the United Nations Operation in Mozambique, deployed in 1993, successfully monitored the ceasefire, the demobilization of forces and the country's first multiparty elections, held in 1994.

Angola. An intermittent yet devastating civil war in Angola, between the government and the National Union for the Total Independence of Angola (UNITA), had plagued the country since its independence from Portugal in 1975. The UN played an important role in ending the conflict — through such efforts as mediation by the Secretary-General and his envoys, the organization of peace talks, the imposition of a Security Council arms and oil embargo and travel restrictions against UNITA, and the monitoring of national elections.

The Security Council established several successive peacekeeping and political missions in Angola. The first, in 1989, monitored the withdrawal of pro-government Cuban troops from the country. The second, starting in 1991, sought to monitor a ceasefire, verify demobilization of combatants, and observe the 1992 elections. But when the election results were rejected by UNITA, the country again plunged into war.

Mediation by the Secretary-General's special representative, Mr. Alioune Blondin Beye, resulted in the 1994 Lusaka Protocol — and a fragile peace. The accord provided for a ceasefire and for UNITA's integration into the government and the armed forces. A third mission was established to support the accord and to help the parties to achieve

81

Africa: a United Nations priority

Africa has been a major focus of United Nations action in the past decade. The Organization has addressed the challenge posed by protracted conflicts and long-standing disputes on the continent in innovative ways and at the highest level. In their Millennium Declaration in September 2000, world leaders resolved to give full support, including special measures to help Africa tackle its peace and development issues.

The Security Council has held several special meetings on Africa at the ministerial level. In 1997, it expressed grave concern over the number and intensity of conflicts on the continent and called for an international effort to promote peace and security. In 1998, meeting at the level of Foreign Ministers, it adopted resolutions on the destabilizing effects of illicit arms flows, on arms embargoes, and on conflict prevention in Africa.

In January 2000, the Security Council drew world attention to Africa's plight through a month-long series of meetings on the subject. Issues addressed included conflict resolution, HIV/AIDS, refugees and internally displaced persons, and UN peace efforts in Africa which, over the years, have involved close collaboration with the African Union and subregional organizations such as the Economic Community of West African States (ECOWAS) and the Southern Africa Development Community (SADC); the Council called for a strengthening such cooperation.

The Secretary-General has made Africa one of his priorities. Both personally and through his 18 special representatives, advisers and envoys to the continent, he has acted to prevent and contain disputes. In a 1998 report on the causes of conflict in Africa and on promoting durable peace, he urged African nations to rely on political rather than military responses; embrace good governance, including respect for human rights, democratization and accountable public administration; and enact reforms to promote economic growth. He called on the international community to provide stronger political support for Africa, including debt relief and market access for its exports.

UN action for Africa over the years has included its campaign against apartheid in South Africa, active support for Namibia's independence, and some 20 peacekeeping operations. Three peacekeeping operations in Somalia, deployed from 1992 to 1995, attempted to restore peace and provide relief aid. Another operation, deployed in 2003, is helping Liberia restore its national life after a 14-year civil war.

The wider economic and social context has a major impact on peace and security in Africa — evident in the obvious link between dire poverty and war. This link is also apparent in such problems as the situation of refugees and internally displaced persons, HIV/AIDS, foreign debt, environmental degradation, human rights abuses, and the persistent economic crisis. In the economic and social sphere as well, Africa is a priority concern of the United Nations.

peace and national reconciliation. (Several years later, in June 1998, the special representative was killed in a plane crash while on a peace mission.)

The Secretary-General visited Angola in 1997 to promote reconciliation and the installation of a government of national unity and reconciliation, which was inaugurated in April 1997. Also during 1997, the **United Nations Observer Mission in Angola (MONUA)** was established to help restore peace and assist in the transition. But after four years of relative peace, the conflict flared up again in December 1998, exacting a heavy toll on the civilian population. The Security Council strengthened sanctions against UNITA for failing to meet its obligations under the Lusaka peace accord.

In December 1998, a UN charter flight crashed in an area of military operations, killing all 14 people aboard. One month later, another UN charter plane crashed under fire in the same area, killing all nine people aboard. The Council repeated that the main responsibility for the deterioration of the peace process lay with UNITA. In February 1999, it allowed MONUA's mandate to expire. Nevertheless, in October, it established the **United Nations Office in Angola (UNOA)**, and a representative of the Secretary-General was appointed to explore measures to restore peace and assist in capacity-building, humanitarian assistance and the promotion of human rights.

The protracted war in Angola came to a swift end when UNITA founder and leader Jonas Savimbi was killed in combat with government forces on 22 February 2002. UNITA and the government's armed forces agreed to a ceasefire in March and, in April, signed a Memorandum of Understanding aimed at completing the remaining provisions of the Lusaka Protocol.

This led to a slight expansion of the UN's political presence, with the establishment in August of the **United Nations Mission to Angola (UNMA)** — to assist the parties in completing the remaining tasks of the Lusaka Protocol, and to assist the government with elections, promoting human rights, enhancing the rule of law, supporting reintegration of demobilized soldiers and promoting economic recovery.

By December 2002, the Security Council lifted all sanctions it had imposed on UNITA over the previous nine years. By early 2003, the remaining tasks of the Lusaka Protocol had been implemented. UNMA was dissolved, and responsibility for all its remaining activities was transferred to a strengthened office of the UN resident coordinator.

Central Africa

Rwanda. United Nations involvement in Rwanda began in 1993, when Rwanda and Uganda requested the deployment of military observers along their common border to prevent military use of the area by the Rwandese Patriotic Front (RPF). In response, the Security Council established the **United Nations Observer Mission Uganda-Rwanda (UNOMUR)**.

Fighting had broken out in Rwanda in 1990 between the mainly Hutu government and the Tutsi-led RPF, operating from Uganda. A 1993 peace agreement provided for a transitional government and for elections. At the parties' request, the Security Council set up the **United Nations Assistance Mission for Rwanda (UNAMIR)** to help them implement the agreement. However, as it became clear later, extremist elements of the Hutu majority were planning a campaign to exterminate Tutsis and moderate Hutus. In early April 1994, the death of the Presidents of Rwanda and Burundi in a plane crash caused by a rocket attack ignited several weeks of intense and systemic waves of massacres. The killings, targeting Tutsis and moderate Hutus, were carried out by the Hutu-dominated army and militias.

UNAMIR sought to arrange a ceasefire, without success, and its personnel came under attack. After some countries unilaterally withdrew their contingents, the Security Council in April reduced UNAMIR's strength from 2,548 to 270. However, UNAMIR managed to shelter thousands of Rwandese. In May, the Council imposed an arms embargo against Rwanda and increased UNAMIR's strength to up to 5,500 troops, but it took nearly six months for member states to provide them. In July, RPF forces took control of Rwanda, ending the civil war and establishing a broad-based government.

From a population of 7.9 million, approximately 800,000 people were murdered, some 2 million fled to other countries, and up to 2 million were internally displaced. A United Nations humanitarian appeal raised $762 million to address the enormous humanitarian challenge, and a Commission of Experts established at the request of the Security Council reported "overwhelming evidence" that Hutu elements had perpetrated acts of genocide against the Tutsi group.

In November 1994, the Council established the **International Criminal Tribunal for Rwanda (ICTR)** to prosecute those responsible for genocide and war crimes. And as Rwandan refugees returned to the country en masse, large numbers of Rwandan Hutus took refuge in eastern Zaire, including elements involved in the genocide. From there, the "génocidaires" launched attacks into western Rwanda.

In 1996, at Rwanda's request, the Council terminated UNAMIR's mandate. UN agencies continued to provide humanitarian aid and assist in the return of refugees. In 1999, an independent inquiry commissioned by the Secretary-General found that the responsibility for the failure to stop the genocide was shared by the UN Secretariat, the Security Council and the member states. He expressed deep remorse over the United Nations failure to stop the genocide, and restated his commitment to make sure the Organization never again fails to stop mass slaughter.

The transitional government established following the genocide decided in 1999 to extend the transition four more years to undertake some important tasks. These included decentralization, transition to democracy, a new constitution, promoting reconciliation, and changes to the justice system — including introduction of the "*gacaca*" system, under which those accused of genocide-related charges are judged by their own communities. As of June 2003, some 110,000 individuals accused of genocide-related crimes remained in detention facilities, in extremely poor conditions.

Although the ICTR had already convicted former President Jean Kambanda, among others, and sentenced him to life in prison, its work was seriously hampered by the unavailability of witnesses and lack of full cooperation by the government — which accused it of inefficiency, employing "génocidaires" on defence teams — and the resultant slow pace of trials. Subsequently, the Security Council decided to set up a pool of 18 *ad litem* (short-term) judges, allowing up to nine to serve at any one time — up from the previous maximum of four. As of June 2003, the Tribunal had indicted 81 individuals, of whom 61 were in custody. The ICTR is set to end its term in 2008.

With elections planned for 2003, the UN sent a needs assessment mission to Rwanda, at the request of its national electoral commission. In May, a new constitution was adopted by referendum. In August, voters gave Paul Kagame a landslide victory in presidential elections. A month later, his RPF party won a large majority in the first multiparty, parliamentary elections since independence in 1962. To mark the tenth anniversary of the genocide in Rwanda, the General Assembly declared 7 April 2004 as an International Day of Reflection on the 1994 Genocide in Rwanda.

At the regional level, Uganda and Rwanda intervened in the renamed Democratic Republic of the Congo (DRC), claiming security concerns over sanctuary being given there to remnants of former Hutu militias ("Interahamwe") and Rwandan Armed Forces ("ex-FAR") responsible for the 1994 genocide. In July 1999, after intensive diplomatic efforts by the UN, the OAU and the region, the Lusaka Ceasefire Agreement for the DRC was signed. The Security Council subsequently established the United Nations Mission in the Democratic Republic of the Congo (MONUC).

In July 2002, Presidents Kagame and Kabila agreed on the withdrawal of Rwandan troops from the DRC and the dismantling of the ex-FAR and Interahamwe forces — a major turning point towards peace and stability for the Great Lakes region. Rwanda completed the withdrawal of its troops on 7 October. MONUC had voluntarily repatriated some 900 Rwandese combatants and their dependants by the end of 2003.

Burundi. The United Nations Office in Burundi has participated in international efforts to help resolve the crisis in that country, where a long-standing internal conflict led in 1993 to a coup attempt in which the first democratically elected President, a Hutu, and six ministers were killed. This ignited factional fighting in which at least 150,000 people died in the following three years.

In 1996, the government and President — put in place by a 1994 agreement between the Hutu majority and Tutsi minority — were deposed by a Tutsi-led military coup. The Security Council condemned the coup and urged the military leaders to restore constitutional order. Neighbouring countries imposed an economic embargo. As fighting intensified between the largely Tutsi army and Hutu rebels, some 500,000 people were forcibly transferred to "regroupment camps" and 300,000 fled to Tanzania.

Former Tanzanian President Julius Nyerere then began mediation efforts which led, in 1998, to a new transitional constitution based on political partnership between Hutus and Tutsis, inauguration of a transitional national assembly, and a ceasefire agreement with some parties to the conflict. In 1999, the neighbouring states suspended their economic sanctions. In 2000, following Mr. Nyerere's death, former South African President Nelson Mandela succeeded him as facilitator of the peace process. Through his efforts, a Peace and Reconciliation Agreement was signed in August in Arusha, Tanzania.

Welcoming the agreement, the Security Council urged the parties remaining outside the peace process to participate in it fully. The transitional government was installed in November 2001, followed by the transitional national assembly and senate. South Africa, assisted by Gabon and Tanzania and with the support of the United Nations and the African Union, intensified efforts to negotiate a complete ceasefire. By early 2003, ceasefire agreements had been signed with three major factional groups.

In April 2003, the African Union authorized the deployment of the **African Mission in Burundi (AMIB)**, comprising up to 3,500 troops and including 120 military observers. On 30 April, at the end of the first half of the transitional period, a Hutu President and a Tutsi Vice-President were sworn in — marking a transfer of executive power from the Tutsi minority to the Hutu majority.

At the end of June, however, four members of parliament were abducted by the National Council for the Defence of Democracy-Forces for the Defence of Democracy (CNDD/FDD) rebel faction, as deadly attacks shook Bujumbura, Burundi's capital. Clashes were also reported between government forces and the Palipehutu-Forces Nationales de Libération (Palipehutu-FNL) faction. Sixteen of Burundi's 17 provinces were now subject to sporadic fighting, looting and armed banditry. The UN withdrew its non-essential staff from Bujumbura, where scores of people had been killed and thousands displaced.

Nevertheless, sustained efforts by South African President Thabo Mbeki and other regional leaders resulted in the signing between the transitional government and the CNDD/FDD of a protocol to address political, defence and security power-sharing issues (the Pretoria Protocol) leading to the Global Ceasefire Agreement of 16 November 2003. As a result, the CNDD/FDD joined the transitional institutions. The Security Council urged Palipehutu-FNL (Rwasa), the only armed rebel group which had not yet joined the Arusha Agreement, to do so.

At long last there was real hope that a democratic Burundi would emerge from a decade of civil strife that had left between 250,000 and 300,000 people dead. The presence of AMIB had played a key role in providing an atmosphere of security and in assisting the parties to achieve progress in the disarmament process. But the Mission suffered from a serious lack of funds and logistics support — provided by donor countries on a voluntary basis — which prevented it from fully implementing its mandate. This was particularly a matter of concern, in view of national legislative elections scheduled to take place before 31 October 2004. The African Union requested that AMIB be taken over by the United Nations.

On 21 May 2004, acting under the enforcement provisions of the UN Charter, the Security Council authorized the deployment, on 1 June, of the **United Nations Operation in Burundi (ONUB)** — to be composed, initially, of existing AMIB forces. It authorized ONUB to use all necessary means to ensure respect for ceasefire agreements; to carry out disarmament and demobilization activities; and to monitor the illegal flow of arms across the national borders. ONUB was also to help create the necessary security conditions for the provision of humanitarian assistance, to facilitate the voluntary return of refugees and internally displaced persons, and to contribute to the successful completion of the electoral process by ensuring a secure environment for free, transparent and peaceful elections.

On 1 June, more than 2,000 AMIB troops were "rehatted" as United Nations forces.

Democratic Republic of the Congo. Following the 1994 genocide in Rwanda and the establishment of a new government there, some 1.2 million Rwandese Hutus — including elements who had taken part in the genocide — fled to the Kivu provinces of eastern Zaire, an area inhabited by ethnic Tutsis and others. There, a rebellion began in 1996, pitting rebel forces led by Laurent Désiré Kabila against the army of President Mobutu Sese Seko. Kabila's forces, aided by Rwanda and Uganda, took the capital city of Kinshasa in 1997 and renamed the country the Democratic Republic of the Congo (DRC). The civil war resulted in more than 450,000 refugees and internally displaced persons.

In 1998, a rebellion against the Kabila government started in the Kivus, and within weeks the rebels had seized large areas of the country. Angola, Chad, Namibia and Zimbabwe promised President Kabila military support, but the rebels maintained their grip on the eastern regions. Rwanda and Uganda supported the rebel movement, the Congolese Rally for Democracy (RCD). The Security Council called for a ceasefire and the withdrawal of foreign forces, and urged states not to interfere in the country's internal affairs. In May 1999, the RCD split into two factions.

Diplomatic efforts by the Secretary-General, the OAU and the South African Development Community (SADC) led in July 1999 to the Lusaka Ceasefire Agreement. Signed by the DRC along with Angola, Namibia, Rwanda, Uganda and Zimbabwe, it provided for an end to hostilities and the holding of an inter-Congolese dialogue. The RCD and the Mouvement de Libération du Congo signed it in August. To help implement the agreement, the Council authorized the deployment of 90 United Nations military liaison officers to strategic areas in the country and to the capitals of the signatory states. In November, it established the **United Nations Mission in the Democratic Republic of the Congo (MONUC)** to maintain liaison with the parties, assist in implementing the agreement and monitor security conditions.

On 16 January 2001, President Kabila was assassinated while in his palace in Kinshasa, and was succeeded by his son Joseph Kabila.

In April 2001, an expert panel established by the Security Council reported that the conflict in the DRC was mainly about access by foreign armies to the country's rich mineral resources. Five key minerals in particular — diamonds, copper, cobalt, gold and coltan (a component of electronic chips used in cell phones and laptop computers) — were being exploited by those armies in a systematic fashion, while a number of companies had been trading arms for natural resources or facilitating access to funds to purchase weapons. The DRC also has reserves of gems, timber and uranium.

In May, President Joseph Kabila announced that he was lifting the ban on political parties in the DRC. Nevertheless, fighting continued to intensify in the east, involving armed groups and soldiers from Rwanda, Burundi, local Congolese militia known as the Mayi-Mayi, and the RCD. In October, the Security Council authorized the deployment of UN troops and military observers to that region, as a long-awaited inter-Congolese dialogue began in Addis Ababa.

In July 2002, an agreement was signed by the governments of the DRC and Rwanda on the withdrawal of Rwandan troops from the DRC and the dismantling of the ex-FAR and Interahamwe forces there. In September, a similar agreement was reached between the DRC and Uganda. However, by October, renewed fighting in the eastern part of the DRC threatened to destabilize the entire country.

Diplomatic efforts to assist inter-Congolese dialogue continued, and in December 2002, the parties to the conflict, under UN and South African mediation, agreed to form a transitional government, with the hope of holding transparent and democratic elections at the end of a two-year transition period. The Security Council enlarged MONUC to 8,700 military personnel and expanded its presence eastward, to provide security at disarmament and demobilization sites and assist in the destruction of impounded weapons and munitions.

Unfortunately, new fighting soon erupted in the South Kivu region, sending more than 8,500 Congolese refugees into neighbouring Burundi over a 12-day period. At the end of January 2003, the WFP launched emergency airlifts to provide 892 tons of food for some 115,000 desperate and hungry people forced from their homes by the fighting in Bunia — chief town of the resource-rich Ituri district of Oriental Province. In March, a UN-brokered ceasefire at the local level was signed in Ituri. However, following the withdrawal of the Ugandan army in May, violence resumed in Bunia, with warring Hema and Lendu groups vying for control of the region.

Finally, in May 2003, the parties signed a ceasefire agreement for the Ituri region. With relative calm holding in the region, MONUC continued to patrol Bunia, trying to ease ethnic tensions and reassure the terrified local population — even as the bodies of two UN military observers slain a week earlier were recovered just north of Bunia. The brutal inter-ethnic power struggle had so far claimed more than 400 lives, and was marked by the systematic use of rape, murder and "witnessed cannibalism" as a form of psychological torture. On 30 May, the Security Council authorized the deployment of an **Interim Emergency Multinational Force (IEMF)** to Bunia until

1 September, to help stabilize the situation. It was provided by the European Union — the first such force fielded outside of Europe — and led by France.

On 29 June, the government and the country's main opposition factions — including the RCD and the Movement for the Liberation of the Congo (MLC) — signed an agreement on military and security arrangements. On 17 July, the government of national unity and transition was installed in Kinshasa, with the swearing-in of four Vice-Presidents to head up the DRC's new power-sharing transitional government led by President Kabila. The Security Council extended MONUC's mandate through 30 July 2004 and increased its military strength to 10,800, in preparation for the transfer of security responsibilities from the IEMF in September.

Acting under Chapter VII of the UN Charter, the Council also authorized the mission, for the first time since it was established, to use all necessary means — including force — to fulfil its mandate in Ituri and North and South Kivu Provinces. It also instituted an arms embargo against all foreign and Congolese armed groups in the east of the country. MONUC was authorized to take the necessary measures to protect civilians and humanitarian workers under imminent threat of violence, protect UN personnel and facilities, ensure the freedom of movement of MONUC personnel, and help improve security conditions for humanitarian assistance.

By 5 September 2003, after the handover of responsibilities from the IEMF to MONUC, some 2,500 UN peacekeepers were firmly in place in Bunia. Over the subsequent six months, MONUC's Ituri Brigade increased in strength to some 4,500 troops and expanded its presence to seven locations outside of Bunia. Despite this stabilizing presence, violence has continued in Ituri, including the ambush in February 2004 by a local militia of a MONUC convoy which killed a UN military observer. On 28 October, the UN panel investigating the plunder of the DRC's natural resources reported that such illegal exploitation remained one of the main sources of funding for groups involved in perpetuating the conflict. The Security Council condemned the practice. Meanwhile, preparations were under way for elections to be held in 2005.

Central African Republic. The conflict in the Central African Republic occurred when soldiers staged a series of mutinies in the mid-1990s. In 1998, following an intervention by troops from France, the former colonial power, and later by an African multinational force (MISAB), the UN established the **United Nations Mission in the Central African Republic (MINURCA)** — a peacekeeping operation with a mandate to help improve security in the capital, Bangui. Later, the United Nations also provided support for elections, which were concluded the following year. **The United Nations Peace-building Office in the Central African Republic (BONUCA)** was created in February 2000, following the withdrawal of MINURCA.

But unrest continued, and an attempted coup by army officers was put down in May 2001. Two years later, in March 2003, a group led by General François Bozizé forcefully took power through a coup d'état, ousting elected President Ange Félix Patassé. The Security Council condemned the coup, stressing that the Bangui authorities must elaborate a plan for national dialogue, including a timeframe for the holding of elections as soon as possible.

By the end of June, the UN Secretary-General reported that the new authorities envisaged a process of national dialogue, to be followed by a constitutional referendum and then general elections in 2004 — resulting in a return to constitutional legality in January 2005. The government opted to involve all political factions and civil society in managing the transition, and a dialogue of national reconciliation was begun. In October 2003, the Secretary-General welcomed the spirit of "openness, forgiveness and understanding" that characterized those talks.

Meanwhile, BONUCA's mandate was extended to the end of 2004, to continue supporting the government's efforts to restore constitutional legality through national dialogue, and to strengthen national capacities for promotion of the rule of law during the transitional period leading up to the general elections.

West Africa

Office of the Special Representative of the Secretary-General for West Africa. A United Nations inter-agency mission visited 11 countries in West Africa in March 2001. It recommended that the grave, interlinked political, economic and social problems faced by West African countries would be best addressed through an integrated subregional strategy involving the United Nations and its partners. In November 2001, the Secretary-General decided to establish the Office of the Special Representative of the Secretary-General for West Africa to promote such an integrated approach. Based in Dakar, the Office became operational in September 2002.

The Office also carries out good offices roles and special assignments in West African countries, liaising with subregional organizations and reporting to United Nations Headquarters on key developments of subregional significance. For example, the special representative has been closely involved since late 2002 in international efforts aimed at resolving the conflict in Côte d'Ivoire.

The special representative is also chairperson of the **Cameroon-Nigeria Mixed Commission**, established by the Secretary-General at the request of the Presidents of Nigeria and Cameroon, to consider all aspects of the implementation of a ruling by the International Court of Justice on the boundary between the two countries.

Relations between Cameroon and Nigeria had been strained for some time over issues relating to their 1,600-kilometre land boundary, extending from Lake Chad to the Bakassi peninsula, with a maritime boundary in the Gulf of Guinea. Issues included rights over oil-rich land and sea reserves, and the fate of local populations. Tensions escalated into military confrontation at the end of 1993 with the deployment of Nigerian military to the 1,000-square-kilometre Bakassi peninsula. In 1994, Cameroon brought the border dispute to the World Court.

On 10 October 2002, the Court issued its judgement, and the Mixed Commission held its first meeting in December, meeting every two months thereafter — alternating between Yaoundé, Cameroon and Abuja, Nigeria and making steady progress. In April 2004, it decided that the withdrawal and transfer of authority over the land boundary would take place between 15 June and 15 July. Withdrawal from the Bakassi peninsula and transfer of authority to Cameroon would occur between 15 July and 15 September.

Côte d'Ivoire. In December 1999, a group of officers and soldiers led by General Robert Guei overthrew Côte d'Ivoire's constitutional government led by President Konan Bedié, who had come to power in December 1993. New presidential elections were held in October 2000. Realizing that he was losing in the polls to Laurent Gbagbo, leader of the Front Populaire Ivorien, Guei claimed victory on 23 October. Alassane Ouattara, leader of the Rassemblement Démocratique des Républicains, had been barred from contesting the elections under the provisions of a new, controversial Constitution adopted six months earlier.

As thousands of people demonstrated against Guei's action in Abidjan, Gbagbo declared himself president, and Guei fled the city. Violent clashes ensued in the streets of the capital between Gbagbo's supporters, those backing Ouattara and security forces. Hundreds died. An independent commission of enquiry established by the Secretary-General later concluded that the security forces had been responsible for repressing the protests and were implicated in the killings.

In August 2002, President Gbagbo formed a new, broad-based government. Tensions persisted, despite a national reconciliation process launched in October 2001 under the chairmanship of former Prime Minister Seydou Diarra. On 19 September 2002, groups of disgruntled military personnel attempted a coup and occupied the northern part of the country. An Economic Community of West African States (ECOWAS) summit on 29 September in Accra decided to establish a peacekeeping force and a six-member contact group to help address the crisis in Côte d'Ivoire. The rebel Mouvement Patriotique de Côte d'Ivoire (MPCI) and the government signed a ceasefire agreement on 17 October and the ECOWAS force began to deploy to monitor it.

The attempted coup resulted in a de facto partition of the country, with the government controlling the south, the MPCI the north and north-east, and two other rebel groups which emerged in November 2002 — the Mouvement Populaire du Grand Ouest (MPIGO) and the Mouvement pour la Justice et la Paix (MJP) — controlling the west. The fighting caused massive internal and external displacement of people to neighbouring countries.

Following an impasse in ECOWAS-led talks in late 2002, the government and rebel forces met in Linas-Marcoussis, France, from 15 to 23 January 2003. A peace agreement was reached that addressed issues underlying the conflict and provided for the establishment of a government of national reconciliation. On 11 January, the MPIGO and MJP had signed a ceasefire agreement with the government.

On 4 February, the Security Council adopted resolution 1464 (2003) which called on the Ivorian political forces to immediately implement the Linas-Marcoussis Agreement. It also authorized the ECOWAS forces, together with the French forces supporting them, to act under Chapter VII of the Charter to ensure their security and freedom of movement and ensure protection of civilians within their zones of operation. On 7 February, the Secretary-General appointed Albert Tevoedjre as his special representative for Côte d'Ivoire.

President Gbagbo, in keeping with the Linas-Marcoussis accord, established the national reconciliation government on 13 March with Seydou Diarra as the new Prime Minister, with enlarged powers. The outstanding issue of nominees for the ministers for defence and national security was being addressed through a national security council. On 3 May, the Forces armées nationales de Côte d'Ivoire (FANCI) and the Forces Nouvelles — comprising MPCI, MJP and MPIGO — signed a cease-fire agreement that covered the whole country and authorized the deployment of French and ECOWAS forces to secure the western region.

By its resolution 1479 of 13 May 2003, the Security Council established the **United Nations Mission in Côte d'Ivoire (MINUCI)**, consisting of up to 76 military liaison officers and a civilian component, with a mandate to facilitate the implementation of the Linas-Marcoussis Agreement. But by November, it was clear that the peace process had encountered serious difficulties.

The transitional government had failed to begin restructuring the defence and security forces immediately upon taking office, as required under Linas-Marcoussis. And in September, the Forces Nouvelles, which held control in northern provinces, rejected President Gbagbo's appointment of defence and internal security ministers and pulled out of the government. Along with six other signatories, it protested that President Gbagbo had not delegated enough power to the Prime Minister and the national reconciliation government.

Prior to the current turmoil, Côte d'Ivoire had long been considered West Africa's leading economy and was seen as a beacon of tolerance. But by November 2003, the Security Council was expressing serious concern that the peace process had stalled. It also condemned attacks against UN personnel in October in opposition-held territory, and the murder of a French journalist in Abidjan, the government-controlled commerce centre. As the year ended, the United Nations Emergency Relief Coordinator expressed concern about rising tensions in the country, and the impact of possible renewed conflict on civilians.

Responding to this situation, the Security, on 27 February 2004, established the **United Nations Operation in Côte d'Ivoire (UNOCI)**, with effect from 4 April — asking the Secretary-General to transfer authority from MINUCI and the ECOWAS forces to UNOCI at that time. It also authorized the French forces to use all necessary means to support UNOCI, which has an authorized maximum strength of 6,240 military personnel.

In coordination with the French forces, UNOCI is mandated to observe and monitor implementation of the comprehensive ceasefire of May 2003, including the movements of armed groups; to assist in disarmament, demobilization, reintegration, repatriation and resettlement; to protect UN personnel, institutions and civilians; to provide support for humanitarian assistance and implementation of the peace process; and to assist in the field of human rights, public information, and law and order.

Liberia. In 1997, after eight years of civil strife, a democratically elected government was installed in Liberia and the **United Nations Peace-building Support Office in Liberia (UNOL)** was established. But political instability and insecurity persisted, and in 1999, fighting began between government forces and the rebel group Liberians United for Reconciliation and Democracy (LURD). The fighting spread and intensified in early 2003 with the emergence, in the western region, of a new armed group — the Movement for Democracy in Liberia (MODEL). By May 2003, rebel forces controlled 60 per cent of the country. The humanitarian situation was grave, with thousands of people displaced.

In April 2003, Liberian President Charles Taylor had informed the two co-Chairmen of the International Contact Group on Liberia that his government was ready to negotiate unconditionally with rebel forces towards a ceasefire. As the parties gathered in Accra, Ghana, on 4 June for ECOWAS-sponsored peace talks, the UN-backed Special Court for Sierra Leone announced that it had indicted President Taylor for war crimes in Sierra Leone during its 10-year civil war, and issued an international warrant for his arrest. Addressing the conference, President Taylor offered to remove himself from the process if that would facilitate peace.

Barely two weeks later, the Liberian government delegation at the talks, LURD and MODEL signed a ceasefire accord, providing for immediate dialogue to reach a comprehensive peace agreement within 30 days — and calling for the formation of a transitional government without President Taylor. On hearing the news, citizens in the Liberian capital, Monrovia, rejoiced in the streets. A few days later, Switzerland announced that, at the request of the Special Court, it had frozen or blocked several of the President's personal and business accounts.

Fighting continued in Monrovia and throughout the country despite the accords, and hundreds of innocent civilians were killed. On 28 June, warning of a possible massive humanitarian catastrophe, the Secretary-General urged the Security Council to mandate the deployment of a multinational force. On 7 July, at resumed peace talks in Accra, President Taylor announced his intention to resign from office and leave Liberia. Within days, the Secretary-General appointed Jacques Paul Klein, former head of the UN Mission in Bosnia and Herzegovina, as his special representative for Liberia.

Diplomatic and political efforts intensified. On 23 July, with rebel mortars pounding Monrovia, hundreds of hungry, terrified refugees scrambled for safety inside the walls of the UN compound. ECOWAS decided to send in a vanguard force of 1,000 to 1,500 troops. On their arrival, President Taylor would depart and reinforcements from the United States and other countries would move in to prepare for a UN mission.

On 1 August, the Security Council authorized the ECOWAS multinational force. Three days later, the UN airlifted the first of two battalions from Nigeria to Liberia's main airport to set up a forward headquarters for ECOWAS troops. Taking advantage of a lull in the violence, UN and other relief agencies began rushing food and medical supplies to hundreds of thousands of desperate people crowding the streets of war-ravaged Monrovia. The UN launched an appeal for $69 million in emergency aid for Liberia.

On 11 August, President Taylor resigned his office and departed for exile in Nigeria. He was succeeded by his Vice President, Moses Blah, as head of the interim government. Several days later, at the Accra talks, the Secretary-General's special representative secured a signed agreement by the parties to ensure free and unimpeded access of humanitarian aid to all territories under their control, and to guarantee the security of international aid workers. The government, LURD and MODEL also signed a comprehensive peace agreement, which was witnessed by ECOWAS, the African Union and Mr. Klein for the United Nations.

On 19 September, the Security Council established the **United Nations Mission in Liberia (UNMIL)** — with up to 15,000 military personnel and over 1,000 civilian police officers — to take over from the ECOWAS force on 1 October. Its mandate included monitoring the ceasefire; assisting in disarmament, demobilization, reintegration and repatriation (DDRR) of all armed parties; providing security at key government installations and vital infrastructure; protecting UN staff, facilities and civilians; and assisting in humanitarian aid and human rights — with particular attention to such vulnerable groups as refugees and the internally displaced. UNMIL was also mandated to help the transitional government develop a strategy to consolidate its institutions, with a view to holding free and fair elections by October 2005. It was later announced that the UN Office in Liberia would be replaced by UNMIL.

The transfer took place as scheduled, when 3,500 ECOWAS soldiers were "rehatted" with the UN blue helmet — the first contingent of 15,000 troops to be deployed by UNMIL. Less than two weeks later, the government and rebel leaders declared Monrovia a "weapons-free zone". The following day, 14 October, the national transitional government of Liberia was installed, led by Chairman Gyude Bryant. On 17 October, former President Blah turned over a large quantity of arms to UN peacekeepers, declaring "we do not want to fight anymore". On 7 November, the Secretary-General's special representative launched a $220,000 road rehabilitation project for Monrovia as part of an UNMIL infrastructure project.

On 13 November, UNMIL responded to ceasefire violations in the areas bordering Guinea and Côte d'Ivoire by increasing its air and land patrols there. On 17 November, it began an intensive public information campaign about the DDRR process, which was formally launched on 1 December. More than 8,000 former combatants had turned in their weapons by 14 December, when the process was temporarily suspended to make some adjustments. According to UNHCR, up to 40,000 former fighters were waiting to be demobilized and reintegrated into civilian life after 14 years of fighting.

As the year drew to a close, plans were also under way for an International Conference on the Reconstruction of Liberia, which was held from 5 to 6 February 2004. By June, the Secretary-General's special representative reported that UNMIL troop deployments had significantly stabilized the country and the peace process was "firmly on track", adding that 70 per cent of an estimated 53,000 former combatants had already given up their weapons.

Guinea-Bissau. Following a period of conflict in Guinea-Bissau, a government of national unity was inaugurated in February 1999. In March, the UN established the **United Nations Peace-building Support Office in Guinea-Bissau (UNOGBIS)** to help create an enabling environment for restoring and consolidating peace, democracy and the rule of law and to facilitate the organization of free and transparent elections. The Office helped promote national reconciliation and strengthen democratic institutions; but in May, the peace accord broke down, fighting resumed and rebel troops ousted President João Bernardo Vieira. Following parliamentary and presidential elections in November 1999 and January 2000, the transitional government turned over power to the civilian government under the new President, Koumba Yala.

Although the United Nations Support Office continued to help the new government in the transitional period, the consolidation of peace and economic recovery was severely hampered by political instability within the country, causing donors to limit their assistance. The dire economic situation led to mounting social tensions. In late November 2002, President Yala dissolved the National Assembly, appointing a new "caretaker government". Parliamentary elections scheduled for May 2003 were repeatedly postponed. Finally, on 14 September 2003, he was ousted in a bloodless coup.

Reporting to the Security Council several months later, the Secretary-General said that removal of the democratically elected president, however reprehensible, took place after constitutional norms had been repeatedly violated. Describing the military coup as "the culmination of an untenable situation", he called on the international community to recommend ways of preventing democratically elected governments in post-conflict countries from flouting the principles of basic governance.

On 28 September, a political transitional charter was signed by the military and 23 of the nation's 24 recognized parties. It provided for a civilian transitional government led by a civilian transitional president and prime minister; parliamentary elections to be held within six months; and presidential elections to be organized within one year of the swearing-in of the new deputies. By 6 October, all transitional mechanisms were in place and Henrique Perreira Rosa, an economist and businessman who headed the national election commission for the first multiparty elections in 1994, was sworn in as transitional President.

On 18 November, the President appealed to the Security Council for help in paying the salaries his government owed its civil servants. The previous government had failed to pay salaries, leading to waves of strikes by teachers, health care workers and other government employees — and the 14 September coup. He later announced that parliamentary elections would be held on 28 March 2004. On 19 December, the Council appealed for urgent assistance to Guinea-Bissau. A UNDP-managed emergency fund was established to help the government — then facing an $18.3 million budget shortfall — to resume social services.

Sierra Leone. The United Nations became involved in Sierra Leone in 1995, when the Secretary-General appointed a special envoy to mediate in the civil war. In 1991, fighters of the Revolutionary United Front (RUF) had launched a war from the east of the country to overthrow the government. With the support of Nigerian and Guinean troops, Sierra Leone's army tried to defend the government, but in 1992 the army itself overthrew the government. Despite the change of power, the RUF continued its attacks.

The special envoy, working in collaboration with the OAU and the Economic Community of West African States (ECOWAS), negotiated a settlement and the return to civilian rule. Elections were held in 1996, and the army relinquished power to the winner, Ahmad Tejan Kabbah. But the RUF did not participate in the election, and continued hostilities. The special envoy assisted in negotiating the 1996 Abidjan Peace Accord between the government and the RUF, but it was derailed by another military coup in 1997, in which the army joined with the RUF to form a ruling junta. President Kabbah and his government went into exile in Guinea. The Security Council imposed an oil and arms embargo and authorized ECOWAS to ensure its implementation, using troops of its monitoring group, ECOMOG.

In 1998, responding to an attack by supporters of the junta, ECOMOG launched a military attack that led to the collapse of the junta. President Kabbah was returned to office, and the Security Council terminated the embargo. In June, the Council established the **United Nations Observer Mission in Sierra Leone (UNOMSIL)**, which monitored the security situation and efforts to disarm combatants and restructure the security forces. Unarmed UNOMSIL teams, under ECOMOG protection, documented atrocities and human rights abuses against civilians.

Fighting continued, with the rebel alliance gaining control of more than half of the country. During an offensive to retake Freetown, the capital, the alliance in January 1999 overran most of the city. All UNOMSIL personnel were evacuated, but the special representative and the chief military observer continued to perform their duties, maintaining contacts with all parties and monitoring the situation. Later that month, ECOMOG troops retook Freetown and reinstalled the civilian government. The war resulted in some 700,000 internally displaced persons (IDPs) and some 450,000 refugees in neighbouring countries.

The special representative, in consultation with West African states, started diplomatic efforts to open up a dialogue with the rebels. Negotiations between the government and the rebels led to the Lomé Peace Agreement, signed in July, to end the war and form a government of national unity.

The Security Council in October decided to replace UNOMSIL with a larger mission — the **United Nations Mission in Sierra Leone (UNAMSIL)** — to assist the parties in putting the agreement into effect and to assist in disarming, demobilizing and reintegrating the estimated 45,000 combatants. In February 2000, following the announcement that the ECOMOG troops would be withdrawn, the Council increased the strength of UNAMSIL to 11,000 troops.

But in April, members of the RUF attacked UN forces after ex-combatants came forward to disarm. Four peacekeepers were killed, and close to 500 United Nations personnel were taken hostage by RUF forces amid renewed fighting. In May, British troops, serving under a bilateral arrangement with the government of Sierra Leone, secured the capital and its airport. They also assisted in capturing the RUF leader, Foday Sankoh, who was arrested by the police. By the end of the month, around half of the UN hostages had been released. The Security Council increased UNAMSIL's strength to 13,000 troops to help restore peace. In July, UNAMSIL staged a rescue operation, bringing to safety the remaining hostages. The Security Council in August started the process of setting up a special court to try those responsible for war crimes.

Since 2001, the United Nations has made steady progress in implementing its peacekeeping mandate in Sierra Leone. UNAMSIL completed its deployment to all areas of the country in November, and the disarmament process was completed in January 2002. A total of 57,000 combatants from all parties were disarmed and demobilized, paving the way for presidential and parliamentary elections.

Following the elections in May 2002, UNAMSIL focused on helping the government consolidate peace by facilitating the extension of state authority throughout the country and the reintegration of ex-combatants — a total 46,900 ex-combatants had benefited from short-term reintegration projects as of June 2003 — and supporting the settlement of internally displaced persons and returnees. The resettlement of IDPs was completed in December 2002; the repatriation of Sierra Leonean refugees is ongoing. The Truth and Reconciliation Commission and the Special Court for Sierra Leone began to function in mid-2002.

In September 2002, the Security Council approved a drawdown of UNAMSIL in four phases, to be completed in December 2004. The first two phases were completed on schedule. By February 2004, UNAMSIL's troop strength had been reduced from 17,500 to 11,672. The pace of the drawdown is guided by progress made in developing the capacity of Sierra Leone's security forces to take responsibility for the country's internal and external security. To that end, the Council authorized the deployment of up to 170 civilian police personnel to UNAMSIL to assist in training the Sierra Leone police, while an international military advisory training team has been assisting in the restructuring and reform of the army.

Ethiopia-Eritrea

With the collapse of the military government in Ethiopia in 1991, the Eritrean People's Liberation Front (EPLF) announced the formation of a provisional government and the holding of a referendum to determine the wishes of the Eritrean people regarding their status in relation to Ethiopia. In 1992, the head of its referendum commission invited the United Nations to observe the referendum process.

The General Assembly established the **United Nations Observer Mission to Verify the Referendum in Eritrea (UNOVER)**, which observed the organization and holding of the 1993 referendum. Ninety-nine per cent of the voters favoured independence; shortly thereafter, Eritrea declared independence and joined the United Nations.

In May 1998, fighting broke out between Ethiopia and Eritrea over disputed border areas. The Security Council demanded an end to the hostilities and offered technical support for the delimitation and demarcation of the border. The Secretary-General called for an end to the fighting so as to give a chance to mediation efforts by the United States and Rwanda. The OAU subsequently took the lead in the mediation. In May 2000, the Security Council imposed an arms embargo on the two countries.

In June, following proximity talks under OAU auspices, a cessation of hostilities agreement was reached in Algiers. To assist in its implementation, the Security Council in July established the **United Nations Mission in Ethiopia and Eritrea (UNMEE)**, involving the deployment of liaison officers to each capital and military observers along the border. In September, the Council authorized the deployment of up to 4,200 military personnel to monitor the cessation of hostilities and assist in ensuring observance of the security commitments agreed by the two parties.

With the arrival of the peacekeepers, the Ethiopian and Eritrean forces redeployed and a temporary security zone (TSZ) was created. UNMEE was mandated to patrol and monitor the zone. It was also entrusted to chair the Military Coordination Commission, to coordinate and provide technical assistance for humanitarian mine-action activities in and around the TSZ, and to coordinate its activities there with the humanitarian and human rights efforts of the UN and other organizations.

The parties continued to negotiate their differences, facilitated by Algeria, and in December 2000 signed a peace agreement providing for a permanent end to military hostilities and the release of prisoners of war. It also required the establishment of an independent commission to delimit and demarcate the border based on pertinent colonial treaties and applicable international law. In April 2002, the five-member neutral Boundary Commission reached its final and binding decision on delimitation of the border. To assist in its implementation, the Security Council adjusted UNMEE's mandate to include demining in support of demarcation, and administrative and logistical support for the Commission's field offices.

During 2003, the military situation was generally stable, but the peace process remained at a critical stage, owing to Ethiopia's rejection of the Boundary

Commission's recommendations. The parties generally respected the integrity of the temporary security zone, established as a first step towards demarcation of the border, but some incursions were reported. These culminated in a shooting incident in early November, in which an Eritrean militiaman was killed. Throughout the year, the absence of direct political contacts between the two countries hindered the normalization of bilateral relations — a vital element of any peace process. The Secretary-General and his special representative urged the countries to resume a political dialogue. In September, the Security Council called on them to create the necessary conditions for the boundary demarcation to proceed.

On 30 January 2004, the Secretary-General, very concerned at the lack of progress in arbitrating the border dispute, announced that he had offered his good offices to the two parties, and had appointed Lloyd Axworthy, former Foreign Minister of Canada, as his special envoy for Ethiopia and Eritrea.

The Americas

The United Nations was instrumental in bringing peace to the Central American region, in one of its most complex and successful peacemaking and peacekeeping efforts.

The United Nations became involved in Central America in 1989, when Costa Rica, El Salvador, Guatemala, Honduras and Nicaragua requested its assistance in their agreement to end the conflicts that plagued the region, promote democratic elections and pursue democratization and dialogue. The Security Council established the **United Nations Observer Group in Central America (ONUCA)** to verify compliance with commitments to cease assistance to irregular and insurrectionist forces, and not allow the territory of any country to be used for attacks into other countries.

Nicaragua. The five countries also agreed to draw up a plan for demobilizing the Nicaraguan resistance, and the Nicaraguan government announced it would hold elections under international and United Nations monitoring. The **United Nations Observation Mission for the Verification of Elections in Nicaragua (ONUVEN)** observed the preparation and holding of the 1990 elections — the first to be observed by the UN in an independent country. The success of ONUVEN helped create conditions for the voluntary demobilization of the "contras", which was overseen by ONUCA in 1990.

El Salvador. In El Salvador, negotiations brokered by the Secretary-General and his personal representative culminated in the 1992 peace accords, which put an end to a 12-year conflict that had claimed some 75,000 lives. The **United Nations Observer Mission in El Salvador (ONUSAL)** monitored the accords, including the demobilization of combatants and both parties' compliance with their human rights commitments. ONUSAL also assisted in bringing about reforms needed to tackle the root causes of the civil war — such as judicial reforms and the establishment of a new civilian police force. At the request of the government, ONUSAL observed the 1994 elections. Its mandate ended in 1995.

Guatemala. At the request of the government and the Guatemalan National Revolutionary Unity (URNG), the United Nations, beginning in 1991, assisted in talks aimed at ending the civil war, which had lasted over three decades and resulted in some 200,000 people killed or missing. In 1994, the parties concluded accords providing for the United Nations to verify all agreements reached and to establish a human rights mission. The General Assembly established the **United Nations Human Rights Verification Mission in Guatemala (MINUGUA)**.

In 1996, a ceasefire was reached, and the parties signed a peace agreement — ending the last and longest of Central America's conflicts. For the first time in 36 years, the region was at peace. MINUGUA has remained in the country to verify compliance with the accords, while United Nations agencies have continued to address the social and economic roots of conflict throughout the region.

Haiti. In 1990, following the departure of "life president" Jean-Claude Duvalier and a series of short-lived governments, Haiti's provisional government asked the United Nations to observe that year's elections. The **United Nations Observer Group for the Verification of the Elections in Haiti (ONUVEH)** observed the preparation and holding of the elections, in which Jean-Bertrand Aristide was elected President. But a military coup in 1991 ended democratic rule, and the President went into exile.

The Secretary-General, at the request of the General Assembly, appointed a special envoy for Haiti, who was also appointed special envoy by the OAS. In response to the worsening situation, a joint United Nations/OAS mission, the **International Civilian Mission in Haiti (MICIVIH)**, was deployed in the country in 1993 to monitor the human rights situation and investigate violations.

To encourage the restoration of constitutional rule, the Security Council imposed an oil and arms embargo in 1993 and a trade embargo in 1994. Subsequently, it authorized establishment of a multinational force to facilitate the return to democratic rule. As the force was about to intervene, the United States and the military rulers reached an agreement aimed at avoiding further violence, and the United States-led multinational force deployed peacefully in the country. President Aristide returned, and the embargo was lifted. In 1995, a UN peacekeeping mission took over from the multinational force, to help the government maintain security and stability and create the first national civil police.

Against the background of a continuing political crisis, the General Assembly in 2000 created a new peace-building mission, the **International Civilian Support Mission in Haiti (MICAH)**, which took over from previous peacekeeping missions and MICIVIH. Its task was to help the government develop democratic institutions, with a focus on human rights, justice and public security. It completed its work in February 2001, while United Nations activities in Haiti continued through UNDP and other agencies.

As Haiti celebrated its bicentennial on 1 January 2004, a severe political deadlock threatened the country's stability. Noting that the proclamation of the independent

Republic of Haiti on 1 January 1804 had marked the beginning of the end of slavery in the Americas, the Secretary-General expressed the hope that Haitians would be able to resolve the current impasse peacefully. In the weeks that followed, fatal clashes between pro- and anti-government militias led to a spiral of increasing violence.

On 29 February, President Aristide left the country, amid reports that he had resigned from office. A letter of resignation was delivered to the Security Council. Hours later, through its resolution 1529, the Council authorized the immediate deployment of a **Multinational Interim Force (MIF)**, following a request by newly sworn-in President Boniface Alexandre "for international assistance to support the constitutional political process under way in Haiti". A United States-led force immediately began its deployment to Haiti.

On 30 April, the Security Council adopted resolution 1542, establishing the **United Nations Stabilization Mission in Haiti (MINUSTAH)** — as envisaged in its earlier resolution — to support the continuation of a peaceful and constitutional political process and the maintenance of a secure and stable environment. MINUSTAH was formally launched on 1 June, and took over responsibility from the MIF on 25 June. It has an authorized total force strength of 6,700 troops and 1,622 civilian police, as well as international and local civilian staff.

Colombia. The Secretary-General has been exercising his good offices in Colombia since December 1999, through his special adviser. The special adviser has continued to assist peace efforts through regular contacts with the government, guerrilla groups, civil society and the international community.

In January 2002, the special adviser, along with a group of 10 facilitating countries and the Catholic Church, helped avert a breakdown in the peace talks between the government and the Revolutionary Armed Forces of Colombia (FARC). Similar efforts in February failed to prevent the talks from collapsing. Despite these difficulties, the United Nations continues to lend its assistance in promoting a peaceful resolution to the conflict in Colombia.

Asia and the Pacific

The Middle East

The United Nations has been concerned with the question of the Middle East from its earliest days. It has formulated principles for a peaceful settlement and dispatched various peacekeeping operations, and continues to support efforts towards a just, lasting and comprehensive solution to the underlying political problems.

The question has its origin in the issue of the status of Palestine. In 1947, Palestine was a Territory administered by the United Kingdom under a mandate from the League of Nations. It had a population of some 2 million — two thirds Arabs and one third Jews. The General Assembly in 1947 endorsed a plan, prepared by the

United Nations Special Committee on Palestine, for the partition of the Territory. It provided for creating an Arab and a Jewish state, with Jerusalem under international status. The plan was rejected by the Palestinian Arabs, the Arab states and other states.

On 14 May 1948, the United Kingdom relinquished its mandate and the Jewish Agency proclaimed the state of Israel. The following day, the Palestinian Arabs, assisted by Arab states, opened hostilities against the new state. The hostilities were halted through a truce called for by the Security Council and supervised by a mediator appointed by the General Assembly, assisted by a group of military observers which came to be known as the **United Nations Truce Supervision Organization (UNTSO)** — the first United Nations observer mission.

As a result of the conflict, some 750,000 Palestine Arabs lost their homes and livelihoods and became refugees. To assist them, the General Assembly in 1949 established the **United Nations Relief and Works Agency for Palestine Refugees in the Near East (UNRWA)**, which has since been a major provider of assistance and a force for stability in the region.

The conflict remaining unresolved, Arab-Israeli warfare erupted again in 1956, 1967 and 1973, each time leading member states to call for United Nations mediation and peacekeeping missions. The 1956 conflict saw the deployment of the first full-fledged peacekeeping force — the **United Nations Emergency Force (UNEF I)** — which oversaw troop withdrawals and contributed to peace and stability.

The 1967 war involved fighting between Israel and Egypt, Jordan and Syria, during which Israel occupied the Sinai Peninsula, the Gaza Strip, the West Bank of the Jordan River, including East Jerusalem, and part of Syria's Golan Heights. The Security Council called for a ceasefire, and subsequently dispatched observers to supervise the ceasefire in the Egypt-Israel sector.

The Council, by *resolution 242 (1967)*, defined principles for a just and lasting peace, namely: "withdrawal of Israel armed forces from territories occupied in the recent conflict"; and "termination of all claims or states of belligerency and respect for and acknowledgement of the sovereignty, territorial integrity and political independence of every state in the area and their right to live in peace within secure and recognized boundaries, free from threats or acts of force". The resolution also affirmed the need for "a just settlement of the refugee problem".

After the 1973 war between Israel and Egypt and Syria, the Security Council adopted *resolution 338 (1973)*, which reaffirms the principles of resolution 242 and calls for negotiations aimed at "a just and durable peace". These resolutions remain the basis for an overall settlement in the Middle East.

To monitor the 1973 ceasefire, the Security Council established two peacekeeping forces. One of them, the **United Nations Disengagement Observer Force (UNDOF)**, established to supervise the disengagement agreement between Israel and Syria, is still in place on the Golan Heights. The other operation was UNEF II in the Sinai.

In the following years, the General Assembly called for an international peace conference on the Middle East, under United Nations auspices. In 1974, the Assembly invited the Palestine Liberation Organization to participate in its work as an observer. In 1975, it established the **Committee on the Exercise of the Inalienable Rights of the Palestinian People,** which continues to work as the General Assembly's subsidiary organ supporting the rights of the Palestinian people and a peaceful settlement of the question of Palestine.

Bilateral negotiations between Egypt and Israel, mediated by the United States, led to the Camp David accords (1978) and the Egypt-Israel peace treaty (1979). Israel withdrew from the Sinai, which was returned to Egypt. Israel and Jordan concluded a peace treaty in 1994.

Lebanon. Meanwhile, southern Lebanon had become the theatre of hostilities between Palestinian groups on the one hand, and Israeli forces and its local Lebanese auxiliary on the other. After Israeli forces invaded southern Lebanon in 1978, following a Palestinian commando raid in Israel, the Security Council adopted resolutions 425 and 426, calling upon Israel to withdraw and establishing the **United Nations Interim Force in Lebanon (UNIFIL).** The Force was set up to confirm the Israeli withdrawal, restore international peace and security, and assist Lebanon in re-establishing its authority in the area.

In 1982, after intense exchanges of fire in southern Lebanon and across the Israel-Lebanon border, Israeli forces moved into Lebanon, reaching and surrounding Beirut. Israel withdrew from most of the country in 1985, but kept control of a strip of land in southern Lebanon, where Israeli forces and its local Lebanese auxiliary remained, and which partly overlapped UNIFIL's area of deployment. Hostilities between Lebanese groups and Israeli and auxiliary forces continued.

Over the years, the Security Council maintained its commitment to Lebanon's integrity, sovereignty and independence, while the Secretary-General sought to persuade Israel to leave the security zone. Israel maintained that the zone was a temporary arrangement governed by its security concerns. UNIFIL sought to contain the conflict and protect the population.

Israel withdrew its forces in May 2000, in accordance with the 1978 Security Council resolutions and in cooperation with the United Nations, with the Secretary-General verifying completion of the withdrawal in June. As Israel pulled out, the Security Council endorsed the Secretary-General's operational plan to assist Lebanon in re-establishing its authority. The Council called on all parties to cooperate with the United Nations in its efforts to stabilize the situation.

In two resolutions in 2003, extending the UNIFIL mandate, the Council commended Lebanon for taking steps to "ensure the return of its effective authority" throughout the south of the country, and again called on the parties to fulfil their commitments to fully respect the withdrawal line identified by the United Nations.

The Middle East peace process. In 1987, the Palestinian uprising (*intifada*) began in the occupied territories of the West Bank and Gaza Strip with a call for

Palestinian independence and statehood. The Palestine National Council proclaimed in 1988 the state of Palestine. The General Assembly acknowledged that proclamation and decided to designate the Palestine Liberation Organization as "Palestine", without prejudice to its observer status.

Following talks in Madrid, and subsequent Norwegian-mediated negotiations, Israel and the Palestine Liberation Organization established mutual recognition on 10 September 1993. Three days later, Israel and the Palestine Liberation Organization signed in Washington, D.C., the Declaration of Principles on Interim Self-Government Arrangements. The agreement opened the way to an interim Palestinian self-government and to successive Israeli withdrawals from the occupied Palestinian territory.

Welcoming the agreement, the Secretary-General pledged the assistance of United Nations agencies and programmes. The UN created a task force on the social and economic development of Gaza and Jericho, and appointed a special coordinator for United Nations assistance, who has been overseeing the work of the programmes and agencies involved. The special coordinator's mandate was expanded in 1999 to include good offices assistance to the Middle East peace process.

The transfer of powers from Israel to the Palestinian Authority in the Gaza Strip and Jericho began in 1994. In 1995, Israel and the Palestine Liberation Organization signed an agreement on Palestinian self-rule in the West Bank, providing for the withdrawal of Israeli troops and the handover of civil authority to an elected Palestinian Council. Elections for the Council and the presidency of the Palestinian Authority were held in 1996. Yasser Arafat, Chairman of the Executive Committee of the Palestine Liberation Organization, was elected President of the Authority.

The peace process was reactivated with the signing of a 1999 interim agreement leading to further redeployment of Israeli troops from the West Bank, agreements on prisoners, the opening of safe passage between the West Bank and Gaza, and resumption of negotiations on permanent status issues. In an effort to address outstanding issues, high-level peace talks were held under United States mediation at Camp David in July 2000, but ended inconclusively. Unresolved issues included the status of Jerusalem, the Palestinian refugee question, security, borders and Israeli settlements.

At the end of September 2000, a new wave of protests and violence began in the occupied Palestinian territory. The ensuing period was characterized by increasing violence, significant loss of life and destruction, a reoccupation of Palestinian population centres, and a rising humanitarian crisis in the West Bank and Gaza Strip. The Security Council repeatedly called for an end to the violence and, through its resolution 1397 (2002), affirmed a vision of a region where two states, Israel and Palestine, would live side by side within secure and recognized borders.

International efforts to calm the situation on the ground and bring the two parties back to the negotiating table were increasingly carried out through the mechanism of "the Quartet" — composed of the United States, the United Nations, the European Union and the Russian Federation. On 30 April 2003, the Quartet presented the parties with its "Road Map" to a permanent two-state solution. A performance-based plan with distinct phases and benchmarks, it envisaged parallel and reciprocal steps by the two parties in the political, security, economic, humanitarian and institution-building fields, under the auspices of the Quartet, leading to a resolution of the conflict by 2005. The Security Council endorsed the Road Map in its resolution 1515 (2003).

Although both parties accepted the Road Map, a sharp escalation of violence during the last half of 2003 led to an intensifying cycle of retaliation and revenge. In September, the UN special coordinator for the Middle East Peace Process, and special representative of the Secretary-General to the Palestine Liberation Organization and the Palestinian Authority, Terje Roed-Larsen, said that neither side had actively addressed the other's concerns: for Israel, security and freedom from terrorist attack; for Palestinians, a viable and independent state based on pre-1967-war borders. But Palestinian suicide bombings continued, while Israel pressed on with the construction of a "separation barrier" in the West Bank.

(At the request of the General Assembly for an advisory opinion on the legality of the wall, the International Court of Justice held three days of open hearings in February 2004 and issued its opinion on 9 July. By 14 votes to 1, it held that construction of the wall was contrary to international law and that Israel was under an obligation to cease its construction, dismantle it forthwith, and make reparation for all damage caused by its construction. The Court's advisory opinions are not binding.)

As 2003 drew to a close, a group of prominent Israelis and Palestinians, in an independent effort, drafted the "Geneva Accord", with detailed steps for resolving the Israeli-Palestinian conflict. The Secretary-General welcomed their attempt to break the stalemate. While such private initiatives were not a substitute for official diplomatic negotiations, the Accord, which was compatible with the Road Map, had already stimulated positive debate, he said.

The Road Map envisages a comprehensive settlement of the Middle East conflict, including the Syrian-Israeli and Lebanese-Israeli tracks — based on Security Council resolutions 242 (1967), 338 (1973) and 1397 (2002), the 1991 Madrid Peace Conference, the principle of land for peace, agreements already reached by the parties, and a peace initiative endorsed by the Arab League's Beirut Summit in March 2002.

Afghanistan

The most recent chapter in United Nations involvement in Afghanistan dates back to September 1995, when the Taliban faction in Afghanistan's civil war, having seized most of the country, took Kabul, its capital. President Burhannudin Rabbani fled, joining the "Northern Alliance", which held territory only in the north. In October 1996, the Security Council and the General Assembly condemned the Taliban's abduction of former President Najibullah and his brother from UN premises in Kabul — where they had taken refuge four years earlier — and their brutal execution.

The Security Council repeatedly expressed concern that the Afghan conflict provided fertile ground for terrorism and drug trafficking. As the fighting continued, the Secretary-General, in July 1997, appointed Lakhdar Brahimi, a former Foreign Minister of Algeria, as his special envoy for Afghanistan. In October, along with the Under-Secretary-General for Political Affairs, Brahimi convened a series of informal meetings of the "Six plus Two" group — the six states bordering Afghanistan (China, Iran, Pakistan, Tajikistan, Turkmenistan and Uzbekistan) plus the United States and Russia.

On 7 August 1998, terrorist bomb attacks on United States embassies in Nairobi, Kenya, and Dar-es-Salaam, Tanzania, claimed hundreds of lives. By its resolution 1193, the Council repeated its concern at the continuing presence of terrorists in Afghanistan. By resolution 1214 of 8 December, it demanded that the Taliban stop providing sanctuary and training for international terrorists and their organizations, and that all Afghan factions cooperate in bringing indicted terrorists to justice.

Citing the Taliban's failure to respond to this demand, the Council, on 15 October 1999, applied broad sanctions under the enforcement provisions of the UN Charter. It noted, in resolution 1267, that Osama bin Laden had been indicted by the United States for the embassy bombings and demanded that the Taliban faction — never recognized as Afghanistan's legitimate government — turn him over to the appropriate authorities to be brought to justice.

On 22 October, the Council expressed deep distress over reports that thousands of non-Afghans were involved in the fighting on the Taliban side — some below the age of 14 years. It expressed grave concern at the forced displacements of civilian populations, summary executions, abuse and arbitrary detention of civilians, violence against women and girls, and indiscriminate bombing. It cited the Taliban's capture of the Iranian Consulate-General in Mazar-e-Sharif and the murder there of Iranian diplomats and a journalist. It was deeply disturbed by the significant increase in the cultivation, production and trafficking of drugs, especially in Taliban-controlled areas, and demanded that such illegal activities be halted.

The Taliban's religious intolerance also aroused widespread condemnation. In March 2001, they blew up two statues of the Buddha carved out of the sandstone cliff-face in the Bamiyan Valley some 1,300 years ago, including the largest statue of the Buddha in the world. Humanitarian personnel were subjected to harassment and physical abuse, following unsubstantiated charges of "immoral behaviour". In May, an edict required Hindu women to veil themselves like their Muslim counterparts, and all non-Muslims were required to wear identity labels. In August, eight international aid workers were arrested and subsequently put on trial for "promoting Christianity".

Their trial was under way on 11 September, when members of bin Laden's Al-Qaeda organization hijacked four commercial jets in the United States, crashing two into the World Trade Center in New York, one into the Pentagon in the US capital, and the fourth into a field in Pennsylvania when passengers tried to stop them. Some 3,000 people were killed. In the days that followed, the US administration issued an ultimatum to the Taliban: turn over bin Laden and close the terrorist operations in Afghanistan or risk a massive military assault. The Taliban refused.

Military action. On 7 October, forces of the United States and United Kingdom unleashed missile attacks against Taliban military targets and bin Laden's training camps in Afghanistan. Two weeks of bombings were followed by the deployment of US ground forces. In December, Afghan militiamen, supported by American bombers, began an offensive strike on a suspected mountaintop stronghold of Osama bin Laden and Al-Qaeda forces in Tora Bora, in eastern Afghanistan near the Pakistan border.

In the weeks following 11 September, the Security Council expressed support for the efforts of the Afghan people to replace the Taliban regime, which it again condemned for allowing the country to be used as a base for the export of terrorism and for providing safe haven to Osama bin Laden.

Addressing a week-long special session of the General Assembly on terrorism on 1 October, Secretary-General Kofi Annan said: "As we summon the will and the resources needed to succeed in the struggle against terrorism, we must also care for all the victims of terrorism". To that end, he announced a donor alert and called on the international community to provide $584 million to meet the humanitarian needs of some 7.5 million Afghan civilians over the following six months.

The UN also continued its efforts to promote dialogue among Afghan parties, aimed at the establishment of a broad-based, inclusive government. Towards that end, the Secretary-General reappointed Lakhdar Brahimi as his Special Representative in Afghanistan. He had resigned two years earlier when negotiations reached an impasse.

On 12 November, the "Six plus Two" group, meeting under the chairmanship of the Secretary-General, agreed on the need for a broad-based and freely chosen Afghan government. Its members pledged continued support for UN humanitarian efforts in Afghanistan, as well as in refugee camps in neighbouring states. On 27 November, a conference on Afghanistan's reconstruction, sponsored by UNDP, the World Bank and the Asian Development Bank, opened in Islamabad. A further donor conference, focusing on immediate and longer-term needs, was held in Berlin in early December.

Interim arrangements. Meanwhile, the Northern Alliance had entered Mazar-e-Sharif, Herat and then Kabul — a decisive event in the defeat of the Taliban. The UN organized a meeting of Afghan political leaders in Bonn in late November. When it concluded on 5 December, the four groups represented, including the Northern Alliance, agreed on a provisional arrangement pending re-establishment of permanent government institutions. As a first step, the Afghan Interim Authority was established.

On 20 December 2001, the Security Council, by resolution 1386, authorized the establishment of an **International Security Assistance Force (ISAF)** to help the

Authority maintain security in Kabul and its surrounding areas. On 22 December, the internationally recognized administration of President Rabbani handed power to the new Afghan Interim Authority, established in Bonn and headed by Chairman Hamid Karzai. Mr. Brahimi moved to Kabul for his work in support of the new Afghan administration, and the first ISAF troops were deployed.

With the easing of hostilities, WFP was able to deliver a record 114,000 metric tonnes of food aid in December — enough to feed 6 million people for two months. Still, by 20 December, only $358 million of the nearly $662 million being sought for UN relief work had been received. To maintain the momentum, an International Conference on Reconstruction Assistance to Afghanistan was held in Tokyo in January.

Addressing the Conference on 21 January 2002, Secretary-General Kofi Annan said reconstruction would require $10 billion over 10 years, including $1.3 billion for the current year and $376 million for quick impact and recovery projects that were "ready to go". Such projects would include the return of some 1.5 million Afghan children to school within two months. The Tokyo Conference was remarkably successful, resulting in pledges of over $4.5 billion. The country's reconstruction needs were immense.

A preliminary assessment by the World Bank, UNDP and the Asian Development Bank identified possible high-priority areas, including: mine action; basic health services to reduce child and maternal mortality; enrolling over a million girls and boys in school; a rapid increase in food production and access to safe water; shelter to facilitate resettlement and development of a national urban management capacity; emergency energy supply while restoring the existing power system; urban and rural employment; local-level reconstruction; and creating a conducive socio-economic environment for returning refugees.

The first milestone of the Bonn Agreement was achieved with the announcement that same day of the composition of the Special Independent Commission for the Convening of the Emergency Loya Jirga (Pashto for "Grand Council") — a traditional forum in which tribal elders come together and settle affairs. The Emergency Loya Jirga was to elect a head of state for the transitional administration and approve proposals for the structure and key personnel of that administration. Under the Bonn Agreement, free and fair elections had to be held within two years of the establishment of the Loya Jirga.

In January 2002, the Security Council, through a presidential statement, welcomed the positive changes in Afghanistan as a result of the collapse of the Taliban regime. It decided to adjust its sanctions to reflect the new realities, targeting Al-Qaeda and its supporters.

On 28 March, the Council, acting on the recommendation of the Secretary-General, established the **United Nations Assistance Mission in Afghanistan (UNAMA)**, to fulfil the tasks entrusted to the UN under the Bonn Agreement, in such areas as human rights, the rule of law and gender issues. Headed by the Secretary-General's special representative, it would also promote national reconciliation, while managing all UN humanitarian activities in Afghanistan in coordination with the Interim Authority and its successors.

In April 2002, the process of electing members to the Emergency Loya Jirga began. Afghans in 300 districts were to select potential candidates to form a pool from which 1,500 members would be selected, beginning in May. Special provision was made for the participation of women in the Loya Jirga. The nine-day council was opened on 11 June by Zahir Shah, the former King of Afghanistan, who nominated Hamid Karzai to lead the nation. On 13 June, Mr. Karzai was elected as Afghanistan's head of state, to lead the transitional government for the next two years.

A year later, on 26 April 2003, a 35-member constitutional review commission was inaugurated. It conducted public consultations throughout Afghanistan and abroad to ascertain the views of the Afghan people. The resulting draft constitution addressed such issues as the rights and freedoms of individuals, form of government, the respective powers of the central government and local institutions, equality among all Afghan citizens, the role of Islam, and the status of languages and religious sects. In October, the commission submitted its draft to the Constitutional Loya Jirga. In November, it was published and widely distributed. The Loya Jirga was set to convene in five weeks.

Voter registration began in December 2003 in eight cities across Afghanistan, ahead of general elections for the national parliament and presidency in 2004. Every Afghan citizen who would be 18 or older by 20 June 2004 and who appeared in person could be registered.

On 29 December 2003, the draft constitution was circulated at a plenary session of the Constitutional Loya Jirga. The text, which included changes approved earlier by the Loya Jirga's reconciliation committee, provided for the establishment of a presidency with significant powers and a bicameral legislature with an assured minimum number of women members. It also codified respect for fundamental human rights and called for the laws of the nation to conform with the principles of Islam.

On 4 January 2004, the Loya Jirga reached agreement on the draft. On 26 January, after the Dari and Pashto language versions had been completely reconciled, it was formally adopted as the Constitution of Afghanistan when it was signed by Afghan President Hamid Karzai.

Disarmament. Throughout the transitional period, disarmament efforts were carried out with the assistance of UNAMA, despite many challenges and suspensions of the process. On 18 July 2002, three Afghan factions near Mazar-e-Sharif began turning over their weapons under UN monitoring, in the first such voluntary exercise ever in Afghanistan. On 24 October 2003, UNAMA officially launched its disarmament, demobilization and reintegration programme in the northern province of Kunduz.

Drug control. By the late 1990s, Afghanistan had become notorious as the source of nearly 80 per cent of the world's illicit opium, the source of heroin. Nearly 1 per cent of its total arable land, some 640 square kilometres, was devoted to poppy growing. In October 2003, the UN Office on Drugs and Crime (UNODC) reported that Afghanistan was providing about three-quarters of the world's opium. About 1.7 million Afghans — some 7 per cent of the national population — worked in that industry, and land under opium poppy cultivation had increased by 8 per cent over the past year. In December 2003, Afghanistan's Foreign Minister met with the UNODC in Vienna to discuss drug-control efforts.

Rehabilitation, Reconstruction and Humanitarian Action. In December 2002, the Secretary-General launched an $815 million appeal for humanitarian aid, recovery assistance and capacity-building. UNESCO worked to preserve Afghanistan's cultural heritage — including what was left of the country's great Buddhist statues. A year later, UNICEF reported that, since the fall of the Taliban, 16 million children had been immunized against measles and 12 million against polio. More than 700,000 women had received tetanus vaccinations, some 50,000 primary school teachers had been trained, and 4 million children — including 1.2 million girls — had returned to school. UNHCR helped more than 2.5 million Afghan refugees return home from Iran and Pakistan, and assisted half a million internally displaced persons.

FAO distributed high-quality seeds and fertilizers to some 60,000 Afghan farm families ahead of the new planting season, benefiting more than half a million people. As 2003 drew to a close, the World Bank approved a $95 million interest-free loan for reconstruction. It would also be providing $40 million in interest-free credit to rehabilitate the irrigation system in the country's five river basins, as well as $31 million in interest-free financing to install customs and communications infrastructure at border crossings, inland clearance depots, transit checkpoints and the Kabul airport.

Security. The chief counterpoint to this string of successes in the post-Taliban period was the volatile security situation in the country, which threatened to undermine the political and reconstruction efforts. In the first half of 2002, several government officials were assassinated, and there was an attempt on President Karzai. Increasingly, UN and other humanitarian workers were being targeted — particularly Afghan nationals working with these organizations.

In July 2002, the Secretary-General noted that the Taliban, though significantly weakened, had not formally given up. Although they were being effectively contained by the US-led coalition, they were still present, along with remnants of Al-Qaeda. The various armed factions were also a source of instability. It was crucially important for the international community to provide security while a national police and army were being trained.

Prior to the fall of the Taliban, Afghanistan had been described by the UN Mine Clearance Programme as the most heavily mined country in the world, with a staggering 9.7 million landmines. By May 2003, with some 8,000 deminers working in the country, the UN Mine Action Centre for Afghanistan had to suspend mine clearance along parts of the route connecting Kabul and Kandahar owing to the security situation. Full demining activities were only able to resume thanks to the introduction of a new technology that reduced the amount of work that needed to be done manually.

On 13 October, the Security Council approved the Secretary-General's recommendation to deploy ISAF beyond Kabul.

In the meanwhile, the UN announced in September that a new police academy was set to open in November in Gardez, with others planned for 2004 in Mazar-e-Sharif, Kunduz, Bamiyan, Jalalabad and Herat. Directed at policemen with little or no previous training, the courses would cover the democratic principles of policing, human rights and basic law, as well as such police techniques as arrests. More than 80 Afghan police officers had already begun a three-year forensics programme, learning how to detect forgeries and conduct DNA and blood analyses.

Iraq

The Department of Political Affairs has played a key role in supporting the efforts of the Secretary-General and the UN system, and in implementing the numerous resolutions of the Security Council with regard to Iraq — from resolution 660 of 2 August 1990, up to resolution 1511 of 16 October 2003.

The UN and Iraq during the 1990s. Throughout the 1990s and beyond, the Secretary-General exercised his good offices with a view to overcoming the various impasses between the Iraqi government of Saddam Hussein and the Security Council. The Secretary-General and his envoys met with the leadership of Iraq and other regional countries on numerous occasions, in order to avoid deterioration of the situation and to restore international peace and security to the troubled region.

The United Nations response to Iraq's invasion of Kuwait on 2 August 1990 illustrates the range of options it has at its disposal in the pursuit of restoring international peace and security. In its resolutions 660 and 661, the Security Council immediately condemned the invasion, demanded Iraq's withdrawal and imposed comprehensive sanctions against Iraq, including a trade and oil embargo. The lifting of these sanctions was made conditional upon Iraq's compliance with all its obligations as outlined in resolution 660, which demanded Iraq's immediate withdrawal from Kuwait. At the 1990 General Assembly session, the membership at large joined the Security Council in condemning Iraq's action.

On 29 November 1990, by its resolution 678, the Security Council set 15 January 1991 as the deadline for Iraq's compliance with resolution 660, and authorized member states to use "all necessary means" under Chapter VII of the UN Charter, to restore international peace and security in the area. On 16 January 1991, multinational forces, allied to restore Kuwait's sovereignty, began attacks against Iraq. These forces acted in accordance with the Security Council's authorization, but not under the direction or control of the United Nations. Hostilities were suspended in February 1991, after the Iraqi forces had left Kuwait.

By its resolution 687 of 8 April 1991, the Security Council set the terms of a ceasefire, demanded that Iraq and Kuwait respect the inviolability of their border, called for the deployment of United Nations observers, took action on compensation for war damages, and decided that Iraq's weapons of mass destruction (WMD), including chemical and biological weapons, should be eliminated. To verify the disarmament of Iraq, the Council established the **United Nations Special Commission (UNSCOM)** on the disarmament of Iraq, with powers of no-notice inspection. The **International Atomic Energy Agency (IAEA)** was entrusted with similar verification tasks in the area of nuclear armaments, with UNSCOM assistance.

Resolution 687 also established a demilitarized zone along the Iraq-Kuwait border. To monitor that zone, the Council, by resolution 689, set up the **United Nations Iraq-Kuwait Observation Mission (UNIKOM)**.

Subsequently, the Council established an **Iraq-Kuwait Boundary Demarcation Commission**, composed of one representative from Iraq, one from Kuwait and three independent experts appointed by the Secretary-General. In 1992, Iraq stopped participating in the Commission's work. In 1994, Iraq informed the Secretary-General that it recognized Kuwait's sovereignty, territorial integrity and international boundaries as demarcated by the Commission, in accordance with agreements between the two countries in 1931 and 1963.

Also during 1991, the Council established a **United Nations Compensation Commission** to process claims and compensate governments, nationals or corporations for any loss or damage resulting from Iraq's invasion of Kuwait, out of a percentage of the proceeds from sales of Iraqi oil. By the end of 2003, it had awarded compensation of some $48 billion.

In the course of their inspections, UNSCOM and the IAEA uncovered and eliminated large quantities of Iraq's banned weapons programmes and capabilities in the nuclear, chemical and biological field. Despite their achievements, UNSCOM and IAEA were unable to determine that Iraq had fulfilled all the obligations it had accepted, pursuant to Security Council resolutions 661, 678 and 687.

In 1998, the Secretary-General mediated a dispute with Iraq concerning the lifting of the oil embargo. Iraq stated that there were no more proscribed weapons in the country, while UNSCOM contended that it did not have the evidence that Iraq had fully complied with resolution 687. In October, Iraq suspended cooperation with UNSCOM, again calling on the Security Council to lift its oil embargo.

UNSCOM conducted its final mission in December 1998. In the same month, the United States and the United Kingdom launched air strikes on Iraq.

By its resolution 1284, of 17 December 1999, the Security Council established a new weapons monitoring body to replace UNSCOM: the **United Nations Monitoring, Verification and Inspection Commission (UNMOVIC)**. Iraq was to provide full cooperation, unrestricted access and provision of information to United Nations arms inspection teams. The Security Council expressed its intention to lift economic sanctions, dependent on Iraq's cooperation with UNMOVIC and the IAEA, which would be reviewed every 120 days.

In February 2000, the Secretary General appointed Ambassador Yuli Vorontsov as coordinator for the return of missing persons and archives from Iraq to Kuwait.

Sanctions and oil-for-food programme. In its resolution 986 of 17 December 1995, the Security Council created an "oil-for-food" programme to address the severe humanitarian impact of the economic sanctions and to offer a degree of relief to Iraqis. The programme monitored the sales of oil by the government of Iraq to purchase food and humanitarian supplies, and managed the distribution of food in the country. It served as the sole source of sustenance for 60 per cent of Iraq's estimated 27 million people.

Renewed weapons inspections and military action. Prior to the onset of military action in Iraq on 19 March 2003 by a US-led coalition, the UN Security Council held numerous meetings on the implementation of Security Council resolution 1441 of 8 November 2002, which provided for an enhanced inspection regime and offered Iraq a final opportunity to comply with relevant Security Council resolutions.

Under resolution 1441, Iraq was required to provide immediate, unconditional and unrestricted access for inspections of the Iraqi weapons programmes by UNMOVIC and the IAEA. On 27 November 2002, UN inspectors returned to Iraq. The Security Council was repeatedly briefed by the Executive Chairman of UNMOVIC, Hans Blix, and the Director-General of the IAEA, Mohamed ElBaradei. But the Council remained divided about how to ensure the fulfilment of Iraq's international obligations.

In the midst of negotiations, the United States, the United Kingdom and Spain presented Iraq with a 17 March 2003 deadline to disarm completely. Facing the increasing likelihood of imminent military action, the Secretary-General ordered the withdrawal from Iraq of United Nations international staff on 17 March and the suspension of all operations, including the oil-for-food programme. Military action by a coalition headed by the United States and the United Kingdom began three days later.

By its resolution 1483 of 22 May 2003, the Security Council, following the collapse of Saddam Hussein's regime, stressed the right of the Iraqi people to freely determine their political future. It also recognized the specific authorities, responsibilities and obligations of the United States and the United Kingdom as the occupying powers (the "Authority") until an internationally recognized government was sworn in. By the same resolution, the Council modified the oil-for-food programme, authorizing it to resume the delivery of food and medical supplies for a transition period of six months. United Nations specialized agencies also provided emergency assistance.

United Nations Assistance Mission. Also by resolution 1483, the Security Council lifted international sanctions and provided a legal basis for the UN to resume operations in Iraq. The Council resolved that the UN should play a vital role in humanitarian relief, the reconstruction of Iraq, and the restoration and establishment of institutions of representative government. On 27 May, the Secretary General appointed Sergio Vieira de Mello as his special representative for Iraq.

By its resolution 1500 of 14 August 2003, the Security Council established the **United Nations Assistance Mission for Iraq (UNAMI)** for an initial period of 12 months. UNAMI was mandated to coordinate humanitarian and reconstruction aid and to assist with the political process that would eventually lead to the establishment of an internationally recognized sovereign Iraqi government. The Council also welcomed the establishment of the Iraqi Governing Council — a body composed of Iraqi representatives that was set up in July and was welcomed by the Security Council as an important step towards the formation of a sovereign and representative government.

Days later, on 19 August 2003, the United Nations headquarters in Baghdad was the target of a terrorist attack that resulted in 22 deaths, and more than 150 injured. Fifteen of the dead were United Nations staff. Among them was the head of mission and the Secretary-General's special representative, Sergio Vieira de Mello.

Following the attack, the Secretary-General withdrew most United Nations international personnel based in Baghdad, maintaining only a small team to provide essential humanitarian assistance. From both inside and outside Iraq, the United Nations continued to carry out assistance activities, including the delivery of food, water and health care throughout the country, relying principally on its Iraqi staff.

The Secretary-General also appointed an independent panel of experts — headed by former Finnish President and former UN Under-Secretary-General Martti Ahtisaari — to review safety measures taken prior to 19 August 2003, and make recommendations to improve the security system for United Nations personnel in Iraq and similar high-risk environments. The report of the panel concluded that the UN security management system was in need of reform.

In December 2003, the Secretary-General designated Ross Mountain as his acting special representative for Iraq and chief of UNAMI, to operate with a core team temporarily located in Cyprus, Jordan and Kuwait. The team focused on coordinating and implementing United Nations relief, recovery and reconstruction activities, and on planning for an eventual deployment back to Iraq.

Political developments and the role of the UN. By its resolution 1511 of 16 October 2003, the Security Council authorized a multinational force under unified command to take all necessary measures to contribute to the maintenance of security and stability in Iraq, as well as to contribute to the security of UNAMI, the Governing Council of Iraq and other institutions of the Iraqi Interim Administration. On 15 November, the Iraqi Governing Council and the Coalition Provisional Authority reached agreement on the restoration of sovereignty on 30 June 2004, and on a timetable for the drafting of a new constitution and the holding of elections.

On 15 January 2004, the Secretary-General appointed his outgoing senior envoy to Afghanistan, Lakhdar Brahimi, as his special advisor. Following requests from the Iraqi Governing Council and CPA Administrator L. Paul Bremer for UN help with the transition to sovereignty and future national elections, the Secretary-General sent an electoral assistance team, led by Carina Perelli, to assess what needed to be done to hold credible elections by 31 January 2005. He also asked Mr. Brahimi and his aides to return to the country and work with Iraqis on arrangements for the forth-coming political transition.

The special adviser arrived in Iraq on 4 April, and began a wide-ranging series of consultations with a broad cross-section of Iraqi society, including the Iraqi Governing Council, non-governmental organizations, human rights advocates, academics, trade union representatives, senior representatives of teachers and farmers groups, intellectuals, students and leaders of the Iraqi women's movement. He also continued ad hoc consultations with members of the CPA.

Returning to New York to address the Security Council on 27 April, Mr. Brahimi said he intended to resume talks with Iraqis to reach agreement by the end of May on the composition of a caretaker government to succeed the United States-led Coalition Provisional Authority. Despite the assassination, on 17 May, of the President of the Governing Council, Ezz El-Din Salim, discussions continued. And on 28 May, the Council decided to name Iyad Allawi as Iraq's Prime Minister-designate.

On 1 June, the special adviser announced that Sheikh Ghazi Al-Yawar, the new head of the Governing Council, would be President of the interim government scheduled to take over at the end of the month. On 8 June, the Security Council unanimously adopted resolution 1546, endorsing the formation of the new interim government. The Council also decided that the mandate for the US-led multina-tional force (MNF) would be reviewed at the request of the Iraqi government or twelve months from the date of resolution 1546, and that its mandate would expire upon the holding of direct national elections — by 31 December, if possible, and no later than 31 January 2005. The Council also declared that it would terminate the MNF's mandate earlier if so requested by the Iraqi government.

On 28 June 2004, two days ahead of the announced date, sovereignty was offi-cially transferred from the CPA to the new Iraqi interim government.

India-Pakistan

The United Nations has continued to be concerned with the decades-old dispute between India and Pakistan over Kashmir. The issue dates back to the 1940s, when the state of Jammu and Kashmir was one of the princely states that became free to accede to India or Pakistan under the partition plan and the India Independence Act of 1947. The Hindu Maharaja of mostly Muslim Jammu and Kashmir signed his state's instrument of accession to India in 1947.

The Security Council first discussed the issue in 1948, following India's com-plaint that tribesmen and others, with Pakistan's support and participation, were invading Jammu and Kashmir and that fighting was taking place. Pakistan denied the charges and declared Jammu and Kashmir's accession to India illegal.

The Council recommended measures to stop the fighting, including the use of United Nations military observers. It established a United Nations Commission for India and Pakistan, which made proposals for a ceasefire and troop withdrawals, and proposed that the issue be decided by plebiscite. Both sides accepted, but could not agree on the modalities for the plebiscite. Since 1949, based on a ceasefire agreement signed by India and Pakistan at Karachi, the **United Nations Military Observer Group in India and Pakistan (UNMOGIP)** has been deployed to monitor the ceasefire line in Jammu and Kashmir.

Following an agreement signed by the parties in 1972, they undertook to settle their differences peacefully, but over the years, tension remained. A hope to break the long-standing impasse came in April 2003, when the Prime Minister of India and the President of Pakistan began a series of reciprocal steps aimed at easing tensions and improving bilateral relations. As the process continued, the Secretary-General expressed the hope that the normalization of diplomatic relations and restoration of rail, road and air links, as well as other confidence-building measures being introduced by the two sides, would lead to the resumption of a sustained dialogue.

In November, Pakistan offered to implement a unilateral ceasefire along the Line of Control in Jammu and Kashmir with effect from 25 November, the beginning of the Muslim festival of Eid Al-Fitr, and India responded positively. The Secretary-General urged the two countries to continue their efforts with patience and resolve. Eventually, these measures led to a summit meeting, on 4 and 5 January in Islamabad, between Prime Minister Atal Bihari Vajpayee of India, and Pakistan's President Pervez Musharraf and its Prime Minister Zafarullah Khan Jamali.

The Secretary-General applauded the two leaders, adding that improved relations between the two countries would mean a lot for the entire South Asian region — not just in terms of reducing political tensions, but also in economic and social terms. He urged both sides to continue their efforts, with the hope that the summit meeting would give a new impetus to sustained and serious dialogue.

Tajikistan

Following the break-up of the Soviet Union, Tajikistan became independent in 1991. It soon faced a social and economic crisis, regional and political tensions, and differences between secularists and pro-Islamic traditionalists, plunging the country into civil war. In 1994, talks under the auspices of the Secretary-General's special representative led to a ceasefire agreement; the Security Council established the **United Nations Mission of Observers in Tajikistan (UNMOT)** to assist in monitoring it.

In 1997, UN-sponsored negotiations led to a peace agreement. UNMOT assisted in its implementation, in close cooperation with a peacekeeping force of the Commonwealth of Independent States and a mission of the Organization for Security and Cooperation in Europe. The country's first multiparty parliamentary elections were held in February 2000. UNMOT withdrew in May, and the United Nations established a peace-building office to consolidate peace and promote democracy.

Cambodia

Before the implementation of the United Nations-brokered 1991 Paris Peace Agreements, Cambodia was in a state of deep internal conflict and relative isolation from much of the world. Since its emergence from French colonialism in the 1950s, the country had suffered not only from the spillover of the war in Viet Nam of the 1960s and 1970s, but also devastating civil conflicts and the vastly destructive totalitarian regime of Pol Pot. During his "Khmer Rouge" regime from 1975 through 1979, nearly 2 million people perished of murder, disease or starvation.

In 1993, with the help of the **United Nations Transitional Authority in Cambodia (UNTAC)**, Cambodia held its first democratic elections. Through its agencies and programmes, the United Nations has supported the Cambodian government in strengthening reconciliation and development. The Office of the High Commissioner for Human Rights, which also supports the work of the special representative of the Secretary-General for human rights in Cambodia, continues to help the government and people of Cambodia in the promotion and protection of human rights, which are cornerstones of the rule of law and democratic development in any country.

In 2003, after protracted negotiations, an agreement was reached between the government of Cambodia and the United Nations providing for the UN to help the country set up and run a special court to prosecute crimes committed during the period of the Khmer Rouge. It was approved by the General Assembly and signed on 6 June 2003. The agreement is awaiting ratification by the Cambodian National Assembly. In the meantime, in December 2003, a UN technical assessment team visited Phnom Penh to work out a concept of operations and technical details of the court with the government.

Bougainville / Papua New Guinea

In early 1998, following a decade of armed conflict over the issue of independence for the island of Bougainville, the government of Papua New Guinea and Bougainville leaders concluded the Lincoln Agreement, which established the framework for a peace process. Under the Agreement, a regional truce monitoring team, with monitors from Australia, New Zealand, Fiji and Vanuatu, was transformed into a Peace Monitoring Group.

In accordance with the Lincoln Agreement, the government of Papua New Guinea sought, and obtained, the Security Council's endorsement of the Agreement, as well as of the appointment of a small UN observer mission. The **United Nations Political Office in Bougainville (UNPOB)**, the first UN political mission in the South Pacific, became operational on 1 August 1998.

UNPOB was to work in conjunction with the Peace Monitoring Group to monitor implementation of the Agreement. It was also to chair the Peace Process Consultative Committee — a body empowered to consult on all aspects of the ceasefire, develop plans for the disposal of weapons, promote public awareness and understanding of the peace process, and assist in other areas. The Committee was composed of representatives of the parties to the conflict, UNPOB and the members of the Peace Monitoring Group.

On 30 August 2001, after more than two years of talks facilitated and chaired by UNPOB, the parties signed the Bougainville Peace Agreement — providing for a weapons disposal plan, autonomy and a referendum. UNPOB took the lead in supervising the weapons disposal plan. Completion of the second stage of the plan, as certified by UNPOB, opened the way for the drafting of a Bougainville Constitution, as well as for preparations for the election of an autonomous Bougainville government.

By the end of 2003, there was increased stability on the island, as it moved towards autonomy. On 1 January 2004, responding to increased stability in Bougainville, the UN replaced UNPOB with a smaller mission, the **United Nations Observer Mission in Bougainville (UNOMB)**.

Europe

Cyprus

The **United Nations Peacekeeping Force in Cyprus (UNFICYP)** was established in 1964 to prevent a recurrence of fighting between the Greek Cypriot and Turkish Cypriot communities and to contribute to the maintenance and restoration of law and order and a return to normal conditions.

In 1974, a coup d'état by Greek Cypriot and Greek elements favouring union of the country with Greece was followed by military intervention by Turkey and the de facto division of the island. Since 1974, UNFICYP has supervised a de facto ceasefire which came into effect on 16 August 1974, and maintained a buffer zone between the lines of the Cyprus National Guard and of the Turkish and Turkish Cypriot forces. In the absence of a political settlement, UNFICYP continues its presence on the island.

The Secretary-General has used his good offices in search of a comprehensive settlement, hosting proximity talks between the two leaders in 1999 and 2000, followed by intensive direct talks beginning in January 2002. In November, he submitted a comprehensive proposal aimed at bridging the gaps between them. However, it did not prove possible to secure agreement by both leaders to submit the proposal to referendums on each side in time to allow a reunited Cyprus to sign the Treaty of Accession to the European Union (16 April).

The talks were suspended in March 2003. In April, the Turkish Cypriot authorities began to open crossing points for public travel by Greek Cypriots to the north and Turkish Cypriots to the south for the first time in nearly three decades. As UN engineers worked to improve the roads, the Security Council authorized an increase in UNFICYP's civilian police component to ensure the safe and orderly passage of people and vehicles. By 2 November, there had been some 2 million crossings.

The Secretary-General welcomed the new initiative, but stressed that it could not substitute for a comprehensive settlement. On 10 February 2004, the Greek Cypriot leader and the Turkish Cypriot leader — along with the guarantor nations of Greece, Turkey and the United Kingdom — resumed negotiations in New York on the basis of the Secretary-General's detailed proposals. The aim was to submit a completed text for referendums in April — in time for a reunited Cyprus to accede to the European Union on 1 May.

After six weeks of negotiations, with agreement just out of reach, the Secretary-General stepped in to complete the "Comprehensive Settlement of the Cyprus Problem" — which called for creation of a United Cyprus Republic composed of a Greek Cypriot constituent state and a Turkish Cypriot constitutent state linked by a federal government. On 24 April, 76 per cent of voters in the Greek Cypriot referendum opposed the plan, while 65 per cent of voters in the Turkish Cypriot referendum supported it.

Without the approval of both communities, the plan was defeated, and on 1 May, Cyprus entered the European Union as a divided and militarized island. Nevertheless, a great deal had been achieved through the negotiations. Addressing the Security Council on 8 June 2004, the Secretary-General's special adviser for Cyprus, Alvaro de Soto, stressed the need to better understand the reason for the Greek Cypriot rejection of the plan. "And we need to know how the Greek Cypriot side sees the way forward." In the meanwhile, the good offices mission of the Secretary-General was suspended.

Georgia

Relations between the Abkhaz and the Georgians have been tense for decades. Renewed attempts in 1990 by the local authorities in Abkhazia (north-western region of Georgia) to separate from the Republic, which became independent in 1991, escalated in 1992 into a series of armed confrontations. Hundreds died and some 30,000 fled to the Russian Federation. An envoy of the Secretary-General, appointed in 1993, began mediation among the parties, and a ceasefire agreement was reached later that year.

The Security Council established the **United Nations Observer Mission in Georgia (UNOMIG)** to verify compliance. But fighting resumed, turning into civil war. In 1994, the parties, meeting in Moscow, agreed on a new ceasefire, to be monitored by a peacekeeping force of the Commonwealth of Independent States. UNOMIG would monitor implementation of the agreement and observe the operation of the force.

Over the years, successive special representatives of the Secretary-General have conducted negotiations, and the Security Council has stressed the need for a comprehensive settlement. But the core political issue — the future status of Abkhazia within the state of Georgia — has not yet been resolved. The UN and interested states are working to advance negotiations between the parties.

The Balkans

Former Yugoslavia. The Federal Socialist Republic of Yugoslavia was a founding member of the United Nations. In 1991, two republics of the federation, Slovenia and Croatia, declared independence. Croatian Serbs, supported by the national army, opposed the move, and war between Serbia and Croatia broke out. Responding, the Security Council imposed an arms embargo on Yugoslavia, and the Secretary-General appointed a personal envoy to support peace efforts by the European Community.

To create conditions for a settlement, the Security Council in 1992 established the **United Nations Protection Force (UNPROFOR)**, initially in Croatia. But the war extended to Bosnia and Herzegovina, which had declared independence — a move supported by Bosnian Croats and Muslims but opposed by Bosnian Serbs. The Serb and Croatian armies intervened, and the Council imposed economic sanctions on the Federal Republic of Yugoslavia, consisting by then of Serbia and Montenegro.

The war intensified, generating the largest refugee crisis in Europe since the Second World War. Faced with widespread reports of "ethnic cleansing", the Security Council in 1993 created, for the first time, an international court to prosecute war crimes. It also declared certain places as "safe areas", in an attempt to insulate them from the fighting.

UNPROFOR sought to protect the delivery of humanitarian aid in Bosnia and to protect Sarajevo, its capital, as well as other "safe areas". But while peacekeeping commanders requested 35,000 troops, the Security Council authorized only 7,600. To deter continuing attacks against Sarajevo, the North Atlantic Treaty Organization (NATO) in 1994 authorized air strikes at the Secretary-General's request. Bosnian Serb forces detained some 400 UNPROFOR observers, using some as "human shields".

Fighting intensified in 1995. Croatia launched major offensives against its Serb-populated areas. NATO responded to Bosnian Serb shelling of Sarajevo with massive air strikes. Bosnian Serb forces took over the "safe areas" of Srebrenica and Zepa. They killed some 7,000 unarmed men and boys in Srebrenica, in the worst massacre in Europe since the Second World War. In a 1999 report, the Secretary-General acknowledged the errors of the UN and member states in their response to the ethnic cleansing campaign that culminated in Srebrenica. The tragedy, he said, "will haunt our history forever".

At the talks in Dayton, Ohio, in 1995, agreement was reached between Bosnia and Herzegovina, Croatia and Yugoslavia, ending the 42-month war in which 230 UN personnel died. To ensure compliance, the Security Council authorized a multinational, NATO-led, 60,000-strong Implementation Force.

The Security Council established a UN International Police Task Force, which later became part of a larger **United Nations Mission in Bosnia and Herzegovina (UNMIBH)**. The mission facilitated the return of refugees and displaced persons, fostered peace and security, and helped to build up state institutions. Also in 1996, the Council established the **United Nations Mission of Observers in Prevlaka (UNMOP)**, to monitor the demilitarization of the Prevlaka peninsula, a strategic area in Croatia contested by Yugoslavia. UNMIBH and UNMOP completed their work at the end of 2002.

Kosovo. In 1989, the Federal Republic of Yugoslavia revoked local autonomy in Kosovo, a province in southern Yugoslavia historically important to Serbs which was more than 90 per cent ethnically Albanian. Kosovo Albanians dissented, boycotting Serbian state institutions and authority in a quest for self-rule.

Tensions increased as the Kosovo Liberation Army (KLA), which surfaced in 1996 with a call for armed rebellion for independence, launched attacks against Serb officials and Albanians who collaborated with them. Serb authorities responded with mass arrests. Fighting erupted in March 1998 as Serbian police swept the Drenica region, ostensibly looking for KLA members. The Security Council imposed an arms embargo against Yugoslavia, including Kosovo, but the situation deteriorated into open warfare.

Then, in March 1999, following warnings to Yugoslavia, and against the backdrop of a Serbian offensive in Kosovo, NATO began air strikes against Yugoslavia. The Secretary-General said it was tragic that diplomacy had failed. Although there were times when "the use of force may be legitimate in the pursuit of peace", he said, the Security Council should be involved in any such decisions.

Yugoslavia launched a major offensive against the KLA and began mass deportations of ethnic Albanians from Kosovo, causing an unprecedented outflow of 850,000 refugees. UNHCR and other humanitarian agencies rushed to assist them in Albania and the former Yugoslav Republic of Macedonia.

In June, Yugoslavia accepted a peace plan proposed by the Group of Eight (the seven western industrialized nations and Russia). The Security Council endorsed it and authorized member states to establish a security presence to deter hostilities, demilitarize the KLA and facilitate the return of refugees. It asked the Secretary-General to establish an interim international civilian administration, under which the people could enjoy substantial autonomy and self-government. Yugoslav forces withdrew, NATO suspended its bombings, and a 50,000-strong multinational **Kosovo Force (KFOR)** arrived to provide security.

The **United Nations Interim Administration Mission in Kosovo (UNMIK)** immediately established a presence on the ground. Its task was unprecedented in complexity and scope. The Security Council vested UNMIK with authority over the territory and people of Kosovo, including all legislative and executive powers and administration of the judiciary. It had four pillars: civil administration, under the UN itself; humanitarian assistance, led by UNHCR; democratization and institution-building, led by the OSCE; and economic reconstruction and development, managed by the European Union. It was a unique team effort, bringing together four international organizations under the umbrella of the United Nations.

At least 841,000 refugees of the approximately 850,000 who fled during the war returned, and the first priority was to equip them for the rigours of the coming winter. That accomplished, UNMIK made significant progress towards re-establishing normal life and ensuring long-term economic reconstruction. Regulations were issued covering such issues as the appointment and removal of judges, banking, licensing, establishment of a central fiscal authority, and a Kosovo budget. UNMIK also established a dialogue with leaders of ethnic communities, restored utilities and opened schools.

A joint interim administrative structure was established, with representatives of all ethnic groups. Some 3,000 UNMIK police officers were deployed throughout the territory, and a Kosovo Police Service, including minority representatives, was built up. The KLA was completely demilitarized by September 1999 and its members reintegrated in civil society. In the following months, as some 210,000 non-Albanian Kosovars left Kosovo for Serbia and Montenegro, a joint committee facilitated their safe return.

By the end of June 2000, UNHCR was phased out as an UNMIK pillar, though it maintained a very active presence in the region. In May 2001, UNMIK established a new pillar to strengthen its police and justice capabilities — previously addressed under the heading of civil administration. The new "police and justice" pillar was under the direct leadership of the United Nations.

The overwhelming security challenge remained the protection of non-Albanian minorities. Despite significant progress, intimidation, murders and violence against those populations continued. Remaining ethnic minorities lived in isolated enclaves guarded by KFOR. To break the circle of impunity, aggravated by a dysfunctional judiciary system, UNMIK started appointing international judges and prosecutors.

In April 2001, the International Criminal Tribunal for the former Yugoslavia presented its indictment of former Yugoslav President Slobodan Milosevic and four others for crimes against humanity, during a "systematic attack directed against the Kosovo Albanian civilian population of Kosovo". He was transferred to the Tribunal in June. In September, the Security Council lifted its arms embargo against the Federal Republic of Yugoslavia. In November, Kosovo-wide elections were held, electing a 120-member law-making Assembly. In March 2002, the Assembly elected the province's first President and Prime Minister.

Nevertheless, much remained to be done in developing provisional democratic institutions and ensuring conditions for a peaceful and normal life for all inhabitants. On two occasions, the UN Mission chief felt compelled to overrule the Kosovo Assembly — once for overstepping its authority on a border issue; another time for failing to protect minority rights. The Security Council supported those decisions.

As 2003 drew to a close, senior officials launched a set of standards to prepare UN-administered Kosovo for its final status. They included free, fair and regular elections; free media; and a sound and impartial legal system. On 30 December, UNMIK completed the transfer of specific responsibilities to local provisional institutions. It retained certain powers, including control over security, foreign relations, the protection of minority rights, and energy — pending determination of the province's final status.

Disarmament

(http://disarmament.un.org:8080)

Since the birth of the United Nations, the goals of multilateral disarmament and arms limitation have been central to its efforts to maintain international peace and security. The Organization has given highest priority to reducing and eventually eliminating nuclear weapons, destroying chemical weapons and strengthening the prohibition against biological weapons — all of which pose the greatest threat to humankind. While these objectives have remained constant over the years, the scope of deliberations and negotiations is changing as political realities and the international situation evolve.

The international community is now considering more closely the excessive and destabilizing proliferation of small arms and light weapons and has mobilized to combat the massive deployment of landmines — phenomena that threaten the economic and social fabric of societies and kill and maim civilians, too many of whom are women and children. Consideration is also being given to the need for multilaterally negotiated norms against the spread of ballistic missile technology, the explosive remnants of war, and the impact of new information and telecommunications technologies on international security.

The tragic events of 11 September 2001 in the United States underlined the potential danger of weapons of mass destruction falling into the hands of terrorists. The attack could have had even more devastating consequences had the terrorists been able to acquire and use chemical, biological or nuclear weapons. Reflecting these concerns, the General Assembly adopted at its fifty-seventh session in 2002, for the first time, a resolution on measures to prevent terrorists from acquiring weapons of mass destruction and their delivery means and called upon member states to support international efforts to that end.

In addition to its role in the actual disarmament of weapons and in verifying compliance, the United Nations plays an essential role in multilateral disarmament by assisting member states in establishing new norms and in strengthening and consolidating existing agreements. One of the most effective means of deterring the use or threatened use of weapons of mass destruction by terrorists is to strengthen multilateral regimes already developed to ban those weapons and prevent their proliferation.

Disarmament machinery

The United Nations Charter gives the **General Assembly** the chief responsibility for considering "the general principles of cooperation in the maintenance of international peace and security, including the principles governing disarmament and the regulation of armaments" (article 11). The Assembly has two subsidiary bodies dealing with disarmament issues: the First Committee (Disarmament and International Security), which

Multilateral disarmament and arms regulation agreements

A chronology of important international disarmament and arms regulation measures concluded through negotiations in multilateral and regional forums includes:

- 1959 *Antarctic Treaty*: demilitarizes the continent and bans the testing of any kind of weapon on the continent.

- 1963 *Treaty Banning Nuclear Weapon Tests in the Atmosphere, in Outer Space and under Water (Partial Test-Ban Treaty)*: restricts nuclear testing to underground sites only.

- 1967 *Treaty for the Prohibition of Nuclear Weapons in Latin America and the Caribbean (Treaty of Tlatelolco)*: prohibits testing, use, manufacture, storage, or acquisition of nuclear weapons by the countries of the region.

- 1967 *Treaty on Principles Governing the Activities of States in the Exploration and Use of Outer Space, including the Moon and Other Celestial Bodies (Outer Space Treaty)*: mandates that outer space be used for peaceful purposes only and that nuclear weapons not be placed or tested in outer space.

- 1968 *Treaty on the Non-Proliferation of Nuclear Weapons (NPT)*: the non-nuclear-weapon states agree never to acquire nuclear weapons and, in exchange, are promised access to and assistance in the peaceful uses of nuclear energy. Nuclear-weapon states pledge to carry out negotiations relating to cessation of the nuclear arms race and to nuclear disarmament, and not to assist in any way in the transfer of nuclear weapons to non-nuclear-weapon states.

- 1971 *Treaty on the Prohibition of the Emplacement of Nuclear Weapons on the Sea-Bed and the Ocean Floor and in the Subsoil Thereof (Sea-bed Treaty)*: bans the emplacement of nuclear weapons, or any weapon of mass destruction, on the seabed or ocean floor.

- 1972 *Convention on Bacteriological (Biological) Weapons (BWC)*: bans the development, production and stockpiling of biological and toxin agents, and provides for the destruction of such weapons and their means of delivery.

- 1980 *Convention on Certain Conventional Weapons (CCW)*: prohibits certain conventional weapons deemed excessively injurious or having indiscriminate effects. Protocol I bans weapons which explode fragments that are undetectable by X-ray within the human body. Amended Protocol II (1995) limits the use of certain types of mines, booby-traps and other devices. Protocol III bans incendiary weapons. Protocol IV bans the use of blinding laser weapons.

- 1985 *South Pacific Nuclear Free Zone Treaty (Treaty of Rarotonga)*: bans the stationing, acquisition or testing of nuclear explosive devices and the dumping of nuclear waste within the zone.

- 1990 *Treaty on Conventional Armed Forces in Europe (CFE Treaty)*: limits the numbers of various conventional armaments in a zone stretching from the Atlantic Ocean to the Urals.

- 1993 *Chemical Weapons Convention (CWC)*: prohibits the development, production, stockpiling and use of chemical weapons and requires their destruction.

- 1995 *Southeast Asia Nuclear-Weapon-Free Zone Treaty (Treaty of Bangkok)*: bans the development or stationing of nuclear weapons on the territories of the states party to the treaty.

- 1996 *African Nuclear-Weapon-Free Zone Treaty (Treaty of Pelindaba)*: bans the development or stationing of nuclear weapons on the African continent.

- 1996 *Comprehensive Nuclear-Test-Ban Treaty (CTBT)*: places a worldwide ban on nuclear test explosions of any kind and in any environment.

- 1997 *Mine Ban Convention*: prohibits the use, stockpiling, production and transfer of anti-personnel mines and provides their destruction.

(For status of ratification of these agreements, see *http://disarmament.un.org:8080/TreatyStatus.nsf*)

124

meets during the Assembly's regular session and deals with all disarmament issues on its agenda; and the Disarmament Commission, a specialized deliberative body that focuses on specific issues and meets for three weeks every year.

The **Conference on Disarmament** is the international community's sole multilateral negotiating forum for disarmament agreements. The Conference successfully negotiated both the Chemical Weapons Convention and the Comprehensive Nuclear-Test-Ban Treaty. Since it addresses matters that touch upon the national security interests of states, it works strictly on the basis of consensus. It has a limited membership of 66 states and a unique relationship with the General Assembly. While the Conference defines its own rules and develops its own agenda, it takes into account the recommendations of the General Assembly and reports to it annually. Since 1997, the Conference has been unable to agree on a substantive programme of work due to lack of consensus among its members on disarmament priorities.

In the UN Secretariat, the **Department for Disarmament Affairs** implements the decisions of the Assembly on disarmament matters. The **United Nations Institute for Disarmament Research (UNIDIR)** undertakes independent research on disarmament and related problems, particularly international security issues. The **Advisory Board on Disarmament Matters** advises the Secretary-General on matters relating to arms limitation and disarmament, and serves as the Board of Trustees of UNIDIR. It also advises on the implementation of the recommendations of the **United Nations Disarmament Information Programme**.

Weapons of mass destruction (WMD)

Nuclear weapons

Through sustained efforts, the world community has achieved numerous multilateral agreements aimed at reducing nuclear arsenals, excluding their deployment from certain regions and environments (such as outer space and the ocean floor), limiting their proliferation and ending testing. Despite these achievements, nuclear weapons and their proliferation remain a major threat to peace and a major challenge to the international community.

Issues of concern in this area include in particular the need for reductions in nuclear weapons, upholding the viability of the nuclear non-proliferation regime, and preventing the development and proliferation of ballistic missiles and missile defence systems.

Bilateral agreements on nuclear weapons. While international efforts to contain nuclear weapons continue in different forums, it has been generally understood that the nuclear-weapon powers hold special responsibility for maintaining a stable international security environment. During and after the cold war, the two major powers arrived at agreements that have significantly reduced the threat of nuclear war.

Multilateral agreements on nuclear weapons and non-proliferation. The *Treaty on the Non-Proliferation of Nuclear Weapons (NPT)*, the most universal of all multi-

Bilateral agreements

The 1972 *Treaty on the Limitation of Anti-Ballistic Missile Systems (ABM Treaty)* limited the number of anti-ballistic missile systems of the United States and the Soviet Union to one each. A 1997 "demarcation" agreement between the United States and the Russian Federation distinguished between "strategic", or long-range ABMs, which were prohibited, and "non-strategic", or shorter-range ABMs, which were not. The Treaty ceased to be in effect as of 13 June 2002, when the United States withdrew from it.

The 1987 *United States-Soviet Union Intermediate- and Shorter-Range Nuclear Forces Treaty (INF Treaty)* eliminated an entire class of nuclear weapons, which includes all land-based ballistic and cruise missiles with a range of 500 to 5,500 km. By the end of 1996, all the weapons slated for destruction under the provisions of the Treaty had been eliminated.

The 1991 *United States–Soviet Union Strategic Arms Limitation and Reduction Treaty (START I)* placed a ceiling of 6,000 warheads on 1,600 deployed long-range nuclear missiles for each side by 2001, thereby reducing the 1991 stockpile levels by about 30 per cent.

The 1992 *Lisbon Protocol to START I* committed the Russian Federation, Belarus, Kazakhstan and Ukraine, as successor states to the Soviet Union, to abide by the START I Treaty; Belarus, Kazakhstan and Ukraine were to adhere to the NPT as non-nuclear-weapon states. By 1996, these three states had removed all nuclear weapons from their territories.

The 1993 *Strategic Arms Limitation and Reduction Treaty II (START II)* committed both parties to reduce the number of warheads on long-range nuclear missiles to 3,500 on each side by 2003, and eliminated ICBMs (intercontinental ballistic missiles) equipped with MIRVs (multiple independently targetable re-entry vehicles). A 1997 agreement extended the deadline for destruction of the launching systems — missile silos, bombers and submarines — to the end of 2007.

On 24 May 2002, the Presidents of the Russian Federation and the United States signed the *Strategic Offensive Reductions Treaty (SORT)*, also known as the Moscow Treaty, agreeing to limit the level of their deployed strategic nuclear warheads to between 1,700 and 2,200. The Treaty will remain in force until December 2012, and may be extended or superseded by agreement of the parties.

lateral disarmament treaties, was first opened for signature in 1968 and came into force in 1970. The NPT is the cornerstone of the global nuclear non-proliferation regime and the essential foundation for the pursuit of nuclear disarmament. The 2000 Review Conference of the Parties to the NPT adopted a final document in which the nuclear-weapon states made "an unequivocal undertaking ... to accomplish the total elimination of their nuclear arsenals".

The Conference agreed that there should be increased transparency about nuclear-weapon capabilities, and a diminishing role for nuclear weapons in security policies. Preparations are now under way for the next NPT review conference, scheduled for 2005. The decision by the Democratic People's Republic of Korea to withdraw from the Treaty in January 2003, the first such decision since the Treaty's entry into force 33 years ago, is of great concern to the international community.

To verify obligations assumed under the NPT, states parties are required to accept the nuclear safeguards of the International Atomic Energy Agency (IAEA). In 2003, there were 225 safeguards agreements with 140 states (and with Taiwan, Province of China), including 136 comprehensive safeguards agreements pursuant to the NPT. In addition to the NPT, the treaties of Tlatelolco, Rarotonga, Bangkok and Pelindaba require non-nuclear-weapon states to apply IAEA safeguards.

In 1996, an overwhelming majority of General Assembly members adopted the *Comprehensive Nuclear-Test-Ban Treaty (CTBT)*, to ban any nuclear-test explosions anywhere. Originally proposed in 1954, it had taken four decades to adopt the Treaty, which extended the 1963 partial test ban to all environments. Opened for signature in 1996, the CTBT has not yet entered into force. Of 44 states listed in its Annex II whose ratification is required before the Treaty can enter into force, 12 have not yet signed or ratified the instrument. The United Nations Secretary-General, in his capacity as the Depositary of the Treaty, has convened three Conferences on Facilitating the Entry into Force of the CTBT — in 1999, 2001 and 2003, respectively.

With nearly 170 signatory states participating in the Vienna-based Preparatory Commission for the Comprehensive Nuclear-Test-Ban-Treaty Organization (CTBTO PrepCom), preparations are under way in the Provisional Technical Secretariat, established in 1997, to ensure that an international monitoring system is operational by the time the Treaty enters into force. The Agreement to Regulate the Relationship between the United Nations and the Preparatory Commission for the Comprehensive Nuclear-Test-Ban Treaty Organization was signed in 2000.

In September 2003, the Conference on Facilitating the Entry into Force of the CTBT was held in Vienna and adopted a declaration that stressed the importance of a universal and effectively verifiable Treaty as a major instrument in all aspects of nuclear disarmament and non-proliferation.

Nuclear-weapon-free zones. In a development that was to herald a new movement in regional arms control, the signing of the 1967 *Treaty for the Prohibition of Nuclear Weapons in Latin America and the Caribbean (Treaty of Tlatelolco)* established for the first time a nuclear-weapon-free zone in a populated area of the world. With the deposit of Cuba's instrument of ratification in 2002, the nuclear-weapon-free zone in Latin America and the Caribbean was consolidated to include all states in the region.

Since then, three other zones have been established — in the South Pacific (*Treaty of Rarotonga*, 1985), South-East Asia (*Treaty of Bangkok*, 1995) and Africa

(*Treaty of Pelindaba*, 1996). By virtue of such treaties, the entire southern hemisphere has nuclear-weapon-free status. In September 2002, the five Central Asian states (Kazakhstan, Kyrgyzstan, Tajikistan, Turkmenistan and Uzbekistan) provisionally agreed on a draft text of a treaty to establish a Central Asian nuclear-weapon-free zone. Proposals have also been made for establishing nuclear-weapon-free zones in Central Europe and South Asia, as well as for a zone free of weapons of mass destruction in the Middle East. The concept of an individual country as a nuclear-weapon-free zone was acknowledged by the international community in 1998, when the General Assembly supported Mongolia's self-declaration of its nuclear-weapon-free status.

Preventing nuclear proliferation. The International Atomic Energy Agency (IAEA) plays a prominent role in international efforts to prevent the proliferation of nuclear weapons — serving as the world's inspectorate for the application of nuclear safeguards and verification measures covering civilian nuclear programmes.

Under agreements concluded with states, IAEA inspectors regularly visit nuclear facilities to verify records on the whereabouts of nuclear material, check IAEA-installed instruments and surveillance equipment and confirm inventories of nuclear material. Taken together, these and other safeguards measures provide independent, international verification that governments are abiding by their commitment to peaceful uses of nuclear energy.

To verify the implementation of the 229 safeguards agreements currently in force in 145 states (and in Taiwan, China), 250 IAEA experts conduct daily on-site inspections in every part of the world, for a total of some 2,400 safeguards inspections a year. Their aim is to ensure that the nuclear material held in 900 nuclear installations in some 70 countries is not diverted away from legitimate peaceful uses to military purposes. IAEA thus contributes to international security, and reinforces efforts to halt the spread of arms and move towards a world free of nuclear weapons.

Various types of safeguards agreements can be concluded with IAEA. Those in connection with the NPT, the *Model Protocol Additional to Existing Safeguards Agreements*, as well as those relating to the *Treaty of Tlatelolco*, the *Treaty of Pelindaba* and the *Treaty of Rarotonga* require non-nuclear-weapon states to submit their entire nuclear-fuel-cycle activities to IAEA safeguards. Other agreements cover safeguards at single facilities. IAEA safeguards under the NPT are an integral part of the international regime for non-proliferation and play an indispensable role in ensuring the implementation of the Treaty.

Removing the threat of chemical and biological weapons

The entry into force of the *Chemical Weapons Convention (CWC)* in 1997 completed a process that started in 1925, when the Geneva Protocol prohibited the use of poison gas weapons. The Convention created, for the first time in the history of international arms control, a stringent international verification regime (involving collection of information on chemical facilities and routine global inspections) to oversee compliance with treaty obligations by states parties to the Convention. Established for that purpose at The Hague in the Netherlands, the **Organisation for the Prohibition of Chemical Weapons (OPCW)** had conducted, by August 2003, almost 1,500 inspections in 56 states parties. Through its inspections, 32 of the 61 declared chemical weapons production facilities have been certified as destroyed or converted. The First Special Session of the Conference of the States Parties to Review the Operation of the Chemical Weapons Convention was held in 2003. The Agreement Concerning the Relationship between the United Nations and the OPCW was signed in 2000.

Unlike the CWC, the 1972 *Biological Weapons Convention (BWC)*, which entered into force in 1975, does not provide for a verification mechanism. However, states parties exchange, as a confidence-building measure, detailed information each year on such items as their high-risk biological research facilities. The Fifth Review Conference of the States Parties to the Biological Weapons Convention concluded its resumed session in 2002, agreeing to hold annual meetings of states parties and experts meetings in the three years leading up to the next review conference in 2006.

The objective of these meetings is to discuss and promote common understanding and effective action on issues relating to national measures to implement the BWC, international response to and investigation of the alleged use of biological weapons, improved surveillance of infectious diseases, and codes of conduct for scientists. Universalizing and fully implementing the BWC, as well as the CWC, and preventing the proliferation of biological and chemical weapons, represent a major task for the international community.

Developments in the field of **ballistic missile proliferation and missile defences** continued to be a source of concern for many member states. In 2002, a panel of governmental experts constituted by the Secretary-General tackled this issue for the first time at the international level. It concluded that the subject needed further exploration of all the approaches undertaken at the national, bilateral, regional, plurilateral and multilateral levels.

Conventional weapons, confidence-building and transparency

Small arms, light weapons and practical disarmament. Following the end of the cold war, the international community was confronted with the eruption of intra-state conflicts in many parts of the world, in which small arms and light weapons were the weapons of choice. Though not the root cause of conflict, these weapons exacerbate violence, facilitate the use of child combatants, hinder humanitarian assistance and delay post-conflict reconstruction and development. An estimated 40 to 60 per cent of the world's trade in small arms is or becomes illicit. Controlling the proliferation of illicit weapons is thus a necessary step towards better international, regional or national control over all aspects of the issue of small arms.

Member states initiated action to stem the excessive accumulation and uncontrolled transfer of these weapons by sponsoring two expert studies in 1997 and 1999 that began to focus attention on the topic. As a result of those studies, for the first time, an international Conference on the Illicit Trade in Small Arms and Light Weapons in All Its Aspects was held in 2001 at the United Nations. The UN Conference produced a programme of action with recommendations for action at the national, regional and global levels. A follow-on meeting of member states to assess how the programme was being implemented concluded in 2003 that the programme of action was starting to take effect. One result is that negotiations will begin in 2004 on an international instrument to enable states to identify and trace, in a timely and reliable manner, illicit small arms and light weapons.

The General Assembly in 1996 invited interested states to establish a group to assist states facing problems in post-conflict situations. The group was subsequently set up to examine and support practical disarmament projects, particularly as designed and initiated by affected countries. At its recommendation, the Secretary-General in 1998 created a trust fund which has supported projects such as one in Albania, where the civilian population was encouraged to voluntarily surrender weapons in exchange for community development incentives.

Since the uncontrolled spread of illicit small arms impacts many aspects of the United Nations work — from children to health to refugees to development — a mechanism called "Coordinating Action on Small Arms" was put in place in 1998 to guarantee that the UN system addressed the many sides of small arms control in a coordinated manner. A comprehensive global effort to address the small arms scourge has also been launched and sustained by civil society, thorough research, the promotion of coordinated national action, and global lobbying for an international convention on the arms trade.

Anti-personnel mines. The growing proliferation and indiscriminate use of anti-personnel landmines around the world has been a particular focus of attention. In 1995, a review of the *Convention on Certain Conventional Weapons (CCW)* — also known as the *Inhumane Weapons Convention* —produced Amended Protocol II, which entered into force on 3 December 1998, strengthening restrictions on certain uses, transfers and types (self-destroying and detectable) of landmines. Currently 69 states are bound by this protocol.

Not satisfied with what they considered an inadequate response to a serious humanitarian crisis, a group of like-minded states negotiated an agreement on a total ban on all anti-personnel landmines — the *Convention on the Prohibition of the Use, Stockpiling, Production and Transfer of Anti-personnel Mines and on Their Destruction (Mine-Ban Convention)*, which was opened for signature in 1997 and entered into force on 1 March 1999. As of December 2003, 134 states have become parties to it.

The successful implementation of both instruments led to the destruction of stockpiles, mine clearance in affected countries, and fewer new victims. Some 93 countries are now officially mine free, and 41 out of 55 producing countries have stopped the production of these weapons. Countries not party to either instrument have declared unilateral moratoriums on the use and transfer of landmines.

Explosive Remnants of War and Mines Other than Anti-Personnel Landmines (MOTAPM). While significant steps have been taken to address anti-personnel landmines, many civilians are killed or injured by other explosive munitions. They pose a potential hazard to populations through inadvertent contact or deliberate tampering, especially if the danger is not well understood. MOTAPM can cause severe damage even in small numbers; when placed in strategic locations, a single mine can cause entire roads to be closed and can disrupt normal activities. Combined with other possible characteristics of MOTAPM, such as anti-handling devices and minimum metal content, their humanitarian impact can be quite serious.

A group of governmental experts of the states parties to the Convention on Certain Conventional Weapons is currently negotiating an instrument on post-conflict remedial measures to reduce the risks caused by explosive remnants of war, and exploring the issue of MOTAPM, in order to consider the most appropriate way to reduce the risks posed by their irresponsible use.

Register of Conventional Arms. In order to contribute to confidence building and security among states, the General Assembly established the *United Nations Register of Conventional Arms* in 1992. This voluntary reporting arrangement enables participating governments to provide information on the export and import of seven categories of major conventional weapons systems: warships, including submarines; battle tanks; armoured combat vehicles; combat aircraft; attack helicopters; large-calibre artillery; and missiles and missile-launchers, including short-range man-portable air-defence systems. Such data are compiled and published annually by the UN as official documents available to the general public, as well as through the United Nations website. Thus far, more than 160 states have reported to the Register one or more times.

Another global mechanism designed to promote transparency in military matters is the *United Nations system for the standardized reporting of military expenditures*, introduced in 1980. This voluntary reporting instrument covers national expenditures on military personnel, operations and maintenance, procurement and construction, and research and development. So far, more than 110 states have reported to this instrument at least once.

Prevention of an arms race in outer space. Matters related to outer space have been pursued in international forums along two separate lines: those related to peaceful applications of space technology and those related to the prevention of an arms race in that environment. These issues have been discussed in the General Assembly, the Committee on the Peaceful Uses of Outer Space and its subsidiary bodies, and the Conference on Disarmament. These discussions have contributed to the conclusion of a number of international agreements concerning both peaceful and military aspects of the use of outer space.

Reflecting the importance of preventing the militarization of outer space, the General Assembly's first special session on disarmament (1978) called for international negotiations on the issue. Since 1982, the Conference on Disarmament has had on its agenda an item entitled "Prevention of an arms race in outer space", but little progress has been made to date in negotiating a multilateral agreement, owing to continuing differences in perception among its members.

Relationship between disarmament and development. The question of promoting economic and social progress, especially for less developed nations, by using the resources released through general disarmament under a system of effective international control has long been debated among member states. Eventually, an international conference on the relationship between disarmament and development was held in 1987. In view of the changes in the international situation since then, a group of governmental experts is meeting in 2003-2004 to conduct a reappraisal of this relationship.

Regional approaches to disarmament. The United Nations supports initiatives towards disarmament undertaken at the regional and subregional levels, promoting security and confidence-building measures among states within a region. It also assists them in implementing the guidelines and recommendations for regional approaches to disarmament adopted by the Disarmament Commission in 1993. To foster regional disarmament, the UN works with governmental organizations and arrangements — such as the African Union, the European Union, the Euro-Atlantic Partnership Council, the League of Arab States, the Organization of American States, the Organization of the Islamic Conference, the Organization for Security and Cooperation in Europe, and the Stability Pact for South Eastern Europe — as well as with international, regional and local non-governmental organizations.

Disarmament information and education activities. In 2002, the General Assembly adopted a report by a group of experts on disarmament and non-proliferation education, reaffirming that disarmament education was an integral part of peace education and an important aspect of every citizen's training for participation in civil life. In 2003 and 2004, the United Nations, in partnership with the Hague Appeal for Peace, is conducting a peace and small arms education project aimed at children and youth in four countries (Albania, Cambodia, Niger and Peru). Administrators, teachers and students there will tackle the issue of illicit guns and the threat they pose, in order to improve academic skills, increase interest and attention at school, and reduce crime and violence.

The United Nations undertakes information and education activities on multilateral disarmament issues in the framework of its *Disarmament Information Programme* — through publications, special events, meetings, seminars, panel discussions, exhibits and a comprehensive website on disarmament issues (*disarmament.un.org*). The *United Nations Disarmament Fellowship Programme*, launched by the General Assembly in 1978, has trained over 500 public officials from about 150 countries — many of whom are now in positions of responsibility in the field of disarmament within their own governments.

Gender mainstreaming in disarmament. The face of warfare has changed in recent years as women and girls have increasingly been affected by conflicts, both as victims and perpetrators. The UN promotes understanding of the importance of gender perspectives in all aspects of disarmament — whether collecting and destroying weapons, de-mining, conducting fact-finding missions, or participating in decision-making and peace processes. For instance, a gender perspective would consider how the spread of small arms affects women in particular and what might be done about it.

Peaceful uses of outer space

The United Nations works to ensure that outer space is used for peaceful purposes and that the benefits from space activities are shared by all nations. This concern with the peaceful uses of outer space began soon after the launch of Sputnik — the first man-made satellite — by the Soviet Union in 1957, and has kept pace with advances in space technology. The United Nations has played an important role, by developing international space law and by promoting international cooperation in space science and technology.

The main intergovernmental body in this field is the **United Nations Committee on the Peaceful Uses of Outer Space**. It reviews the scope of international cooperation in peaceful uses of outer space, devises programmes and directs United Nations technical cooperation, encourages research and dissemination of information, and contributes to the development of international space law. Set up by the General Assembly in 1959, it is made up of 65 member states.

The Committee has two subcommittees:

- The **Scientific and Technical Subcommittee** is the focal point of international cooperation in space technology and research.

- The **Legal Subcommittee** works to ensure the development of a legal framework concomitant with the rapid technological development of space activities.

The Committee and its subcommittees meet annually to consider questions put before them by the General Assembly, reports submitted to them and issues raised by member states. Working on the basis of consensus, the Committee makes recommendations to the General Assembly.

Legal instruments

The work of the Committee and its Legal Subcommittee has resulted in the adoption by the General Assembly of five legal instruments, all of which are in force:

- The 1966 *Treaty on Principles Governing the Activities of States in the Exploration and Use of Outer Space, including the Moon and Other Celestial Bodies (Outer Space Treaty)* provides that space exploration shall be carried out for the benefit of all countries, irrespective of their degree of development. It seeks to maintain outer space as the province of all humankind, free for exploration and use by all states, solely for peaceful purposes, and not subject to national appropriation.

- The 1967 *Agreement on the Rescue of Astronauts, the Return of Astronauts and the Return of Objects Launched into Outer Space (Rescue Agreement)* provides for aiding the crews of spacecraft in case of accident or emergency landing, and establishes procedures for returning to the launching authority a space object found beyond the territory of that authority.

- The 1971 *Convention on International Liability for Damage Caused by Space Objects (Liability Convention)* provides that the launching state is liable for damage caused by its space objects on the earth's surface, to aircraft in flight, and to space objects of another state or persons or property on board such objects.

- The 1974 *Convention on Registration of Objects Launched into Outer Space (Registration Convention)* provides that launching states maintain registries of space objects and provide information on objects launched to the United Nations. Under this Convention, the Office for Outer Space Affairs maintains a United Nations Registry on objects launched into outer space. Information has been provided by all launching states and organizations. A searchable online index of objects launched into outer space is maintained by the Office for Outer Space Affairs on its website (*www.oosa.unvienna.org*).

- The 1979 *Agreement Governing Activities of States on the Moon and Other Celestial Bodies (Moon Agreement)* elaborates the principles relating to the moon and other celestial bodies set out in the 1966 Treaty, and sets up the basis to regulate the future exploration and exploitation of natural resources on those bodies.

On the basis of the work of the Committee and its Legal Subcommittee, the General Assembly has adopted sets of principles, including the following, on the conduct of space activities:

- The *Principles governing the use by states of artificial earth satellites for international direct television broadcasting* (1982) recognize that such use has international political, economic, social and cultural implications. Such activities should promote the dissemination and exchange of information and knowledge, foster development, and respect the sovereign rights of states, including the principle of non-intervention.

- The *Principles relating to remote sensing of the earth from outer space* (1986) state that such activities are to be conducted for the benefit of all countries, respecting the sovereignty of all states and peoples over their natural resources, and for the rights and interests of other states. Remote sensing is to be used to preserve the environment and to reduce the impact of natural disasters.

- The *Principles on the use of nuclear power sources in outer space* (1992) recognize that such sources are essential for some space missions, but that their use should be based on a thorough safety assessment. The Principles provide guidelines for the safe use of nuclear power sources and for notification of a malfunction of a space object where there is a risk of re-entry of radioactive material to the earth.

- The *Declaration on international cooperation in the exploration and use of outer space for the benefit and in the interest of all states, particularly developing countries* (1996) provides that states are free to determine all aspects of their participation in international space cooperation on an equitable and mutually acceptable basis, and that such cooperation should be conducted in ways that are considered most effective and appropriate by the countries concerned.

Office for Outer Space Affairs
(*www.oosa.unvienna.org*)

The Vienna-based **United Nations Office for Outer Space Affairs** serves as the secretariat for the Committee on the Peaceful Uses of Outer Space, and assists developing countries in using space technology for development.

The Office disseminates space-related information to member states through its International Space Information System. Through its *United Nations Programme on Space Applications*, the Office provides technical advisory services to member states in conducting pilot projects, and undertakes training and fellowship programmes in such areas as remote sensing, satellite communication, satellite meteorology, satellite navigation, basic space science and space law. The Office is also a cooperating body to the International Charter, "Space and Major Disasters" — a mechanism through which UN agencies can request satellite imagery to support their response to disasters.

The Office provides technical assistance to the regional centres for space science and technology education and to the network of space science and technology education and research institutions for central-eastern and south-eastern Europe affiliated with the United Nations. These bodies help to develop the skills and knowledge of scientists and researchers in aspects of space science and technology that can contribute to sustainable development. The centre in Asia and the Pacific became operational in India in 1996; the centres in Morocco and Nigeria in 1999. In 2003, the Latin America and Caribbean centres in Mexico and Brazil became operational. The Office is providing technical support to the government of Jordan in its preparations for the establishment of a west Asia centre.

The Office works in close cooperation with international organizations such as the European Space Agency (ESA), the International Astronautical Federation (IAF), the Committee on Earth Observation Satellites (CEOS), and the Committee on Space Research (COSPAR).

In addition, other United Nations organizations are active in areas such as space communication, satellite meteorology, space science and remote sensing. To coordinate the space-related activities of the United Nations system, an inter-agency meeting on outer space activities convenes annually.

Latest developments

In a publication of this kind, it is impossible to remain entirely up to date with the rapid changes taking place in the political and security sphere — including, for example, the developing situation in and around the Darfur region of the Sudan. For the latest developments in this and all areas of UN involvement, please consult the UN website (*www.un.org*) and, in particular, the UN News website (*www.un.org/News*).

Chapter 3
Economic and
Social Development

ECONOMIC AND SOCIAL DEVELOPMENT

Although most people associate the United Nations with the issues of peace and security, the vast majority of the Organization's resources are in fact devoted to advancing the Charter's pledge to "promote higher standards of living, full employment and conditions of economic and social progress and development". United Nations development efforts have profoundly affected the lives and well-being of millions of people throughout the world. Guiding the United Nations endeavours is the conviction that lasting international peace and security are possible only if the economic and social well-being of people everywhere is assured.

Many of the economic and social transformations that have taken place globally in the last five decades have been significantly affected in their direction and shape by the work of the United Nations. As the global centre for consensus-building, the United Nations has set priorities and goals for international cooperation to assist countries in their development efforts and to foster a supportive global economic environment.

This consensus has been expressed through a series of *International Development Decades*, the first beginning in 1961. These broad statements of policy and goals, while emphasizing certain issues of particular concern in each decade, have consistently stressed the need for progress on all aspects of development, social as well as economic, and the importance of narrowing the disparities between industrialized and developing countries.

Since the 1990s, the United Nations has provided a platform for formulating and promoting key new developmental objectives on the international agenda, through a series of global conferences. It has articulated the need for incorporating issues such as the advancement of women, human rights, sustainable development, environmental protection and good governance into the development paradigm. The focus now is on implementing the commitments made at these conferences in an integrated and coordinated manner.

At their Millennium Summit in 2000, member states adopted a set of wide-ranging Millennium Development Goals, supported by a series of specific, attainable targets. Together, the goals and targets aim at: eradicating extreme poverty and hunger; achieving universal primary education; promoting gender equality and the empowerment of women; reducing child mortality; improving maternal health; combatting HIV/AIDS, malaria and other diseases; ensuring environmental sustainability; and developing a global partnership for development.

International debate on economic and social issues has increasingly reflected the commonality of interests between rich and poor countries in solving the many problems that transcend national boundaries. Issues such as refugee populations, organized crime, drug trafficking and AIDS are seen as global problems requiring coordinated action. The impact of persistent poverty and unemployment in one region can

Making globalization work for all

In their Millennium Declaration, in September 2000, world leaders stressed that ensuring globalization becomes a positive force for all represents the central challenge before the international community. People must feel included if globalization is to succeed, Secretary-General Kofi Annan said in his report to the Millennium Summit.*

The benefits of globalization — including faster growth, higher living standards, and new opportunities for countries and individuals — are obvious, he said:. Yet a backlash has begun, because these benefits are so unequally distributed, and because the global market is not yet underpinned by rules based on shared social objectives.

Global companies should be guided by the concept of global "corporate citizenship", and apply good practices wherever they operate — promoting equitable labour standards, respect for human rights and protection of the environment.

For its part, the United Nations must "ensure that globalization provides benefits not just for some, but for all; that opportunity exists not merely for the privileged, but for every human being everywhere". The Organization must "broker differences among states" and forge "coalitions for change" by opening up further to the participation of the many actors involved in globalization — civil society, the private sector, parliamentarians, local authorities, scientific associations and educational institutions.

Above all, "we must put people at the centre of everything we do", Mr. Annan said. "Only when that begins to happen will we know that globalization is indeed becoming inclusive, allowing everyone to share its opportunities."

---

* We the Peoples: the role of the United Nations in the 21st century. United Nations, 2000, ISBN 92-1-100844-1, E.00.1.16. Also available at www.un.org/millennium/sg/report.

be quickly felt in others, not least through migration, social disruption and conflict. Similarly, in the age of a global economy, financial instability in one country is immediately felt in the markets of others.

There is also growing consensus on the role played by democracy, human rights, popular participation, good governance and the empowerment of women in fostering economic and social development.

Coordinating development activities

Despite advances on many fronts, gross disparities in wealth and well-being continue to characterize the world. Reducing poverty and redressing inequalities, both within and between countries, remain fundamental goals of the United Nations.

The United Nations system works in a variety of ways to promote its economic and social goals — by formulating policies, advising governments on their development plans, setting international norms and standards, and mobilizing funds for development programmes totalling over $30 billion annually. It is through the work of its various funds and programmes and its family of specialized agencies, in areas as diverse as education, air safety, environmental protection and labour conditions, that the work of the Organization touches the lives of people everywhere.

The **Economic and Social Council (ECOSOC)** is the principal body coordinating the economic and social work of the United Nations and its operational arms. It is also the central forum for discussing international economic and social issues and for formulating policy recommendations.

Under ECOSOC, the **Committee for Development Policy,** made up of 24 experts working in their personal capacity, acts as an advisory body on emerging economic, social and environmental issues. It also sets the criteria for the designation of "least developed countries" (LDCs).

The **United Nations Development Group**, comprised of Secretariat bodies as well as the development funds and programmes, assists in the management and coordination of development work within the Organization. This executive body works to enhance cooperation between policy-making entities and the distinct operational programmes. The Executive Committee on Economic and Social Affairs, comprised of Secretariat bodies and including the regional commissions, is also an instrument for policy development and management.

Within the United Nations Secretariat, the **Department of Economic and Social Affairs (DESA)** gathers and analyses economic and social data; carries out policy analysis and coordination, and provides substantive and technical support to member states in the social and economic sphere. Its substantive support to intergovernmental processes facilitates member states' role in setting norms and standards and in agreeing on common courses of action in response to global challenges. DESA provides a crucial interface between global policies and national action, and among research, policy and operational activities.

The five **regional commissions** facilitate similar exchanges of economic and social information and policy analysis in the regions of Africa, Asia and the Pacific, Europe, Latin America and the Caribbean, and Western Asia.

The various **United Nations funds and programmes** deal with operational activities for development in programme countries, while the **United Nations specialized agencies** provide support and assistance for countries' development efforts. At a time of increasingly limited resources, both human and financial, enhanced coordination and cooperation among the various arms of the system are vital if development goals are to be realized.

Economic development

The world has witnessed enormous economic development in recent decades, but the generation of wealth and prosperity has been very uneven — so uneven that economic imbalances are seen to exacerbate social problems and political instability in virtually every region of the world. The end of the cold war and the accelerating integration of the global economy have not solved persistent problems of extreme poverty, indebtedness, underdevelopment and trade imbalance.

One of the founding principles of the United Nations is the conviction that economic development for all peoples is the surest way to achieve political, economic and social security. It is a central preoccupation of the Organization that nearly half of the world's population — mostly in Africa, Asia, and Latin America and the Caribbean — still must make do on less than $2 per day. Some 860 million people are illiterate, over 100 million children have no access to school, over 1 billion lack access to safe water, and some 2.4 billion people — more than a third of the world's population — lack access to proper sanitation. At the end of 2002, some 180 million workers were unemployed worldwide, while the "working poor" — those who earn less than $1 a day — had risen to 550 million.

The United Nations continues to be the sole institution dedicated to finding ways to ensure that economic expansion and globalization are guided by policies aimed at ensuring human welfare, sustainable development, the eradication of poverty, fair trade and the reduction of crippling foreign debt.

The United Nations urges the adoption of macroeconomic policies that address current imbalances — particularly the growing gap between the North and South —

as well as the persistent problems of the least developed countries, and the unprecedented needs of countries in transition from centralized to market economies. All over the world, United Nations programmes of assistance promote poverty reduction, child survival, environmental protection, women's progress and human rights. For millions in poor countries, these programmes are the United Nations.

Official development assistance

Through their policies and loans, the lending institutions of the United Nations system have, collectively, an enormous influence on the economies of developing countries. This is especially true for the least developed countries (LDCs), which include 49 nations whose extreme poverty and indebtedness have marginalized them from global growth and development. These nations, most of which are in Africa, are given priority attention in several United Nations assistance programmes.

Small island developing states, landlocked developing countries and countries with economies in transition also suffer from critical problems requiring special attention from the international community. These, too, are given priority in the assistance programmes of the United Nations system, as well as through official development assistance (ODA) from member states.

In 1970, the General Assembly set an ODA target of 0.7 per cent of gross national income (GNI). For years, the collective effort of members of the Development Assistance Committee (DAC) of the Organization for Economic Cooperation and Development (OECD) — now comprising 22 industrialized countries and the European Commission — hovered at around half that level.

During the 1990s, ODA fell sharply, bringing it to an all-time low. Within the reduced total, however, more assistance went to basic social services — up from 4 per cent of ODA in 1995, to 14 per cent by the year 2000 (nearly $4 billion). And more than four-fifths of aid was no longer tied to the procurement of goods and services in the donor country.

ODA levels began to recover during the new century. Among DAC members, total ODA had risen to some 0.25% of combined GNI by 2003. At some $68.5 billion, this was its highest level ever, both in nominal and real terms.

To date, only five countries — Denmark, Luxembourg, Netherlands, Norway and Sweden — have met and maintained the 0.7 per cent target for ODA. They have also attained the benchmark figure of 0.15 per cent of their gross national product, set in 1981 at the first United Nations Conference on the Least Developed Countries.

The International Conference on Financing for Development, held at Monterrey, Mexico in 2002, stimulated commitments from major donors to increase ODA as a first step towards reversing its decline in the 1990s. It also sought to shift

International Conference on Financing for Development
(www.un.org/esa/ffd)

The *International Conference on Financing for Development* was held from 18 to 22 March 2002 in Monterrey, Mexico. This UN-hosted Conference on key financial and development issues attracted 50 heads of state or government and over 200 ministers, as well as leaders from the private sector, civil society and all the major intergovernmental financial, trade, economic and monetary organizations.

The Monterrey Conference also marked the first quadripartite exchange of views between governments, civil society, the business community and the institutional stakeholders on global economic issues. These global discussions involved over 800 participants in 12 separate roundtables — co-chaired by heads of governments, the heads of the World Bank, International Monetary Fund, the World Trade Organization and the regional development banks, as well as ministers of finance, trade and foreign affairs. The outcome of the Conference, known as the Monterrey Consensus, provides a picture of the new global approach to financing development.

Subsequently, the General Assembly decided to reconstitute its high-level dialogue on strengthening international cooperation for development as the intergovernmental focal point for follow-up on the Conference and related issues — to be held during odd-numbered years beginning in 2003. It includes a policy dialogue, with the participation of the relevant stakeholders, on implementation of the results of the Conference, as well as on the coherence and consistency of the international monetary, financial and trading systems in support of development.

The Assembly also decided that interactions between representatives of the Economic and Social Council, the directors of the executive boards of the World Bank and the International Monetary Fund, and representatives of the appropriate intergovernmental body of the World Trade Organization would continue each spring. The April 2002 consultation was expanded to include roundtables with representatives from civil society and the business community.

The Fourth World Trade Organization (WTO) Ministerial Conference, held at Doha, Qatar, in 2001, also addressed the means of implementing sustainable development. The Fifth WTO Ministerial Conference, held at Cancun, Mexico, in September 2003, built on the Doha Declaration.

the focus of such assistance more towards poverty reduction, education and health (*see box*).

United Nations ODA is derived from two sources: grant assistance from United Nations specialized agencies, funds and programmes; and support from lending institutions of the United Nations system, such as the World Bank and the International Fund for Agricultural Development (IFAD).

The World Bank provided $18.5 billion in 2003, working in more than 100 developing countries. IFAD provides some $450 million a year in loans and grants, and has financed 633 projects worldwide since its establishment in 1977 — through $7.7 billion in loans and $35.4 million in grants. In addition, the International Monetary Fund works to ensure the viability of the international monetary and financial system through dialogue and policy advice, technical assistance and lending.

Funding for United Nations development activities reached an all-time high of $7.1 billion in 2001, up by almost 17 per cent from 2000 (excluding the World Bank Group). That was the second highest growth rate recorded by the UN system during the previous decade — the highest level of 19 per cent having been achieved in 1998 when expenditures reached $5.7 billion. ODA from the UN agencies, funds and programmes is widely distributed among the many countries in need.

Promoting development worldwide

The **United Nations Development Programme (UNDP)** is the developing countries' development agency, committed to making a pivotal contribution to halving world poverty by 2015. UNDP provides sound policy advice and helps build institutional capacity that generates equitable economic growth.

With a global network of 166 country offices, UNDP works on the ground to help people help themselves. Its focus is on helping countries build and share solutions to the challenges of: democratic governance; poverty reduction; crisis prevention and recovery, whether stemming from violent conflicts or natural disasters; energy, environment and sustainable development; information and communications technology; and preventing the spread of HIV/AIDS. In each of these areas, UNDP advocates for the protection of human rights and, especially, the empowerment of women. It is a hands-on organization, with the vast majority of its staff working in the countries where people need help.

The majority of UNDP's core programme funds go to those countries which are home to the world's extremely poor. In 2002, nearly 1.2 billion people lived in extreme poverty, defined as an income of less than $1 per day. Funding for UNDP development assistance exceeded $2.8 billion in 2002, its highest level ever. Contributions to UNDP are voluntary, and come from nearly every government in the world. Countries that receive UNDP-administered assistance contribute to project costs through personnel, facilities, equipment and supplies.

To ensure maximum impact from global development resources, UNDP coordinates its activities with other United Nations funds and programmes and the international financial institutions, including the World Bank and the International Monetary Fund. In addition, UNDP's country and regional programmes draw on the expertise of developing country nationals and NGOs. Seventy-five per cent of all UNDP-supported projects are implemented by local organizations.

Africa: a United Nations priority

The United Nations, reflecting the concern of the international community, has made the critical socio-economic conditions in Africa a priority concern. In affirming its commitment to support the region's development, it has devised special programmes to find durable solutions to external debt and debt-service problems, to increase foreign direct investment, to enhance national capacity-building, to deal with the shortage of domestic resources for development, to facilitate the integration of the African countries into international trade, and to tackle HIV/AIDS.

In 1996, the General Assembly launched the United Nations System-wide Special Initiative on Africa. Under that Initiative, ILO's Jobs for Africa Programme aimed to develop and strengthen national and regional capacity to combat poverty by generating employment. UNDP's Africa 2000 Initiative provided support to rural women for sustainable development activities, while UNESCO-, UNICEF- and World Bank-led activities focused on improving primary education in countries where primary school enrolment was low.

The Special Initiative was brought to a close in 2002 following a review by the Assembly, which then adopted the New Partnership for Africa's Development (NEPAD) — an African-owned and led initiative, launched by the Organization of African Unity (now the African Union) in July 2001, as the framework of international efforts for Africa's development.

The UN participates at the country, regional and global levels, through such efforts as the United Nations Development Assistance Framework, as well as programmes led by the Economic Commission for Africa, which provide a framework for increased coordination and collaboration at the subregional and regional levels. The Office of the Special Adviser on Africa reports on support provided by the UN system and the international community and coordinates global advocacy in support of the New Partnership.

The Joint United Nations Programme on HIV/AIDS (UNAIDS) has intensified its campaign against HIV/AIDS in Africa. Seeking as broad a base as possible for its campaign, UNAIDS has brought together governments, regional bodies, development agencies, non-governmental organizations and the corporate sector, including pharmaceutical corporations, under an umbrella group known as the International Partnership Against AIDS in Africa.

The Secretary-General and United Nations agencies have called on industrialized countries to ease Africa's economic hurdles — by arranging deeper debt relief, by lowering tariffs that penalize African exports and by increasing official development assistance. The United Nations efforts are also linked with other development undertakings, such as the Tokyo International Conference on African Development, the Heavily Indebted Poor Countries Debt Initiative and the Alliance for African industrialization.

At the country level, UNDP promotes an integrated approach to the provision of United Nations development assistance. In several developing countries, it has established a **United Nations Development Assistance Framework (UNDAF)** made up of United Nations teams under the leadership of the local United Nations resident coordinator, who is usually the resident representative of UNDP. The frameworks articulate a coordinated response to the main development challenges identified for the United Nations by governments. Resident coordinators serve as coordinators of humanitarian assistance in cases of human disasters, natural disasters and complex emergency situations.

UNDP, together with the World Bank and the United Nations Environment Programme, is one of the managing partners of the **Global Environment Facility** and is one of the sponsors of the **Joint United Nations Programme on HIV/AIDS (UNAIDS)**.

Lending for development

The **World Bank**, formally known as the **International Bank for Reconstruction and Development (IBRD)**, works in more than 100 developing countries, bringing finance and/or technical expertise to help them reduce poverty. It is currently involved in more than 1,800 projects in virtually every sector and developing country — from providing microcredit in Bosnia and Herzegovina and raising AIDS awareness in Guinea, to supporting the education of girls in Bangladesh and improving health care delivery in Mexico; from helping Timor-Leste rebuild after independence, to helping India rebuild after a devastating earthquake in Gujarat.

One of the world's largest sources of development assistance, the Bank supports the efforts of developing country governments to build schools and health centres, provide water and electricity, fight disease and protect the environment. It does this through the provision of loans, which are repaid. Developing countries borrow from the Bank because they need capital, technical assistance and policy advice.

There are two types of World Bank lending. The first type is for higher-income developing countries, some of which can borrow from commercial sources, but generally only at high interest rates. These countries receive loans from the IBRD, which allow them more time to repay than if they borrowed from a commercial bank — 15 to 20 years with a three-to-five-year grace period before the repayment of principal begins. Funds are borrowed for specific programmes in support of poverty reduction, delivery of social services, environmental protection and economic growth. In fiscal year 2003, IBRD provided loans totalling $11.2 billion in support of 99 new projects in 37 countries. The Bank, which has a AAA credit rating, raises nearly all its money through the sale of its bonds in the world's financial markets.

The second type of loan goes to the poorest countries, which are usually not creditworthy in the international financial markets and are unable to pay near-market interest rates on the money they borrow. Lending to the poorest countries is done by a World Bank affiliate, the **International Development Association (IDA)**. Funded largely by contributions from 40 rich member countries, IDA helps the world's poorest countries by providing grant financing and credits. These "credits" are actually interest-free loans with a 10-year grace period and maturities of 35 to 40 years. In fiscal year 2003, IDA provided $7.3 billion in financing for 141 new projects in 55 low-income countries. It is the world's largest source of concessional assistance.

Under its regulations, the Bank can lend only to governments, but it works closely with local communities, NGOs and private enterprise. Its projects are designed to assist the poorest sectors of the population. Successful development requires that governments and communities "own" their development projects. The Bank encourages governments to work closely with NGOs and civil society to strengthen participation by people affected by Bank-financed projects. NGOs based in borrowing countries collaborate in about half of these projects.

The Bank encourages the private sector by advocating stable economic policies, sound government finances, and open, honest and accountable governance. It supports many sectors in which private-sector development is making rapid inroads — finance, power, telecommunications, information technology, oil and gas and industry. The Bank's regulations prohibit it from lending directly to the private sector, but a Bank affiliate — the **International Finance Corporation (IFC)** — exists expressly to promote private sector investment by supporting high-risk sectors and countries. Another affiliate, the **Multilateral Investment Guarantee Agency (MIGA)**, provides political risk insurance (guarantees) to those who invest in or lend to developing countries.

But the World Bank does much more than lend money. It also routinely includes technical assistance in the projects it finances. This may include advice on such issues as the overall size of a country's budget and where the money should be allocated, or how to set up village health clinics, or what sort of equipment is needed to build a road. The Bank funds a few projects each year devoted exclusively to providing expert advice and training. It also trains people from borrowing countries on how to create and carry out development programmes.

The IBRD supports sustainable development projects in such areas as reforestation, pollution control and land management; water, sanitation and agriculture; and conservation of natural resources. It is also the main funder of the Global Environment Facility. In recent years, the Bank has put significant resources into the **Heavily Indebted Poor Countries (HIPC)** Initiative, by which 26 poor countries have received debt relief which will save them $41 billion over time. It is also the world's largest long-term financer of HIV/AIDS programmes, with current commitments exceeding $1.3 billion — half of which is for sub-Saharan Africa.

Lending for stability

Many countries turn to the **International Monetary Fund (IMF)**, a United Nations specialized agency, when internal or external factors seriously undermine their balance-of-payments position, fiscal stability or capacity to meet debt service commitments. The IMF offers advice and policy recommendations to overcome these problems, and often makes financial resources available to member countries in support of economic reform programmes.

Members with balance-of-payments problems generally avail themselves of the IMF's financial resources by "purchasing" reserve assets — in the form of other members' currencies and Special Drawing Rights — with an equivalent amount of their own currencies. The IMF levies charges on these loans, and requires that members repay the loans by repurchasing their own currencies from the IMF over a specified time.

The main IMF facilities are:

- *Stand-by arrangements*, designed to provide short-term balance-of-payments assistance for deficits of a temporary or cyclical nature; these must be repaid within 5 years.

- *Extended Fund Facility*, designed to support medium-term programmes aimed at overcoming balance-of-payments difficulties stemming from macroeconomic and structural problems; these must be repaid within 10 years.

- *Poverty Reduction and Growth Facility*, a concessional facility designed for low-income member countries with the explicit goal of reducing poverty. Members qualifying for funding may borrow up to 140 per cent of their quota under a three-year arrangement (and up to 185 per cent under exceptional circumstances). Loans carry an annual interest rate of 0.5 per cent; repayments are made beginning 5 1/2 years and ending 10 years after disbursement.

- *Compensatory Financing Facility*, which provides timely financing for members experiencing temporary export shortfalls or excesses in cereal import costs.

- *Contingent Credit Lines*, which aim to prevent the spread of a crisis by enabling countries that are pursuing sound policies to have quick access to financing should a crisis threaten.

- *Supplemental Reserve Facility*, which provides financial assistance in financial crises for exceptional balance-of-payments difficulties due to a large short-term financing need resulting from a sudden and disruptive loss of market confidence; repayments are expected within 2 1/2 years but can be extended to 3 years.

To provide debt relief to heavily indebted poor countries following sound policies, the IMF and the World Bank jointly provide, under the Heavily Indebted Poor Countries Initiative, exceptional assistance to eligible countries to reduce their external debt burdens to sustainable levels, enabling them to service their debts without the need for further debt relief. It is a comprehensive approach, involving multilateral, official, bilateral and commercial creditors.

Surveillance is the process by which the IMF appraises its members' exchange rate policies through a comprehensive analysis of the general economic situation and

151

policies of each member. The IMF carries out surveillance through annual consultations with individual countries; multilateral surveillance twice a year; regional surveillance through discussion with regional groupings; as well as precautionary arrangements, enhanced surveillance and programme monitoring, which provide a member with close IMF monitoring in the absence of the use of IMF resources.

The IMF provides technical assistance to its members in several broad areas: the design and implementation of fiscal and monetary policy; institution-building, such as the development of central banks or treasuries; and the collection and refinement of statistical data. It also provides training to member countries' officials at the IMF institutes in Washington, D.C., Abidjan, Singapore and Vienna.

Investment and development

As foreign direct investment has continued to expand dramatically, developing countries have increasingly opened up their economies to such investment. Various parts of the United Nations system monitor and assess developments, such as FAO, UNDP and UNIDO, and assist developing country governments in attracting investment.

Two affiliates of the World Bank — the International Finance Corporation and the Multilateral Investment Guarantee Agency — help promote investment in developing countries. Through its advisory work, the **International Finance Corporation (IFC)** helps governments create conditions that stimulate the flow of both domestic and foreign private savings and investment. IFC stimulates and mobilizes private investment in the developing world by demonstrating that investments there can be profitable. As of fiscal year 2002, IFC had committed more than $34 billion of its own funds, and had arranged $21 billion in syndications for some 2,825 companies in 140 developing countries since its founding in 1956.

The **Multilateral Investment Guarantee Agency (MIGA)** is an investment insurance affiliate of the Bank. Its goal is to facilitate the flow of private investment for productive purposes to developing member countries, by offering investors long-term political risk insurance — that is, coverage against the risks of expropriation, currency transfer, war and civil disturbance — and by providing advisory services. MIGA carries out promotional programmes, disseminates information on investment opportunities, and provides technical assistance that enhances the investment promotion capabilities of countries. Since its inception in 1988, MIGA has issued more than 650 guarantees for projects in 85 developing countries, facilitating more than $50 billion in foreign direct investment.

The **United Nations Conference on Trade and Development (UNCTAD)** helps developing countries and economies in transition promote foreign direct investment and improve their investment climate. It also assists government agencies to improve the general understanding of global trends in foreign direct investment and related policies, as well as the interrelationship between foreign direct investment, trade, technology and development. The results of its work are presented

Foreign direct investment and development

Foreign direct investment continues to be a driving force in the global economy. The continuing expansion of investment flows underscores the central role played by transnational corporations in both industrialized and developing countries. According to UNCTAD's *World Investment Report 2003*:

- Foreign direct investment inflows by transnational corporations rose to a peak of $1,393 billion in 2000, before declining to $650 billion in 2002.

- The number of transnational corporations worldwide has continued to expand — up to 64,000 in 2002.

- Some 870,000 foreign affiliates of the world's transnationals sold about $18 trillion of goods and services in 2002 — more than double the volume of global exports. International production has become more important than international trade in delivering goods and services to foreign markets.

- The largest 100 non-financial transnationals hold a dominant position in the global production system. In 2001, they held over $3 trillion in foreign assets, had foreign sales amounting to $2 trillion and employed almost 7 million people in their foreign affiliates.

- In 2001, four corporations from developing countries were on the list of the world's 100 biggest transnational corporations, measured by foreign assets: Hutchison Whampoa Limited (Hong Kong, China), Singtel Ltd. (Singapore), Cemex S.A. (Mexico) and LG Electronics Inc. (Republic of Korea).

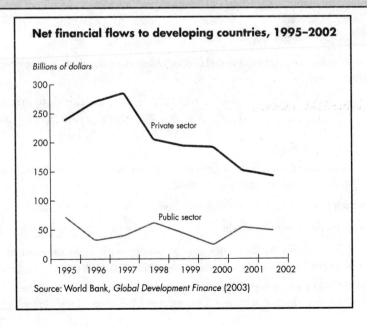

Net financial flows to developing countries, 1995–2002

Billions of dollars

Private sector

Public sector

Source: World Bank, *Global Development Finance* (2003)

153

in the annual *World Investment Report, Investment Policy Reviews, World Investment Directory* and other studies, which are the basis for policy discussions in UNCTAD's Commission on Investment, Technology and Related Financial Issues.

UNCTAD, through its **Division on Investment Technology and Enterprise Development**, promotes understanding on investment, enterprise development and technological capacity building, and assists governments in formulating and carrying out policies and activities in this area.

Trade and development

International trade has been growing strongly by an annual average of 6.5 per cent since the early 1990s, enabling various developing countries to enjoy remarkable gains in prosperity and growth. But major disparities persist, with many of the poorest countries still participating only marginally in international trade.

The **United Nations Conference on Trade and Development (UNCTAD)** is tasked with ensuring the integration of all countries in global trade. As the focal point within the United Nations for dealing with development-related issues in the areas of trade, finance, technology, investment and sustainable development, UNCTAD works to maximize the trade, investment and development opportunities of developing countries. It helps them face the challenges arising from globalization and integrate with the world economy on an equitable basis.

UNCTAD pursues these goals through research and policy analysis, intergovernmental deliberations, technical cooperation, and interaction with civil society and the business sector.

In particular, UNCTAD:

- examines trends in the global economy and evaluates their impact upon development;

- helps developing countries, particularly the least developed, to maximize the positive impact of globalization and liberalization, helping them integrate with the international trading system and become actively involved in international trade negotiations;

- examines global trends in foreign direct investment flows and their impact on trade, technology and development;

- helps developing countries attract investment;

- helps developing countries develop enterprises and entrepreneurship; and

- helps developing countries and countries with economies in transition improve the efficiency of their trade-supporting services.

UNCTAD promotes enterprise development, particularly for small and medium-sized enterprises, through regular intergovernmental discussions and through technical

154

Promoting equitable trade

Intergovernmental negotiations under UNCTAD's auspices have resulted in the following:

- Agreement on a Generalized Systems of Preferences (1971), which facilitates the preferential treatment of over $70 billion of developing-country exports to industrialized countries annually.

- Agreement on a Global System of Trade Preferences among developing countries (1989).

- International commodity agreements, including those for cocoa, sugar, natural rubber, jute and jute products, tropical timber, tin, olive oil and wheat.

- The Common Fund for Commodities, which provides financial backing for the operation of international stocks and for research and development projects in the area of commodities.

- Debt relief: More than 50 developing countries have benefited from debt relief of over $6.5 billion since a resolution on the retroactive adjustment of terms of the ODA debt of low-income developing countries was approved in 1978.

- Guidelines for international action on debt rescheduling (1980) .

- Agreement on a Global Framework for Transit Transport Cooperation between Landlocked and Transit Developing Countries and the Donor Community (1995).

- United Nations conventions in the area of maritime transport: including a code of conduct for liner conferences (1974), on international carriage of goods by sea (1978), on international multimodal transport of goods (1980), on conditions for registration of ships (1986) and on maritime liens and mortgages (1993).

UNCTAD also brought about the only universal, voluntary code on competition — the 1980 agreement on a set of multilateral principles and rules to control restrictive business practices — which is reviewed every five years. The agreement was reviewed most recently in 2000, in close cooperation with the World Bank and the World Trade Organization, to increase both efficiency and equity in competition matters.

cooperation. Its **Commission on Enterprise, Business Facilitation and Development**, examines ways to formulate and carry out effective enterprise development strategies.

UNCTAD's technical cooperation activities involve over 300 projects in more than 100 countries, for which it provides about $24 million annually. They include:

- The *Automated System for Customs Data,* using state-of-the-art technology, helps governments modernize customs procedures and management. Used by more than 60 countries, the system is fast becoming the internationally accepted standard for customs automation.

- The *Advance Cargo Information System* helps African countries develop their transport sector, using computer technology to track cargo along land and sea routes.

- The EMPRETEC *Programme* promotes small and medium-sized enterprise development. An information network provides entrepreneurs with access to business databases.

The **International Trade Centre UNCTAD/WTO (ITC)** is the focal point in the United Nations system for technical cooperation with developing countries in trade promotion. It works with developing countries and countries with economies in transition in setting up trade promotion programmes to expand their exports and improve their import operations.

ITC's field of specialization covers six areas:

- product and market development;

- development of trade support services;

- trade information;

- human resources development;

- international purchasing and supply management; and

- needs assessment and programme design for trade promotion.

Technical cooperation projects in trade promotion are carried out by ITC specialists working in close liaison with local trade officials. National projects often take the form of a broad-based package of services to expand country exports and improve import operations.

Agricultural development

The majority of people on the planet continue to live in rural areas and derive their livelihood, directly or indirectly, mostly from agriculture. In recent decades, rural poverty has spread and deepened and, in the rush to industrialization, insufficient investment has been made in the agricultural sector. The United Nations has addressed this imbalance in a variety of ways.

The **Food and Agriculture Organization of the United Nations (FAO)** is the lead agency for agriculture, forestry, fisheries and rural development. It gives practical help to developing countries through a wide range of technical assistance projects. A specific priority is to encourage rural development and sustainable agriculture — a long-term strategy for increasing food production and food security while conserving and managing natural resources.

In promoting sustainable agricultural development, FAO encourages an integrated approach, with environmental, social and economic considerations included in the formulation of development projects. In some areas, for example, particular combinations of crops can improve agricultural productivity, provide a source of fuel wood for local villagers, improve soil fertility and reduce the impact of erosion.

On average, FAO has some 2,000 field projects operating at any given time. They range from integrated land management projects, to emergency response, to policy and planning advice to governments in areas as diverse as forestry and marketing strategies. FAO usually takes one of three roles: implementing its own programme; executing a programme on behalf of other agencies and donors; or providing advice and management assistance to national projects.

FAO's Investment Centre assists developing countries in formulating investment projects in agricultural and rural development. Each year, this assistance helps mobilize some $3 billion for investment projects, including external funds of over $2 billion.

FAO is active in land and water development, plant and animal production, forestry, fisheries, economic, social and food security policy, investment, nutrition, food standards and food safety, and commodities and trade. For example:

- A programme in nine southern African countries helps rural populations to improve their living standards and nutrition by fish farming. Small bodies of water are brought into the production process, integrating aquaculture with farming. Small farmers have thus expanded food production for consumption and trade.

- Poor farmers in Sri Lanka have been encouraged to form informal groups for income-generating activities, such as land reclamation or small-scale processing. Groups are taught how to gain economic advantages by, for example, buying fertilizer in bulk and marketing crops together. Some 4,000 poor farmers have benefited from the project.

- A project in Mali has established revolving funds to allow women's groups to buy seeds, fertilizers, water pumps and grinding mills. The women have created home and market gardens, selling surplus vegetables in newly established weekly markets. Village women have thus developed activities to expand food production, increase income, improve health and gain access to water.

- Using integrated pest management techniques promoted by FAO, 200,000 Indonesian rice farmers have increased yields and reduced the use of pesticides, helping protect the environment and food quality while saving the government $120 million a year in pesticide subsidies.

The **International Fund for Agricultural Development (IFAD)** finances agricultural development projects that alleviate rural poverty and improve nutrition in the developing world. The Fund's participatory, grass-roots approach is a distinguishing feature of its work. Its small but efficient institutional structure enables the Fund to detect and react to new demands in the rural sector in a flexible and timely manner. In fulfilling its mandate, IFAD provides direct funding and mobilizes resources for programmes specifically designed to promote the economic advancement of the rural poor, mainly by improving the productivity of farm activities.

IFAD's beneficiaries are the poorest of the world's people: small farmers, the rural landless, nomadic pastoralists, artisanal fisherfolk, indigenous people and — across all groups — poor rural women. Most of IFAD's resources are made available to poor countries on highly concessional terms, repayable over 40 years, including a grace period of 10 years, and a 0.75 per cent service charge per annum.

Since its establishment in 1977, IFAD has financed 633 projects in 115 countries and independent territories, to which it has committed over $7.7 billion in loans and $35.4 million in grants. Recipient countries have contributed $7.9 billion, and donors have provided $6.6 billion in cofinancing. These projects have helped some 50 million rural poor households, or approximately 250 million people.

Industrial development

Globalization of industry has created unprecedented industrial challenges and opportunities for developing countries and countries with economies in transition. The **United Nations Industrial Development Organization (UNIDO)** is the specialized agency helping these countries to pursue sustainable industrial development in the new global environment. UNIDO provides tailor-made solutions to today's industrial problems by assisting governments, business associations and the private industrial sector with packages of integrated services addressing three priority areas:

- *Competitive economy*, including industrial policy formulation and implementation, continuous improvements and quality management, and investment and technology promotion.

- *Sound environment*, including environmental policies, energy efficiency and cleaner production.

- *Productive employment*, including policies supporting small and medium-sized enterprises, entrepreneurship development and women entrepreneurs.

Acting as a global forum for industrial development, UNIDO brings together representatives of government, industry and the public and private sectors from developed and developing countries, as well as from countries with economies in transition. Through its technical cooperation programmes, UNIDO puts into effect the task of sustaining an economically efficient, socially desirable and ecologically sound pace of industrial development.

Together with member states, UNIDO has developed integrated packages of service modules designed to meet the specific requirements of countries in strengthening industrial capacities and achieving a cleaner and sustainable industrial development.

UNIDO's 13 investment and technology promotion offices, financed by the countries in which they are located, promote business contacts between industrialized countries and developing countries and countries with economies in transition. It has 5 investment promotion units, 27 national cleaner production centres and 10 international technology centres. Headquartered in Vienna, UNIDO is represented in 35 developing countries, through 9 regional offices, 20 country offices and 6 focal points.

Labour

Concerned with both the economic and social aspects of development, the **International Labour Organization (ILO)** is one of the specialized agencies that pre-dates the United Nations, as it was established in 1919. Its long and diverse work in the setting and monitoring of labour standards in the workplace has provided a framework of international labour standards and guidelines which have been adopted in national legislation by virtually all countries.

ILO is guided by the principle that social stability and integration can be sustained only if they are based on social justice — particularly the right to employment with fair compensation in a healthy workplace. Over the decades, ILO has helped to create such hallmarks as the eight-hour day, maternity protection, child-labour laws, and a whole range of policies that promote safety in the workplace and peaceful industrial relations.

Specifically, ILO engages in:

- the formulation of international policies and programmes to promote basic human rights, improve working and living conditions and enhance employment opportunities;
- the creation of international labour standards — backed by a unique system to supervise their application — to serve as guidelines for national authorities in putting sound labour policies into practice;
- an extensive programme of technical cooperation, formulated and carried out in partnership with beneficiaries, to help countries make these policies effective; and
- training, education, research and information activities to help advance all these efforts.

Decent work. The central purpose of ILO is to promote opportunities for decent work for all people. The International Labour Conference has approved four objectives that must converge on this primary goal. They are:

- to promote and realize fundamental principles and rights at work;
- to create greater opportunities for women and men to secure decent employment and income;
- to enhance the coverage and effectiveness of social protection for all; and
- to strengthen dialogue among governments, labour and business.

To implement these objectives, ILO is focusing on such areas as the progressive abolition of child labour, safety and health at work; socio-economic security; promoting small and medium-sized enterprises; developing skills, knowledge and employability; eliminating discrimination and gender inequality; and promoting the *ILO Declaration on Fundamental Principles and Rights at Work*, adopted by the International Labour Conference in 1998.

Technical cooperation. ILO's technical cooperation focuses on support for democratization, poverty alleviation through employment creation, and the protection of workers. In particular, ILO helps countries to develop their legislation and take practical steps towards putting ILO standards into effect — for instance, by developing occupational health and safety departments, social security systems and worker education programmes. Projects are carried out through close cooperation between recipient countries, donors and the ILO, which maintains a network of area and regional offices worldwide. ILO has technical cooperation programmes in some 140 countries and territories; in the last decade, it spent an average of $130 million annually on technical cooperation projects.

ILO's **International Training Centre**, located in Turin, Italy, carries out training for senior and mid-level managers in private and public enterprises, leaders of workers' and employers' organizations, government officials and policy makers. Some 80,000 people from 172 countries have been trained since the Centre opened in 1965.

ILO's **International Institute for Labour Studies**, located in Geneva, promotes policy research and public discussion of emerging issues of concern to ILO. The organizing theme is the relationship between labour institutions, economic growth and social equity. The Institute acts as a global forum on social policy, maintains international research networks and carries out educational programmes.

International aviation

In 2002 alone, some 1.6 billion passengers flew on over 20 million flights, while nearly 30 million tonnes of manufactured goods were shipped by air — not to mention freight, foodstuffs and more. The safe and orderly growth of international flight is overseen by a United Nations specialized agency, the **International Civil Aviation Organization (ICAO)**.

ICAO aims to meet the need of the public for safe, regular, efficient and economic international air transport, and to ensure the safe and orderly growth of international civil aviation throughout the world. It encourages the arts of aircraft design and operation for peaceful purposes, as well as the development of airways, airports and air navigation facilities.

To meet these objectives, ICAO:

- has adopted international standards and recommendations which are applied to the design and performance of aircraft and much of their equipment; the performance of airline pilots, flight crews, air traffic controllers, and ground and maintenance crews; and security requirements and procedures at international airports;

- formulates visual and instrument flight rules, as well as the aeronautical charts used for international navigation. Aircraft telecommunications systems, radio frequencies and security procedures are also its responsibility;

- works towards minimizing the impact of aviation on the environment through reductions in aircraft emissions and through noise limits; and

- facilitates the movement of aircraft, passengers, crews, baggage, cargo and mail across borders, by standardizing customs, immigration, public health and other formalities.

As acts of unlawful interference continue to pose a serious threat to the safety and security of international civil aviation, ICAO continues to pursue policies and programmes designed to prevent them. In the wake of the terrorist attacks on 11 September 2001 in the United States, ICAO has developed an aviation security plan of action and a training programme for aviation security, currently comprising seven training packages. ICAO maintains 10 aviation security training centres to promote regional cooperation in this crucial area.

In addition, ICAO meets requests from developing countries for help in improving air transport systems and training for aviation personnel. It has helped to establish regional training centres in several developing countries, and has enabled thousands of students to attend training schools registered with ICAO. The agency has dispatched technical cooperation experts to more than 100 countries, and is involved in some 120 projects each year, with average annual expenditures of $54 million.

ICAO is now developing a satellite-based system to meet the future communications, navigation, surveillance and air traffic management needs of civil aviation. The system applies the latest technology in satellites and computers, data links and deck avionics to cope with expanding operational needs. This integrated global system will increase safety and improve the way air traffic services are organized and operated. The system, which has been endorsed by ICAO member states, is now in its implementation phase.

ICAO cooperates with the International Air Transport Association, the Airports Council International, the International Federation of Airline Pilot Associations and the International Council of Aircraft Owner and Pilot Associations.

International shipping

When the **International Maritime Organization (IMO)** held its first Assembly in 1959, it had less than 40 member states. Today it has 162 member states and over 98 per cent of the world's merchant fleets adhere to the key international shipping conventions developed by IMO.

The adoption of maritime legislation is IMO's best known responsibility. IMO has adopted around 40 conventions and protocols, most of them updated in line with changes taking place in world shipping. Maritime security has been added to IMO's objectives of improving the safety of international shipping and preventing marine pollution from ships. Key environmental concerns being addressed include the transfer of harmful aquatic organisms in ballast water and sediments, the emission of greenhouse gases from ships, and ship recycling.

Initially, IMO focused on developing international treaties and other legislation concerning ship safety and marine pollution prevention. Today, the main focus is on implementation of IMO's international standards, while continuing to amend and update existing legislation and to fill in any gaps in the regulatory framework.

The main IMO treaties on maritime safety and prevention of marine pollution by ships which are in force worldwide include:

- *International Convention on Load Lines* (LL), 1966

- *International Regulations for Preventing Collisions at Sea* (COLREG), 1972

- *International Convention for Safe Containers* (CSC), 1972

- *International Convention for the Prevention of Pollution from Ships*, 1973, as modified by the Protocol of 1978 relating thereto (MARPOL 73/78)

- *International Convention for the Safety of Life at Sea* (SOLAS), 1974

- *International Convention on Standards of Training, Certification and Watchkeeping for Seafarers* (STCW), 1978

- *International Convention on Maritime Search and Rescue* (SAR), 1979

Numerous codes, some of which have been made mandatory, address specific issues, such as carriage of dangerous goods and high-speed craft. The International Safety Management Code, made mandatory by means of SOLAS amendments adopted in 1994, addresses the people who operate and run ships. Special attention has been paid to crew standards, including the complete revision in 1995 of the 1978 seafarers' training and certification convention, which for the first time gave IMO the task of monitoring compliance with the Convention.

Safety of life at sea remains one of the key objectives of IMO. In 1999, the *Global Maritime Distress and Safety System* became fully operational, guaranteeing assistance to a ship in distress virtually anywhere in the world; even if its crew does not have time to radio for help, the message is transmitted automatically.

Various IMO conventions address liability and compensation issues. The most significant include the 1992 *Protocol of the International Convention on Civil Liability for Oil Pollution Damage* (CLC Convention, 1969) and the 1992 *Protocol of the International Convention on the Establishment of an International Fund for Compensation for Oil Pollution Damage* (IOPC Fund, 1971), which together provide compensation to victims of oil pollution damage. The *Athens Convention relating to the Carriage of Passengers and their Luggage by Sea* (PAL, 1974) sets compensation limits for passengers on ships.

In December 2002, the IMO adopted an International Ship and Port Facility Security Code, which requires compliance with new measures aimed at protecting shipping against terrorist attacks. Adopted under amendments to the *International Convention for the Safety of Life at Sea* (SOLAS), the Code became mandatory on 1 July 2004.

IMO's technical cooperation programme aims to support the implementation of its international standards and regulations, particularly in developing countries, and to assist governments in operating a shipping industry successfully. The emphasis is on training, and IMO has under its auspices the **World Maritime University** in Malmö, Sweden, the International Maritime Law Institute in Malta and the International Maritime Academy in Trieste, Italy.

Telecommunications

Telecommunications have become a key to the global delivery of services. Banking, tourism, transportation and the information industry all depend on quick and reliable global telecommunications. The sector is being revolutionized by powerful trends, such as globalization, deregulation, restructuring, value-added network services, intelligent networks and regional arrangements. Such developments have transformed telecommunications from its earlier status as a public utility to one having strong links with commerce and trade. It has been projected that the global telecommunications market will grow from nearly $1.4 trillion in 2001 to some $1.7 trillion by 2007.

Against this background works the **International Telecommunication Union (ITU)**, the world's oldest intergovernmental organization, dating back to 1865. Within ITU, the public and private sectors coordinate global telecommunications networks and services.

Specifically, ITU:

- develops standards which foster the interconnection of national communications infrastructures into global networks, allowing the seamless exchange of information — be it data, faxes or phone calls — around the world;

- works to integrate new technologies into the global telecommunications network, allowing for the development of new applications, such as the Internet, electronic mail, multimedia and electronic commerce;

- adopts international regulations and treaties governing the sharing of the radio frequency spectrum and satellite orbital positions — finite natural resources which are used by a wide range of equipment including television and radio broadcasting, mobile telephones, satellite-based communications systems, aircraft and maritime navigation and safety systems, and wireless computer systems;

The telephone gap shrinks...

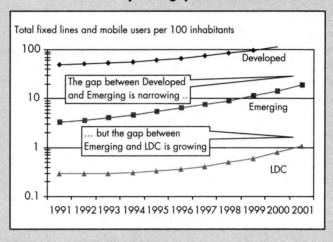

Total fixed lines and mobile users per 100 inhabitants

The gap between Developed and Emerging is narrowing ..

... but the gap between Emerging and LDC is growing

but the Internet gap grows

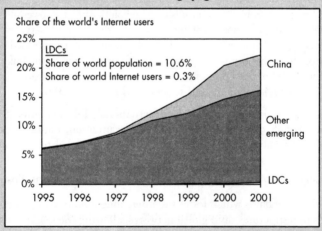

Share of the world's Internet users

LDCs
Share of world population = 10.6%
Share of world Internet users = 0.3%

China

Other emerging

LDCs

Note: Top chart is logarithmic. Developed refers to the European Union, Iceland, Norway, Switzerland, Canada, United States, Japan, Australia, New Zealand, Hong Kong SAR, the Republic of Korea, Singapore and Taiwan-China. LDC refers to the 49 least developed countries. Emerging refers to all other countries.

Source: ITU, *World Telecommunication Development Report* (2002)

- strives to expand and improve telecommunications in the developing world by providing policy advice, technical assistance, project management and training, and by fostering partnerships between telecommunications administrations, funding agencies and private organizations.

The ITU also has the leading managerial role for the **World Summit on the Information Society**. During its first phase, held at Geneva from 10 to 12 December 2003, participants adopted a declaration of principles and plan of action aimed at building a people-centred, inclusive and development-oriented information society, where everyone can create, access, use and share information and knowledge. The concluding phase of the Summit meets at Tunis from 16 to 18 November 2005.

In today's fast-moving telecommunications environment, membership in the ITU gives governments and private organizations a unique opportunity to make an important and valued contribution to the developments rapidly reshaping the world. ITU membership represents a cross-section of the telecommunications and information technology industry — from the world's largest manufacturers and carriers, to small, innovative new players working in new fields like Internet Protocol (IP) networking.

In addition to its 189 member states, ITU has over 640 sector members and some 95 associates, representing scientific and industrial companies, public and private operators and broadcasters, and regional and international organizations. Founded on the principle of international cooperation between government and the private sector, the ITU is a global forum through which government and industry can work towards consensus on a wide range of issues affecting the future of this increasingly important industry.

International postal service

More than 6 million postal employees working in over 700,000 post offices all over the world ensure the processing and delivery of some 430 mail items every year. The United Nations specialized agency regulating this service is the **Universal Postal Union (UPU)**.

The UPU forms a single postal territory of countries for the reciprocal exchange of letter-post items. Every member state agrees to transmit the mail of all other members by the best means used for its own mail. As the primary vehicle of cooperation between national postal services, the UPU works to improve international postal services, provide postal customers in every country with harmonized and simplified procedures for their international mail, and make available a universal network of up-to-date products and services.

The UPU sets indicative rates, maximum and minimum weight and size limits, and the conditions of acceptance of letter-post items, including priority and non-priority items, letters, aerogrammes, postcards, printed matter and small packets. It prescribes the methods for calculating and collecting transit charges (for letter-post items passing through one or more countries) and terminal dues (for imbalance of mails). It also establishes regulations for registered and air mail, and for items requiring special precautions, such as infectious and radioactive substances.

Thanks to UPU, new products and services are integrated into the international postal network. In this way, such services as registered letters, postal money orders, international reply coupons, small packets, postal parcels and expedited mail services have been made available to most of the world's citizens.

The agency has taken a strong leadership role in certain activities, such as the application of electronic data interchange (EDI) technology by the postal administrations of member countries and the monitoring of quality of postal services worldwide.

The UPU provides technical assistance through multi-year projects aimed at optimizing national postal services. It also conducts short projects which may include study cycles, training fellowships, and the expertise of development consultants who carry out on-the-spot studies on training, management or postal operations. The UPU has also made international financial institutions increasingly aware of the need for investment in the postal sector.

Around the world, postal services are making a determined effort to revitalize the postal business. As part of a communications market that is experiencing explosive growth, they have to adapt to a rapidly changing environment, becoming more independent, self-financing enterprises and providing a wider range of services. The UPU is playing a leadership role in promoting this revitalization.

Intellectual property

Intellectual property in various forms — including books, feature films, artistic performance media and computer software — has become a central issue in international trade relations. Millions of patent, trademark and industrial design registrations are currently in force worldwide. In today's knowledge-based economy, intellectual property is a tool for promoting wealth creation as well as economic, social and cultural development.

A United Nations specialized agency, the **World Intellectual Property Organization (WIPO)**, is responsible for promoting the protection of intellectual property all over the world through cooperation among states, and for administering various international treaties dealing with the legal and administrative aspects of intellectual property. Intellectual property comprises two main branches: industrial property, which primarily means inventions, trademarks, industrial designs and appellations of origin; and copyright, covering chiefly literary, musical, artistic, photographic and audiovisual works.

WIPO administers 23 treaties covering crucial aspects of intellectual property, some dating back to the 1880s. Two key treaties are the *Paris Convention for the Protection of Industrial Property* (1883) and the *Berne Convention for the Protection of Literary and Artistic*

Works (1886). Its new policy of adopting recommendations — on the protection of well-known marks (1999), trademark licenses (2000) and marks on the Internet (2001) — complements the treaty-based approach to international legal standard-setting.

The agency assists governments, organizations and the private sector, monitors developments, and seeks to harmonize and simplify rules and practices. It remains alert to the need to develop new international norms and standards in line with advances in technology and business practices, as well as in response to such concerns as traditional knowledge, folklore, biodiversity and biotechnology.

WIPO's **Arbitration and Media Centre** helps individuals and companies from around the world resolve their disputes. It is also the leading dispute resolution service for challenges relating to abuses in the registration and use of Internet domain names — commonly known as "cybersquatting". It provides this service both for the generic top-level domains, such as .com, .net, .org, and .info, and for certain country-code domains. The entire procedure is conducted online, resulting in enforceable decisions within two months, while greatly reducing the cost of reaching a settlement.

Through its "digital agenda", WIPO seeks to encourage the dissemination of such intellectual property as music, films, trade identifiers and knowledge on the Internet, while protecting the rights of their creators and owners. The agenda aims to integrate developing countries into the Internet environment, including through the use of WIPOnet — a global, intellectual property information network — and the electronic delivery of information and services.

WIPO offers expert advice to developing countries on international patent applications, trademark registration and deposits of industrial designs — encouraging them to make full use of the intellectual property system to foster domestic creative activity, attract investment and facilitate the transfer of technology. It provides legal and technical advice and expertise in drafting and revising national legislation. Training programmes are organized for a range of beneficiaries, including policy makers, officials and students. Assistance is offered to countries for automation of their national intellectual property offices.

WIPO also provides services for international applications of industrial property rights. Four WIPO treaties, covering inventions (patents), trademarks and industrial design, ensure that the filing of one international registration will have effect in any of the signatory states. The services provided by WIPO under these treaties simplify and reduce the cost of making individual applications or filings in all the countries in which protection for a given intellectual property right is sought.

Global statistics

Governments, public institutions and the private sector rely heavily on relevant, accurate, comparable and timely statistics at national and global levels, and the United Nations has served as a global focal point for statistics since its founding.

The **Statistical Commission** is the United Nations intergovernmental body mandated to strengthen the harmonization of official statistics worldwide. Composed of 24 member states, it seeks to develop methodologies relating to demographic, social and housing statistics, including principles and recommendations for population and housing censuses, sample surveys, and the production of vital statistics from civil registries, national accounts, industrial commodities production, energy, international trade and environmental data.

Guided by the Commission, the **Statistics Division** of the Secretariat offers a broad range of services for producers and users of statistics. Its data and analytical publications, CD-ROMs and Internet services include the *Statistical Yearbook*, *Monthly Bulletin of Statistics, World Statistics Pocketbook, UN Statistics Newsletter* and the *official database of the United Nations Millennium Development Goals indicators*. Its specialized publications cover demographic, social and housing statistics, national accounts, industrial commodities production, energy, international trade, the environment, and methodological and technical guidelines.

The Division also aims to improve national capabilities in developing countries by providing technical advisory services, training programmes and workshops organized throughout the world on various topics (see *http://unstats.un.org/unsd*).

Public administration

A country's public sector is arguably the most important component in the successful implementation of its national development programmes. The new opportunities created by globalization, the information revolution and democratization have dramatically affected the state and how it functions. Managing the public sector in an environment of unremitting change has become a demanding challenge for national decision-makers, policy developers and public administrators.

The United Nations, through its *Programme in Public Administration and Finance*, assists countries in their efforts to strengthen, improve and reform their governance systems and administrative institutions. Managed by DESA's **Division for Public Administration and Development Management**, the Programme helps governments ensure that their governance — including their public economic, administrative and financial institutions — functions in an effective, responsive, pro-poor and democratic manner. The Division promotes sound public policies, effective and responsive public administration, efficient, engaging service delivery, and openness to change.

Activities include helping governments in developing countries design national programmes for improving ethics; transparency and accountability in public policies; strengthening capacities for local governments and decentralized governance; innovations in the delivery of public services; civil service reforms; reconstructing governance and public administration institutions after severe conflict; human resources development and management in the public sector; and redesigning and strengthening governance systems and institutions.

Many activities foster South-South cooperation by emphasizing the success of such cooperation and disseminating best practices — including through the United Nations Online Network of Public Administration and Finance. The Division also helps to introduce systems, tools, techniques, procedures and processes, including the use of information technology in government operations and service delivery, to achieve the Millennium Development Goals.

Science and technology for development

Since the 1960s, the United Nations has been promoting the application of science and technology for the development of its member states. The **Commission on Science and Technology for Development**, a functional commission of ECOSOC, examines science and technology questions and their implications for development; promotes the understanding of science and technology policies in respect of developing countries; and formulates recommendations on science and technology matters within the UN system. Composed of 33 member states and meeting annually, the Commission selects different themes for its intersessional work and its deliberations. The theme for 2003-2004 was "Promoting the application of science and technology to meet the development goals contained in the Millennium Declaration".

UNCTAD provides substantive and secretariat support to the Commission. It promotes policies favouring technological capacity-building, innovation and technology flows to developing countries. It also provides technical assistance in the area of information technologies, and promotes technological capacity-building to individual enterprises through cooperative arrangements among firms, such as partnerships and networking. Its recent work has focused on the linkages between foreign direct investment (FDI) and technology transfer, as well as the role of technology and innovation in enhancing productive capacity and export competitiveness. It also looks at the implications of technology-related issues for trade negotiations.

FAO, IAEA, ILO, UNDP, UNIDO and WMO all address scientific and technological issues within their specific mandates. Science for development is also an important element in the work of UNESCO.

Social development

Inextricably linked to economic development, social development has been a cornerstone of the work of the United Nations from its inception. Over the decades, the United Nations has emphasized the social aspects of development to ensure that the aim of better lives for all people remains at the centre of development efforts.

In its early years, the United Nations organized ground-breaking research and data gathering in the areas of demographics, health and education, which witnessed the compilation, often for the first time, of reliable data on global social indicators.

Major world conferences since 1990

- World Conference on Education for All, 1990, Jomtien, Thailand
- World Summit for Children, 1990, New York
- International Conference on Nutrition, 1992, Rome
- United Nations Conference on Environment and Development (UNCED), 1992, Rio de Janeiro
- World Conference on Human Rights, 1993, Vienna
- International Conference on Population and Development, 1994, Cairo
- Global Conference on the Sustainable Development of Small Island Developing States, 1994, Barbados
- World Summit for Social Development, 1995, Copenhagen
- Fourth World Conference on Women: Action for Equality, Development and Peace, 1995, Beijing
- Second United Nations Conference on Human Settlements (Habitat II), 1996, Istanbul
- World Food Summit, 1996, Rome
- World Education Forum, 2000, Dakar
- Third United Nations Conference on the Least Developed Countries, 2001, Brussels
- World Conference against Racism, 2001, Durban
- World Food Summit: five years after, 2001, Rome
- International Conference on Financing for Development, 2002, Monterrey
- Second World Assembly on Ageing, 2002, Madrid
- World Summit for Sustainable Development, 2002, Johannesburg

Special sessions of the General Assembly have reviewed progress made five years after the United Nations Conferences on Environment and Development (1997), Small Island Developing States (1999), Population and Development (1999), Women (2000), Social Development (2000), Human Settlements (2001) and Children (2001). Another special session addressed the problems of HIV/AIDS (2001).

It also undertook efforts to protect the cultural heritage, from architectural monuments to languages, reflecting concern for those societies particularly vulnerable to the rapid processes of change.

The Organization has been in the forefront of supporting government efforts to extend social services relating to health, education, family planning, housing and sanitation to all people. In addition to developing models for social programmes, the United Nations has helped to integrate economic and social aspects of development. Its evolving policies and programmes have always stressed that the components of development — social, economic, environmental and cultural — are interconnected and cannot be pursued in isolation.

Globalization and liberalization are posing new challenges to social development. There is a growing desire to see a more equitable sharing of the benefits of globalization. Many governments which have made great sacrifices in economic reforms and liberalization feel they have yet to reap the anticipated benefits of globalization. These benefits, moreover, have not been equally distributed, not even in the developed countries.

For more than half of the world's population who have not benefited from the new global economy, it has often deepened feelings of despair that the weak will never be able to compete with the already strong and powerful. There is a need to better direct the benefits of liberalized trade and investment towards reducing poverty, increasing employment and promoting social integration.

The United Nations work in the social area has become ever more closely associated with a "people-centred" approach that places individuals, families and communities at the centre of development strategies. The Organization has placed new emphasis on social development, in part out of concern that economic and political problems have dominated the international agenda, sometimes at the expense of social issues, such as health, education and population, or of social groups, such as women, children and the elderly.

Reflecting this concern, most of the recent global conferences convened by the United Nations have focused on the problems of social development. The World Summit for Social Development (Copenhagen, 1995) marked the first time that all members of the international community gathered to carry forward the struggle against poverty, unemployment and social disintegration, and to create new awareness of social responsibility and solidarity for the 21st century.

The originality of the Summit lay in its universality, the scope it gave to social development, its ethical basis, and its call for renewed forms of partnership and solidarity within and among nations. The 10 commitments contained in the Copenhagen Declaration for Social Development represent a social contract at the global level.

The diverse issues of social development represent a challenge for developing and developed countries alike. To differing degrees, all societies are confronted by the problems of unemployment, social fragmentation and persistent poverty. And a growing number of social problems — from forced migration to drug abuse, organized crime and the spread of diseases — can be successfully tackled only through concerted international action.

The United Nations addresses the issues of social development through the General Assembly and the **Economic and Social Council (ECOSOC)**, where system-

World Summit for Social Development

The World Summit for Social Development (Copenhagen, 1995) was part of a series of global conferences convened by the United Nations with the objective of enriching the international agenda and to raise awareness of major issues, through cooperation by member states and with the participation of other development actors. Some 117 heads of state or government, supported by ministers representing another 69 countries, adopted the *Copenhagen Declaration on Social Development* and the *Programme of Action*.

Governments pledged to confront the profound social problems of the world by addressing three core issues common to all countries: eradication of poverty, promotion of full employment, and promotion of social integration, particularly of the disadvantaged groups. The Summit signalled the emergence of a collective determination to treat social development as one of the highest priorities of national and international policies, and to place the human person at the centre of development.

Five years later, a special session of the General Assembly (Geneva, 2000) reaffirmed the centrality of more equitable, socially just and people-centred societies. It agreed on new initiatives, including creating a coordinated international strategy on employment, developing innovative sources of public and private funding for social development and poverty eradication programmes, and setting for the first time a global target for poverty reduction — halving the proportion of people living in extreme poverty by 2015.

Many new national policies and programmes have been initiated following the Summit. Social development has been given increased priority in national and international policy objectives. States have recognized the importance of making social improvement an integral part of development strategy at the national and international levels, as well as of placing people at the centre of development. The Summit has also led the United Nations system to refocus its activities.

However, national and international policy responses have been uneven. Despite these advances, there has been little progress in some key areas, and evident regress in others. Inequality within and among states has continued to grow.

wide policies and priorities are set and programmes endorsed. One of the Assembly's six main committees, the **Social, Humanitarian and Cultural Committee**, takes up agenda items relating to the social sector. Under ECOSOC, the main intergovernmental body dealing with social concerns is the **Commission for Social Development**. Composed of 46 member states, the Commission advises ECOSOC and governments on social policies and on the social aspects of development.

Within the Secretariat, the **Division for Social Policy and Development** of the Department of Economic and Social Affairs services these bodies, providing research, analysis and expert guidance. Throughout the UN system, there are many specialized agencies, funds, programmes and offices that address different aspects of social development.

Reducing poverty

The United Nations system has made poverty reduction a priority. The General Assembly has proclaimed 1997-2006 the **International Decade for the Eradication of Poverty**. Its objective is to eradicate absolute poverty, and substantially reduce overall global poverty through decisive national action and international cooperation. In their Millennium Declaration, world leaders resolved to halve, by 2015, the number of people living on less than $1 a day, and also set targets in the fight against poverty and disease.

A key player in this effort is the **United Nations Development Programme (UNDP)**, which has made poverty alleviation its chief priority. UNDP sees poverty as a complex phenomenon, involving people's lack of empowerment, income and basic services.

UNDP works to strengthen the capacity of governments and civil society organizations to address the whole range of factors that contribute to poverty. These include increasing food security; improving the availability of shelter and basic services; generating employment opportunities; increasing people's access to land, credit, technology, training and markets; and enabling people to participate in the political processes that shape their lives. The heart of UNDP's anti-poverty work lies in empowering the poor.

The World Bank estimates the number of people living in extreme poverty dropped by about 125 million from 1990 to 1999, and the proportion of total population living on less than $1 a day fell from 29 to 22.7 per cent. Nevertheless, at current rates of decline, the Millennium Development Goal of halving extreme poverty by 2015 is unlikely to be met in all regions of the world. In addition, the average under-five mortality rate in the developing countries in the year 2000 was 10 times higher than in the developed countries. In sub-Saharan Africa, where the highest rate is found, under-five mortality was reduced by only 3 per cent during the 1990s, which may be attributed, in part, to mother-to-child transmission of HIV.

According to estimates by FAO, undernourishment in developing countries declined from 29 to 17 per cent between 1979-81 and 1997-99, but still left some 777 million people undernourished. Many developing countries, especially those in sub-Saharan Africa, showed only a marginal decline. The number of people with access to safe drinking water increased from 77 to 82 per cent during the 1990s. Although more than 40 per cent of the population in sub-Saharan Africa still lack such access, the millennium goal of reducing by half the proportion of people without sustainable access to safe drinking water appears attainable.

Millennium Declaration targets for poverty, disease and the environment

At the Millennium Summit in September 2000, world leaders committed themselves to the following targets:

- By 2015, cut in half the proportion of the world's people whose income is less than one dollar a day and the proportion of people unable to reach or afford safe drinking water.

- Also by 2015, ensure that both male and female children everywhere will be able to complete a full course of primary schooling and have equal access to all levels of education.

- Reduce maternal mortality by three quarters and under-five child mortality by two thirds.

- Halt and reverse the spread of HIV/AIDS, malaria and other major diseases.

- Provide special assistance to children orphaned by HIV/AIDS.

- By 2020, achieve significant improvement in the lives of at least 100 million slum dwellers.

- Promote gender equality and the empowerment of women as ways to combat poverty, hunger and disease and to stimulate sustainable development.

- Develop and implement strategies that give young people everywhere a chance to find decent and productive work.

- Encourage the pharmaceutical industry to make essential drugs more widely available and affordable for all who need them in developing countries.

- Develop partnerships with the private sector and civil society organizations in pursuit of development and poverty eradication.

- Ensure that the benefits of new technologies — especially information and communication technologies — are available to all.

In the Millennium Declaration, world leaders also resolved to take action on a number of environmental issues, namely:

- Ensure the entry into force of the Kyoto Protocol, preferably by 2002, and begin the required reduction in emissions of greenhouse gases.

- Press for full implementation of the Convention on Biological Diversity and the Convention to Combat Desertification, especially in Africa.

- Stop unsustainable exploitation of water resources by developing water management strategies at the regional, national and local levels.

- Intensify cooperation to reduce the number and effects of natural and man-made disasters.

- Ensure free access to information on the human genome sequence.

There has been progress in achieving the goal of universal education by 2015, as seen in the increase of about 82 million in the total number of pupils in primary education between 1990 and 1998. The world's youth literacy rate increased from an estimated 84 per cent to 87 per cent from 1990 to 2000, and will likely reach 91 per cent by the year 2015 if the current trend continues. While there have been signs of progress in promoting gender equality in education, a gender gap in enrolment remains at all levels of education in developing countries.

The international financial institutions of the United Nations system play a central role in funding numerous programmes that focus on the social aspects of poverty eradication. In support of the Millennium Development Goals, the World Bank has focused on four priority areas: education for all; HIV/AIDS; water and sanitation; and health. Out of $11.2 billion in total lending for the fiscal year ending 30 June 2003, World Bank loan and grant approvals for education reached a record $2.3 billion. Approvals for health and social services projects totalled $3.4 billion, while loans for water, sanitation and flood prevention projects reached $1.4 billion, compared with $546 million in the previous fiscal year.

The Bank's **International Development Association (IDA)** is the largest source of donor funds for basic social services in the poorest countries. Funds from IDA, for example, have ensured that African pupils have received over 5 million textbooks, that over 6,700 health-care centres have been built and staffed in Asia, and that 9.5 million poor people in Latin America have benefited from social investment projects. In fiscal year 2003, IDA provided some $7.3 billion for development projects. Since its establishment in 1960, IDA has provided some $142 billion, supporting country-led poverty reduction strategies in key policy areas — such as raising productivity, providing accountable governance, improving the private investment climate, and improving access to education and health care for the poor.

Fighting hunger

Food production has increased at an unprecedented rate since the United Nations was founded in 1945, outpacing the doubling of the world's population over the same period. Since the early 1960s, the proportion of hungry people in the developing world has been reduced from more than 50 per cent to less than 20 per cent. But despite these gains, hunger remains a massive global challenge.

There is enough food in the world today for every man, woman and child to lead healthy and productive lives. And yet, hunger afflicts one out of every seven people on earth. More than 800 million people go to bed hungry every night — well over the entire population of Europe. Some 24,000 people, nearly half of them children, die every day from hunger and related causes. That's one child every eight seconds.

Most of the United Nations bodies fighting hunger have important social programmes to advance food security for the poorer sectors of the population, particularly in rural areas. Since its establishment, the **Food and Agriculture Organization** of the United Nations (FAO) has been working to alleviate poverty and hunger by promoting agricultural development, improved nutrition and the pursuit of food security —access by all people at all times to the food they need for an active and healthy life.

FAO's **Committee on World Food Security** is responsible for monitoring, evaluating and consulting on the international food security situation. It analyses food needs, assesses availability and stock levels, and monitors policies aimed at food security. FAO, through its *Global Information and Early Warning System*, also oversees an extensive monitoring system with the assistance of satellite surveillance, which monitors conditions affecting food production and alerts governments and donors to any potential threat to food supplies.

FAO's *Special Programme for Food Security* targets the 83 countries that are home to the vast majority of the world's chronically hungry people. The programme seeks to increase food production and to make conditions better for farming families. During a pilot phase, farmers choose and demonstrate selected technologies to increase food production. Successful strategies are then made widely available during an expansion phase.

At the World Food Summit (Rome, 1996), hosted by FAO, 186 countries approved a *Declaration and Plan of Action on World Food Security* aiming to halve hunger by 2015 and outlining ways to achieve universal food security. The "World Food Summit: five years later" (Rome, 2002) was attended by 179 countries plus the European Community, including 73 heads of state or government or their deputies. The Summit called for an international alliance to accelerate action to reduce world hunger. It unanimously adopted a declaration calling on the international community to fulfil the pledge made at the 1996 Summit to reduce the number of hungry by half, to about 400 million, by 2015.

The **International Fund for Agricultural Development (IFAD)** provides development funding to combat rural poverty and hunger in the poorest regions of the world. Some 900 million people — 75 per cent of the world's 1.2 billion extremely poor — live in rural areas. IFAD therefore gives priority to rural poverty. To ensure that development aid actually reaches those who need it most, IFAD involves the rural poor, both men and women, in their own development. Its local-level operations in 114 countries keep IFAD in continuous and direct contact with the rural poor, where their own opportunities and constraints form the backbone of IFAD's knowledge base.

The social dimensions of IFAD's work include the organization and mobilization of farming and fishing associations in poor communities. Using loans to finance basic inputs such as seeds, fertilizers, tools and nets, to buy food-processing equipment or to start up micro-enterprises, millions of rural women and men have been able to organize beyond the levels of subsistence and lift their families and communities out of poverty. Since 1977, IFAD has financed 633 projects in 115 countries. For every dollar of its own resources channelled to the poor, IFAD has mobilized two dollars from other donors and host governments, for a total of more than $22.2 billion in project costs.

IFAD has helped more than 250 million rural poor, once marginalized, to participate in their national economies. Once organized, the rural poor are excellent repayers, with a loan-repayment rate of approximately 97 per cent, a fact that has stimulated the establishment of small-loan programmes around the world.

The World Food Programme (WFP), the largest food-aid organization in the world, provided food to more than 72 million people in 82 countries during 2002, and in 2003 reached a record 110 million people with food aid. WFP buys more goods and services from developing countries, in an effort to reinforce their economies, than any other UN agency or programme.

Over the past three decades, WFP has invested some $27.8 billion and more than 43 million metric tonnes of food to combat hunger, focusing on emergency assistance, relief and rehabilitation, development aid and special operations. In emergencies, WFP is on the front line, delivering food aid to the victims of war, civil conflict, drought, crop failures and natural disasters. After the cause of the emergency has passed, WFP uses food aid to help communities rebuild their shattered lives.

WFP sees food aid as one of the most effective deterrents against poverty. Its development projects, which benefited 14 million people in 55 countries in 2002, focus on nutrition, school feeding, building for the future, disaster mitigation, and supporting sustainable livelihoods. It transports more food aid than any other international organization — 90 per cent of it by ship.

"Food-for-work" projects encourage self-sufficiency, paying workers with food to build roads and ports, hospitals and schools, start small businesses and replant degraded forests. WPF pays workers with food to build, and provides free lunches that lure children to school and give them the energy to study. Food also encourages pregnant mothers and pre-school children to visit health care clinics.

"Food-for-growth" projects target needy people at the most critical time of their lives — babies, schoolchildren, pregnant women and the elderly — using food aid as preventive medicine. In countries like Haiti, Pakistan, Morocco and Mozambique, WFP food aid is also used to draw vulnerable mothers and children to health clinics, as well as to literacy and nutrition classes.

United Nations programmes have proven over and over again that hunger and poverty can be overcome with socially relevant and carefully planned programmes that address the longer-term needs of the affected populations. WFP is committed to such assistance. It also has a special commitment to helping women gain equal access to life's basic necessities, and to providing food aid to address issues relating to HIV/AIDS.

WFP relies entirely on voluntary contributions to finance its humanitarian and development projects. Despite having no independent source of funds, it has the largest budget of any major UN agency or programme — as well as the smallest headquarters staff and lowest overhead. Governments are its principal source of funding, but businesses and individuals are making an increasingly vital contribution to its mission. WFP also works with more than 1,000 NGOs, whose grass-roots and technical knowledge is invaluable in assessing how to deliver its food aid to the right people.

Health

In most parts of the world, people live longer, infant mortality is decreasing and illnesses are kept in check as more people have access to basic health services, immunization, clean water and sanitation. The United Nations has been deeply involved in many of these advances, particularly in developing countries, by supporting health services, delivering essential drugs, making cities healthier, providing health assistance in emergencies and fighting infectious diseases. The Millennium Declaration includes measurable targets to be achieved by countries in nutrition, access to safe water, maternal and child health, infectious disease control, and access to essential medicines by 2015.

Infectious diseases, in particular, remain a major global threat. Up to 45 per cent of deaths in Africa and South-East Asia in 1998 are thought to have been due to an infectious disease, while 48 per cent of premature deaths (under age 45) worldwide are thought to have an infectious cause. Factors have included increased drug resistance, constantly expanding global travel, and the emergence of such new diseases as "severe acute respiratory syndrome" (SARS). However, the causes and the solutions for most infectious diseases are known, and illness and death can in most cases be avoided at an affordable cost. The major infectious diseases are HIV/AIDS, malaria and tuberculosis (see boxes). Stopping and reversing transmission is a key Millennium Development Goal.

For decades, the United Nations system has been in the forefront of the fight against disease through the creation of policies and systems that address the social dimensions of health problems. The **United Nations Children's Fund (UNICEF)** focuses on child and maternal health, and the **United Nations Population Fund (UNFPA)** focuses on reproductive health and family planning. The specialized agency coordinating global action against disease is the **World Health Organization (WHO)**. WHO has set ambitious goals for achieving health for all, making reproductive health available, building partnerships and promoting healthy lifestyles and environments.

WHO was the driving force behind various historic achievements, including the global eradication of smallpox in 1980, achieved after a 10-year campaign. Together with its partners, WHO eliminated poliomyelitis from the Americas in 1994 — the first step towards the goal of certifying the world polio-free by 2005.

Another achievement was the adoption of a ground-breaking public health treaty to control tobacco supply and consumption. The WHO Framework Convention on Tobacco Control covers tobacco taxation, smoking prevention and treatment, illicit trade, advertising, sponsorship and promotion, and product regulation. It was

On the verge of a polio-free world

When the Global Polio Eradication Initiative was launched in 1988, there were an estimated 350,000 cases of the disease worldwide — paralysing more than 1,000 children in more than 125 countries on 5 continents every day. After a concerted campaign, including National Immunization Days to immunize millions of children under five, that figure has dropped to 677 reported cases in 2003 — more than a 99 per cent reduction.

Today, some 3 million people in the developing world, who would have been paralysed, are walking because they have been immunized against polio. Tens of thousands of public health workers and millions of volunteers have been trained, and transport and communications systems for immunization have been strengthened. Since 1988, some 2 billion children worldwide have been immunized — thanks to the cooperation of more than 200 countries and 20 million volunteers, and an investment of $3 billion.

This success has been possible through an unprecedented partnership for health spearheaded by WHO, UNICEF, the United States Centers for Disease Control and Prevention, and Rotary International, which alone will have contributed $500 million to the campaign by 2005. Health ministries, donor governments, foundations, corporations, celebrities, the UN Secretary-General, former South African President Nelson Mandela, philanthropists, health workers and volunteers have each played their part.

Today, only six countries remain polio endemic — Nigeria, India, Pakistan, Egypt, Niger and Afghanistan. A series of massive campaigns in 2004 aims at immunizing 250 million children multiple times, in order to completely wipe out the disease. The public health savings of polio eradication, once immunization stops, are estimated to be $1.5 billion a year.

adopted unanimously by WHO's 192 member states and opened for signature in June 2003. The Convention is a key part of the global strategy to reduce the worldwide epidemic of tobacco use. In 2002, tobacco killed 4.9 million people — up sharply from estimates only two years earlier, as the true toll of tobacco in developing countries is becoming known. If action is not taken, annual tobacco-related deaths will reach 10 million by the late 2020s — with more than 70 per cent of these in developing countries.

Between 1980 and 1995, a joint UNICEF-WHO effort raised global immunization coverage against six killer diseases — polio, tetanus, measles, whooping cough, diphtheria and tuberculosis — from 5 to 80 per cent, saving the lives of some 2.5 million children a year. A similar initiative is the Global Alliance for Vaccines and Immunization. It extends immunization services to include protection against hepatitis B, which kills some 1 million people a year, and haemophilus influenza type B, which kills 900,000 children under age five each year. Launched in 1999 with initial

The UN combats HIV/AIDS

(*www.unaids.org*)

HIV/AIDS has become a development disaster of global proportions. In 2003, this epidemic killed more than 3 million people — an average of 8,000 deaths every day — while 5 million were newly infected by the HIV virus. That's 10 people every minute. By the end of 2003, there were some 40 million people living with the virus, 2.5 million of them under 15 years of age. To date, an estimated 28 million people have already died.

In Africa, AIDS has already orphaned more than 11 million children, half between the ages of 10 and 14. In the hardest-hit regions, life expectancy is plummeting. HIV/AIDS is spreading at an alarming rate among women, who now account for half of those infected worldwide. The epidemic is expanding most rapidly in regions which had, for the most part, been spared — especially in Eastern Europe and across all of Asia, from the Urals to the Pacific Ocean.

To tackle this threat, nine UN agencies have pooled their resources in the Joint United Nations Programme on HIV/AIDS (UNAIDS) — the leading advocate for a worldwide response aimed at preventing transmission, providing care and support, reducing the vulnerability of individuals and communities, and alleviating the impact of the epidemic. Funded by voluntary contributions from governments, foundations, corporations, private groups and individuals, UNAIDS operates as a catalyst and coordinator of action rather than as a direct funding or implementing agency. Its budget for 2003 was $95 million.

In addition, the Secretary-General has issued a call to action to address the HIV/AIDS epidemic, describing it as a personal priority. He also proposed the establishment of a Global AIDS and Health Fund, which became operational in 2002. The Fund aims to support some of the increased spending needed to help developing countries confront the crisis.

Priority areas for UNAIDS include women (comprising 50% of all those living with HIV worldwide), young people (half of all new infections worldwide are among youth, aged 15-24 years), vulnerable populations, mother-to-child transmission, standards of care, vaccine development, and special initiatives for hard-hit regions, including Africa. UNAIDS also seeks to increase involvement by political leaders, promote research, and foster an environment supportive of those affected by the disease.

UNAIDS works with governments, corporations, media, religious bodies, community groups and networks of people living with HIV/AIDS. In developing countries, UNAIDS staff and representatives of sponsoring organizations share information, plan coordinated action and decide on joint financing of major activities. The main objective is to support the host country's efforts to mount an effective response.

In recent years, AIDS mortality rates have declined steadily in high-income countries, largely due to widespread access to antiretroviral treatment. On World Aids Day 2003 (1 December), UNAIDS and WHO unveiled a detailed plan to train tens of thousands of community workers in developing and transition countries to provide antiretroviral treatment to 3 million HIV-infected people by 2005.

The participating agencies of UNAIDS are UNICEF, WFP, UNDP, UNFPA, UNODC, ILO, UNESCO, WHO and the World Bank. In their Millennium Declaration, world leaders resolved by 2015 to have halted and begun to reverse the spread of HIV/AIDS and to provide special assistance to children orphaned by the disease.

funds from the Bill and Melinda Gates Foundation, the Alliance incorporates WHO, UNICEF, the World Bank, the United Nations Foundation and private sector partners.

Guinea-worm disease is on the threshold of eradication and, thanks to new and better methods of treatment, leprosy is also being overcome. River blindness has been virtually eliminated from the 11 West African countries once affected — an achievement benefiting millions. WHO is now targeting elephantiasis for elimination as a public health problem.

WHO's priorities in the area of communicable diseases are: to reduce the impact of malaria and tuberculosis through global partnership; to strengthen surveillance, monitoring and response to global communicable disease problems; to reduce the impact of diseases through intensified and routine prevention and control; and to generate new knowledge, intervention methods, implementation strategies and research capabilities for use in developing countries.

In addition to fighting infectious disease, WHO is a key player in promoting primary health care, delivering essential drugs, making cities healthier, and promoting healthy lifestyles and environments. It also plays a key role in tackling health emergencies, such as outbreaks of EBOLA haemorrhagic fever.

A motor for health research. Working with its partners in health research, WHO gathers data on current conditions and needs, particularly in developing countries. These range from epidemiological research in remote tropical forests to monitoring the progress of genetic research. WHO's tropical disease research programme is tackling the resistance of the malaria parasite to the most commonly used drugs, and is fostering the development of new drugs and diagnostics against tropical infectious diseases. Research also helps to improve national and international surveillance of epidemics, and to develop preventive strategies for new and emerging diseases that integrate laboratory discoveries with the latest information from the field.

Standard-setting. WHO establishes international standards on biological and pharmaceutical substances. It has developed the concept of "essential drugs" as a basic element of primary health care.

WHO works with countries to ensure the equitable supply of safe and effective drugs at the lowest possible cost and with the most effective use. To this end, it has developed a "model list" of some 306 drugs and vaccines considered essential to help prevent or treat over 80 per cent of all health problems. Nearly 160 countries have adapted the list to their own requirements. WHO also cooperates with member states, civil society and the pharmaceutical industry to develop new essential drugs for priority health problems in poor and middle-income countries, and to continue production of established essential drugs.

Through the international access afforded to the United Nations, WHO oversees the global collection of information on communicable diseases, compiles comparable health and disease statistics, and sets international standards for safe food, as well as for biological and pharmaceutical products. It also provides unmatched evaluation

Malaria, SARS and tuberculosis

The Roll Back Malaria initiative, sponsored by WHO, was launched in 1998 with the declared objective of halving the global burden of malaria by 2010. Its founding partners — UNDP, UNICEF, the World Bank and WHO — agreed to share their expertise and resources in a concerted effort to tackle malaria worldwide, with a particular focus on Africa. Since 1998, international spending on malaria has more than trebled, to some $200 million a year, and strategic plans have been developed in more than 30 endemic African countries. Significant additional resources have come from the new Global Fund to Fight AIDS, Tuberculosis and Malaria.

Severe acute respiratory syndrome (SARS), the first new disease of the 21st century, does not yet have a vaccine or treatment other than isolation and quarantine. It has resulted in major economic losses, particularly in the Far East, and demonstrated the havoc that can be caused by an easily transmitted disease in the era of globalization. In June 2003, WHO launched a public-private initiative to fight SARS and build capacity for surveillance, epidemiology and public health laboratory facilities worldwide. The global business community has pledged to mobilize the initial resources needed through a special fund. Such funding initiatives will help prepare the world to respond to future emerging diseases, as well as to bioterrorist threats.

The Global Plan to Stop Tuberculosis was produced in 2001 as a five-year action plan of the Global Stop TB Partnership, which has been hosted by WHO since 1998. Today, over 250 national governments, organizations, donor agencies and institutions are working together to eliminate TB, through a health strategy known as DOTS ("Directly Observed Treatment, Short-course").

The Global Plan proposes expanding DOTS so that all have access to effective diagnosis and treatment; adapting the strategy to meet the challenges of HIV/AIDS and TB drug resistance; developing better diagnostics, new drugs and a new vaccine; and strengthening the Global Partnership so that proven control strategies can be applied worldwide. Effective TB control will cost some $9.1 billion through 2005. If the Global Plan goals are met, some 12.8 million additional people will be treated for TB by 2005, saving 3.4 million additional lives.

of the cancer-producing risks of pollutants, and has put into place the universally accepted guidance for global control of HIV/AIDS.

Human settlements

In 1950, New York City was the only metropolitan area with a population of over 10 million. By the year 2000, there were 19 such "mega-cities" — all but four in developing countries. In 1950, only 30 per cent of the world's population was urban. Today, nearly half of its 6.1 billion people live in towns and cities. More than 1 billion of the world's people live in slums; in developing countries, 40 per cent of the urban population live in slums.

The **United Nations Human Settlements Programme (UN-HABITAT)** — formerly known as the United Nations Centre for Human Settlements — is the lead agency within the United Nations system for addressing this situation. It is mandated by the United Nations General Assembly to promote socially and environmentally sustainable towns and cities, with the goal of providing adequate shelter for all. To that end, it has 154 technical programmes and projects in 61 countries, most of them in the least developed countries. Its annual budget for 2002-2003 was $300 million.

At Habitat II, the Second United Nations Conference on Human Settlements (Istanbul, 1996), agreement was reach on the Habitat Agenda — a global plan of action in which governments committed themselves to the goals of adequate shelter for all and sustainable urban development. UN-HABITAT is the focal point for implementing the Agenda, assessing progress in its implementation at the international, regional, national and local levels, and monitoring global trends and conditions.

UN-HABITAT runs two major worldwide campaigns — the Global Campaign on Urban Governance, and the Global Campaign for Secure Tenure:

- *Global Campaign on Urban Governance.* In many cities, poor governance and inappropriate policies have led to environmental degradation, increased poverty, low economic growth and social exclusion. This campaign aims to increase local capacity for good urban governance — the efficient, effective response to urban problems by democratically elected and accountable local governments, working in partnership with civil society. The campaign focuses on inclusiveness, addressing the needs of the excluded urban poor and promoting the involvement of women in decision-making at all levels.

- *Global Campaign for Secure Tenure.* This campaign is designed to take forward the commitment of governments to providing "adequate shelter for all" — one of the two main themes of the Habitat Agenda. It identifies the provision of secure tenure as essential for a sustainable shelter strategy and as vital to the promotion of housing rights. The campaign has been designed to spearhead a shelter strategy that promotes the rights and interests of the poor, recognizing that the vast majority of their shelter is provided by the urban poor themselves. It also aims to promote the rights and role of women in successful shelter policy.

Through various means, the agency focuses on a range of issues and special projects which it helps implement. Together with the World Bank, it is engaged in a slum upgrading initiative called the *Cities Alliance*. Other programmes aim at promoting effective housing development policies and strategies, campaigning for housing rights, promoting sustainable cities and urban environmental planning and management, and post-conflict land management and reconstruction in countries devastated by war or natural disasters.

UN-HABITAT activities address water and sanitation and solid waste management for towns and cities, training and capacity-building for local leaders, ensuring that women's rights and gender issues are brought into urban development and management policies, and helping fight crime through its *Safer Cities Programme*. The agency helps strengthen rural-urban linkages, as well as infrastructure development and public service delivery. It is also engaged in research and monitoring of urban economic development, employment, poverty reduction, municipal and housing finance systems, and urban investment.

Its programmes include:

- *Best Practices and Local Leadership Programme* — a global network of government agencies, local authorities and civil society organizations dedicated to identifying and disseminating best practices to improve the living environment and apply lessons learned to policy development and capacity-building.

- *Sustainable Cities Programme* — a joint UN-HABITAT-UNEP initiative that builds capacities in urban environmental planning and management, using participatory methods. The programme currently operates in some 45 cities around the world.

- *Managing Water in African Cities* — a UN-HABITAT-UNEP initiative that supports effective water management and protection of water resources from urban pollution.

- *Risk and Disaster Management Unit* — assists national and local governments, as well as communities, in carrying out post-disaster reconstruction and rehabilitation programmes.

- *Localizing Agenda 21* — translates the human settlements components of *Agenda 21* into action at the local level, by stimulating joint venture initiatives in selected medium-sized cities. (*Agenda 21* is the global plan of action for sustainable development adopted at the 1992 "Earth Summit", described later in this chapter.)

- *Global Urban Observatory and Statistics* — monitors the implementation of the Habitat Agenda by developing and applying policy-oriented urban indicators, while building local capacity to select, collect, manage and apply indicators and statistics in policy analysis.

Education

Great strides have been made in education in recent years, marked by a significant increase in the number of children in schools. Nevertheless, more than 115 million children — nearly 56 per cent of them girls in developing countries — have no access to primary education, and many who start attending are forced to leave because of poverty or family and social pressures. Despite enormous literacy efforts, 862 million adults remain illiterate, some two thirds of whom are women. The United Nations Literacy Decade (2003-2012) seeks to draw greater attention to this pressing issue.

Research has shown the close relationship between access to education and improved social indicators. Schooling has a special multiplier effect for women. A woman who is educated will typically be healthier, have fewer children and have more opportunities to increase household income. Her children, in turn, will experience lower mortality rates, better nutrition and better overall health. For this reason, girls and women are the focus of the education programmes of many United Nations agencies.

Many parts of the United Nations system are involved in the funding and development of a variety of education and training programmes. These range from traditional basic schooling to technical training for human resources development in areas such as public administration, agriculture and health services, to public awareness campaigns to educate people about HIV/AIDS, drug abuse, human rights, family planning, and many other issues. **UNICEF**, for example, devotes more than 20 per cent of its annual programme expenditure to education, paying special attention to girls' education.

The lead organization in the area of education is the **United Nations Educational, Scientific and Cultural Organization (UNESCO)**. Together with other partners, it works to ensure that all children are enrolled in schools that are child-friendly and have trained teachers providing quality education.

UNESCO is providing the secretariat for the most ambitious United Nations interagency campaign ever launched to achieve universal, quality-based primary education by 2015 — based on a framework for action adopted by more than 160 nations at the World Education Forum in Dakar, Senegal in the year 2000. This goal was reconfirmed by world leaders in their Millennium Declaration in September of that year.

At the Forum, governments committed themselves to the achievement of quality education for all, with particular emphasis on girls and such groups as working children and children affected by war. Donor countries and institutions pledged that no nation committed to basic education would be thwarted by lack of resources. The Forum drew from the results of the largest, most comprehensive and statistically rigorous stocktaking of education in history — the two-year "Education for All Assessment" and six high-level regional conferences.

UNESCO's innovative interdisciplinary project, "Educating for a sustainable future", helps member states improve and reorient their national education and training activities on environment, population and development, including health education and the prevention of drug abuse and AIDS.

Under its programme of promoting lifelong education for all, UNESCO supports and fosters national projects to renovate educational systems and develop alternative strategies to make lifelong education accessible to all. The programme also seeks to widen access to basic education and improve its quality, reform higher education worldwide, and promote adult and continuing education.

Some 7,500 schools in 171 countries are involved in UNESCO's Associated Schools Project, an international network elaborating ways and means for enhancing the role of education in learning to live together in a world community. Some 5,000 UNESCO Clubs in more than 120 countries, mainly comprising teachers and students, carry out a wide range of educational and cultural activities.

Research and training

Academic work in the form of research and training is carried out by a number of specialized United Nations organizations. This work is aimed at enhancing understanding of the global problems we face, as well as fostering the human resources required for the more technical aspects of economic and social development.

The mission of the **United Nations University (UNU)** is to contribute, through research and capacity-building, to efforts to resolve the pressing global problems of concern to the United Nations, its peoples and member states. An international community of scholars, UNU is a bridge between the UN and the international academic community — a think-tank for the United Nations system, and a builder of capacities, particularly in developing countries. The UNU cooperates with over 30 United Nations entities and more than 100 research institutions around the world.

UNU's academic work addresses specific issues of concern to the United Nations. Its current thematic focus covers five areas: peace, governance, development, the environment, and science, technology and society. Academic activities are carried out at the UNU Centre in Tokyo, and through research and training centres and programmes located in various parts of the world. These include:

- *UNU Food and Nutrition Programme for Human and Social Development*, Ithaca, New York, United States (1975) — focuses on food and nutrition capacity-building.
- *UNU Geothermal Training Programme*, Reykjavik, Iceland (1979) — geothermal research, exploration and development.
- *UNU World Institute for Development Economics Research* (UNU-WIDER), Helsinki, Finland (1985).
- *UNU Programme for Biotechnology in Latin America and the Caribbean*, Caracas, Venezuela (1988) — focuses on biotechnology and society.
- *UNU Institute for New Technologies, Maastricht*, the Netherlands (1990) — examines the social and economic impact of new technologies.
- *UNU International Institute for Natural Resources in Africa*, Accra, Ghana (1990) — natural resources management.
- *UNU International Institute for Software Technology*, Macau, China (1992) — software technologies for development.
- *UNU Institute of Advanced Studies*, Tokyo, Japan (1995) economic restructuring for sustainable development.

- *UNU International Leadership Academy*, Amman, Jordan (1995) — focuses on leadership development.

- *UNU International Network on Water, Environment and Health*, Hamilton, Ontario, Canada (1996).

- *UNU Fisheries Training Programme*, Reykjavik, Iceland (1998) — fisheries research and development.

- *UNU Programme on Comparative Regional Integration Studies*, Bruges, Belgium (2001) — for the development of a global network on comparative regional integration studies.

- *UNU Programme on Science and Technology for Sustainability*, Kwangju, Republic of Korea (2001) — science and technology for environmental sustainability.

- *UNU Pantanal Regional Environment Programme*, State of Mato Grosso, Brazil (2002) —works on fragile ecosystems in wetlands.

- *UNU Institute for Environment and Human Security*, Bonn, Germany (2003).

The **United Nations Institute for Training and Research (UNITAR)** works to enhance the effectiveness of the UN through appropriate training and research. It conducts training programmes in multilateral diplomacy and international cooperation for diplomats accredited to the United Nations, as well as for national officials involved in UN-related work. It also carries out a wide range of training programmes in the field of social and economic development.

Each year, UNITAR conducts some 120 different fellowships, seminars and workshops, benefiting more than 5,500 participants on five continents. It also carries out results-oriented research relating to training and the development of pedagogical materials — including distance learning training packages, workbooks, software and video training packs. UNITAR is supported entirely from voluntary contributions.

The **United Nations System Staff College (UNSSC)** is mandated to help strengthen leadership and management development capacities throughout the UN system. It has three main programmes. One provides staff training and learning services, usually on an inter-agency basis. Another offers capacity-building services to assist UN organizations in knowledge management, human resources management and operational effectiveness. A third programme aims at promoting collaboration and raising awareness on the issues of performance and quality, with the aim of strengthening the management culture across the UN system. All these activities are geared to supporting the Millennium Development Goals and the Secretary-General's reform agenda. The College was established in January 2002 and is a distinct entity within the UN system (*see www.unssc.org*).

The **United Nations Research Institute for Social Development (UNRISD)** engages in research on the social dimensions of contemporary problems affecting development. Working through an extensive network of national research centres, the

Institute collaborates with governments, development agencies, grass-roots organizations and scholars on the formulation of development policies. Current research themes include social policy and development; democracy, governance and human rights; civil society and social movements; and technology, business and society.

Population and development

The United Nations estimates that despite a projected decrease in global fertility levels, population is expected to increase dramatically over the next 50 years. Rapid population growth weighs heavily on the earth's resources and environment, often outstripping efforts towards development. The UN has addressed the relationship between population and development in many ways, placing special emphasis on advancing the rights and status of women, which is seen as key to social and economic progress.

Over the decades, the United Nations has been carrying out operational activities in many developing countries. Various parts of the Organization have worked together to build national statistical offices, take censuses, make projections and disseminate reliable data. The United Nations quantitative and methodological work, particularly its authoritative estimates and projections of population size and change, has been pioneering. This has led to a significant increase in national capacities to plan ahead, incorporate population policies into development planning, and take sound economic and social decisions.

The **Commission on Population and Development**, composed of 47 member states, is charged with studying and advising ECOSOC on population changes and their effects on economic and social conditions. It has primary responsibility for reviewing the implementation of the programme of action of the 1994 International Conference on Population and Development.

The **Population Division** of the United Nations Department of Economic and Social Affairs serves as the secretariat of the Commission. It also provides the international community with up-to-date and scientifically objective information on population and development. It undertakes studies on population levels, trends, estimates and projections, as well as on population policies and the link between population and development. The Division maintains major databases, including the *World Population Projections to 2150* and the *Global Review and Inventory of Population Policies* (GRIPP). It also coordinates the *Population Information Network* (POPIN), which promotes use of the Internet to facilitate global sharing of population information.

The **United Nations Population Fund (UNFPA)**, which leads the operational activities of the UN system in this field, helping developing countries and those with economies in transition find solutions to their population problems. It assists states in improving reproductive health and family planning services on the basis of individual choice, and in formulating population policies in support of sustainable development. It also promotes awareness of population problems, and helps governments deal with them in ways best suited to each country's needs.

As the largest internationally funded source of population assistance, UNFPA manages one fourth of such assistance worldwide. It is primarily a funding organization for population projects and programmes carried out by governments, UN agencies and NGOs.

Its core programme areas are:

- *Reproductive health, including safe motherhood, family planning and sexual health,* which helps people achieve their desired family size and enjoy greater freedom in planning their future, saves lives, supports the fight against HIV/AIDS, and contributes to slower and more balanced population growth.

- *Population and development strategies,* which helps countries incorporate population issues in policy making, design strategies to improve the quality of life of their people, and improve their own capacity to develop population programmes.

- *Advocacy,* to promote women's equality, maintain political commitment, and increase awareness and resources for population and development.

Other special programmes cover youth, ageing, HIV/AIDS prevention, emergency obstetric care, fistula prevention and treatment, as well as population and the environment. UNFPA does not provide any support for abortion services. Rather, it seeks to prevent abortion by helping to increase access to family planning.

UNFPA is the lead United Nations organization for advancing the programme of action adopted at the International Conference on Population and Development (Cairo, 1994) and reviewed by a special session of the General Assembly in 1999. The programme focuses on meeting the needs of individual women and men rather than achieving demographic targets. Key to this approach is empowering women and providing them with more choices, through expanded access to education, health services and employment opportunities.

UNFPA also addresses the reproductive health needs of adolescents. Programmes seek to prevent teenage pregnancy, prevent and treat fistula, prevent HIV/AIDS and other sexually transmitted infections, reduce recourse to abortion, and improve access to reproductive health services and information.

The ability of parents to choose the number and spacing of their children is an essential component of reproductive health and an internationally recognized basic human right. While the number of couples using family planning has risen dramatically in recent years, at least 350 million couples worldwide lack access to a full range of family planning methods.

Surveys show that an additional 120 million women would currently be using a modern family planning method if more accurate information, affordable services and appropriate counselling were available, and if their husbands, extended families and communities were more supportive. UNFPA works with governments, the private sector and NGOs to meet people's family planning needs.

Advancement of women

Promotion of equality between women and men is central to the work of the United Nations. Gender equality is not only a goal in its own right, but is also recognized as a critical means for achieving all other development goals. Efforts to overcome poverty and to reduce hunger are increasingly built around women's critical role in economic and social development. The promotion of education for girls is necessary for the achievement of universal primary education. The fight against the HIV/AIDS pandemic, where women account for nearly 50 per cent of those infected with HIV worldwide, requires the full involvement of women and girls. The United Nations actively supports women's empowerment and enjoyment of their human rights through adoption of global norms, standards and policies, and through its development assistance activities.

The **Commission on the Status of Women**, under ECOSOC, examines progress towards women's equality throughout the world, makes recommendations for promoting women's rights in the political, economic, social and educational fields, and addresses women's rights problems requiring immediate attention. It also drafts treaties and other instruments aimed at improving the status of women in law and practice. The 45-member commission has prepared four global conferences on women's issues and gender equality, including the Fourth World Conference on Women (Beijing, 1995), and monitors implementation of the resulting platform for action and the outcome of the twenty-third special session of the General Assembly held in 2000.

The **Committee on the Elimination of Discrimination against Women (CEDAW)** monitors adherence to the *United Nations Convention on the Elimination of All Forms of Discrimination against Women*. The recommendations of the 23-expert committee have contributed to a better understanding of women's economic and social rights, their political and civil rights, and the means to ensure the enjoyment of those rights.

The **Division for the Advancement of Women**, in the Department of Economic and Social Affairs, supports the efforts of the Commission on the Status of Women and the Committee on the Elimination of Discrimination against Women to advance the global agenda for gender equality and strengthen the mainstreaming of gender issues.

The **special adviser to the Secretary-General** on gender issues and the advancement of women oversees the work of the Division. She provides support at the senior level to intergovernmental and expert bodies, including to the Security Council, on such critically emerging issues as women, peace and security. She plays a leadership and catalytic role within the Organization on all gender equality issues, including gender mainstreaming in all programmatic and operational activities. She offers policy advice to the United Nations system on the achievement of 50/50 gender balance and on improving the status of women.

The special adviser also coordinates inter-agency mechanisms and chairs the Inter-Agency Network on Women and Gender Equality of the United Nations system, which works to strengthen implementation of the platform for action and its

World conferences on women

United Nations conferences, building on the energy of national women's movements, have galvanized understanding, interest and action concerning the advancement of women around the world.

Three world conferences — in Mexico City (1975), Copenhagen (1980) and Nairobi (1985) — greatly enhanced international awareness of the concerns of women and created invaluable links between national women's movements and the international community.

At the Fourth World Conference on Women (Beijing, 1995), representatives of 189 governments adopted the *Beijing Declaration and Platform for Action*, aimed at removing obstacles to women's participation in all spheres of public and private life. The Platform identifies 12 critical areas of concern:

- the persistent and increasing burden of poverty on women;
- unequal access to and inadequate educational opportunities;
- inequalities in health status, inadequate health-care services, and unequal access to health care;
- violence against women;
- effects of conflict on women;
- inequality in women's participation in the definition of economic structures and policies, and in the production process;
- inequality in the sharing of power and decision-making;
- insufficient mechanisms to promote the advancement of women;
- lack of awareness of, and commitment to, internationally and nationally recognized women's human rights;
- insufficient mobilization of mass media to promote women's contribution to society;
- lack of adequate recognition and support for women's contribution to managing natural resources and safeguarding the environment;
- the girl child.

At the twenty-third special session of the General Assembly in 2000 to follow up on the implementation of the Beijing Declaration and Programme of Action, countries pledged additional initiatives, such as strengthening legislation against all forms of domestic violence, and enacting laws and policies to eradicate such harmful practices as early and forced marriage and female genital mutilation. Targets were set to ensure free compulsory primary education for both girls and boys, and to improve women's health through wider access to health care and prevention programmes.

follow-up, and of the *Convention on the Elimination of All Forms of Discrimination against Women.*

Beyond the Secretariat, all the organizations of the United Nations family address issues relating to women and gender in their policies and programmes. Women are central to UNICEF's work for children. Much of UNFPA's mandate revolves around women's health and reproductive rights. UNDP, UNESCO, WFP, ILO and others have programmes focused on women and the promotion of gender equality. In addition, two other entities have an exclusive focus on women's issues: UNIFEM and INSTRAW.

The **United Nations Development Fund for Women (UNIFEM)** is a voluntary fund that provides financial support and technical assistance to innovative programmes which promote women's human rights, their economic and political empowerment, and gender equality. UNIFEM works primarily in three areas: strengthening women's economic capacity as entrepreneurs and producers; increasing women's participation in governance, leadership and decision-making; and promoting women's human rights to make development more equitable.

The **International Research and Training Institute for the Advancement of Women (INSTRAW)** undertakes research and training that uses new information and communication technologies to contribute to the advancement of women and support their access into the information society of the 21st century.

Promoting the rights of the child

Eleven million children die every year before their fifth birthday, and tens of millions more are left physically or mentally disabled because they lack what is needed to survive and flourish. Many of the deaths are caused by preventable or easily treated illnesses; others by the pernicious effects of poverty, ignorance, discrimination and violence. In their entirety, they represent an acute loss to families, communities, nations and the world.

Beyond infancy, the young still confront forces that threaten their lives and well-being. They are made more vulnerable because their rights are often denied them, including their right to education, participation and protection from harm.

The **United Nations Children's Fund (UNICEF)** acts to protect children's rights. It advocates for full implementation of the *Convention on the Rights of the Child* and the *Convention on the Elimination of All Forms of Discrimination against Women.* UNICEF's objective is to see that children get the best possible start in life. It works in partnership with governments, sister UN agencies and NGOs to advance health, education, nutrition and protection for every child. In its work in 158 countries and territories, UNICEF emphasizes sustainable, low-cost programmes in which communities are encouraged to take an active part.

Special Session on Children

From 8 to 10 May 2002, more than 7,000 people participated in the most important international conference on children in more than a decade — the special session of the United Nations General Assembly on children. It was convened to review progress since the World Summit for Children in 1990 and re-energize global commitment to children's rights. The special session was a landmark — the first one devoted exclusively to children and the first to include them as official delegates.

The special session culminated in the official adoption, by some 180 nations, of its outcome document, "A World Fit for Children". The new agenda for, and with, the world's children comprised 21 specific goals and targets for the next decade. It was the result of more than two years of consensus-building, in which the nations of the world committed themselves to improving the situation of children and young people. "A World Fit for Children" sets out four key priorities:

- promoting healthy lives;
- providing quality education for all;
- protecting children against abuse, exploitation and violence;
- combating HIV/AIDS.

The document's declaration commits leaders to completing the unfinished agenda of the 1990 World Summit for Children, and to achieving other goals and objectives, in particular those of the UN Millennium Declaration. It reaffirms leaders' obligation to promote and protect the rights of each child, acknowledging the legal standards set by the Convention on the Rights of the Child and its Optional Protocols. All of society is called upon to join a global movement to build a world fit for children, based on a 10-point rallying call that also formed the core of UNICEF's "Say Yes for Children" campaign.

The plan of action sets out three necessary outcomes: the best possible start in life for children; access to a quality basic education, including free and compulsory primary education; and ample opportunity for children and adolescents to develop their individual capacities. There are strong calls to support families, eliminate discrimination and tackle poverty.

A wide range of actors and partners are called upon to play key roles in this plan, including: children themselves; parents, families and other caregivers; local governments; parliamentarians; NGOs; the private sector; religious, spiritual, cultural and indigenous leaders; the mass media; regional and international organizations; and people who work with children.

To achieve these goals and targets, "A World Fit for Children" calls for the mobilization and allocation of new resources at both national and international levels. It supports the development of local partnerships, as well as the pursuit of global targets and actions, such as allocation by industrialized countries of 0.7 per cent of their gross national product for official development assistance (ODA). It also supports the 20/20 Initiative — a compact between developing and industrialized countries that calls for 20 per cent of developing countries' budgets and 20 percent of ODA to be allocated to basic social services.

UNICEF's current priorities are early childhood development, girls' education, immunization, fighting HIV/AIDS, and protecting children from violence, abuse, exploitation and discrimination. These aims are congruent with the Millennium Development Goals and with the objectives expressed within "A World Fit for Children", the outcome document of the 2002 special session of the General Assembly on children.

The UN Children's Fund is widely engaged in every facet of child health, from before birth through adolescence. It acts to ensure that pregnant women have access to proper prenatal and delivery care, strengthens families' ability to manage childhood illnesses at home, and offers guidance to communities in achieving the best health care possible. UNICEF works to reduce the risks of HIV/AIDS to young people by sharing information that will keep them safe. It makes special efforts to see that children who lose their parents to HIV/AIDS receive the same kind of care as their peers. And it helps women and children afflicted with AIDS to live their lives with dignity.

UNICEF is also involved worldwide in the process of immunization, from the purchase and distribution of vaccines to safe inoculation. More than 100 million children are now immunized against the most common illnesses, a programme that saves 2.5 million lives every year. UNICEF buys 65 per cent of all the world's vaccines and is the main supplier of vaccines to developing countries.

In its support for many different initiatives that educate children from pre-school age through adolescence, UNICEF mobilizes teachers, registers children, prepares school facilities and organizes curricula, sometimes rebuilding educational systems from the ground up. It makes sure that children have the chance to play and learn, even in times of conflict, because sports and recreation are equally important to a child's progress. UNICEF also works to ensure that every child is registered at birth, so that he or she has access to health care and education. It encourages proper nutrition for pregnant mothers and breastfeeding after birth. It improves water and sanitation facilities at kindergartens and child-care centres.

The UN Children's Fund helps create protective environments for the young. It encourages legislation that bans child labour, condemns female genital mutilation, and acts to make it more difficult to exploit children for sexual and economic ends. UNICEF designs landmine awareness campaigns and helps to demobilize child soldiers. In addition, it helps reunite parents with their children when they've been separated by conflict, and makes certain that children who are orphaned receive care and protection. UNICEF pioneered the idea of "days of tranquillity", when hostile forces agree to ceasefires for long enough to allow all children to be vaccinated.

Social integration

There are several social groups that the United Nations has come to recognize as deserving special attention, including youth, older persons, persons with disabilities, minorities and indigenous populations. Their concerns are addressed by the General Assembly, ECOSOC and the Commission for Social Development. Specific programmes for these groups are carried out within the United Nations Department of Economic and Social Affairs.

The United Nations has been instrumental in defining and defending the human rights of vulnerable groups. It has helped to formulate international norms, standards and recommendations for action regarding these groups, and strives to highlight their concerns through research and data gathering, as well as through the declaration of special years and decades aimed at encouraging awareness and international action.

Families

Families are basic units of society and have been transformed to a great degree over the past 50 years as a result of changes in their structure (e.g., smaller-sized households, delayed marriage and childbearing, increased divorce rates and single parenthood), global trends in migration, the phenomenon of demographic ageing, the HIV/AIDS pandemic and the impacts of globalization. These dynamic social forces have had a manifest impact on the capacities of families to perform such social functions as the socialization of children and caregiving for its younger and older members.

By proclaiming 1994 as the International Year of the Family, with the theme, "Family: Resources and Responsibilities in a Changing World", the General Assembly helped to bring the subject of the family into the international dialogue on development. As a result, governments formulated national action plans on the family, established ministries devoted to the family and passed family-oriented legislation. The Assembly also convened an International Conference on Families (New York, 1994).

The two main objectives of the UN programme on the family are to strengthen family-centred components of integrated development policies and programmes, and to ensure the successful observance of the tenth anniversary of the International Year of the Family in 2004 at all levels. The programme focuses on five areas: technology and its impact on the family; indicators and statistics for family well-being; approaches to the development of family policies; parental roles and intra-familial support systems; and HIV/AIDS and its impact on families.

The United Nations also promotes the annual worldwide observance of the International Day of Families on 15 May of each year. Proclaimed by the General Assembly in 1993, the observance is intended to increase awareness of issues relating to the family and to encourage appropriate action.

Youth

The General Assembly has adopted several resolutions and campaigns specific to youth, and the Secretariat has overseen the related programmes and information campaigns:

- In 1965, the General Assembly adopted the *Declaration on the Promotion among Youth of the Ideals of Peace, Mutual Respect and Understanding between Peoples*, stressing the importance of the role of youth in today's world.

- Two decades later, the Assembly proclaimed 1985 as International Youth Year, adopting guidelines for further planning, as well as a global long-term strategy on youth employment. The UN has promoted implementation of these guidelines, helping governments to develop policies and programmes relating to youth.

- In 1995, the United Nations adopted a world programme of action for youth to the year 2000 and beyond — an international strategy to address the problems of young people and increase opportunities for their participation in society. It also called for a World Conference of Ministers Responsible for Youth to meet regularly under the aegis of the United Nations. Its first session, held in Lisbon in 1998, adopted the **Lisbon Declaration on Youth** and recommended initiatives at the national, regional and global levels.

- At the initiative of the General Assembly, a World Youth Forum of the United Nations system has held four sessions so far, aimed at promoting joint initiatives relating to youth. The Forum has focused on increasing the channels of communication between youth NGOs and the youth-related bodies of the UN system and promoting NGO-United Nations system initiatives on youth.

- The United Nations Youth Fund supports projects involving young people and provides seed-money grants to governments and NGOs for innovative programmes relating to youth.

- Various UN forums also consider the social and economic impact of globalization on young people, with particular attention to its policy implications.

In their Millennium Declaration, the heads of state or government at the Millennium Summit resolved to "develop and implement strategies that give young people everywhere a real chance to find decent and productive work". At the request of the Secretary-General, a Youth Employment Network was established in 2001 as a joint initiative of the United Nations, the ILO and the World Bank. Its 12-member, high-level panel serves in an ongoing advisory capacity, and has issued recommendations on translating the Summit commitments into action. (For additional information, see *www.ilo.org/public/english/employment/strat/yen/index.htm*)

Older persons

Between the years 2000 and 2050, the proportion of older persons worldwide (aged 60 years and older) is expected to more than double, from 10 to 22 per cent — equalling the proportion of children (aged 0 to 14 years). As a result of this historic demographic transition — from high birth and death rates to low birth and death rates — the old and the young will represent an equal share of the world's population for the first time in history.

In many developed countries, the number of older persons now exceeds the number of children, and birth rates have fallen below replacement levels. In some countries, older persons will outnumber children by more than two to one by 2050.

In developing countries, the proportion of older persons is expected to rise from 8 per cent currently to 21 per cent in 2050, while the proportion of children is expected to drop from 33 to 20 per cent. Even more compelling is the rapid pace of the ageing process, and the fact that in less than three decades, three quarters of the world's older persons will live in developing countries. Moreover, despite increasing urbanization, the majority of older persons in developing countries will continue to live in rural areas.

The world community is recognizing the need to integrate the emerging process of global ageing into the larger context of development. Policies on ageing should be designed within a broader "life course" and society-wide perspective, taking note of recent global initiatives and the guiding principles which have emerged from major United Nations conferences. Most importantly, older persons represent contributors to development. Recognition of their ability to take action for the betterment of themselves and their societies should be woven into policies and programmes at all levels.

In response to global ageing, the United Nations has taken several initiatives:

- The first World Assembly on Ageing (Vienna, 1982) adopted the International Plan of Action on Ageing. The Plan recommended action in such sectors as employment and income security, health and nutrition, housing, education and social welfare. It sees older persons as a diverse and active population group with wide-ranging capabilities and, at times, particular health-care needs.

- The *United Nations Principles for Older Persons*, adopted by the General Assembly in 1991, established universal standards pertaining to the status of older persons in five areas: independence, participation, care, self-fulfilment and dignity.

- In 1992 — the tenth anniversary of the adoption of the Plan of Action — the Assembly held an International Conference on Ageing. It adopted the *Proclamation on Ageing*, laying out the main direction for further action on ageing, and proclaimed 1999 as the International Year of Older Persons.

- The General Assembly in 1999 met to follow up on the International Year. Sixty-four countries spoke, offering wide support for the objectives of the Year and its theme, "Towards a society for all ages".

- The second World Assembly on Ageing met at Madrid in 2002 to design international policy on ageing for the 21st century. It adopted a new international plan of action on ageing, by which member states committed themselves to action at all levels in three priority areas: older persons and development; advancing health and well-being into old age; and ensuring the existence of enabling and supportive environments.

Indigenous issues

There are more than 370 million indigenous peoples worldwide, many of whom live in poverty. They have the shortest life expectancy, the highest infant-mortality rates, the poorest school retention and graduation rates, and the highest unemployment. They live mostly in overcrowded, poor quality housing and suffer endemic environmental health problems. As a result, they are grossly overrepresented in prisons, as well as in statistics on poverty.

In the late 1980s, discussions began on establishing a permanent, high-level body to consider global issues relating to indigenous peoples, with their effective participation. In response, the Economic and Social Council, in July 2000, decided to establish the **Permanent Forum on Indigenous Issues**, with a mandate to discuss indigenous issues relating to economic and social development, culture, education, health and human rights. The Forum was asked to provide expert advice and recommendations to the Council and, through it, to the programmes, funds and agencies of the United Nations. It was asked to raise awareness, promote the integration and coordination of activities relating to indigenous issues within the UN system, and prepare and disseminate information on indigenous issues.

The expectations of the Forum are enormous. Indigenous peoples and the Forum would like to see focused and targeted recommendations, characterized by enormous political wisdom, resulting in catalytic policies on the ground. The UN system is called upon to engage systematically with the Forum, inviting its input and responding to its recommendations, to help improve lives. Also to be considered is how indigenous issues may best be pursued in meeting the Millennium Development Goals. In many countries, attention to indigenous communities will directly contribute to the goal of halving extreme poverty by 2015.

The Permanent Forum on Indigenous Issues is composed of 16 members — eight nominated by member states and elected by the Economic and Social Council, and eight nominated through indigenous regional consultation processes and appointed by the Council President. The secretariat of the Permanent Forum was launched early in 2003 within the UN Department of Economic and Social Affairs. It has been working with an inter-agency support group made up of UN agencies, funds and programmes, to assist in implementing the Forum's recommendations. The second session of the Forum was held in May 2003, with some 1,000 participants in attendance (*see www.un.org/esa/socdev/pfii*).

Persons with disabilities

Persons with disabilities are often excluded from the mainstream of society. Discrimination takes various forms, ranging from invidious discrimination, such as the denial of educational opportunities, to more subtle forms of discrimination, such as segregation and isolation because of the imposition of physical and social barriers. Society also suffers, since the loss of the enormous potentials of persons with disabilities impoverishes humankind. Changes in the perception and concepts of disability involve both changes in values and increased understanding at all levels of society.

Since its inception, the United Nations has sought to advance the status of persons with disabilities and to improve their lives. The concern of the United Nations for the well-being and rights of such persons is rooted in its founding principles, which are based on human rights, fundamental freedoms and the equality of all human beings.

In the 1970s, the concept of the human rights of persons with disabilities gained wider international acceptance. The General Assembly adopted, in 1971, the *Declaration on the Rights of Mentally Retarded Persons* and, in 1975, the *Declaration on the Rights of Disabled Persons*, which set the standards for equal treatment and equal access to services.

The International Year of Disabled Persons (1981) led to the adoption of the *World Programme of Action concerning Disabled Persons*, a policy framework for promoting the rights of persons with disabilities. It calls for international cooperation in support of equality and the full participation of persons with disabilities in social life and development. In 1992, the General Assembly proclaimed 3 December as the International Day of Disabled Persons.

A major outcome of the United Nations Decade of Disabled Persons (1983-1992) was the adoption of the United Nations *Standard Rules for the Equalization of Opportunities for Persons with Disabilities*. These rules serve as an instrument for policy making and as a basis for technical and economic cooperation.

In recent years, the General Assembly has reaffirmed its commitment to adopting and implementing effective public policies and programmes for persons with disabilities, with a focus on accessibility, employment, sustainable livelihoods, social services and social safety nets. In 2001, the Assembly established an ad hoc committee to consider proposals for a comprehensive international convention to promote and protect the rights and dignity of persons with disabilities. In June 2004, the committee began negotiations on the draft convention, based on a text prepared by its working group.

A growing body of data suggests the need to address issues concerning persons with disabilities in the context of overall national development and within the broad framework of human rights. The United Nations works with governments, the nongovernmental community, academic institutes and professional societies to compile international resources, promote awareness and build national capacities for broad human rights approaches to this issue.

International action on disability is increasingly focused on outreach, building national capacities for improved information services and institutional mechanisms to promote equal opportunities. The United Nations continues its efforts to strengthen national capacities to promote the disability perspective in mainstream development and human rights activities (*see www.un.org/esa/socdev/enable*).

Uncivil society: crime, illicit drugs and terrorism

Transnational organized crime, illicit drug trafficking and terrorism have become social, political and economic forces capable of altering the destinies of countries and regions.

Recent trends include large-scale bribery of public officials, the growth of "criminal multinationals" and trafficking in human beings. The use of terrorism to intimidate communities large and small and to sabotage economic development is a further threat that requires effective international cooperation. The United Nations is addressing these threats to good governance, social equity and justice for all citizens, and is orchestrating a global response.

The Vienna-based **United Nations Office on Drugs and Crime (UNODC)** leads the international effort to combat drug trafficking and abuse, organized crime and international terrorism — what the Secretary-General has called the "uncivil" elements of society. The Office is composed of a crime programme — which also addresses terrorism and its prevention — and a drug programme.

Drug control

More than 200 million people abuse drugs worldwide. Drug abuse is responsible for lost wages, soaring health-care costs, broken families and deteriorating communities. In particular, drug use by injection is fuelling the rapid spread of HIV/AIDS and hepatitis in many parts of the world.

There is a direct link between drugs and an increase in crime and violence. Drug cartels undermine governments and corrupt legitimate businesses. Revenues from illicit drugs fund some of the most deadly armed conflicts.

The financial toll is staggering. Enormous sums are spent to strengthen police forces, judicial systems and treatment and rehabilitation programmes. The social costs are equally jarring: street violence, gang warfare, fear, urban decay and shattered lives.

The United Nations is addressing the global drug problem on many levels. The **Commission on Narcotic Drugs**, a functional commission of ECOSOC, is the main intergovernmental policy making and coordination body on international drug control. Made up of 53 member states, it analyses the world drug abuse and trafficking problem and develops proposals to strengthen international drug control. It monitors implementation of the international drug control treaties and the guiding principles and measures adopted by the General Assembly.

The Commission has five subsidiary bodies to promote cooperation and coordination at the regional level in Africa, Asia and the Pacific, Europe, Latin America and the Caribbean, and the Near and Middle East.

The **International Narcotics Control Board (INCB)** is a 13-member, independent, quasi-judicial body that monitors governments' compliance with international drug control treaties and assists them in this effort. It strives to ensure that drugs are available for medical and scientific purposes and to prevent their diversion into illegal channels. It sets limits on the amounts of narcotic drugs needed by countries for medical and scientific purposes. It also sends investigative missions and technical visits to drug-affected countries.

A series of treaties, adopted under United Nations auspices, require that governments exercise control over the production and distribution of narcotic and psychotropic substances, combat drug abuse and illicit trafficking, and report to international organs on their actions. These treaties are:

- The *Single Convention on Narcotic Drugs* (1961), which seeks to limit the production, distribution, possession, use and trade in drugs exclusively to medical and scientific purposes, and obliges states parties to take special measures for particular drugs such as heroin. The 1972 Protocol to the Convention stresses the need for treatment and rehabilitation of drug addicts.

- The *Convention on Psychotropic Substances* (1971), which establishes an international control system for psychotropic substances. It responds to the diversification and expansion of the spectrum of drugs, and introduces controls over a number of synthetic drugs.

- The *United Nations Convention against Illicit Traffic in Narcotic Drugs and Psychotropic Substances* (1988), which provides comprehensive measures against drug trafficking, including provisions against money laundering and the diversion of precursor chemicals. As the main instrument for international cooperation against drug trafficking, it provides for the tracing, freezing and confiscation of proceeds and property derived from drug trafficking; the extradition of drug traffickers; and the transfer of criminal prosecution proceedings. States parties commit themselves to eliminate or reduce drug demand.

Through its drug programme, UNODC provides leadership for all United Nations drug control activities. It helps to prevent developments that could aggravate drug production, trafficking and abuse; assists governments in establishing drug control structures and strategies; provides technical assistance in drug control; promotes the implementation of drug control treaties; and acts as a worldwide centre of expertise and repository of information.

UNODC's approach to the global drug problem is multifaceted. Community-based programmes for drug abuse prevention, treatment and rehabilitation involve NGOs and civil society. Alternative development assistance provides new economic opportunities to populations economically dependent on the cultivation of illicit crops. Better training and technology to curb drug trafficking makes law enforcement agencies more effective. And assistance to the business community and NGOs helps them create programmes to reduce drug demand. For instance:

- The *Global Illicit Crops Monitoring Programme*, carried out in Afghanistan, Laos, Myanmar, Bolivia, Colombia and Peru, integrates satellite sensing, aerial surveillance and on-the-ground assessment, in order to enable countries to gain a wide-ranging picture of illicit growing areas and trends.

- The *Global Assessment Programme* supplies accurate and current statistics on illicit drug consumption worldwide. Such a picture of drug abuse trends is crucial for finding the best strategies for prevention, treatment and rehabilitation.

- The *Legal Assistance Programme* works with states to implement drug control treaties by helping to draft legislation and train judicial officials. More than 1,700 key personnel have received legal training, and over 140 countries have received legal assistance.

At the 1998 special session of the General Assembly devoted to countering the world drug problem, the world's governments pledged to work together to streamline strategies and strengthen activities aimed at curtailing illicit production and consumption. These included: campaigns to reduce drug demand; programmes to restrict availability of materials that can be used in drug production; efforts to improve judicial cooperation among countries to better control drug trafficking; and stepped-up efforts to eradicate illicit drug crops.

Crime prevention

Crime is increasing in scope, intensity and sophistication. It threatens the safety of citizens around the world and hampers the social and economic development of countries. Globalization has opened up new forms of transnational crime. Multinational criminal syndicates have expanded the range of their operations from drug and arms trafficking to money laundering. Traffickers move as many as 4 million illegal migrants each year, generating gross earnings of up to $7 billion. A country plagued by corruption is likely to attract investment levels 5 per cent lower than those of a relatively uncorrupt country, and to lose up to 1 per cent of economic growth per year.

The **Commission on Crime Prevention and Criminal Justice**, made up of 40 member states, is a functional body of ECOSOC. It formulates international policies and coordinates activities in crime prevention and criminal justice.

Through its crime programme, UNODC carries out the mandates established by the Commission, and is the United Nations office responsible for crime prevention, criminal justice and criminal law reform. It pays special attention to combating transnational organized crime, corruption, terrorism and trafficking in human beings. Its strategy is based on international cooperation and the provision of assistance for those efforts. It fosters a culture based on integrity and respect for the law, and promotes the participation of civil society in combating crime and corruption.

UNODC supports the development of new international legal instruments on global crime, including the *United Nations Convention against Transnational Organized Crime* and its three protocols, which entered into forced in September 2003; and the *United Nations Convention against Corruption*, adopted by the General Assembly in 2003. It is now promoting their ratification and helping states put their provisions into effect.

UNODC also provides technical cooperation to strengthen the capacity of governments to modernize their criminal justice systems. In 1999, in cooperation with United Nations Interregional Crime and Justice Research Institute (UNICRI), it launched three programmes addressing major priority concerns: the *Global*

Programme against Corruption, the *Global Programme in Trafficking in Human Beings* and *Global Studies on Organized Crime*.

The UN Office on Drugs and Crime promotes and facilitates the application of United Nations standards and norms in crime prevention and criminal justice as cornerstones of humane and effective criminal justice systems — basic requisites for fighting national and international crime. More than 100 countries have relied on these standards for elaborating national legislation and policies, leading to a common foundation for the fight against international crime that is respectful of human rights and the needs of individuals.

In addition, the Office analyses emerging trends in crime and justice, develops databases, issues global surveys issued, gathers and disseminates information. It also undertakes country-specific needs assessments and early warning measures — for example, on the escalation of terrorism.

A *Global Programme against Terrorism* was launched in October 2002. In its first year it provided legal technical assistance to more than 30 countries on becoming party to and implementing the 12 universal instruments on the prevention and suppression of international terrorism. The programme works with regional and other international organizations, such as the OSCE and the IMF, and maintains regular contact with the Counter-Terrorism Committee established pursuant to Security Council resolution 1373 (2001). It coordinates its work with the Committee and, where appropriate, involves the Committee in its activities.

The *Global Programme against Money Laundering* assists governments in confronting criminals who launder the proceeds of crime through the international financial system. Estimates of laundered money are as high as $500 billion a year. In close cooperation with international anti-money laundering organizations, the programme provides governments, law enforcement and financial intelligence units with anti-money laundering schemes, advises on improved banking and financial policies, and assists national financial investigation services.

The **United Nations Interregional Crime and Justice Research Institute (UNI-CRI)** operates as the interregional research arm of UNODC's crime programme. It undertakes and promotes action-oriented research aimed at the prevention of crime and the treatment of offenders. It contributes, through the dissemination of research and information, to the formulation of improved policies on crime prevention and control.

As decided by the General Assembly, a **United Nations Congress on the Prevention of Crime and the Treatment of Offenders** is held every five years, as a forum to exchange policies and stimulate progress in the fight against crime. Participants include criminologists, penologists and senior police officers, as well as experts in criminal law, human rights and rehabilitation. The Eleventh Crime Congress will meet in Bangkok in April 2005, on the theme, "Synergies and responses: strategic alliances in crime prevention and criminal justice".

Science, culture and communication

The United Nations sees cultural and scientific exchanges, as well as communication, as instrumental to the advancement of international peace and development. In addition to its central work concerning education, the **United Nations Educational, Scientific and Cultural Organization (UNESCO)** focuses its activities on three other areas: science in the service of development; cultural development — heritage and creativity; and communication and information.

Science

UNESCO's major programme on science in the service of development fosters the advancement, transfer and sharing of knowledge in the natural, physical, social and human sciences. UNESCO's intergovernmental programmes include *Man and the Biosphere*; a programme of the Intergovernmental Oceanographic Commission; the *Project on Environment and Development in Coastal Regions*; the *Management of Social Transformations Programme*; the *International Hydrological Programme*; and the *International Geological Correlation Programme*. In addition, through education and training initiatives, UNESCO helps to correct the imbalance in scientific and technological manpower, 90 per cent of which is concentrated in the industrialized countries.

In the wake of advances in cloning living beings, the UNESCO member states in 1997 adopted the *Universal Declaration on the Human Genome and Human Rights* — the first international text on the ethics of genetic research. The declaration sets universal ethical standards on human genetic research and practice, balancing the freedom of scientists to pursue their work with the need to safeguard human rights and protect humanity from potential abuses.

In the social and human sciences, UNESCO focuses on promoting philosophy and social sciences research; promoting and teaching human rights and democracy; combating all forms of discrimination; improving the status of women; and encouraging action to solve the problems faced by youth, including education for the prevention of AIDS.

Cultural development

UNESCO's cultural activities are concentrated on safeguarding cultural heritage. Under the 1972 *Convention on the Protection of the World Cultural and Natural Heritage*, 175 states have pledged their cooperation to protect 730 outstanding sites in 125 countries — towns, monuments and natural environments that have been placed on the *World Heritage List* of sites threatened by neglect. A 1970 UNESCO convention prohibits the illicit import, export and transfer of cultural property, and a 1995 convention favours the return of stolen or illegally exported cultural objects to their country of origin.

UNESCO is also drafting a convention to safeguard intangible heritage, which includes oral traditions, customs, languages, music, dance, rituals, festivities, traditional medicine, the culinary arts and all kinds of traditional skills. It is also considering the possibility of developing a normative instrument that would extend and complete the *Universal Declaration on Cultural Diversity*, adopted in November 2001. UNESCO's activities also focus on promoting the cultural dimension of development; encouraging creation and creativity; preserving cultural identities and oral traditions; and promoting books and reading.

Communication and information

UNESCO has asserted itself as a world leader in promoting press freedom and pluralistic, independent media. Its major programme in this area seeks to promote the free flow of information and to strengthen the communication capacities of developing countries. It assists member states in adapting their media laws to democratic standards, and in pursuing editorial independence in public and private media. When violations of press freedom occur, UNESCO's Director-General intervenes through diplomatic channels or public statements.

At the initiative of UNESCO, 3 May is observed annually as **World Press Freedom Day.**

With the aim of reinforcing developing countries' communication infrastructures and human resources, UNESCO provides training and technical expertise and helps develop national and regional media projects — especially through its *International Programme for the Development of Communication.*

UNESCO helps developing countries set up their own informatics systems and secure access to global information flows, in order to bridge the digital divide. Its emphasis is on training, as well as on establishing computer networks to link scientific and cultural institutions and hook them up to the Internet.

The new information and communication technologies (ICTs), by multiplying the possibilities for producing, disseminating and receiving information on an unprecedented scale, are extending the principle of the free flow of ideas. UNESCO seeks to ensure that as many people as possible benefit from these opportunities. Additional issues being addressed by UNESCO include the social and cultural impact of these technologies, and policy approaches to legal and ethical issues relating to cyberspace.

Information and Communication Technologies Task Force. The UN Millennium Declaration pledged "to ensure that the benefits of new technologies, especially information and communication technologies, are available to all". In an increasingly global economy, such technologies can accelerate development, economic growth, productivity and the eradication of poverty.

Responding to this challenge, the Secretary-General, in November 2001, launched the UN Information and Communication Technologies Task Force. Its mandate is to promote awareness, inclusive policies, and innovative technological and business models, while building public-private-civil society partnerships that contribute to realizing development goals through the widespread use of ICT.

The Task Force is a global platform for placing ICT at the service of all the world's citizens, not just the privileged few. It is not an operational or funding agency. Rather, it serves as a catalyst, as well as a focal point for establishing strategic direction, policy coherence and advocacy — for the common goal of a global ICT-based development agenda.

The Task Force has created working groups to address specific ICT/development themes, including: ICT policy and governance; national and regional e-strategies; human resources development and capacity-building; low-cost connectivity access; and business enterprise and entrepreneurship. It has also created regional nodes for Africa, Latin America and the Caribbean, Asia, the Arab states, Europe and Central Asia — providing region-specific support while enhancing synergies among existing regional endeavours.

Decreasing the digital divide requires cross-sectoral efforts in both the public and private spheres, at the global, regional and local levels. As the Task Force continues its work, the challenge is to make the new economy productive and sustainable over the long term, to spread it worldwide, and to respond to the needs and demands of the people of the world.

Sustainable development

In the first decades of the United Nations, environmental concerns rarely appeared on the international agenda. The related work of the Organization emphasized the exploration and use of natural resources, while seeking to ensure that developing countries in particular would maintain control over their own resources. During the 1960s, agreements were made concerning marine pollution, especially oil spills. Since then, there has been increasing evidence of the deterioration of the environment on a global scale, and the international community has shown escalating alarm over the impact of development on the ecology of the planet and on human well-being. The United Nations has been a leading advocate for environmental concerns, and a leading proponent of "sustainable development".

The relationship between economic development and environmental degradation was first placed on the international agenda in 1972, at the United Nations Conference on the Human Environment, held in Stockholm. After the Conference, governments set up the **United Nations Environment Programme (UNEP)**, which remains the world's leading environmental agency.

In 1973, the **United Nations Sudano-Sahelian Office (UNSO)** was set up to spearhead efforts to reverse the spread of desertification in West Africa. But efforts to integrate environmental concerns with national economic planning and decision-making moved slowly. Overall, the environment has continued to deteriorate, and such problems as global warming, ozone depletion and water pollution have grown more serious, while the destruction of natural resources has accelerated rapidly.

Sustainable development summits

At the United Nations Conference on Environment and Development (UNCED) (Rio de Janeiro, 1992), also known as the Earth Summit, it was agreed that environmental protection and social and economic development are fundamental to *sustainable* development, based on the "Rio Principles". To achieve such development, world leaders adopted a global programme entitled *Agenda 21*.

In *Agenda 21*, governments outlined a detailed blueprint for action that could move the world away from its present unsustainable model of economic growth towards activities that will protect and renew the environmental resources on which growth and development depend. The blueprint also recommended ways to strengthen the part played by such major groups as women, trade unions, farmers, children and young people, indigenous peoples, the scientific community, local authorities, business, industry and NGOs, in achieving sustainable development.

In 1997, the General Assembly held a special session (Earth Summit + 5) on the implementation of *Agenda 21*. Member states grappled with differences among them on how to finance sustainable development globally, but emphasized that putting *Agenda 21* into practice was more urgent than ever. The session's final document recommended measures to this end, including: adopting legally binding targets to reduce emission of greenhouse gases leading to climate change; moving more forcefully towards sustainable patterns of energy production, distribution and use; and focusing on poverty eradication as a prerequisite for sustainable development.

The World Summit on Sustainable Development (Johannesburg, 2002) reviewed progress since the 1992 Earth Summit. Its "Johannesburg Declaration on Sustainable Development" and 54-page "Plan of Implementation" reaffirmed the central importance of sustainable development and paved the way for addressing its most pressing challenges. Commitments were made on specific time-bound goals, including new targets relating to sanitation, chemical use and production; the maintenance and restoration of fish stocks; and reducing the rate of biodiversity loss. The special needs of Africa and the small island developing states were specifically addressed, while such new issues as sustainable production and consumption patterns, energy and mining were brought into sharper focus.

The 1980s witnessed landmark negotiations among member states on environmental issues, including treaties protecting the ozone layer and controlling the movement of toxic wastes. The World Commission on Environment and Development, established in 1983 by the General Assembly, brought a new understanding and sense of urgency to the need for a new kind of development that would ensure economic well-being for present and future generations, while protecting the environmental resources on which all development depends. The Commission's 1987 report to the General Assembly put forward this new concept of *sustainable development*, as an alternative to development based simply on unconstrained economic growth.

After considering the report, the General Assembly called for the United Nations Conference on Environment and Development — the *Earth Summit*.

Today, awareness of the need to support and sustain the environment is reflected in virtually all areas of United Nations work. Dynamic partnerships between the Organization and governments, NGOs, the scientific community and the private sector are bringing new knowledge and specific action to the global environmental problems. The UN maintains that environment protection must be part of all economic and social development activities. Development cannot be achieved unless the environment is protected.

Agenda 21

Governments took an historic step towards ensuring the future of the planet when the 1992 Earth Summit adopted *Agenda 21*, a comprehensive plan for global action in all areas of sustainable development.

In *Agenda 21*, governments outlined a detailed blueprint for action that could move the world away from its present unsustainable model of economic growth towards activities that will protect and renew the environmental resources on which growth and development depend. Areas for action include: protecting the atmosphere; combating deforestation, soil loss and desertification; preventing air and water pollution; halting the depletion of fish stocks; and promoting the safe management of toxic wastes.

Agenda 21 also addresses patterns of development which cause stress to the environment, including: poverty and external debt in developing countries; unsustainable patterns of production and consumption; demographic stress; and the structure of the international economy. The action programme also recommends ways to strengthen the part played by major groups — women, trade unions, farmers, children and young people, indigenous peoples, the scientific community, local authorities, business, industry and NGOs — in achieving sustainable development.

The United Nations has acted to integrate the concept of sustainable development in all relevant policies and programmes. Income-generating projects increasingly take environmental consequences into account. Development assistance programmes are more than ever directed towards women, in view of their central roles as producers of goods, services and food, and as caretakers of the environment. The moral and social imperatives for alleviating poverty are given additional urgency by the recognition that poverty eradication and environmental quality go hand in hand.

To ensure full support for the goals of *Agenda 21* worldwide, the General Assembly in 1992 established the **Commission on Sustainable Development**. A functional commission of ECOSOC, the 53-member body monitors and reports on implementation of *Agenda 21* and the other Earth Summit agreements, including the outcome of the 2002 World Summit on Sustainable Development. It promotes an active and continuous dialogue with governments, civil society and other interna-

Changing human behaviour

Achieving sustainable development worldwide entails changing patterns of production and consumption — what we produce, how it is produced and how much we consume. Finding ways to do this, particularly in the industrialized countries, was first put on the international agenda at the Earth Summit. Since then, the Commission on Sustainable Development has spearheaded a work programme aimed at challenging the behaviour of individual consumers, households, industrial concerns, businesses and governments. Its actions have included expanding the UN Guidelines for Consumer Protection to include a section on the promotion of sustainable consumption.

In 2002, the World Summit on Sustainable Development reaffirmed the importance of such efforts. It identified changing unsustainable patterns of consumption and production as essential for sustainable development. It expressed a renewed commitment to accelerate change in that direction, with developed countries taking the lead through such measures as the development and implementation of policies; increasing eco-efficiency; promoting cleaner production; increasing awareness; and enhancing corporate responsibility. Discussions on these issues involved business and industry, governments, consumer organizations, international bodies, the academic community and NGOs.

Using fewer resources and wasting less is simply better business. It saves money and generates higher profits. It protects the environment by conserving natural resources and creating less pollution, thus sustaining the planet for the enjoyment and well-being of future generations.

tional organizations aimed at building partnerships to address key issues relating to sustainable development, and to help coordinate environment and development activities within the United Nations.

The **Division for Sustainable Development** of the UN Department of Economic and Social Affairs provides the secretariat for the Commission and monitors progress in the implementation of *Agenda 21*, the *Programme for the Further Implementation of Agenda 21*, and the *Johannesburg Plan of Implementation*. It responds to requests for policy recommendations, and provides technical services for capacity-building in sustainable development. It also provides analytical and information services.

World Summit on Sustainable Development

The World Summit on Sustainable Development was held in Johannesburg, South Africa, from 26 August to 4 September 2002, to take stock of achievements, challenges and new issues arising since the 1992 Earth Summit. It was an "implementation" Summit, designed to turn the goals, promises and commitments of *Agenda 21* into concrete, tangible actions.

The Summit brought together a wide range of interests. Over 22,000 people participated, including 100 heads of state, more than 8,000 representatives from NGOs, business and other major groups, and 4,000 members of the press. At least as many people attended related parallel events.

Member states agreed to the *Johannesburg Declaration on Sustainable Development* and a 54-page *Plan of Implementation* detailing the priorities for action. The Summit reaffirmed sustainable development as a central element of the international agenda and paved the way for the practical, sustained measures needed to address many of the world's most pressing challenges. The concept of sustainable development was broadened and strengthened, particularly with respect to the links between economic and social development and the conservation of natural resources.

Commitments were made on specific time-bound targets and goals, including important new targets relating to basic sanitation, the use and production of chemicals, the maintenance and restoration of fish stocks, and a reduction in the rate of biodiversity loss. New issues were brought into sharper focus, including sustainable production and consumption patterns, energy and mining. The special needs of Africa and the small island developing states were specifically addressed. A unique and important outcome of the Summit was that the internationally agreed commitments were complemented by a range of voluntary partnership initiatives for sustainable development.

Financing sustainable development

At the Earth Summit, it was agreed that most financing for *Agenda 21* would come from within each country's public and private sectors. However, new and additional external funds were deemed necessary to support developing countries' efforts to implement sustainable development practices and protect the global environment.

Launched in 1991 and restructured in 1994, the **Global Environment Facility (GEF)** has twice been entrusted with channelling these funds. In 1994, 34 nations pledged $2 billion to the GEF. In 1998, 36 nations pledged $2.75 billion more. And in 2002, 32 nations pledged nearly $3 billion for the next four years. GEF funds are the primary means by which the goals of the conventions on biological diversity, climate change and persistent organic pollutants are achieved.

GEF projects — principally carried out by UNDP, UNEP and the World Bank — conserve and make sustainable use of biological diversity, address global climate change, reverse the degradation of international waters, phase out substances that deplete the ozone layer, combat land degradation and drought, and reduce and eliminate the production and use of certain persistent organic pollutants.

GEF currently funds close to 1,200 projects in 140 developing nations and countries with economies in transition. It has allocated $4.5 billion and raised another $13 billion in co-financing from recipient governments, international development agencies, private industry and NGOs.

In 1991, a Multilateral Fund was set up to assist developing countries in complying with their obligations under the Montreal Protocol — the international treaty enacted to phase out substances that damage the ozone layer. Since then, the Fund has provided over $1.5 billion worth of assistance to 130 developing countries. Some 4,000 Fund projects, implemented by UNDP, UNEP, UNIDO and the World Bank and a number of bilateral government agencies, have resulted in the phase-out of approximately 180,000 tonnes of ozone-depleting substances.

Action for the environment

The entire United Nations system is engaged in environmental protection in diverse ways. Its lead agency in this area is the **United Nations Environment Programme (UNEP)**. As the environmental conscience of the UN system, UNEP assesses the state of the world's environment and identifies issues requiring international cooperation. It helps formulate international environmental law, and helps integrate environmental considerations in the social and economic policies and programmes of the UN system.

UNEP, with its motto of "Environment for Development", helps solve problems that cannot be handled by countries acting alone. It provides a forum for building consensus and forging international agreements. In doing so, it strives to enhance the participation of business and industry, the scientific and academic communities, NGOs, community groups and others in achieving sustainable development.

One of UNEP's functions is to promote scientific knowledge and information on the environment. Research and synthesis of environmental information, promoted and coordinated at the regional and global levels by UNEP, has generated a variety of reports on the state of the environment. Reports such as the 2002 *Global Environment Outlook* have generated created worldwide awareness of emerging environmental problems. Some reports have triggered international negotiations on environmental conventions.

Through a worldwide network of collaborating and resource centres, including the *Global and Regional Integrated Data* (GRID) network and the *World Conservation and Monitoring Centre*, UNEP facilitates and coordinates the collection and dissemination of the best possible scientific data and information at the global and regional levels. Decision-makers, scientists and members of civil society can also have online access to targeted regional and sectoral environmental data, through the *UNEP.net* system.

UNEP acts to protect oceans and seas and promote the environmentally sound use of marine resources under its *Regional Seas Programme*, which now covers over 140 countries. This programme works towards the protection of shared marine and water resources through 13 conventions or action plans, the most recent one dealing with the north-east Pacific region. Regional conventions and action plans for which UNEP provides the secretariat cover eastern Africa, West and Central Africa, the Mediterranean, the Caribbean, the East Asian seas and the north-west Pacific.

Coastal and marine areas cover some 70 per cent of the earth's surface and are vital to the planet's life-support system. Most pollution comes from industrial wastes, mining, agricultural activities and emissions from motor vehicles, some of which occurs thousands of miles inland. The *Global Programme of Action for the Protection of the Marine Environment from Land-based Activities*, adopted in 1995 under UNEP auspices, is considered a milestone in international efforts to protect oceans, estuaries and coastal waters from pollution caused by human activities on land. The programme, which has a coordination office in The Hague, addresses what might be the most serious threat to the marine environment: the flow of chemicals, pollutants and sewage into the sea.

UNEP's Paris-based **Division of Technology, Industry and Economics** is active in UN efforts aimed at encouraging decision-makers in government, industry and business to adopt policies, strategies and practices that are cleaner and safer, use natural resources more efficiently, and reduce pollution risks to people and the environment. The Division facilitates the transfer of safer, cleaner and environmentally sound technologies, especially those which deal with urban and freshwater management; helps countries to build capacities for the sound management of chemicals and the improvement of chemical safety worldwide; supports the phase-out of ozone-depleting substances in developing countries and countries with economies in transition; assists decision-makers to make better, more informed energy choices which fully integrate environmental and social costs; and works with governments and the private sector to integrate environmental considerations in their activities, practices, products and services.

UNEP Chemicals provides countries with access to information about toxic chemicals; assists countries in building their capacities to produce, use and dispose of chemicals safely; and supports international and regional actions needed to reduce or eliminate chemical risks.

In collaboration with FAO, UNEP facilitated the negotiation of the *Rotterdam Convention on Prior Informed Consent Procedures for Certain Hazardous Chemicals and Pesticides in International Trade* (1998). The Convention gives importing countries the power to decide which chemicals they want to receive and to exclude those they cannot manage safely. UNEP also facilitated the completion, in 2001, of the *Stockholm Convention on Persistent Organic Pollutants* — a legally binding treaty to reduce and eliminate releases of certain chemicals that remain intact in the environment for long periods, become widely distributed geographically, accumulate in the fatty tissue of living organisms and are toxic to humans and wildlife. This include highly toxic pesticides and industrial chemicals and by-products that are highly mobile and accumulate in the food chain.

Over the years, UNEP has been the catalyst for the negotiation of other international agreements that form the cornerstone of UN efforts to halt and reverse damage to the planet. The historic *Montreal Protocol* (1987) and its subsequent amendments seek to preserve the ozone layer in the upper atmosphere. The *Basel*

Convention on the Control of Hazardous Wastes and Their Disposal (1989) has reduced the danger of pollution from toxic waste.

The *Convention on International Trade in Endangered Species* (1973) is universally recognized for its achievements in controlling the trade in wildlife products. UNEP assisted African governments in developing the *Lusaka Agreement on Cooperative Enforcement Operations Directed at Illegal Trade in Wild Fauna and Flora* (1994). The *Convention on Biological Diversity* (1992), and the *Cartagena Protocol on Biosafety* (2000), seek to conserve, and encourage the sustainable and equitable use of the planet's wide variety of plants, animals and micro-organisms, UNEP also helped to negotiate and implement the conventions on desertification and climate change.

Climate change and global warming

There is substantial evidence that human activities contribute to the build-up of "greenhouse gases" in the atmosphere, leading to a gradual rise in global temperatures. In particular, carbon dioxide is produced when fossil fuels are burned to generate energy, or when forests are cut down and burned. According to the Intergovernmental Panel on Climate Change, climate models predict that global temperatures will rise by about 1.4 and 5.8 degrees C (2.5-10.4 F) by 2100. This projected increase is larger than any climate change experienced over the past 10,000 years — with potentially significant impact on the global environment.

To counter global warming, the 1992 *United Nations Framework Convention on Climate Change* was developed and signed in Rio de Janeiro. Under the Convention, developed countries agreed to reduce emissions of carbon dioxide and other greenhouse gases they release into the atmosphere to 1990 levels by 2000. These countries, which together account for 60 per cent of annual carbon dioxide emissions, also agreed to transfer to developing countries technology and information to help them respond to the challenges of climate change. By May 2004, 189 countries had ratified the Convention.

United Nations negotiations on climate change are supported by the work the **Intergovernmental Panel on Climate Change (IPCC)**, which was organized jointly in 1988 by UNEP and WMO. The Panel, a worldwide network of 2,500 leading scientists and experts, reviews scientific research on the issue. In 1989, its finding that human activities could possibly cause changes in the global climate system led to negotiations on the climate change convention. By 2001, with access to new and more powerful computer models, the Panel found that there is "new and stronger evidence that most of the warming observed over the last 50 years is attributable to human activities".

The evidence presented by IPCC scientists in 1995 made it clear that the 1992 target, even if reached on time, would not prevent global warming and its associated problems. Additional reductions would be necessary. In 1997, countries that had ratified the Convention met in Kyoto, Japan, and agreed on a legally binding *Protocol* under which developed countries are to reduce their collective emissions of six green-

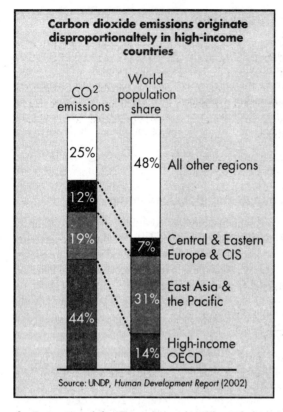

Carbon dioxide emissions originate disproportionaltely in high-income countries

CO² emissions	World population share

25% | 48% All other regions

12% |

19% | 7% Central & Eastern Europe & CIS

| East Asia &
44% | 31% the Pacific

| High-income
| 14% OECD

Source: UNDP, *Human Development Report* (2002)

house gases by 5.2 per cent between 2008 and 2012, taking 1990 levels as the baseline. The Protocol also establishes several innovative "mechanisms" aimed at reducing the costs of curbing emission levels.

Ozone depletion. The ozone layer is a thin layer of gas in the upper atmosphere, about 12 to 45 kilometres above the ground, that shields the earth's surface from the sun's damaging ultraviolet rays. Exposure to increased ultraviolet radiation is known to result in skin cancer, and to cause unpredictable damage to plants, algae, the food chain and the global ecosystem.

UNEP helped to negotiate and now administers the historic *Vienna Convention for the Protection of the Ozone Layer* (1985), and the *Montreal Protocol* (1987) and its amendments. Under these agreements, developed countries have banned the production and sale of chlorofluorocarbons — chemicals that deplete the ozone layer. Developing countries must stop their production by 2010. Schedules are also in place to phase out other ozone-depleting substances.

In 2002, a UNEP–WMO assessment of ozone depletion, prepared by more than 250 scientists from around the world, confirmed the effectiveness of the *Montreal Protocol*. According to the assessment, the combined total of ozone-depleting compounds in the lowest part of the atmosphere peaked in 1994 and is now slowly declining. If measures had not been taken in accordance with the Protocol, the ozone depletion would have been much more serious and would have continued for many more decades. But even though the Protocol is working well to reduce the use and release of ozone-depleting substances, the continuing influence of chemicals already released into the atmosphere means that the ozone depletion will continue for years to come.

Scientists predict that the earth's protective ozone shield will start to recover in the near future and will fully recover by 2050 — *if* the Protocol continues to be vigorously enforced.

Small islands

More than 40 small island developing states and territories share specific disadvantages and vulnerabilities. Their ecological fragility, small size, limited resources and isolation from markets have not allowed them to take advantage of globalization — a major obstacle in their socio-economic development. This makes sustainable development a unique challenge for the island states and the international community at large. Since the 1992 Earth Summit, these states and islands have been considered "a special case both for environment and development".

At the Global Conference on the Sustainable Development of Small Island Developing States (Barbados, 1994), a programme of action was adopted that set forth policies, actions and measures at all levels to promote sustainable development for these states. In 1999, the General Assembly reviewed implementation of that programme, and called for further action in priority areas. In 2005, the international community will again take stock of progress at an international meeting to be held in Mauritius, where it expected to recommend further practical measures.

Sustainable forest management

Since the adoption of a non-binding statement of forest principles at the 1992 Earth Summit, there has been significant progress in international forest policy. Many initiatives have been launched, both within and outside the UN system. From 1995 to 2000, the Intergovernmental Panel on Forests and the Intergovernmental Forum on Forests — under the UN Commission on Sustainable Development — were the main intergovernmental forums for the development of forest policy.

In October 2000, the Economic and Social Council established the **United Nations Forum on Forests**, a high-level intergovernmental body with universal membership. Its mission is to promote the management, conservation and sustainable development of forests and to strengthen long-term political commitment to that end. It meets annually to address issues of priority concern and to review progress in implementing actions proposed by the earlier intergovernmental bodies.

At the invitation of ECOSOC, the heads of relevant international organizations have also formed a 14-member **Collaborative Partnership on Forests**, which fosters increased cooperation and coordination in support of the goals of the UN Forum on Forests and the implementation of sustainable forest management worldwide.

Desertification

One quarter of the earth's land is threatened by desertification, according to UNEP estimates. Over 250 million people are directly affected, and the livelihoods of over 1 billion people in more than 100 countries are jeopardized, as farming and grazing land becomes less productive. Drought can trigger desertification, but human activities —

overcultivation, overgrazing, deforestation and poor irrigation — are usually the main causes.

A United Nations treaty, the *Convention to Combat Desertification in those Countries Experiencing Serious Drought and/or Desertification, Particularly in Africa* (1994), seeks to address this problem. The treaty, to which 186 countries are party, provides the framework for all activity to combat desertification. It focuses on improving land productivity, rehabilitation of land, and the conservation and management of land and water resources. It emphasizes popular participation and an enabling environment for local people to help themselves reverse land degradation. It contains criteria for the preparation by affected countries of national action programmes, and gives an unprecedented role to NGOs in preparing and carrying out action programmes.

Various United Nations agencies provide assistance to combat desertification. UNDP funds activities to combat desertification through the Nairobi-based Drylands Development Centre, which helps develop policies, provides technical advice, and supports desertification control and dryland management programmes. A special IFAD programme has mobilized $400 million, plus another $350 million in co-financing, for projects in 25 African countries threatened by desertification. Similarly, the World Bank organizes and funds programmes aimed at protecting fragile drylands and increasing their agricultural productivity on a sustainable basis, while FAO promotes sustainable agricultural development through a wide range of practical help to governments. UNEP supports regional action programmes, data assessment, capacity-building and public awareness of the problem.

Biodiversity, pollution and overfishing

Biodiversity — the variety of plant and animal species — is essential for human survival. The protection and conservation of the diverse range of species of animal and plant life and their habitats is the aim of the *United Nations Convention on Biological Diversity* (1992), to which 180 states are party. The Convention obligates states to conserve biodiversity, ensure its sustainable development, and provide for the fair and equitable sharing of benefits from the use of genetic resources. A protocol to ensure the safe use of genetically modified organisms was adopted in 2000.

Protection of endangered species is also enforced under the 1973 *Convention on International Trade in Endangered Species*, administered by UNEP. The 162 states parties meet periodically to update the list of which plant and animal species or products, such as ivory, should be protected by quotas or outright bans. The 1979 *Bonn Convention on the Conservation of Migratory Species of Wild Animals*, and a series of associated agreements, aims to conserve terrestrial, marine and avian migratory species and their habitats. At the end of 2003, the treaty had 84 states parties.

Acid rain. Caused by emissions of sulphur dioxide from industrial manufacturing processes, "acid rain" has been significantly reduced in much of Europe and North

America thanks to the 1979 *Convention on Long-Range Transboundary Air Pollution*. The Convention, to which 48 states are party, is administered by the United Nations Economic Commission for Europe.

Hazardous wastes and chemicals. To regulate the 3 million tons of toxic waste that crosses national borders each year, member states negotiated in 1989 the *Basel Convention on the Control of Transboundary Movements of Hazardous Wastes and their Disposal*, administered by UNEP. The treaty, to which 157 states are party, was strengthened in 1995 to ban the export of toxic waste to developing countries, which often do not have the technology for safe disposal. In 1999, governments adopted the *Basel Protocol on Liability and Compensation* to deal with who is financially responsible in the event of the illegal dumping or accidental spills of hazardous wastes.

High-seas fishing. The overfishing and near exhaustion of many species of commercially valuable fish, along with the increasing incidence of illegal, unregulated and unreported fishing on the high seas, led governments to call for measures to conserve and sustainably manage fish resources — especially those which migrate across broad areas of the ocean or move through the economic zone of more than one country. The 1995 *United Nations Agreement on Straddling Fish Stocks and Highly Migratory Fish Stocks*, which entered into force in December 2001, provides a regime for the conservation and management of these stocks, with a view to ensuring their long-term survival.

Protecting the marine environment

The oceans cover two thirds of the earth's surface, and protecting them has become one of the United Nations primary concerns. UNEP's work, particularly its diverse efforts to protect the marine environment, has focused world attention on the oceans and seas. The **International Maritime Organization (IMO)** is the United Nations specialized agency responsible for measures to prevent marine pollution from ships and to improve the safety of international shipping. In spite of the dramatic expansion of world shipping, oil pollution from ships was cut by around 60 per cent during the 1980s, and the number of oil spills during the past two decades has been greatly reduced. This is partly due to the introduction of better methods of controlling the disposal of wastes, and partly to the tightening of controls through conventions.

The pioneer *International Convention for the Prevention of Pollution of the Sea by Oil* was adopted in 1954, and IMO took over responsibility for it in 1959. In the late 1960s, a number of major tanker accidents led to further action. Since then, IMO has developed many measures to prevent accidents at sea and oil spills, to minimize their consequences, and to combat marine pollution — including that caused by the dumping into the seas of wastes generated by land-based activities.

The main treaties are: the *International Convention Relating to Intervention on the High Seas in Cases of Oil Pollution Casualties*, 1969; the *Convention on the Prevention of Marine Pollution by Dumping of Wastes and Other Matters*, 1972; and the *International Convention on Oil Pollution Preparedness, Response and Cooperation*, 1990.

IMO has also tackled the environmental threats caused by routine operations such as the cleaning of oil cargo tanks and the disposal of engine-room wastes — in tonnage terms a bigger menace than accidents. The most important of these measures is the *International Convention for the Prevention of Pollution from Ships, 1973, as modified by its 1978 Protocol* (MARPOL 73/78). It covers not only accidental and operational oil pollution, but also pollution by chemicals, packaged goods, sewage and garbage. Amendments to the Convention adopted in 1992 oblige all new tankers to be fitted with double hulls or a design that provides equivalent cargo protection in the event of a collision or grounding.

Two IMO treaties — the *International Convention on Civil Liability for Oil Pollution Damage* (CLC) and the *International Convention on the Establishment of an International Fund for Oil Pollution Damage* (FUND) — establish a system for providing compensation to those who have suffered financially as a result of pollution. The treaties, adopted in 1969 and 1971 and revised in 1992, enable victims of oil pollution to obtain compensation much more simply and quickly than had been possible before.

Weather, climate and water

From weather prediction to climate-change research and early warnings on natural hazards, the **World Meteorological Organization (WMO)** coordinates global scientific efforts to provide timely and accurate weather information and other services for the user community, including the airline and shipping industries. WMO's activities contribute to the safety of life and property, economic and social development, and the protection of the environment.

Within the United Nations, WMO is the authoritative scientific voice on the earth's atmosphere and climate. The agency facilitates international cooperation in establishing networks of stations for making meteorological, hydrological and other observations. It promotes the rapid exchange of meteorological information, standardization of meteorological observations, and uniform publication of observations and statistics. It also furthers the application of meteorology to aviation, shipping, water problems, agriculture and other weather-sensitive socio-economic activities; promotes operational hydrology; and encourages research and training.

The *World Weather Watch* is the backbone of WMO's activities. It offers up-to-the-minute worldwide weather information through observation systems and telecommunication links operated by member states and territories — with 16 satellites, 3,000 aircraft, 10,000 land observation stations, 7,300 ship stations, and 900 moored and drifting buoys carrying automatic weather stations. Each day, high-speed links transmit data and weather charts through 3 world, 34 regional and 187 national meteorological centres, which cooperate in preparing weather analyses and forecasts. Thus, ships and airplanes, research scientists, the media and the public are given a constant supply of timely weather data.

It is through WMO that the complex agreements on weather standards, codes, measurements and communications are established internationally. A *Tropical Cyclone Programme* helps more than 50 countries vulnerable to cyclones to minimize destruction and loss of life by improving forecasting and warning systems and disaster preparedness. WMO's *Natural Disaster Prevention and Mitigation Programme* ensures the integration of various WMO programme activities in this area and coordinates them with related activities of international, regional and national organizations, including civil defence bodies. It also provides scientific and technical support for WMO's response to disaster situations.

The *World Climate Programme* collects and preserves climate data, helping governments plan for climate change. Such information can improve economic and social planning for and understanding of climate processes. It can also detect and warn governments of impending climate variations (such as the El Niño and La Niña phenomena) and their impact several months ahead — as well as of changes, natural or man-made, which could affect critical human activities. To assess all available information on climate change, WMO and UNEP established in 1988 the Intergovernmental Panel on Climate Change.

The *Atmospheric Research and Environment Programme* coordinates research on the structure and composition of the atmosphere, the physics and chemistry of clouds, weather modification, tropical meteorology, and weather forecasting. It helps member states to conduct research projects, disseminate scientific information, and incorporate the results of research into forecasting and other techniques. Under the *Global Atmosphere Watch*, a global network of some 340 stations in 80 countries monitors the levels of greenhouse gases, ozone, radionuclides and other traces of gases and particles in the atmosphere.

Weather-related agricultural losses may approach 20 per cent of annual production in some countries. The *Applications of Meteorology Programme* helps countries apply meteorology to the protection of life and property and to social and economic development. It seeks to improve public weather services; increase the safety of sea and air travel; reduce the impact of desertification; and improve agriculture and the management of water, energy and other resources. In agriculture, for instance, prompt meteorological advice can mean a substantial reduction in losses caused by droughts, pests and disease.

The *Hydrology and Water Resources Programme* helps to assess, manage and conserve global water resources. It promotes global cooperation in evaluating water resources and in developing hydrological networks and services, including data collection and processing, hydrological forecasting and warning, and the supply of meteorological and hydrological data for design purposes. The programme, for instance, facilitates cooperation with respect to water basins shared between countries, and provides specialized forecasting in flood-prone areas, thus helping to preserve life and property.

WMO's *Space Programme* was created to contribute to the development of the Global Observing System of the *World Weather Watch* programme, as well as to other

WMO-supported programmes and associated observing systems. Its purpose is to provide improved data, products and services continuously, and to facilitate their wider availability and meaningful use worldwide. The *Education and Training Programme* encourages the exchange of scientific knowledge through courses, seminars and conferences, curriculum development, the introduction of new techniques and training materials, and support to training centres. It place several hundred specialists from all over the world in advanced courses each year.

The *Technical Cooperation Programme* helps developing countries obtain technical expertise and equipment to improve their national meteorological and hydrological services. It fosters the transfer of technology, as well as of meteorological and hydrological knowledge and information. The *Regional Programme* supports the implementation of programmes and activities having a regional focus, through eight WMO regional and subregional offices worldwide.

Natural resources and energy

The United Nations has long been assisting countries in managing their natural resources. As early as 1952, the General Assembly declared that developing countries have "the right to determine freely the use of their natural resources" and that they must use such resources towards realizing economic development plans in accordance with their national interests.

An ECOSOC body composed of government-nominated experts, the 24-member **Committee on Energy and Natural Resources for Development** develops guidelines on policies and strategies for ECOSOC and governments in cooperation with the Commission on Sustainable Development. It is divided into two sub-groups of 12 members each. The **Sub-group on Energy** reviews trends and issues in energy development, as well as coordination of UN system activities in the field of energy. The **Sub-group on Water Resources** considers issues relating to the integrated management of land and water resources, as well as the coordination of related UN system activities.

Water resources. The United Nations has long been addressing the global crisis caused by growing demands on the world's water resources to meet human, commercial and agricultural needs. The 1977 United Nations Water Conference, the International Conference on Water and the Environment and the Earth Summit (1992), and the International Drinking Water Supply and Sanitation Decade (1981-1990) all focused on this vital resource. The Decade helped some 1.3 billion people in the developing countries gain access to safe drinking water. The United Nations International Year of Freshwater, 2003, aimed at raising public awareness globally, while the first United Nations *World Water Development Report* (2003) analysed data and trends affecting the world's freshwater resources.

It is estimated that 1.1 billion people do not have sufficient drinking water and 2.4 billion have no access to sanitation. By 2050, at least one in four people is likely to live in a country affected by chronic or recurring shortages of fresh water. Causes of water shortage include inefficient use, degradation of water by pollution, and over-exploitation of groundwater reserves. Action is needed to achieve better management of scarce freshwater resources — with a particular focus on such issues as supply and demand, and quantity and quality.

UN system activities are geared towards the sustainable development of fragile and finite freshwater resources. These resources are under increasing stress from population growth, pollution and the demands of agricultural and industrial uses, which continue to increase. The Department of Economic and Social Affairs has a sizeable programme of technical cooperation in water resources development. The Commission on Sustainable Development has considered ways to increase access to water through market mechanisms, including pricing, while ensuring that poor people can afford water.

Energy. As a driving force for development, energy, in adequate supply, is essential to economic advancement and poverty eradication. However, the environmental and health consequences of the generation and use of conventional energy systems have become a serious concern. Moreover, the increasing demand for energy per capita, coupled with the rising global population, is resulting in consumption levels that cannot be sustained using current energy systems.

While efforts are being made to move towards renewable sources of energy that are significantly less polluting, additional demand still outpaces the introduction of capacity based on renewable energy. Thus, serious efforts are needed to improve energy efficiency and move towards cleaner fossil fuel technologies in the transition towards sustainable development. Although global energy consumption is projected to double by 2060, special efforts will be needed for this to benefit the 2 billion people, mostly in rural areas of developing countries, who currently lack access to modern commercial energy services.

The UN system is active in a broad range of activities to assist developing countries in the field of energy — ranging from education, training and capacity-building, to assistance on policy reforms and the provision of energy services. These activities focus on meeting energy needs within the context of sustainable development.

Technical cooperation. The United Nations maintains an active programme of technical cooperation in the field of water, minerals, energy and relating to small island developing states. Technical cooperation assistance and advisory services relating to water and mineral resources emphasize environmental protection, investment promotion, legislation and sustainable development. Technical cooperation relating to energy deals with access to energy, energy sector reform, energy efficiency, renewable energy, rural energy, cleaner fossil fuel technologies and energy for transportation.

During the past two decades, hundreds of technical cooperation and pre-investment projects in water, minerals and energy involving hundreds of millions of dollars have been implemented by the United Nations and its family of organizations. Complementary resources have been provided by recipient governments in the form of national staff, facilities and local operating costs. As a result, each year hundreds of field projects assist developing countries in the sustainable development of their natural resources, through projects which strengthen national capacity and stimulate further investment.

Nuclear safety

Today, 441 nuclear power reactors produce almost 16 per cent of the world's electricity. In nine countries, over 40 per cent of energy production comes from nuclear power. The **International Atomic Energy Agency (IAEA)**, an international organization in the United Nations family, fosters the development of the safe, secure and peaceful uses of atomic energy, and plays a prominent role in international efforts aimed at ensuring the use of nuclear technology for sustainable development. In the current debate on energy options to curb carbon dioxide emissions which contribute to global warming, IAEA has stressed the benefits of nuclear power as an energy source free of greenhouse and other toxic gas emissions.

IAEA serves as the world's central intergovernmental forum for scientific and technical cooperation in the nuclear field. It is a focal point for the exchange of information and the formulation of guidelines and norms in the area of nuclear safety, as well as for the provision of advice to governments, at their request, on ways to improve the safety of reactors and avoid the risk of accidents.

The Agency's responsibility in the area of nuclear safety has increased as nuclear-power programmes have grown and public attention has focused on safety aspects. IAEA formulates basic standards for radiation protection and issues regulations and codes of practice on specific types of operations — including the safe transport of radioactive materials. It facilitates emergency assistance to member states in the event of a radiation accident, under the *Convention on Assistance in the Case of a Nuclear Accident or Radiological Emergency* (1986) and the *Convention on Early Notification of a Nuclear Accident* (1986). Other international treaties for which IAEA is the depositary include the *Convention on Physical Protection of Nuclear Material* (1987), the *Vienna Convention on Civil Liability for Nuclear Damage* (1963), the *Convention on Nuclear Safety* (1994), and the *Joint Convention on the Safety of Spent Fuel Management and on the Safety of Radioactive Waste Management* (1997).

The IAEA's technical cooperation programme provides assistance in the form of in-country projects, experts, and training in the application of peaceful nuclear techniques, which help countries in such critical areas as water, health, nutrition, medicine and food production. Examples include work related to mutation breeding, through which nearly 2,000 new beneficial varieties of crops have been developed using radiation-based technology — thereby improving food production. Another example is the use of isotope hydrology to map underground aquifers, manage ground and surface waters, detect and control pollution, and monitor dam leakage and safety — thus improving access to safe drinking water. Still another example concerns medical treatment, in which the Agency supplies radiotherapy equipment and trains staff to safely treat cancer patients in some 80 developing countries which are IAEA members.

The IAEA collects and disseminates information on virtually every aspect of nuclear science and technology through its *International Nuclear Information System* (INIS) in Vienna. With UNESCO, it operates the International Centre for Theoretical Physics in Trieste, Italy, and maintains three laboratories. IAEA works with FAO in research on atomic energy in food and agriculture, and with WHO on radiation in medicine and biology. Its Marine Environment Laboratory in Monaco carries out worldwide marine pollution studies with UNEP and UNESCO.

The **United Nations Scientific Committee on the Effects of Atomic Radiation (UNSCEAR),** a separate body established in 1955, assesses and reports on the levels and effects of exposure to ionizing radiation. Governments and organizations worldwide rely on its estimates as the scientific basis for evaluating radiation risk, establishing radiation protection and safety standards, and regulating radiation sources.

Chapter 4
Human Rights

One of the great achievements of the United Nations is the creation of a comprehensive body of human rights law — a universal and internationally protected code to which all nations can subscribe and to which all people can aspire. The Organization has defined a broad range of internationally accepted rights, including economic, social and cultural rights and political and civil rights. It has also established mechanisms to promote and protect these rights and to assist governments in carrying out their responsibilities.

The foundations of this body of law are the United Nations Charter and the Universal Declaration of Human Rights, adopted by the General Assembly in 1945 and 1948, respectively. Since then, the United Nations has gradually expanded human rights law to encompass specific standards for women, children, persons with disabilities, minorities, migrant workers and other vulnerable groups, who now possess rights that protect them from discriminatory practices that had long been common in many societies.

Rights have been extended through ground-breaking General Assembly decisions that have gradually established their universality, indivisibility and interrelatedness with development and democracy. Education campaigns have informed the world's public of their inalienable rights, while numerous national judicial and penal systems have been enhanced through UN training programmes and technical advice. The United Nations machinery to monitor compliance with human rights treaties has acquired a remarkable cohesiveness and weight among member states.

The United Nations High Commissioner for Human Rights works to strengthen and coordinate United Nations efforts for the protection and promotion of all human rights of all persons around the world. The Secretary-General has made human rights the central theme that unifies the Organization's work in the key areas of peace and security, development, humanitarian assistance, and economic and social affairs. Virtually every United Nations body and specialized agency is involved to some degree in the protection of human rights.

Human rights instruments

At the San Francisco Conference in 1945 at which the United Nations was established, some 40 non-governmental organizations (NGOs) representing women, trade unions, ethnic organizations and religious groups joined forces with government delegations, mostly from smaller countries, and pressed for more specific language on human rights than had been proposed by other states. Their determined lobbying resulted in the inclusion of some provisions on human rights in the **United Nations Charter,** laying the foundation for the post-1945 era of international law-making.

Thus, the Preamble to the Charter explicitly reaffirms "faith in fundamental human rights, in the dignity and worth of the human person, in the equal rights of men and women and of nations large and small". Article 1 establishes that one of the four principal tasks of the United Nations is to promote and encourage "respect for human rights and for fundamental freedoms for all without distinction as to race, sex, language, or religion". Other provisions commit states to take action in cooperation with the UN to achieve universal respect for human rights.

International Bill of Human Rights

Three years after the United Nations was created, the General Assembly laid the cornerstone of contemporary human rights law: the **Universal Declaration of Human Rights**, intended as a "common standard of achievement for all peoples". It was adopted on 10 December 1948, the day now observed worldwide as **International Human Rights Day**. Its 30 articles spell out basic civil, cultural, economic, political and social rights that all human beings in every country should enjoy (*see box*).

The provisions of the Universal Declaration are considered by many scholars to have the weight of customary international law because they are so widely accepted and used to measure the conduct of states. Many newly independent countries have cited the Universal Declaration or included its provisions in their basic laws or constitutions.

The broadest legally binding human rights agreements negotiated under United Nations auspices are the International Covenant on Economic, Social and Cultural Rights, and the International Covenant on Civil and Political Rights. These agreements, adopted by the General Assembly in 1966, take the provisions of the Universal Declaration a step further by translating these rights into legally binding commitments, while committees monitor the compliance of states parties.

The Universal Declaration, together with the two International Covenants on Human Rights and the Optional Protocols to the International Covenant on Civil and Political Rights, comprise the **International Bill of Human Rights**.

Economic, social and cultural rights

The **International Covenant on Economic, Social and Cultural Rights** entered into force in 1976, and has 148 states parties. The human rights that the Covenant seeks to promote and protect include:

- The right to work in just and favourable conditions.

- The right to social protection, to an adequate standard of living and to the highest attainable standards of physical and mental well-being.

- The right to education and the enjoyment of benefits of cultural freedom and scientific progress.

Defining universal rights

The Universal Declaration of Human Rights is the cornerstone of the wide-ranging body of human rights law created over the decades.

Its Articles 1 and 2 state that "all human beings are born equal in dignity and rights" and are entitled to all the rights and freedoms set forth in the Declaration "without distinction of any kind such as race, colour, sex, language, religion, political or other opinion, national or social origin, property, birth or other status".

Articles 3 to 21 set forth the civil and political rights to which all human beings are entitled, including:

- The right to life, liberty and security.
- Freedom from slavery and servitude.
- Freedom from torture or cruel, inhuman or degrading treatment or punishment.
- The right to recognition as a person before the law; the right to judicial remedy; freedom from arbitrary arrest, detention or exile; the right to a fair trial and public hearing by an independent and impartial tribunal; the right to be presumed innocent until proved guilty.
- Freedom from arbitrary interference with privacy, family, home or correspondence; freedom from attacks upon honour and reputation; the right to protection of the law against such attacks.
- Freedom of movement; the right to seek asylum; the right to a nationality.
- The right to marry and to found a family; the right to own property.
- Freedom of thought, conscience and religion; freedom of opinion and expression.
- The right to peaceful assembly and association.
- The right to take part in government and to equal access to public service.

Articles 22 to 27 set forth the economic, social and cultural rights to which all human beings are entitled, including:

- The right to social security.
- The right to work; the right to equal pay for equal work; the right to form and join trade unions.
- The right to rest and leisure.
- The right to a standard of living adequate for health and well-being.
- The right to education.
- The right to participate in the cultural life of the community.

Finally, Articles 28 to 30 recognize that everyone is entitled to a social and international order in which the human rights set forth in the Declaration may be fully realized; that these rights may only be limited for the sole purpose of securing recognition and respect of the rights and freedoms of others and of meeting the requirements of morality, public order and the general welfare in a democratic society; and that each person has duties to the community in which she or he lives.

The Covenant provides for the realization of these rights without discrimination of any kind. In 1985, the **Committee on Economic, Social and Cultural Rights** was established by the Economic and Social Council (ECOSOC) to monitor implementation of the Covenant by states parties. This 18-member body of experts studies reports submitted under special procedures and discusses them with representatives of the governments concerned. The Committee makes recommendations to states based on its review of their reports. It also adopts general comments which seek to outline the meaning of human rights or cross-cutting themes, and the steps required by states parties to implement the Covenant's provisions.

Civil and political rights

The *International Covenant on Civil and Political Rights* and its *First Optional Protocol* entered into force in 1976. The Covenant has 151 states parties; the Protocol, 104.

- The Covenant deals with such rights as freedom of movement; equality before the law; the right to a fair trial and presumption of innocence; freedom of thought, conscience and religion; freedom of opinion and expression; peaceful assembly; freedom of association; participation in public affairs and elections; and protection of minority rights.

- It prohibits arbitrary deprivation of life; torture, cruel or degrading treatment or punishment; slavery and forced labour; arbitrary arrest or detention; arbitrary interference with privacy; war propaganda; and advocacy of racial or religious hatred.

The Covenant has two protocols. The *First Optional Protocol* (1966), a procedural instrument, provides the right of petition to individuals who comply with admissibility criteria. The *Second Optional Protocol* (1989) establishes substantive obligations towards abolition of the death penalty and has 50 states parties.

The Covenant established an 18-member **Human Rights Committee**, which considers reports submitted periodically by states parties on measures taken to implement the Covenant's provisions. For states parties to the *First Optional Protocol*, the Committee also considers communications from individuals who claim to be victims of violations of any of the rights set forth in the Covenant. The Committee considers such communications in closed meetings; all related and documents remain confidential. The findings of the Committee, however, are made public and are reproduced in its annual report to the General Assembly.

Other conventions

The Universal Declaration has served as the inspiration for some 80 conventions and declarations that have been concluded within the United Nations on a wide range of issues. Seven of the conventions are monitored for compliance by states parties. When states become party to these treaties, they agree to have their human rights legislation and practices reviewed by independent expert bodies:

- The *Convention on the Prevention and Punishment of the Crime of Genocide* (1948), a direct response to the atrocities of the Second World War, defines the crime of genocide as the commission of certain acts with intent to destroy a national, ethnic, racial or religious group, and commits states to bringing to justice alleged perpetrators. It has 135 states parties.

- The *Convention Relating to the Status of Refugees* (1951) defines the rights of refugees, especially their right not to be forcibly returned to countries where they are at risk, and makes provisions for various aspects of their everyday lives, including their right to work, education, public assistance and social security, and their right to travel documents. It has 142 states parties. The *Protocol relating to the Status of Refugees* (1967) ensures the universal application of the Convention, which was originally designed for refugees from the Second World War. The Protocol has 141 states parties. A total of 145 states have acceded to one or both of these instruments.

- The *International Convention on the Elimination of All Forms of Racial Discrimination* (1966) is accepted by 169 states parties. Beginning with the premise that any policy of superiority based on racial differences is unjustifiable, scientifically false and morally and legally condemnable, it defines "racial discrimination" and commits states parties to take measures to abolish it in both law and practice. The Convention established a monitoring body, the **Committee on the Elimination of Racial Discrimination**, to consider reports from states parties — as well as petitions from individuals alleging a violation of the Convention, if the state concerned has accepted this optional procedure of the Convention.

- The *Convention on the Elimination of All Forms of Discrimination against Women* (1979), with 175 states parties, guarantees women's equality before the law and specifies measures to eliminate discrimination against women with respect to political and public life, nationality, education, employment, health, marriage and the family. The Convention established the **Committee on the Elimination of Discrimination against Women** as the body to monitor its implementation and consider reports from states parties. The *Optional Protocol to the Convention* (1999), with 59 states parties, allows individuals to submit to the Committee complaints on violations of the Convention.

- The *Convention against Torture and Other Inhuman or Degrading Treatment or Punishment* (1984), with 134 states parties, defines torture as an international crime, holds states parties accountable for preventing it and requires them to punish the perpetrators. No exceptional circumstances may be invoked to justify torture, nor may a torturer offer a defence of having acted under orders.

The monitoring body set up by the Convention, the **Committee against Torture**, reviews reports of states parties, may receive and consider petitions from individuals whose states have accepted this procedure, and can initiate investigations regarding countries where it believes the practice of torture is serious and systematic.

- The *Convention on the Rights of the Child* (1989) recognizes the particular vulnerability of children and brings together in one comprehensive code protections for children in all categories of human rights. The Convention guarantees non-discrimination and recognizes that the best interests of the child must guide all actions. Special attention is paid to children who are refugees, disabled or members of minorities. States parties are to provide guarantees for children's survival, development, protection and participation. The Convention is the most broadly ratified treaty, with 192 states parties. The **Committee on the Rights of the Child**, established by the Convention, oversees its implementation and considers reports submitted by states parties.

- The *International Convention on the Protection of the Rights of All Migrant Workers and Members of Their Families* (1990) defines basic rights and principles as well as measures to protect migrant workers, whether legal or illegal, throughout the process of migration. The Convention, which entered into force on 1 July 2003, has 24 states parties. The first meeting of its monitoring body, the **Committee on Migrant Workers**, was held in March 2004.

The Universal Declaration and other United Nations instruments have also formed part of the background to several regional agreements, such as the European *Convention on Human Rights*, the *American Convention on Human Rights* and the *African Charter of Human and Peoples' Rights*.

Other standards

In addition, the United Nations has adopted many other standards and rules on the protection of human rights. These "declarations", "codes of conduct" and "principles" are not treaties to which states become party. Nevertheless, they have a profound influence, not least because they are carefully drafted by states and adopted by consensus. Among the most important of these:

- The *Declaration on the Elimination of All Forms of Intolerance and of Discrimination Based on Religion and Belief* (1981) affirms the right of everyone to freedom of thought, conscience and religion and the right not to be subject to discrimination on the grounds of religion or other beliefs.

- The *Declaration on the Right to Development* (1986) established that right as "an inalienable human right by virtue of which each person and all peoples are entitled to participate in, contribute to and enjoy economic, social, cultural and political development in which all human rights and fundamental freedoms can be fully realized". It adds that "equality of opportunity for development is a prerogative both of nations and of individuals".

- The *Declaration on the Rights of Persons Belonging to National or Ethnic, Religious and Linguistic Minorities* (1992) proclaims the right of minorities to enjoy their own culture; to profess and practise their own religion; to use their own language; and to leave any country, including their own, and to return to their country. The Declaration calls for action by states to promote and protect these rights.

- The *Declaration on Human Rights Defenders* (1998) seeks to recognize, promote and protect the work of human rights activists all over the world. It enshrines the right of everyone, individually and in association with others, to promote and strive to protect human rights at the national and international levels, and to participate in peaceful activities against human right violations. States are to take all necessary measures to protect human rights defenders against any violence, threats, retaliation, pressure or other arbitrary action.

Other important non-treaty standards include the *Standard Minimum Rules for the Treatment of Prisoners* (1957), the *Basic Principles on the Independence of the Judiciary* (1985), the *Body of Principles for the Protection of All Persons under Any Form of Detention or Imprisonment* (1988) and the *Declaration on the Protection of All Persons from Enforced Disappearance* (1992).

Human rights machinery

Commission on Human Rights

The major United Nations body working to promote and protect human rights is the **Commission on Human Rights**, which was established in 1946. The Commission provides overall policy guidance, studies human rights problems, develops new international norms, and monitors the observance of human rights around the world. As the principal intergovernmental policy-making body for human rights at the United Nations, the Commission is authorized to discuss human rights situations anywhere in the world and to examine information from states, NGOs and other sources.

The Commission provides a forum for states, intergovernmental organizations and NGOs to voice their concerns about human rights issues. Made up of 53 member states elected for three-year terms, the Commission meets for six weeks each year in Geneva. States and NGOs present information on situations of concern to them, and the governments involved often submit replies. In response, the Commission may designate experts or fact-finding groups, organize on-the-spot visits, pursue discussions with governments, provide assistance, and condemn violations it has uncovered.

If a particular situation is deemed sufficiently serious, the Commission may order an investigation by either a group of independent experts (working group) or an indi-

Special rapporteurs and working groups

The special rapporteurs and working groups on human rights are on the front lines in the protection of human rights. They investigate violations and intervene in individual cases and emergency situations, in what are referred to as "special procedures". Human rights experts are independent. They serve in their personal capacity for a maximum of six years and are not remunerated. The number of such experts has grown steadily over the years. There are currently over such 30 special procedure mandates.

In preparing their reports to the Commission on Human Rights and the General Assembly, these experts use all reliable resources, including individual complaints and information from NGOs. They may also activate "urgent-action procedures", to intercede with governments at the highest level. A significant portion of their research is done in the field, where they meet both with authorities and victims, and gather on-site evidence. Their reports are made public, thus helping to publicize violations and to emphasize the responsibility of governments for the protection of human rights.

These experts examine, monitor and publicly report on human rights situations in specific countries, or on major human rights violations worldwide.

- **Country-specific special rapporteurs, independent experts and representatives** — currently report on Afghanistan, Burundi, Cambodia, Cuba, the Democratic Republic of the Congo, Haiti, Iraq, Liberia, Myanmar, the occupied Palestinian territories and Somalia. In addition, the Secretary-General has been mandated to prepare reports on Cyprus, East Timor, Kosovo and the occupied Arab territories.

- **Thematic special rapporteurs, representatives and working groups** — currently report on enforced or involuntary disappearances, summary executions, torture, arbitrary detention, racial discrimination, violence against women, the sale of children, religious intolerance, internally displaced persons, migrants, human rights defenders, freedom of expression, independence of the judiciary, restitution and compensation of victims, mercenaries, structural adjustment and foreign debt, extreme poverty, adverse effects of the illicit movement and dumping of toxic and dangerous products and wastes, and the rights to development, education, food, housing and health.

vidual (special rapporteur or representative). Based on information received from these experts, the Commission then calls upon the government concerned to bring about needed changes.

In 1947, the Commission on Human Rights established the **Subcommission on the Promotion and Protection of Human Rights** (formerly the Subcommission on Prevention of Discrimination and Protection of Minorities). Meeting annually, it consists of 26 experts who serve in their personal capacity, not as representatives of their government. Originally dedicated to the issues of discrimination and minority protection, the Subcommission has over the years greatly expanded its scope to cover a broad range of human rights issues. It has initiated many studies, particularly on the development of legal rules, and makes recommendations to the Commission. NGOs also take part in its work.

The Subcommission's three major working groups deal with indigenous populations, contemporary forms of slavery, and minorities.

UN High Commissioner for Human Rights

The **United Nations High Commissioner for Human Rights** is the official with principal responsibility for UN human rights activities. Appointed for a four-year term, the High Commissioner is charged with many tasks, including: promoting and protecting the effective enjoyment by all of all human rights; promoting international cooperation for human rights; stimulating and coordinating action on human rights in the UN system; assisting in the development of new human rights standards; and promoting the ratification of human rights treaties. The High Commissioner is also mandated to respond to serious violations of human rights and to undertake preventive action.

On 25 February 2004, the General Assembly approved the appointment of Louise Arbour of Canada as the latest UN High Commissioner for Human Rights. Ms. Arbour was the Chief Prosecutor of the UN International Criminal Tribunals for the former Yugoslavia and for Rwanda from October 1996 to September 1999 — a period of intense activity for both courts. Her four-year term as High Commissioner began on 1 July, following her retirement from Supreme Court of Canada in June. Her predecessor, Mr. Sergio Vieira de Mello (Brazil), was killed in the 19 August 2003 attack on UN headquarters in Baghdad, where he was on assignment as head of the UN mission in Iraq. In the interim, Mr. Bertrand Ramcharan (Guyana) served as Acting High Commissioner.

Under the direction and authority of the Secretary-General, the High Commissioner reports to the Commission on Human Rights, and through ECOSOC to the General Assembly. With the aim of securing respect for human rights and preventing violations, the High Commissioner engages in dialogue with governments. Within the UN system, the High Commissioner works to strengthen and streamline the United Nations human rights machinery to make it more efficient and effective.

The **Office of the High Commissioner for Human Rights (OHCHR)** is the focal point for United Nations human rights activities. It serves as the secretariat for the Commission on Human Rights, the treaty bodies (expert committees that monitor treaty compliance) and other UN human rights organs. It also undertakes human rights field activities, and provides advisory services and technical assistance. In addition to its regular budget, some of the Office's activities are financed through extrabudgetary resources.

World Conference on Human Rights

The Second World Conference on Human Rights (Vienna, 1993) reaffirmed the universality and central role of human rights.

The Conference revealed tensions around many issues — such as national sovereignty, universality, the role of NGOs, and the question of impartiality and non-selectivity in the application of international human rights standards. In the *Vienna Declaration and Programme of Action*, 171 states proclaimed that human rights had become the "legitimate concern of the international community" and that "all human rights are universal, indivisible, interdependent and interrelated".

The Declaration states that "while the significance of national and regional particularities and various historical, cultural and religious backgrounds must be borne in mind, it is the duty of states, regardless of their political, economic and cultural systems, to promote and protect all human rights and fundamental freedoms."

"Democracy, development and respect for human rights and fundamental freedoms are interdependent and mutually reinforcing", the Declaration states. It thus reaffirms both the universal right to development and the inextricable relationship between development and human rights.

The High Commissioner has taken specific steps to institutionalize cooperation and coordination with other UN bodies involved in human rights, such as the United Nations Children's Fund (UNICEF), the United Nations Educational, Scientific and Cultural Organization (UNESCO), the United Nations Development Programme (UNDP), the Office of the United Nations High Commissioner for Refugees (UNHCR) and the United Nations Volunteers (UNV). Similarly, the Office works in the area of peace and security in close cooperation with the departments of the United Nations Secretariat. The Office is also part of the Inter-agency Standing Committee, which oversees the international response to humanitarian emergencies.

Education and information. For the United Nations, education is a fundamental human right and one of the most effective instruments for the promotion of human rights. Human rights education, whether in formal or non-formal settings, seeks to advance a universal culture of human rights through innovative teaching methods, the spreading of knowledge and the modification of attitudes.

The **United Nations Decade for Human Rights Education (1995-2004)** seeks to increase global awareness and foster a universal culture of human rights. It has already led some 40 countries to promote human rights education, among other things by including it in their school curriculums. Various countries have adopted national action plans and involved national institutions in this effort.

A key source of human rights information is the OHCHR website (*www.unhchr.ch*).

Promoting and protecting human rights

The role and scope of UN action in promoting and protecting human rights continue to expand. Its central mandate is to ensure full respect for the human dignity of the "peoples of the United Nations", in whose name the Charter was written. Through its international machinery, the United Nations is at work on many fronts:

- **As global conscience** — The United Nations has set the pace in establishing international standards of acceptable behaviour by nations. It has kept the world's attention focused on practices that threaten to undermine human rights standards. And the General Assembly, through a wide range of declarations and conventions, has underscore the universality of human rights principles.

- **As lawmaker** — The United Nations has given impetus to an unprecedented codification of international law. Human rights pertaining to women, children, prisoners, detainees and mentally disabled persons, as well as to such violations as genocide, racial discrimination and torture, are now a major feature of international law, which once focused almost exclusively on inter-state relations.

- **As monitor** — The United Nations plays a central role in ensuring that human rights are not only defined but also protected. The International Covenants on Civil and Political Rights and on Economic, Social and Cultural Rights (1966) are among the earliest examples of treaties that empower international bodies to monitor how states live up to their commitments. Treaty bodies, special rapporteurs and working groups of the Commission on Human Rights each have procedures and mechanisms to monitor compliance with international standards and to investigate alleged violations. Their decisions on specific cases carry a moral weight that few governments are willing to defy.

- **As nerve centre** — OHCHR receives communications from groups and individuals claiming violations of their human rights. More than 100,000 complaints are received every year. OHCHR refers these communications to the appropriate UN bodies and mechanisms, taking into account the implementation procedures established by conventions and resolutions. Requests for urgent intervention can be addressed to OHCHR by fax (41-22-917-9022) and e-mail (*tb-petitions@ohchr.org*).

- **As defender** — When a rapporteur or the chairman of a working group learns that a serious human rights violation, such as torture or imminent extrajudicial execution, is about to occur, he or she addresses an urgent message to the state concerned, requesting clarification and seeking guarantees that the alleged victim's rights will be protected.

- **As researcher** — The United Nations compiles data that is indispensable to the development and application of human rights law. For example, several country studies provided the basis for an instrument that is being drafted to protect the rights of indigenous peoples. Studies and reports prepared by OHCHR at the request of UN bodies point the way towards new policies, practices and institutions to enhance respect for human rights.

- **As forum of appeal** — Under the First Optional Protocol to the International Covenant on Civil and Political Rights, as well as the International Convention on the Elimination of All Forms of Racial Discrimination, the Convention Against Torture and the Optional Protocol to the Convention on the Elimination of All Forms of Discrimination against Women, individuals can bring complaints against states that have accepted the relevant appeal procedure, once all domestic remedies have been exhausted. In addition, the Commission on Human Rights hears numerous complaints annually, submitted by NGOs or individuals.

- **As fact-finder** — The Commission on Human Rights has established mechanisms to monitor and report on the incidence of certain kinds of abuses, as well as on violations in a specific country. The special rapporteurs or representatives and working groups are entrusted with this politically sensitive, humanitarian and sometimes dangerous task. They gather facts, keep contact with local groups and government authorities, conduct on-site visits when governments permit, and make recommendations on how respect for human rights might be strengthened.

- **As discreet diplomat** — The Secretary-General and the UN High Commissioner for Human Rights raise human rights concerns with member states on a confidential basis, on such issues as the release of prisoners and the commutation of death sentences. The Commission on Human Rights may ask the Secretary-General to intervene or send an expert to examine a specific human rights situation, with a view to preventing flagrant violations. The Secretary-General may also undertake quiet diplomacy in the exercise of his "good offices", to communicate the United Nations legitimate concern and curb abuses.

Right to development

The principle of equality of opportunity for development is deeply embedded in the United Nations Charter and the Universal Declaration on Human Rights. The *Declaration on the Right to Development*, adopted by the General Assembly in 1986, marked a turning point, by proclaiming this as an inalienable human right, by which each person and all peoples are entitled to participate in, contribute to and enjoy economic, social, cultural and political development.

The right to development is given prominence in the 1993 Vienna declaration of the Second World Conference on Human Rights, and is cited in the outcomes of other major UN summits and conferences as well, including the Millennium Declaration. In 1998, the Commission on Human Rights established a dual mechanism to address this issue, namely: a working group to monitor progress, analyse

Technical cooperation programme

Since human rights are best protected when they are rooted in the local culture, the United Nations has increased its efforts to promote and protect these rights at the national and local level. International human rights norms cannot be applied unless they are incorporated in national legislation and supported by national institutions.

Many obstacles at the national level still hinder the universal enjoyment of human rights. Various member states do not have the infrastructure that would allow them to effectively promote and protect the rights of their citizens. This is particularly true of countries that are just recovering from deadly civil wars or emerging from humanitarian crises.

The United Nations has therefore strengthened its advisory services to governments and expanded its technical cooperation programmes — in the wider framework of promoting democracy, development and human rights, and of strengthening the capacity of states to advance such rights in their laws and practice.

The Programme of Technical Cooperation for Human Rights, supervised by the Office of the High Commissioner, manages some 50 projects annually in some 30 countries. They are carried out mainly in developing countries and countries in transition towards democracy. The programme, with an annual budget of some $9 million, is mainly financed by voluntary contributions, which totalled $7.6 million in 2002.

The programme reflects national development objectives and UN-coordinated assistance in support of those objectives. It encourages ratification and supports implementation of the international human rights instruments. The focus is on four core areas: the administration of justice; human rights education; national institutions; and national plans of action. Special attention is paid to such issues as economic, social and cultural rights; the right to development; racism; the rights of indigenous people; trafficking of women and children; gender and the human rights of women; and the rights of the child.

As OHCHR does not have the capacity to be present in all countries, it has developed regional strategies through which intergovernmental cooperation is fostered, experience is shared, and common policies and programmes can be developed. OHCHR regional representations serve as resource centres responding to country-level demands.

In addition to national and regional projects, the Office supports implementation of the Secretary-General's United Nations reform programme, which identifies human rights as a cross-cutting element of UN system activities. OHCHR supports this integration of human rights standards and is actively engaged in capacity building. It supports a human rights approach to assessments and planning, as well as to the development of policy and methodology.

obstacles and develop strategies for implementing the right to development; and an independent expert on the right to development, who reports on the current state of progress in implementing the right to development.

The rights of labour

The **International Labour Organization (ILO)** is the UN specialized agency entrusted with defining and protecting the rights of labour. Its tripartite **International Labour Conference** — made up of government, employer and worker representatives — has adopted some 185 conventions and 194 conventions on all aspects of work life, comprising a system of international labour standards. While its recommendations provide guidance on policy, legislation and practice, its conventions create binding obligations for those states which ratify them.

Conventions and recommendations have been adopted on such matters as labour administration, industrial relations, employment policy, working conditions, social security, occupational safety and health. Some seek to ensure basic human rights in the workplace, while others address such issues as the employment of women and children, and such special categories as migrant workers and the disabled.

ILO's supervisory procedure to ensure that its conventions are applied both in law and in practice is based on objective evaluations by independent experts, and on the examination of cases by the ILO's tripartite bodies. There is a also special procedure for investigating complaints of infringement of the freedom of association.

The ILO has brought about many landmark conventions:

- *On forced labour* (1930) — requires the suppression of forced or compulsory labour in all its forms.

- *On freedom of association and protection of the right to organize* (1948) — establishes the right of workers and employers to form and join organizations without prior authorization, and lays down guarantees for the free functioning of such organizations.

- *On the right to organize and collective bargaining* (1949) — provides for protection against anti-union discrimination, for protection of workers' and employers' organizations, and for measures to promote collective bargaining.

- *On equal remuneration* (1951) — calls for equal pay and benefits for work of equal value.

- *On discrimination* (1958) — calls for national policies to promote equality of opportunity and treatment, and to eliminate discrimination in the workplace on grounds of race, colour, sex, religion, political opinion, extraction or social origin.

- *On minimum age* (1973) — aims at the abolition of child labour, stipulating that the minimum age for employment shall not be less than the age of completion of compulsory schooling.

- *On the worst forms of child labour* (1999) — prohibits child slavery, debt bondage, prostitution and pornography, dangerous work, and forcible recruitment for armed conflict.

The General Assembly has also taken a number of measures to protect the rights of migrant workers.

The struggle against discrimination

Apartheid

One of the great successes that demonstrated the ways in which the United Nations can bring an end to major injustices in the world is its role in the abolition of South Africa's apartheid rule. Practically from its inception, the United Nations was involved in the struggle against apartheid, a system of institutionalized racial segregation and discrimination imposed by the South African government.

When, in 1994, the newly elected President of South Africa, Nelson Mandela, addressed the General Assembly, he observed that it was the first time in its 49 years that the Assembly had been addressed by a South African head of state drawn from among the African majority. Welcoming the vanquishing of apartheid, he said: "That historic change has come about not least because of the great efforts in which the United Nations engaged to ensure the suppression of the apartheid crime against humanity."

Condemned by the United Nations in 1966 as a "crime against humanity" incompatible with the Charter and the Universal Declaration of Human Rights, apartheid remained on the General Assembly's agenda from 1948 until its demise in 1994:

- During the 1950s, the General Assembly repeatedly appealed to the South African government to abandon apartheid in the light of the principles of the Charter.

- In 1962, it established the United Nations **Special Committee against Apartheid**, to keep the racial policies of South Africa. The Special Committee became the focal point of international efforts to promote a comprehensive programme of action against apartheid.

- In 1963, the Security Council instituted a voluntary arms embargo against South Africa.

- The General Assembly refused to accept South Africa's credentials to its regular sessions from 1970 through 1974. Following this ban, South Africa did not participate in further proceedings of the Assembly until the end of apartheid in 1994.

- In 1971, the General Assembly called for a sports boycott of South Africa, a move which had continuing impact on public opinion within the country and abroad.

- In 1973, the Assembly adopted the *International Convention on the Suppression and Punishment of the Crime of Apartheid.*

- In 1977, the Security Council made its arms embargo against South Africa mandatory, after determining that the country's aggressions against its neighbours and its potential nuclear capability constituted a threat to international peace and security. This was the first such action by the Council against a member state.

- In 1985, the General Assembly adopted the *International Convention Against Apartheid in Sports.*

- Also in 1985, when the South African government proclaimed a state of emergency and escalated repression, the Security Council, for the first time, called on governments to take significant economic measures against South Africa under Chapter VII of the Charter.

The transition from the apartheid government to a non-racial democracy was facilitated by a 1990 national peace accord between the government and major political parties, with the full support of the United Nations. Two Security Council resolutions in 1992 emphasized the involvement of the international community in facilitating that transition.

To strengthen the structures of the peace accord, the Security Council in 1992 deployed the **United Nations Observer Mission in South Africa (UNOMSA)**, which observed the 1994 elections that led to the establishment of a non-racial and democratic government. With the installation of a new government and adoption of the country's first non-racial, democratic constitution, apartheid had come to an end.

Racism

In 1963, the General Assembly adopted the *United Nations Declaration on the Elimination of All Forms of Racial Discrimination.* The Declaration affirms the fundamental equality of all persons and confirms that discrimination between human beings on the grounds of race, colour or ethnic origin is a violation of the human rights proclaimed in the Universal Declaration and an obstacle to friendly and peaceful relations among nations and peoples.

Two years later, the General Assembly adopted the *International Convention on the Elimination of All Forms of Racial Discrimination,* which obliges states parties to adopt legislative, judicial, administrative and other measures to prevent and punish racial discrimination.

In 1993, the General Assembly proclaimed the **Third Decade to Combat Racism and Racial Discrimination (1993-2003)** and called on all states to take measures to combat new forms of racism, especially through laws, administrative measures, education and information.

Also in 1993, the Commission on Human Rights appointed a special rapporteur on contemporary forms of racism, racial discrimination, xenophobia and related intolerance. The special rapporteur's mandate is to examine incidents of contemporary forms of racism worldwide; racial discrimination; any form of discrimination against blacks, Arabs and Muslims; xenophobia; anti-Semitism; and related expressions of intolerance, as well as governmental measures to overcome them.

As decided by the General Assembly, the third **World Conference against Racism, Racial Discrimination, Xenophobia and Related Intolerance** was held in South Africa in 2001. It focused on practical measures to eradicate racism, including measures of prevention, education and protection, and adopted the Durban declaration and programme of action. Previous such conferences had been held in Geneva in 1978 and 1983.

The rights of women

Equality for women has been a focus of the work of the United Nations since its founding in 1945. The Organization has played a leading role in the global struggle for the promotion and protection of women's human rights, and in efforts to ensure that women have equal access to public life and to opportunities in all aspects of economic and social development.

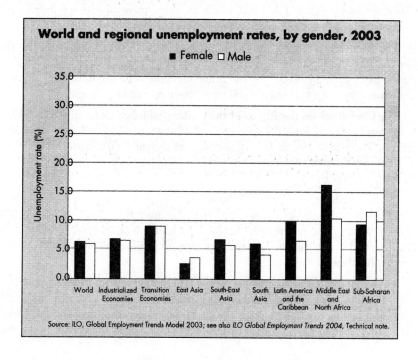

World and regional unemployment rates, by gender, 2003

■ Female □ Male

Source: ILO, Global Employment Trends Model 2003; see also ILO *Global Employment Trends 2004*, Technical note.

The **Commission on the Status of Women** has elaborated international guidelines and law for women's equality and non-discrimination — notably, the 1979 *Convention on the Elimination of Discrimination against Women* and the 1999 Optional Protocol to the Convention. It also prepared the *Declaration on the Elimination of All Forms of Violence against Women*, adopted by the General Assembly in 1993, which includes a clear definition of violence as being physical, sexual or psychological violence occurring in the family or the community and perpetrated or condoned by the state.

The **Committee on the Elimination of Discrimination against Women**, a body made up of 23 independent experts and serviced by the United Nations Secretariat's Division for the Advancement of Women, monitors implementation of the Convention, by such means as examining individual communications and carrying out enquiries under the provisions of the Optional Protocol. (On women's rights, see *www.un.org/womenwatch*)

The rights of children

Millions of children die every year from malnutrition and disease. Countless others become victims of war and extreme forms of exploitation and abuse, such as sexual exploitation. The **United Nations Children's Fund** (UNICEF), the only UN agency mandated to advocate for children's rights, strives to sustain global commitment to the *Convention on the Rights of the Child*, which embodies universal ethical principles and international legal standards of behaviour towards children.

The General Assembly in 2000 adopted two Optional Protocols to the Convention: one prohibits the recruitment of children under 18 into armed forces or their participation in hostilities; the other strengthens prohibitions and penalties concerning the sale of children, child prostitution and child pornography.

The **Committee on the Rights of the Child**, established under the Convention, meets regularly to monitor the progress made by states parties in fulfilling their obligations. The Committee makes suggestions and recommendations to governments and to the General Assembly on ways in which children's rights under the Convention may be met.

On child labour, the United Nations seeks to protect working children from exploitation and hazardous conditions that endanger their physical and mental development; to ensure children's access to at least minimum levels of education, nutrition and health care; and, in the long term, to achieve the progressive elimination of child labour.

- The International Programme on the Elimination of Child Labour, an initiative of the **International Labour Organization (ILO),** seeks to raise awareness and mobilize action through the provision of technical cooperation. Direct interventions focus on the prevention of child labour; the search for alternatives, including decent employment for parents; and rehabilitation, education and vocational training for children.

- UNICEF supports programmes providing education, counselling and care to children working in very hazardous conditions — whether as sex slaves or even as domestic workers — and vigorously advocates against the violation of their rights.

- The General Assembly has urged governments to take action on the problem of street children, who are increasingly involved in and affected by crime, drug abuse, violence and prostitution.

- The Subcommission on the Promotion and Protection of Human rights has called for steps to halt the recruitment or conscription of children into armed forces. The Secretary-General's special representative for children and armed conflict works to enhance child protection during conflicts.

- The Commission on Human Rights has appointed a special rapporteur on the sale of children, child prostitution and child pornography.

The rights of minorities

Almost one billion people worldwide are estimated to belong to minorities. It has been well documented that many minorities are often the subject of discrimination and exclusion, as well as victims of violent conflict.

A well-defined interest has emerged in meeting the legitimate aspirations of national, ethnic, religious and linguistic groups, not only in protecting and accommodating cultural diversity, but also as a means of strengthening the stability of society.

The United Nations has from its inception placed minority rights high on its human rights agenda. The protection of the human rights of members of minorities is guaranteed specifically in article 27 of the International Covenant on Civil and Political Rights, as well as in the principles of non-discrimination and participation, which are basic to all United Nations human rights law.

The adoption of the *Declaration on the Rights of Persons Belonging to National or Ethnic, Religious and Linguistic Minorities* by the General Assembly in 1992 gave new impetus to the United Nations human rights agenda. In 1995, the Commission on Human Rights approved the establishment by its Subcommission of a working group on minorities — the only such forum to which minority representatives have access. It seeks to reach out to minority communities so they can raise their voices in a United Nations meeting and have their concerns heard — and even make suggestions for remedying their situation. The working group is mandated to offer solutions for minority problems, recommending practical measures to improve the promotion and protection of minority rights.

Indigenous peoples

The United Nations has increasingly taken up the cause of indigenous peoples, who are considered one of the world's most disadvantaged groups. Indigenous peoples are also called first peoples, tribal peoples, aboriginals and autochthons. There are at least 5,000 indigenous groups, made up of 300 million people, living in over 70 countries on five continents. Excluded from decision-making processes, many have been marginalized, exploited, forcefully assimilated and subjected to repression, torture and murder when they speak out in defence of their rights. Fearing persecution, they often become refugees and sometimes must hide their identity, abandoning their languages and traditional customs.

In 1982, the Subcommission of the Commission on Human Rights established a working group on indigenous populations, which reviews developments pertaining to the rights of indigenous peoples and promotes international standards concerning their rights. It also prepared a draft *Declaration on the Rights of Indigenous Peoples* for eventual adoption by the General Assembly, which is now being considered by the Commission.

In 2000, ECOSOC established the **Permanent Forum on Indigenous Issues** as a subsidiary organ. This 16-expert forum, composed of an equal number of governmental and indigenous experts, will advise ECOSOC; help to coordinate United Nations activities; and discuss indigenous concerns relating to development, culture, the environment, health and human rights. The Forum held its first session in May 2002.

The 1992 Earth Summit heard the collective voice of indigenous peoples as they expressed their concerns about the deteriorating state of their lands and environment. UNDP, UNICEF, IFAD, UNESCO, the World Bank and WHO all have programmes directed at specific indigenous groups, working to improve health and literacy and to combat environmental degradation of their native lands.

At the conclusion of the International Year of the World's Indigenous People (1993), the General Assembly proclaimed the **International Decade of the World's Indigenous People (1995-2004)**, which aims at fostering partnerships to improve the living conditions of those peoples.

Persons with disabilities

More than 600 million persons — approximately 10 per cent of the world's population, of whom some 80 per cent live in the developing world — suffer from some type of physical, mental or sensory impairment.

Persons with disabilities are often excluded from the mainstream of society. Discrimination takes various forms, ranging from the denial of education opportunities to more subtle forms, such as segregation and isolation through the imposition of physical and social barriers. Society also suffers, since the loss of their enormous potential impoverishes humankind. Changing the perception and concept of disability requires changing values and increasing understanding at all levels of society.

Since its inception, the United Nations has sought to advance the status of persons with disabilities and to improve their lives. United Nations concern for the well-being and rights of persons with disabilities is rooted in its founding principles of human rights, fundamental freedoms and equality of all human beings.

In the 1970s, the concept of human rights for persons with disabilities gained wider international acceptance. Through its adoption of the *Declaration on the Rights of Mentally Retarded Persons* (1971) and the *Declaration on the Rights of Disabled Persons* (1975), the General Assembly established the standards for equal treatment and equal access to services, thus accelerating the social integration of disabled persons.

The **International Year of Disabled Persons** (1981) led to the adoption by the General Assembly of the *World Programme of Action Concerning Disabled Persons*, a policy framework for promoting the rights of persons with disabilities. The programme identifies two goals for international cooperation: equality of opportunity; and full participation of persons with disabilities in social life and development.

A major outcome of the **United Nations Decade of Disabled Persons** (1983-1992) was the adoption by the General Assembly in 1993 of the *Standard Rules on the Equalization of Opportunities for Persons with Disabilities*, which serve as an instrument for policy-making and as a basis for technical and economic cooperation.

A new set of standards for the protection of people with mental illness — the *Principles for the protection of persons with mental illness and the improvement of health care* — was adopted by the Assembly in 1991.

In 1994, the General Assembly endorsed a long-term strategy to further the implementation of the *World Programme of Action*, with the goal of "a society for all". In 1997, it set forth accessibility, employment, social services and social safety nets as the priority policy issues.

In 2003, the Assembly decided to begin drafting a "Comprehensive and Integral International Convention on Protection and Promotion of the Rights and Dignity of Persons with Disabilities", as part of its efforts to fulfil the goal of the full participation and equality of persons with disabilities in social life and development.

United Nations activities. A growing body of data suggests the need to address disability issues in the context of national development, within the broad framework of human rights. The United Nations works with governments, NGOs, academic institutions and professional societies to promote awareness and build national capacities for broad human rights approaches to persons with disabilities.

Growing public support for disability action has focused on the need to improve information services, outreach and institutional mechanisms to promote equal opportunity. The UN has been increasingly involved in helping countries strengthen their national capacities to promote such action in their overall development plans. (For further information, see *www.un.org/esa/socdev/disabled* and *www.unhchr.ch/disability/index.htm*)

Migrant workers

With increasing movement of people across international frontiers in search of work, a new human rights convention was approved to curb discrimination against migrant workers. In 1990, following 10 years of negotiations, the *International Convention on the Protection of the Rights of All Migrant Workers and Members of Their Families* was adopted by the General Assembly. The Convention:

- covers the rights of both documented and undocumented migrant workers and their families;

- makes it illegal to expel migrant workers on a collective basis or to destroy their identity documents, work permits or passports;

- entitles migrant workers to receive the same remuneration, social benefits and medical care as nationals; to join or take part in trade unions; and, upon ending their employment, to transfer earnings, savings and personal belongings;

- grants children of migrant workers the right to registration of birth and nationality, as well as access to education.

The Convention entered into force on 1 July 2003. The **Committee on Migrant Workers**, established to monitor its implementation by states parties, held its first session in March 2004.

Administration of justice

The United Nations is committed to strengthening the protection of human rights in the judicial process. When individuals are under investigation by state authorities, when they are arrested, detained, charged, tried or imprisoned, there is always a need to ensure that the law is applied with due regard for the protection of human rights.

The United Nations has worked to develop standards and codes that serve as models for national legislation. They cover such issues as the treatment of prisoners, the protection of detained juveniles, the use of firearms by police, the conduct of law-enforcement officials, the role of lawyers and prosecutors, and the independence of the judiciary. Many of these standards have been developed through the United Nations Commission on Crime Prevention and Criminal Justice and the Centre for International Crime Prevention.

The OHCHR has a programme of technical assistance that focuses on human rights training for legislators, judges, lawyers, law enforcement officers, prison officials and the military.

Future priorities

Despite the efforts of the United Nations, there continue to be massive and widespread violations of human rights worldwide. Five decades after the adoption of the Universal

Declaration of Human Rights, violations across the broad spectrum of human rights continue to dominate the news. At least part of this can be attributed to the heightened awareness of human rights and the stepped-up monitoring of problem areas. These include, in particular, child abuse, violence against women, and abuses that until only recently were considered acceptable behaviour by traditional standards.

Indeed, measures to promote and protect human rights are stronger than ever, and are increasingly linked to the fight for social justice, economic development and democracy. In his reform programme for the United Nations, Secretary-General Kofi Annan declared that human rights would be the cross-cutting theme in all its policies and programmes. And so they are. The vigorous actions taken by the UN High Commissioner for Human Rights, together with the enhanced cooperation and coordination among UN partners, are tangible expressions of the strengthened ability of the United Nations system to fight for human rights.

Chapter 5
Humanitarian Action

HUMANITARIAN ACTION

Since it first coordinated humanitarian relief operations in Europe following the devastation and massive displacement of people in the Second World War, the United Nations has been relied upon by the international community to respond to natural and man-made disasters that are beyond the capacity of national authorities alone. Today, the Organization is a major provider of emergency relief and longer-term assistance, a catalyst for action by governments and relief agencies, and an advocate on behalf of people struck by emergencies.

Conflicts and natural disasters continue to drive civilians from their homes. During 2002, some 5.8 million people were displaced within their own countries and another 14.8 million people had become refugees by fleeing across international borders.

Natural disasters, mostly weather-related, killed roughly 50,000 people and caused economic losses exceeding $60 billion in 2003. UNDP reports that 94 per cent of natural disasters are caused by cyclones, floods, earthquakes and drought. Heat waves and forest fires have also taken a toll in human suffering. And according to a report issued by UNDP in February 2004,* an overwhelming 98.2 per cent of those killed as a result of natural disasters live in developing countries — a striking indicator of how poverty, population pressures and environmental degradation exacerbate suffering and destruction.

Confronted with renewed conflict and the escalating human and financial costs of natural disasters, the United Nations has been engaged on two fronts. On one hand, it has sought to bring immediate relief to the victims, primarily through its operational agencies; on the other hand, it has sought more effective strategies to prevent emergencies from arising in the first place.

When disaster strikes, the United Nations and its agencies rush to deliver humanitarian assistance. In 2002 alone, the Office for the Coordination of Humanitarian Affairs launched 24 inter-agency appeals that raised more than $4.2 billion to assist 35 million people in 18 countries and regions. For example, the Office of the United Nations High Commissioner for Refugees has been providing international protection and assistance to more than 20 million people annually — refugees as well as a growing number of internally displaced persons. In 2003, the UN World Food Programme fed 110 million people, including most of the world's refugees and internally displaced persons (IDPs).

Disaster prevention seeks to reduce the vulnerability of societies to disaster and to address their man-made causes. Early warning is especially important for short-term prevention, and United Nations agencies are increasing their capacity in this area.

---

* "Reducing Disaster Risks: A Challenge for Development", UNDP Bureau for Crisis Prevention and Recovery, 2004.

The Food and Agriculture Organization monitors impending famines, while the World Meteorological Organization carries out tropical cyclone forecasting and drought monitoring. Preparedness is equally vital, and the United Nations Development Programme assists disaster-prone countries in developing contingency planning and other preparedness measures.

Conflict prevention involves strategies such as preventive diplomacy, preventive disarmament and the promotion of human rights. Recent crises have illustrated dramatically the link between war, human rights abuses and refugee flows. Longer-term prevention strategies address the root causes of conflict in a comprehensive manner, fostering security, economic growth, good governance and respect for human rights. These remain the best protection against disaster, whether natural or, as is increasingly the case, man-made.

Coordinating humanitarian action

The past decade has seen an upsurge in the number and intensity of civil wars. These have caused large-scale humanitarian crises — with extensive loss of life, massive displacements of people and widespread damage to societies, in complicated political and military environments. To address these "complex emergencies", the United Nations has upgraded its capacity to respond quickly and effectively.

In 1991, the General Assembly established an inter-agency standing committee to coordinate the international response to humanitarian crises. The **United Nations Emergency Relief Coordinator** is the Organization's focal point for this endeavour, acting as the system's principal policy adviser, coordinator and advocate on humanitarian emergencies. The Emergency Relief Coordinator heads the **Office for the Coordination of Humanitarian Affairs (OCHA)**, which coordinates United Nations assistance in humanitarian crises that go beyond the capacity and mandate of any single agency.

Many actors — including governments, non-governmental organizations (NGOs) and United Nations agencies — seek to respond simultaneously to complex emergencies. OCHA works with them to ensure that there is a coherent framework within which everyone can contribute promptly and effectively to the overall effort.

When an emergency strikes, OCHA coordinates the international response. It consults with the relevant United Nations country team and undertakes inter-agency consultations at Headquarters to reach agreement on the priorities for action. OCHA then provides support for the coordination of activities in the affected country.

Specifically, the Office coordinates field missions by United Nations agencies to assess needs; helps mobilize resources by launching consolidated inter-agency appeals; organizes donor meetings and follow-up arrangements; monitors the status of contributions in response to its appeals; and issues situation reports to keep donors and others updated on developments. Inter-agency appeals have raised over $14 billion for emergencies since 1992.

Responding to emergencies and disasters requires rapid deployment of resources — human, financial and logistical. OCHA has developed mechanisms to make that possible.

A 24-hour disaster response system provides round-the-clock readiness for disasters. It monitors field situations to identify natural disasters, environmental emergencies and industrial accidents, to help coordinate the actions of the international community.

United Nations disaster assessment and coordination teams permit rapid response to complex emergencies. Made up of specially trained national emergency management experts, as well as OCHA staff, the teams can be deployed within hours to help authorities assess the situation and coordinate relief.

When disaster occurs, OCHA coordinates the mobilization and deployment of military and civil protection assets — such as specialized personnel and disaster-relief equipment — from countries and international organizations. OCHA maintains a central register of disaster management capacities that may be available for international assistance. A warehouse in Brindisi, Italy, stocks relief items ready for airlift.

In many disaster-prone developing countries, United Nations disaster management teams have been established, consisting of country-level heads of UN agencies under the leadership of a resident coordinator, usually from UNDP. Such teams make arrangements to coordinate relief activities in anticipation of an emergency.

In collaboration with international agencies and NGOs, the United Nations has helped launch programmes aimed at improving disaster preparedness in more than 70 countries.

OCHA works with its partners in the humanitarian community to build consensus around policies and to identify specific humanitarian issues arising from operational experiences in the field. It tries to ensure that major humanitarian issues are addressed, including those that fall between the mandates of existing humanitarian bodies — such as the plight of internally displaced persons.

By advocating on humanitarian issues, OCHA gives voice to the silent victims of crises, and ensures that the views and concerns of the humanitarian community are reflected in overall efforts towards recovery and peace-building. OCHA promotes greater respect for humanitarian norms and principles, and draws attention to such specific issues as access to affected populations, the humanitarian impact of sanctions, anti-personnel landmines, and the unchecked proliferation of small arms.

OCHA's **Central Emergency Revolving Fund** is a cash-flow mechanism that facilitates an immediate response to an emergency. It is used to help humanitarian agencies with cash-flow problems until donor contributions become available. The

Coordinating emergency relief

The Inter-Agency Standing Committee brings together all major humanitarian agencies, both within and outside the United Nations. Chaired by the United Nations Emergency Relief Coordinator, it oversees the international response to emergencies. Its participants are:

- United Nations High Commissioner for Refugees — provides humanitarian assistance to refugees and displaced persons (programme budget in 2003: $1.15 billion).

- World Food Programme — provides food aid to victims of emergencies (budget for 2003: $4.3 billion).

- United Nations Children's Fund — focuses on assistance to children and women (humanitarian assistance expenditures: $243.3 million in 2002).

- Food and Agriculture Organization of the United Nations — helps to re-establish agricultural production (budget for 2004-2005: $749 million).

- World Health Organization — provides assistance in the area of health (humanitarian assistance budget for 2004-2005: $71.4 million).

- United Nations Development Programme — provides funds for assistance and coordinates humanitarian aid in countries in crisis.

- United Nations Population Fund — supports reproductive health projects in crisis situations.

- World Bank — supports projects for emergency recovery assistance and post-conflict reconstruction.

- Office of the UN High Commissioner for Human Rights, which fosters the protection of human rights through legal expertise and field presence.

- Major intergovernmental humanitarian organizations — the International Organization for Migration, the International Committee of the Red Cross, the International Federation of Red Cross and Red Crescent Societies.

- The Secretary-General's representative on internally displaced persons.

- Three international consortia of non-governmental organizations: InterAction, the International Council of Voluntary Agencies, and the Steering Committee for Humanitarian Response.

Other agencies may be invited on an ad hoc basis.

borrowing agency must reimburse the amount loaned within one year. Since 1992, the Fund has been used more than 160 times, disbursing over $288 million.

OCHA also manages ReliefWeb, the world's foremost humanitarian website — providing the latest information on emergencies worldwide (see *www.reliefweb.int*).

Providing assistance and protection

Four United Nations entities —UNICEF, UNDP, WFP and UNHCR — have primary roles in providing protection and assistance in humanitarian crises.

Children and women constitute the majority of refugees and displaced persons. In acute emergencies, the **United Nations Children's Fund (UNICEF)** works alongside other relief agencies to help re-establish basic services such as water and sanitation, set up schools, and provide immunization services, medicines and other supplies to uprooted populations.

UNICEF also consistently urges governments and warring parties to act more effectively to protect children. Its programmes in conflict zones have included the negotiation of ceasefires to facilitate the provision of such services as child immunization. To this end, UNICEF has pioneered the concept of "children as zones of peace" and created "days of tranquillity" and "corridors of peace" in war-affected regions. Special programmes assist traumatized children and help reunite unaccompanied children with parents or extended families. In 2002, UNICEF provided humanitarian assistance in 51 countries.

The **United Nations Development Programme (UNDP)** is the agency responsible for coordinating activities for natural disaster mitigation, prevention and preparedness. When emergencies occur, UNDP resident coordinators oversee relief and rehabilitation efforts at the national level. Governments frequently call on UNDP to help design rehabilitation programmes and direct donor aid.

UNDP and humanitarian agencies work together to integrate concern for long-term development in their relief operations. UNDP also supports programmes for the demobilization of former combatants, comprehensive mine action, the return and reintegration of refugees and internally displaced persons, and the restoration of the institutions of governance.

To ensure that the resources provided will have the greatest possible impact, each project is carried out in consultation with local and national government officials. UNDP offers rapid assistance to whole communities, while helping to establish the social and economic foundations for durable peace, development and the alleviation of poverty. This community-based approach has helped provide urgent and lasting relief for hundreds of thousands of victims of war and civil upheaval. Today, many conflict-scarred communities have improved their living standards thanks to training programmes, credit schemes and infrastructure projects.

In emergencies, the **World Food Programme (WFP)** provides fast, efficient relief to millions of people who are victims of natural or man-made disasters, including most of the world's refugees and internally displaced persons. Such crises consume most of WFP's resources. A decade ago, two out of three tons of food aid provided by WFP was used to help people become self-reliant. Today, the picture is reversed, with nearly 80 per cent of WFP resources going to victims of humanitarian crises.

Protecting children in war

In over 30 countries, more than 300,000 young persons under 18 are ruthlessly exploited as soldiers — some as young as seven or eight, girls as well as boys. Two million children have been killed in war and civil strife during the past decade, and 6 million have been maimed or disabled. Many others, orphaned by war or separated from their parents, have been traumatized by the struggle for survival.

To tackle this tragedy, the Security Council has called for stronger efforts to end the use of children as soldiers and to protect children in armed conflict. Peacekeeping operations now include the protection of children in their mandate, and several peacekeeping missions — such as in Sierra Leone, the Democratic Republic of the Congo and Côte d'Ivoire — include civilian specialists on the protection of children.

The Secretary-General's special representative for children and armed conflict, Mr. Olara Otunnu, has been working since 1997 to increase global awareness of the impact of conflict on children, and to mobilize the political support of governments and civil society to strengthen their protection. He has been a key advocate for such measures as the strengthening of monitoring and reporting mechanisms on violations of children's rights in armed conflict; placing the welfare of children on peace agendas; and putting children's needs at the centre of post-conflict recovery programmes.

Travelling to war zones, Mr. Otunnu has sought and obtained important commitments from governments and insurgents for the protection and well-being of children in conflict and post-conflict situations. In addition, UNICEF has long worked with governments and rebel movements to demobilize child soldiers, reunite them with their families and foster their social reintegration.

Through short- and long-term emergency operations in 2002, WFP assisted 58 million people, including IDPs, refugees, children orphaned by AIDS, and victims of such natural disasters as floods and drought. The agency is responsible for mobilizing food and funds for all large-scale refugee-feeding operations managed by UNHCR.

WFP is increasingly involved in projects using food aid to support the demobilization of ex-combatants and demining of war zones. After war or disaster strikes, WFP moves in with reconstruction and rehabilitation projects aimed at repairing the damaged infrastructure.

The majority of those affected by disasters live in rural areas. The **Food and Agriculture Organization of the United Nations (FAO)** works with WFP in providing early warning of impending food crises and in assessing food supply problems worldwide.

FAO's *Global Information and Early Warning System* provides regular and updated information on the global food situation. It also carries out assessments of the food situation in food-insecure countries resulting from man-made or natural disasters.

Children in war — legal norms and standards

A framework of norms and standards for the protection of children during conflict has evolved over the years. It includes:

- The Rome Statute of the International Criminal Court — classifies conscription, enlistment or use in hostilities of children under 15 as a war crime.

- The Optional Protocol to the Convention on the Rights of the Child — sets an age limit of 18 years for compulsory recruitment and direct participation in hostilities, and requires states parties to raise the minimum age for voluntary recruitment to at least 16.

- Four Security Council resolutions — 1261 (1999), 1314 (2000), 1379 (2001) and 1460 (2003) — on the protection of children during conflict.

- ILO Convention 182 — defines child soldiering as one of the worst forms of child labour and sets 18 as the minimum age for forced or compulsory recruitment.

- The Geneva Conventions and their Additional Protocols — stipulate that children shall be the object of special respect and shall be protected against any form of assault during conflict, and that they should be provided "with the care and aid they require".

Other international instruments providing for the protection of children are the Ottawa Convention on the Prohibition of the Stockpiling, Production and Transfer of Anti-Personnel Land Mines and on their Destruction, and the African Charter on the Rights and Well-being of the Child — the first regional treaty establishing 18 as the minimum age for all recruitment and participation in hostilities.

Based on assessments made in collaboration with WFP, emergency food aid operations are prepared and jointly approved with FAO, which provides agricultural inputs for rehabilitating food production and gives technical advice in agricultural emergencies. Its special relief operations service provides considerable support to disaster-stricken farmers.

The assistance programmes of the **World Health Organization (WHO)** focus on assessing the health needs of those affected by emergencies and disasters, providing health information and assisting in coordination and planning. WHO carries out emergency programmes in such areas as nutritional and epidemiological surveillance, control of epidemics (including HIV/AIDS), immunizations, management of essential drugs and medical supplies, reproductive health and mental health. WHO makes special efforts to eradicate polio and to control tuberculosis and malaria in countries affected by emergencies.

Protecting UN staff and humanitarian workers

Attacks against United Nations personnel and other humanitarian workers have increased dramatically in the past few years, with scores of staff members killed, taken hostage or detained while working in conflict areas. Violent incidents against UN staff have included armed robbery, assault and rape.

Since 1992, 196 civilian staff have lost their lives as a result of malicious acts and another 18 died in aircraft accidents in the line of duty. Some 240 have been taken hostage or kidnapped while serving in United Nations operations worldwide. There are also 34 outstanding cases of persons arrested, under detention or missing, some dating back over 20 years, in which the UN has been unable to exercise fully its right to protection.

In the year ended 30 June 2003 alone (the cut-off date for these figures), there were five malicious deaths, more than 258 assaults on United Nations and NGO personnel, and some 270 violent attacks against their compounds and convoys. There were at least 83 incursions into UN compounds, more than 550 incidents of theft at official UN sites and staff residences, and 168 incidents of harassment. UN staff are also frequently the targets of street crime, because of the dangerous environments in which they work.

"The safety and security of United Nations personnel continues to be threatened on an alarmingly frequent basis", the Secretary-General reported in September 2003. "Due to their heightened visibility as representatives of the international community, United Nations personnel are placed at substantial risk of being targeted by many diverse entities and individuals."

This was strikingly brought home on 19 August 2003, when the UN headquarters in Baghdad suffered a devastating bomb attack which left 22 dead and over 150 persons injured. It was the most deliberate and devastating attack on civilian staff of the United Nations in its 58-year history. Among those killed was Sergio Vieira de Mello, the UN High Commissioner for Human Rights, who was on assignment as head of the UN mission in Iraq.

The 1994 Convention on the Safety of United Nations and Associated Personnel obliges the governments of countries where the UN is at work to safeguard its staff, and to take preventive measures against murders and abductions. Unfortunately, of the 196 malicious deaths reported above, only 24 perpetrators have been apprehended. Very few countries have investigated fully attacks or threats against international and locally recruited UN and associated staff, or held perpetrators accountable.

Please note that the figures cited above relate only to civilian staff and do not include the 1,934 UN peacekeepers killed since 1948 — including 68 in the first six months of 2004.

International protection and assistance to refugees

At the end of 2003, the Office of the **United Nations High Commissioner for Refugees (UNHCR)** was providing international protection and assistance to some 17.1 million people who had fled war or persecution. A year earlier, it was providing support to some 20.6 million — of whom 10.4 million were refugees, 5.8 million were internally displaced persons, 2.4 million were returnees, 1 million were asylum-seekers, and 951,000 were stateless persons and others of concern to the agency. As the nature of war has changed in the past few decades, with more and more internal conflicts replacing inter-state wars, the number of internally displaced persons has increased significantly, and they are now the second largest group of concern to UNHCR.

UNHCR has been one of the lead humanitarian agencies for some of the major emergencies in post-war history — in the Balkans, which produced the largest refugee flows in Europe since the Second World War; in the aftermath of the Gulf War; in Africa's Great Lakes region; in the massive exoduses in Kosovo and East Timor, and, more recently, West Africa; and in the repatriation operation in Afghanistan.

Refugees are defined as those who have fled their countries because of a well-founded fear of persecution because of their race, religion, nationality, political opinion or membership in a particular social group, and who cannot or do not want to return.

The legal status of refugees is defined in two international treaties, the 1951 *Convention relating to the Status of Refugees* and its 1967 *Protocol*, which spell out their rights and obligations. At the end of 2003, 145 states were party to one or both treaties.

UNHCR's most important function is international protection — trying to ensure respect for refugees' basic human rights, including their ability to seek asylum, and to ensure that no one is returned involuntarily to a country where he or she has reason to fear persecution. Other types of assistance include:

- help during major emergencies involving the movement of large numbers of refugees;
- regular programmes in such fields as education, health and shelter;
- assistance to promote the self-sufficiency of refugees and their integration in host countries;
- voluntary repatriation;
- resettlement in third countries for refugees who cannot return to their homes and who face protection problems in the country where they first sought asylum.

Although UNHCR's mandate is to protect and assist refugees, it has been called upon more and more to come to the aid of a wider range of people living in refugee-like situations. These include people displaced within their own countries; former refugees who may need UNHCR monitoring and assistance once they have returned

261

Refugees in their own country

Internally displaced persons (IDPs) are those who have been forced to flee their homes to escape war, generalized violence, human rights violations or natural and man-made disasters, but who have not crossed an international border. Civil wars have created large groups of such persons all over the world. Today, there are an estimated 20 to 25 million of them — more than the number of refugees.

Refugees usually find in a second country a place of safety, food and shelter. They are protected by a well-defined body of international laws and conventions, and are assisted by UNHCR and other organizations. But the internally displaced often face far more insecure conditions. They may be trapped in an ongoing internal conflict at the mercy of warring parties, making the provision of relief hazardous or impossible.

Primary responsibility for internally displaced persons lies with national governments. Sometimes, however, governments are unable — or unwilling — to meet that responsibility. The government, which retains ultimate control over their fate, may view them as "enemies of the state". There are no specific international conventions to protect such persons, and until recently, donors have been reluctant to intervene in internal conflicts to help them.

Yet the needs of internally displaced persons are similar to those of refugees. Both need immediate protection and assistance, as well as long-term solutions, such as return or resettlement.

Effective coordination is particularly important in assisting the internally displaced, since there is no single international lead agency to address their needs. Work in this area is carried out jointly by the International Committee of the Red Cross, UNHCR, OCHA, the Secretary-General's representative for internally displaced persons, and the Office of the United Nations High Commissioner for Human Rights.

The Secretary-General's representative, Mr. Francis M. Deng, has issued guiding principles on the internally displaced — defining who they are; outlining a large body of international law protecting a person's basic rights; and setting out the responsibility of states. These principles have been accepted by an every-greater number of states.

UNHCR has been called on to assist an estimated 5.8 million internally displaced persons in various regions. Increasingly — in the former Yugoslavia, Timor-Leste, Colombia, Chechnya and, more recently, Afghanistan — UNHCR has decided to assist all uprooted persons on the basis of humanitarian need rather than refugee status.

Notwithstanding these efforts, many internally displaced persons remain without humanitarian assistance or protection — underlining the selective, uneven and, in many cases, inadequate response of national authorities and the international community. Efforts continue to find more effective ways to help these persons.

People in flight
Number of people of concern to UNHCR*

Total:	17.1 million
By region:	
Africa	4.3 million
Asia	6.2 million
Europe	4.3 million
Latin America and Caribbean	1.3 million
North America	962 thousand
Oceania	74 thousand

Some 4 million Palestinians, who are assisted by UNRWA, are not included. However, Palestinians outside the UNRWA area of operations, such as those in Iraq or Libya, are of concern to UNHCR. At the end of 2002, their number was 428,700.

* Includes refugees, asylum-seekers, returnees, internally displaced persons and others of concern as of 1 January 2004. Source: UNHCR

home; stateless persons; and those who receive temporary protection outside their home countries but do not receive the full legal status of refugees. Today, refugees comprise just over half of the people of concern to UNHCR.

Asylum-seekers are persons who have left their countries of origin and have applied for recognition as refugees in other countries, and whose applications are still pending. UNHCR is currently assisting 1 million people in this category. The largest groups of asylum-seekers are living in industrialized countries.

Most refugees want to return home as soon as circumstances permit. At the end of 2002, UNHCR was assisting some 2.4 million returnees. During the year, it helped some 3.6 million refugees and other groups to return home. These included nearly 2 million Afghans from neighbouring Pakistan and Iran, and a further 750,000 civilians who had been uprooted within Afghanistan. There were also significant homecomings in Angola (90,000), Sierra Leone (76,000), Burundi (54,000) and Bosnia and Herzegovina (42,000).

However, the sudden return of large numbers of people can quickly overwhelm fragile economic and social infrastructures. To ensure that returnees can rebuild their lives after they return home, UNHCR works with a range of organizations to facilitate reintegration. This requires emergency assistance for those in need, development programmes for the areas that have been devastated, and job-creation schemes.

The links between peace, stability, security, respect for human rights and sustainable development are increasingly seen as crucial for the achievement of durable solutions to the refugee problem.

Palestine refugees

The **United Nations Relief and Works Agency for Palestine Refugees in the Near East (UNRWA)** has been providing education, health, relief and social services to Palestine refugees since 1950. The General Assembly created UNRWA to provide emergency relief to some 750,000 Palestine refugees who had lost their homes and livelihoods as a result of the 1948 Arab-Israeli conflict. By 2003, UNRWA was providing essential services to more than 4 million registered Palestine refugees in Jordan, Lebanon, Syria, and the West Bank and Gaza Strip.

UNRWA's humanitarian role has been reinforced by recurrent conflicts in the Middle East — such as the civil war in Lebanon and the Palestinian uprising (*intifada*) of 1987, and the second uprising which started in September 2000 (the *Al-Aqsa intifada*).

Education is UNRWA's largest area of activity, accounting for half of its regular budget and two-thirds of its staff. Its 656 elementary and junior secondary schools accommodated more than 490,900 pupils in the 2002/2003 school year, while the eight UNRWA vocational training centres had over 5,100 trainees.

The Agency's network of 122 health centres handled 9.4 million patient visits in 2002. Environmental health services were provided to the 1.3 million refugees living in 59 refugee camps.

Some 229,000 people received special hardship assistance in 2002, which sought to ensure minimum standards of nutrition and shelter and to promote self-reliance through poverty-alleviation programmes. The income-generation programme in the West Bank and Gaza Strip has provided more than 54,900 loans worth $66.2 million to small businesses and micro-enterprises in the West Bank and the Gaza Strip.

UNRWA cooperates closely with the Palestinian Authority. After the 1993 accords between Israel and the Palestine Liberation Organization and the establishment of the Palestinian Authority in the West Bank and Gaza Strip, UNRWA started its *Peace Implementation Programme* to ensure that the benefits of the peace process were realized at the local level. The programme has helped to upgrade infrastructure, create employment, and improve socio-economic conditions in refugee communities throughout its area of operations. By the end of 2002, UNRWA projects had received more than $297.8 million in contributions and pledges.

The international community considers UNRWA a stabilizing factor in the Middle East. The refugees themselves look upon UNRWA's programmes as a symbol of the international community's commitment to a solution of the Palestine refugee issue.

Chapter 6
International Law

Among the United Nations most pervasive achievements has been the development of a body of international law — conventions, treaties and standards — that play a central role in promoting economic and social development, as well as international peace and security. Many of the treaties brought about by the United Nations form the basis of the law that governs relations among nations. While the United Nations work in this area does not always receive attention, it has a daily impact on the lives of people everywhere.

The United Nations Charter specifically calls on the Organization to help in the settlement of international disputes by peaceful means, including arbitration and judicial settlement (Article 33), and to encourage the progressive development of international law and its codification (Article 13). Over the years, the United Nations has sponsored over 500 multilateral agreements, which address a broad range of common concerns among states and are legally binding for the countries that ratify them.

In many areas, the United Nations legal work has been pioneering, addressing problems as they take on an international dimension. It has been in the forefront of efforts to provide a legal framework in such areas as protecting the environment, regulating migrant labour, curbing drug trafficking and combating terrorism. This work continues today, as international law assumes a more central role across a wider spectrum of issues, including human rights law and international humanitarian law.

Judicial settlement of disputes

The primary United Nations organ for the settlement of disputes is the **International Court of Justice**. Popularly known as the World Court, it was founded in 1946. By the end of 2003, it had delivered 78 judgments on disputes brought to it by states and issued 24 advisory opinions in response to requests by duly authorized United Nations organizations. Most cases have been dealt with by the full Court, but since 1981 six cases have been referred to special chambers at the request of the parties (see the Court's site at *www.icj-cij.org*).

In its judgments, the Court has addressed international disputes involving economic rights, rights of passage, the non-use of force, non-interference in the internal affairs of states, diplomatic relations, hostage-taking, the right of asylum and nationality. States bring such disputes before the Court in search of an impartial solution to their differences, on the basis of law. By achieving peaceful settlement on such questions as land frontiers, maritime boundaries and territorial sovereignty, the Court has often helped to prevent the escalation of disputes.

In a typical case of territorial rights, the Court in 2002 settled a sovereignty dispute between Cameroon and Nigeria over the oil-rich Bakassi peninsula, and then over the whole land and sea boundary between the two states. Earlier that year, it resolved a sovereignty dispute between Indonesia and Malaysia over two islands in the Celebes Sea, granting them to Malaysia. In 2001, the Court ended a maritime and territorial dispute between Qatar and Bahrain, which had been a strain on their relations.

In 1999, the Court resolved a sensitive frontier dispute between Botswana and Namibia, with a ruling accepted by both countries. In 1992, it settled a nearly century-old dispute between El Salvador and Honduras, which had led to a short but bloody war in 1969. In 1994, the Court acted on a dispute that had been jointly referred to it by Libya and Chad, ruling that their territory was defined by a 1955 treaty between Libya and France. As a result, Libya withdrew its forces from an area along its southern border with Chad.

Various cases have been referred to the Court against the background of conflict or political upheaval. In 1980, the United States brought a case arising from the seizure of its embassy in Tehran and the detention of its staff. The Court held that Iran must release the hostages, hand back the embassy and make reparation. However, before the Court could set the amount of reparation, the case was withdrawn following an agreement between the two countries. In 1989, Iran asked the Court to condemn the shooting down of an Iranian airliner by a United States warship, and to find the United States responsible for the payment of compensation to Iran. The case was closed in 1996, following a compensation settlement between the parties.

In 1986, Nicaragua brought a case against the United States over the latter's support for Nicaragua's "contras". The Court found that by supporting the contras and laying mines outside Nicaraguan ports — which could not be justified as "collective self-defence" — the United States had violated its international legal obligations not to intervene in the affairs of another state, not to use force against another state, and not to infringe on its sovereignty. Accordingly, the Court decided that the United States had to make reparation. However, in 1991, before the amount was determined, Nicaragua requested that the case be dismissed.

In 1992, Libya brought two cases — one against the United Kingdom and one against the United States — concerning the interpretation or application of the Convention for the Suppression of Unlawful Acts against the Safety of Civil Aviation, arising out of the crash, in 1988, of Pan American flight 103 at Lockerbie, Scotland. The cases were removed from the Court's docket in September 2003, as part of a larger agreement reached between the parties.

In 1993, Bosnia and Herzegovina brought a case against the Federal Republic of Yugoslavia (Serbia and Montenegro) concerning the application of the Convention on the Prevention and Punishment of the Crime of Genocide. The Court called upon the parties to prevent further genocide and further aggravation of the dispute. The case is still pending.

The Court in 1996 rejected objections by the United States to its jurisdiction in a 1992 case concerning the destruction of Iranian oil platforms by United States warships. In November 2003, the Court held that the United States actions could not be justified as necessary to protect its national security interests. However, as those actions did not constitute a breach of its obligations regarding freedom of commerce, Iran's claim for reparation could not be upheld. It also refused to uphold a United States counterclaim.

States have often submitted questions relating to economic rights. In 1995, in the midst of a dispute over fisheries jurisdiction between Canada and the European Union, Spain instituted a case against Canada after that country seized a Spanish fishing trawler on the high seas. More recently, Liechtenstein filed a case against Germany regarding certain property seized during the Second World War.

A case involving claims of environmental protection was brought by Hungary and Slovakia concerning a dispute over the validity of a 1997 treaty that they had concluded on the building of a barrage system on the Danube River. In 1997, the Court found both states in breach of their legal obligations, and called on them to carry out that treaty.

Over the past decade, the number of judicial cases submitted to the Court has increased significantly. While in the 1970s, the Court had only one or two cases on its docket at any one time, between 1990 and 1997 this number varied between 9 and 13. Since then, the number of cases has exceeded 20. At the end of 2003, there were 22 pending cases on the Court's docket, including one under active consideration.

The Court's advisory opinions have dealt with, among other things, admission to United Nations membership, reparation for injuries suffered in the service of the United Nations, the territorial status of Western Sahara, the expenses of certain peacekeeping operations and, more recently, the status of UN human rights rapporteurs. Two opinions, rendered in 1996 at the request of the General Assembly and the World Health Organization, concerned the legality of the threat or use of nuclear weapons.

In a 1971 advisory opinion requested by the Security Council, the Court stated that the continued presence of South Africa in Namibia was illegal and that South Africa was under obligation to withdraw its administration and end its occupation — clearing the way for the independence of Namibia in March 1990.

Development and codification of international law

The **International Law Commission** was established by the General Assembly in 1947 to promote the progressive development of international law and its codification. The Commission, which meets annually, is composed of 34 members elected by the General Assembly for five-year terms. Collectively, the members represent the world's principal legal systems, and serve as experts in their individual capacity, not as representatives of their governments. They address a wide range of issues relevant to the regulation of relations among states.

Most of the Commission's work involves the preparation of drafts on aspects of international law. Some topics are chosen by the Commission, others are referred to it by the General Assembly. When the Commission completes work on a topic, the

General Assembly usually convenes an international conference of plenipotentiaries to incorporate the draft into a convention. It is then opened to states to become parties — meaning that countries formally agree to be bound by its provisions. Some of these conventions form the very foundation of the law governing relations among states. For example:

- The *Convention on the Non-navigational Uses of International Watercourses*, adopted by the General Assembly in 1997, which regulates the equitable and reasonable utilization of watercourses shared by two or more countries.

- The *Convention on the Law of Treaties between States and International Organizations or between International Organizations*, adopted at a conference in Vienna in 1986.

- The *Convention on the Succession of States in Respect of State Property, Archives and Debts*, adopted at a conference in Vienna in 1983.

- The *Convention on the Prevention and Punishment of Crimes against Internationally Protected Persons, including Diplomatic Agents*, adopted by the General Assembly in 1973.

- The *Convention on the Law of Treaties*, adopted at a conference in Vienna in 1969.

- The *Convention on Diplomatic Relations* (1961) and the *Convention on Consular Relations* (1963), adopted at conferences held in Vienna.

In 1999, the Commission adopted a draft declaration aimed at preventing people from becoming stateless in such situations as dissolution of a state or separation of a territory. State responsibility had been a major subject of study by the Commission since its first session in 1949. In 2001, it completed its study of the subject with the adoption of draft articles on "Responsibility of States for internationally wrongful acts". Also in 2001, the Commission adopted draft articles on the prevention of transboundary damage resulting from hazardous activities. It is currently addressing international liability for injurious consequences arising out of acts not prohibited by international law, including such transboundary harm.

Other topics currently being considered by the Commission include: unilateral acts of states; diplomatic protection; reservations to treaties; responsibility of international organizations; shared natural resources of states; and fragmentation of international law, focusing on difficulties arising from the diversification and expansion of international law (see the Commission's website at *www.un.org/law/ilc/index.htm*).

International trade law

The **United Nations Commission on International Trade Law (UNCITRAL)** facilitates world trade by developing conventions, model laws, rules and legal guides designed to harmonize international trade law. Established by the General Assembly in

1966, this 60-nation body brings together representatives of the world's geographic regions and principal economic and legal systems. Over the years, UNCITRAL has become the core legal body of the UN system in the field of international trade law. The international trade law branch of the United Nations Office of Legal Affairs serves as its secretariat.

Over its 37-year history, the Commission has developed widely accepted texts that are viewed as landmarks in various fields of law. These include the UNCITRAL Arbitration Rules (1976); the *UNCITRAL Conciliation Rules* (1980); the *United Nations Convention on Contracts for the International Sale of Goods* (1980); the *UNCITRAL Model Law on International Commercial Arbitration* (1985); the *UNCITRAL Model Law on Procurement of Goods, Construction and Services* (1994); the *UNCITRAL Notes on Organizing Arbitral Proceedings* (1996); and the *Model Law on Electronic Commerce* (1996).

Other notable texts include: the *Convention on the Limitation Period in the International Sale of Goods* (1974); the *United Nations Convention on the Carriage of Goods by Sea (Hamburg Rules)* (1978); the *United Nations Convention on International Bills of Exchange and International Promissory Notes* (1988); the *UNCITRAL Legal Guide on Drawing Up International Contracts for the Construction of Industrial Works* (1988); the *United Nations Convention on the Liability of Operators of Transport Terminals in International Trade* (1991); the *UNCITRAL Legal Guide on International Countertrade Transactions* (1992); the *United Nations Convention on Independent Guarantees and Standby Letters of Credit* (1995); and the *UNCITRAL Model Law on Cross-Border Insolvency* (1997).

More recently adopted texts include the *UNCITRAL Legislative Guide on Privately Financed Infrastructure Projects* (2000); the *United Nations Convention on the Assignment of Receivables in International Trade* (2001); the *UNCITRAL Model Law on Electronic Signatures* (2001); and the *UNCITRAL Model Law on International Commercial Conciliation* (2002).

The Commission's current work includes: preparation of a set of draft model legislative provisions to supplement the *UNCITRAL Legislative Guide on Privately Financed Infrastructure Projects*; compilation and publication of Case Law on UNCITRAL Texts (CLOUT); a draft legislative guide on insolvency laws; a draft instrument on the carriage of goods by sea; and a draft legislative guide on security interests. Work is also continuing on the preparation of international instrument dealing with issues of electronic contracting, and consideration of ways of removing possible legal barriers to electronic commerce in existing international instruments relating to international trade.

In addition, UNCITRAL is continuing to focus on issues relating to the writing requirement as stated in the *UNCITRAL Model Law on International Commercial Arbitration* (1985) and the *Convention on the Recognition and Enforcement of Foreign Arbitral Awards* (1958), as well as a new provision relating to the recognition and enforcement of interim measures of protection to amend article 17 of the *UNCITRAL Model Law on International Commercial Arbitration*.

Environmental law

The United Nations has pioneered the development of international environmental law, brokering major treaties that have advanced environmental protection everywhere. The **United Nations Environment Programme (UNEP)** administers many of these treaties, while the rest are administered by other bodies, including treaty secretariats.

- The *Convention on Wetlands of International Importance Especially as Waterfowl Habitat* (1971) obligates states parties to use wisely all wetlands under their jurisdiction. This Convention was promoted by the United Nations Educational, Scientific and Cultural Organization (UNESCO).

- The *Convention Concerning the Protection of the World Cultural and Natural Heritage* (1972) obligates states parties to protect unique natural and cultural areas. Also promoted by UNESCO.

- The *Convention on International Trade in Endangered Species of Wild Fauna and Flora* (1973) controls international trade in selected wild animal and plant species or products through quotas or outright bans, to ensure their survival.

- The *Bonn Convention on the Conservation of Migratory Species of Wild Animals* (1979), and a series of associated regional and species-specific agreements, aims to conserve terrestrial, marine and avian migratory species and their habitats.

- The *Convention on Long-range Transboundary Air Pollution (Acid Rain Convention)* (1979) and its protocols, negotiated under the auspices of the United Nations Economic Commission for Europe (ECE), provide for the control and reduction of air pollution in Europe and North America.

- The *United Nations Convention on the Law of the Sea* (1982) regulates in a comprehensive way numerous maritime issues. These include rights of civil and naval navigation; the protection of coasts and the marine environment; rights to living and non-living resources; and marine scientific research.

- The *Vienna Convention for the Protection of the Ozone Layer* (1985), the *Montreal Protocol* (1987) and its amendments seek to reduce damage to the ozone layer, which shields life from the sun's harmful ultraviolet radiations.

- The *Basel Convention on the Control of Transboundary Movement of Hazardous Wastes and their Disposal* (1989) and its amendment obligates states parties to reduce shipping and dumping of dangerous wastes across borders; to minimize the amount and toxicity generated by hazardous waste; and to ensure their environmentally sound management as close as possible to the source of generation. In 1999, states parties adopted a protocol on liability and compensation resulting from cross-border movement of hazardous wastes.

- The *Multilateral Fund for the Implementation of the Montreal Protocol* (1991) was established to assist developing country parties to the *Montreal Protocol* whose annual per capita consumption and production of ozone-depleting substances (ODS) is less than 0.3kg — referred to as Article 5 countries — to comply with its control measures. Contributions to the Multilateral Fund from non-Article 5 countries are determined according to the United Nations scale of assessments.

- The *Agreement on the Conservation of Small Cetaceans of the Baltic and North Seas* (1991), concluded under the auspices of the *Convention on Migratory Species*, aims to promote close cooperation among parties with a view to achieving and maintaining a favourable conservation status for small cetaceans. States parties are obligated to engage in habitat conservation and management, surveys and research, pollution mitigation and public information.

- The *Convention on Biological Diversity* (1992) seeks to conserve biological diversity, promote the sustainable use of its components, and encourage equitable sharing of the benefits arising from the use of genetic resources. Its *Cartagena Protocol on Biosafety* (2000) seeks to protect biological diversity from potential risks that might be posed by living modified organisms (LMOs) resulting from modern biotechnology. It establishes an advance inform agreement procedure for ensuring that countries are provided with prior written notification and information necessary to make informed decisions before agreeing to the first import of LMOs that are to be intentionally introduced into the environment.

- The *Framework Convention on Climate Change* (1992) obligates states parties to reduce emissions of greenhouse gases that cause global warming and related atmospheric problems. The Convention's *Kyoto Protocol* (1997) strengthens the international response to climate change by calling on industrialized countries to meet legally binding emission targets during the period 2008-2012. The protocol also establishes several mechanisms that allow some flexibility in how the industrialized countries make and measure their emissions reductions.

- The *International Convention to Combat Desertification in Those Countries Experiencing Serious Drought and/or Desertification, Particularly in Africa* (1994) seeks to promote international cooperation for action to combat desertification and to mitigate the effects of drought.

- The *Agreement on the Conservation of Cetaceans in the Black Sea, Mediterranean Sea and Contiguous Atlantic area* (1996) seeks to reduce the threat to cetaceans in Mediterranean and Black Sea waters. It requires that states implement a detailed conservation plan for cetaceans, including legislation banning the deliberate capture of cetaceans; measures to minimize their incidental capture; and the creation of protected zones.

- The *Rotterdam Convention on the Prior Informed Consent Procedure for Certain Hazardous Chemicals and Pesticides in International Trade* (1998) obligates the exporters of a hazardous chemical or pesticide to provide to the importing country information on the substance's potential health and environmental dangers.

- The *Stockholm Convention on Persistent Organic Pollutants* (2001) aims to reduce and eliminate releases of certain highly toxic pesticides, industrial chemicals and by-products — such as DDT, PCBs and dioxin — that are highly mobile and accumulate in the food chain.

- The UNESCO *Man the Biosphere Programme* develops the basis, within the natural and the social sciences, for the sustainable use and conservation of biological diversity, and for the improvement of the relationship between people and their environment worldwide. The programme encourages interdisciplinary research, demonstration and training in natural resources management.

The **International Maritime Organization (IMO)** has promoted conventions that have helped to reduce marine pollution. A series of Regional Seas Programmes helps governments protect their shared marine and water resources through UNEP-sponsored conventions and protocols in 13 regions.

Law of the sea

The *United Nations Convention on the Law of the Sea* is one of the most comprehensive instruments of international law. Its 320 articles and 9 annexes contain an all-encompassing legal regime for the world's oceans and seas, establishing rules governing all activities in the oceans and the use of their resources — including navigation and over-flight, exploration and exploitation of minerals, conservation and pollution, fishing and shipping. It enshrines the notion that all problems of ocean space are closely interrelated and need to be addressed as a whole. It embodies in one instrument the codification of traditional rules for the use of the oceans, as well as the development of new rules governing emerging concerns. It is a unique instrument, often referred to as the "constitution for the oceans".

It is now universally accepted that any action in the area of ocean affairs and the law of the sea must be in conformity with the provisions of the Convention, whose authority is based on its near-universal acceptance. The Convention has more than 140 states parties, and many more are in the process of ratifying or acceding to it. Nearly all states recognize and adhere to its provisions.

The twentieth anniversary of the opening for signature of the Convention was celebrated in 2002 with a two-day plenary meeting of the General Assembly.

Impact of the Convention

Through national and international legislation and related decision-making, States have consistently upheld the Convention as the pre-eminent international legal instrument in the field. Its implicit authority has resulted in the near-universal acceptance of some of its key provisions, including: 12 nautical miles as the limit of the territorial sea; coastal states' jurisdiction over the resources of an "exclusive economic zone" up to the limit of 200 nautical miles; and their jurisdiction over the resources of the continental shelf extending beyond the limits of that zone. And it has brought stability in the area of navigation — establishing the right of innocent passage through the territorial sea, and the right of transit passage through narrow straits used for international navigation.

The near-universal acceptance of the Convention was facilitated in 1994 by the General Assembly's adoption of the *Agreement Relating to the Implementation of Part XI of the Convention,* which removed certain obstacles that had prevented mainly industrialized countries from signing the Convention. The agreement is now widely accepted, having more than 110 states parties.

The Convention has been acknowledged for its impact on coastal states' control over marine scientific research, the prevention of pollution, and access by landlocked states to and from the sea. Moreover, it is now recognized as the framework and foundation for any future instruments that seek to further define rights and obligations in the oceans — as reflected in the adoption of the 1995 *Agreement on Straddling Fish Stocks and Highly Migratory Fish Stocks.*

That agreement sets out a regime for the conservation and management of those fish stocks which remain within a coastal state's **exclusive economic zone (EEZ)** and those in areas beyond and adjacent to that zone. It establishes that such management must be based on a precautionary approach, as well as the best scientific evidence available. It also elaborates on the legal provision that states should cooperate to ensure long-term sustainability and promote the optimum utilization of fisheries resources, both within and beyond their exclusive economic zone.

Bodies established under the Convention

The Convention established three specific organs to deal with various aspects of the law of the sea.

The **International Seabed Authority** is the organization through which states parties organize and control activities relating to the deep seabed's mineral resources in the international seabed area, beyond the limits of national jurisdiction. Inaugurated in 1994, it is located in Kingston, Jamaica. In 2002, the Authority adopted a "mining code", which contains regulations on prospecting and exploration for polymetallic nodules in the Area (defined as "the seabed and ocean floor and subsoil thereof, beyond the limits of national jurisdiction").

Following adoption of the code, which includes standard clauses for exploration contracts, the first 15-year contracts for exploration for polymetallic nodules in the deep seabed were signed in 2001 with the registered pioneer investors: the State Enterprise Yuzhmorgeologiya (Russian Federation); the Interoceanmetal Joint Organization (a consortium formed by Bulgaria, Cuba, the Czech Republic, Poland, the Russian Federation and the Slovak Republic); the Republic of Korea; the China Ocean Minerals Research and Development Association (COMRA); the Institut français de recherche pour l'exploitation de la mer (IFREMER)/Association française pour l'étude et la recherche des nodules (AFERNOD); the Deep Ocean Resources Development Company (DORD-Japan); and the Department of Ocean Development, India.

The pioneer investors are state-owned enterprises or multinational consortia that — having undertaken prospecting activities and having located economically exploitable deposits of polymetallic nodules in the Area before the adoption of the Convention — were accorded preferential treatment in the granting of production authorizations over other applicants, except the Enterprise itself. The Enterprise is the organ of the International Seabed Authority which carries out activities in the Area as enumerated in the Convention — as well as the transport, processing and marketing of minerals recovered from the Area.

The **International Tribunal for the Law of the Sea**, operational since 1996, was established to settle disputes relating to the interpretation or application of the Convention. Composed of 21 judges elected by the states parties, it is located in the German seaport of Hamburg. The Tribunal received its first application instituting a case in November 2001. Since then, 11 cases have been submitted to it, most of them seeking the prompt release of vessels and their crews, allegedly arrested in breach of the Convention. Some cases have dealt with the conservation of living resources — namely, southern blue-fin tuna stocks, in *New Zealand v. Japan* and *Australia v. Japan*; and swordfish stocks in the south-eastern Pacific Ocean, in a case between Chile and the European Community. Another case dealt with the prevention of land-based pollution from a plant designed to reprocess spent nuclear fuel into a new fuel known as "mixed oxide fuel" (MOX), in *Ireland v. United Kingdom*.

The purpose of the **Commission on the Limits of the Continental Shelf** is to facilitate implementation of the Convention with respect to delineation of the outer limits of the continental shelf beyond 200 nautical miles from the baselines from which the breadth of the territorial sea is measured. Under the Convention, a coastal state establishes the outer limits of its continental shelf where it extends beyond 200 miles on the basis of the Commission's recommendation.

The Commission held its first session at United Nations Headquarters in 1997. Its 21 members, elected by the states parties to the Convention, serve in their personal capacity. They are experts in the fields of geology, geophysics, hydrography and geodesy. The Commission received its first submission by a state party, the Russian Federation, in December 2001.

Meeting of states parties

Although the Convention does not provide for a periodic conference of states parties, the annual meeting of states parties, which is convened by the Secretary-General, has served as a forum where issues of concern have been discussed. This is in addition to its assigned administrative functions, such as election of members of the Tribunal and the Commission, as well as other budgetary and administrative actions.

The General Assembly performs an oversight function with respect to ocean affairs and the law of the sea. In 2000, it established an open-ended, informal, consultative process to facilitate its own annual review of developments in the field. That process, convened annually, makes suggestions to the Assembly on particular issues, with an emphasis on identifying areas where coordination and cooperation among governments and agencies should be enhanced — particularly in the fields of safety of navigation and the protection of vulnerable marine ecosystems. The consultative process, originally instituted for three years, has been extended for three additional years because of the positive results it has achieved.

International humanitarian law

International humanitarian law encompasses the principles and rules that regulate the means and methods of warfare, as well as the humanitarian protection of civilian populations, sick and wounded combatants, and prisoners of war. Major instruments include the 1949 *Geneva Conventions for the Protection of War Victims* and two additional protocols, concluded in 1977 under the auspices of the International Committee of the Red Cross.

In the past few years, the United Nations has taken a leading role in efforts to advance international humanitarian law. The Security Council has become increasingly involved in protecting civilians in armed conflict, promoting human rights and protecting children in wars. The establishment of the International Criminal Tribunals for the Former Yugoslavia and for Rwanda, as well as tribunals in Timor-Leste, Sierra Leone and Cambodia, not only contribute to ensuring accountability but also in the strengthening and wider appreciation of humanitarian law. The elaboration by the preparatory commission for the International Criminal Court of the "elements of crimes" with respect to genocide, war crimes and crimes against humanity, is another tangible contribution in understanding international humanitarian law.

The General Assembly, as a political forum of the United Nations, has contributed to elaborating a number of instruments. Among them are the *Convention on the Prevention and Punishment of the Crime of Genocide* (1948); the *Convention on the Non-Applicability of Statutory Limitations to War Crimes and Crimes Against Humanity* (1968); the *Convention on Prohibition and Restrictions on the Use of Certain Conventional Weapons which may be deemed to be Excessively Injurious or to have Indiscriminate Effects* (1980) and its four protocols; and the *Principles of International*

Cooperation in the Detection, Arrest, Extradition and Punishment of Persons Guilty of War Crimes and Crimes Against Humanity, which the Assembly adopted in 1973. The Assembly also facilitated the convening of the diplomatic conference that adopted the **Rome Statute of the International Criminal Court** in 1998.

International tribunals

Mass violations of international humanitarian law in the former Yugoslavia and in Rwanda led the Security Council to establish two international tribunals to prosecute persons responsible for such violations. Both tribunals were established under Chapter VII of the Charter, which deals with enforcement measures, and are subsidiary organs of the Council.

- The **International Criminal Tribunal for the Former Yugoslavia**, established in 1993, is composed of four chambers (three trial chambers and an appeals chamber), a prosecutor and the registry. Under its Statute, it can prosecute four kinds of offences: grave breaches of the Geneva Conventions; violations of the laws or customs of war; genocide; and crimes against humanity. The Tribunal is located at The Hague, in the Netherlands.

- The **International Criminal Tribunal for Rwanda**, established in 1994, is composed of four chambers (three trial chambers and an appeals chamber), a prosecutor and the registry. In 1998, the Tribunal handed down the first-ever conviction of genocide by an international court. The Tribunal is located in Arusha, Tanzania; the Office of the Prosecutor is in Kigali, Rwanda.

The tribunals have a common appeals chamber and originally had a common prosecutor. They are engaged in a number of trial proceedings and have between them indicted more than 150 individuals. In August 2003, the Security Council decided that each Tribunal shall have its own prosecutor.

The **Special Court for Sierra Leone**, an independent judicial body, was established in January 2002 pursuant to an agreement between the government of Sierra Leone and the United Nations to prosecute persons who bear the greatest responsibility for the commission of crimes against humanity, war crimes and other serious violations of international humanitarian law, as well as crimes committed under relevant Sierra Leonean law within the territory of Sierra Leone since 30 November 1996. The Court is located in Freetown, Sierra Leone. The Secretary-General of the United Nations appoints the prosecutor and the registrar. The Secretary-General and the government of Sierra Leone each get to appoint judges of both the trial and appeals chambers of the Court.

International terrorism

The United Nations has consistently addressed the problem of terrorism, at both the legal and political level.

In the legal sphere, the UN and its related bodies — such as the International Civil Aviation Organization (ICAO), the International Maritime Organization (IMO) and the International Atomic Energy Agency (IAEA) — have developed a network of international agreements that constitute the basic legal instruments against terrorism. These are the:

- *Convention on Offences and Certain Other Acts Committed on Board Aircraft* (Tokyo, 1963).

- *Convention for the Suppression of Unlawful Seizure of Aircraft* (The Hague, 1970).

- *Convention for the Suppression of Unlawful Acts against the Safety of Civil Aviation* (Montreal, 1971) .

- *Convention on the Prevention and Punishment of Crimes against Internationally Protected Persons, including Diplomatic Agents* (New York, 1973) .

- *Convention on the Physical Protection of Nuclear Material* (Vienna, 1980) .

- *Protocol for the Suppression of Unlawful Acts of Violence at Airports Serving International Civil Aviation* (Montreal, 1988) .

- *Convention for the Suppression of Unlawful Acts against the Safety of Maritime Navigation* (Rome, 1988) .

- *Protocol for the Suppression of Unlawful Acts against the Safety of Fixed Platforms located on the Continental Shelf* (Rome, 1988) .

- *Convention on the Marking of Plastic Explosives for the Purpose of Detection* (Montreal, 1991).

The General Assembly has also concluded the following four conventions:

- The *Convention against the Taking of Hostages* (1979), in which states parties agree to make the taking of hostages punishable by appropriate penalties. They also agree to prohibit certain activities within their territories, to exchange information and to enable any criminal or extradition proceedings to take place. If a state party does not extradite an alleged offender, it must submit the case to its own authorities for prosecution.

- The *Convention on the Safety of United Nations and Associated Personnel* (1994), adopted by the Assembly following many instances of attacks against UN personnel in the field which resulted in injury and death.

- The *International Convention for the Suppression of Terrorist Bombings* (1997). It is aimed at denying "safe havens" to persons wanted for terrorist bombings by obligating each state party to prosecute such persons if it does not extradite them to another state that has issued an extradition request.

- The *International Convention for the Suppression of the Financing of Terrorism* (1999) obligates states parties either to prosecute or extradite persons accused of funding terrorist activities, and requires banks to enact measures to identify suspicious transactions.

A committee established by the Assembly in 1996 is elaborating a convention for the suppression of acts of nuclear terrorism and a comprehensive convention against international terrorism.

In the political sphere, the General Assembly in 1994 adopted the *Declaration on Measures to Eliminate International Terrorism*. In 1996, it adopted the *Declaration to Supplement the 1994 Declaration*, which condemned all acts and practices of terrorism as criminal and unjustifiable, wherever and by whomever committed. The Assembly urged states to take measures at the national and international levels to eliminate international terrorism.

Other legal questions

The General Assembly has adopted legal instruments on various other questions. Among them are the *International Convention against the Recruitment, Use, Financing and Training of Mercenaries* (1989); the *Body of Principles for the Protection of All Persons under Any Form of Detention or Imprisonment* (1988); and the *Declaration on the Enhancement of the Effectiveness of the Principle of Refraining from the Threat or Use of Force in International Relations* (1987).

The Assembly has adopted many international instruments on the recommendation of the **Special Committee on the Charter of the United Nations and on the Strengthening of the Role of the Organization**, established by the Assembly in 1974. These include the *United Nations Model Rules for the Conciliation of Disputes between States* (1995); the *Declaration on the Enhancement of Cooperation between the United Nations and Regional Arrangements or Agencies in the Maintenance of International Peace and Security* (1994); the *Declaration on Fact-finding by the United Nations in the Field of the Maintenance of International Peace and Security* (1991); the *Declaration on the Prevention and Removal of Disputes and Situations Which May Threaten International Peace and Security and on the Role of the United Nations in this Field* (1988); and the *Declaration on the Peaceful Settlement of International Disputes* (1982).

Under the Article 102 of the UN Charter, member states should register international agreements they enter into with the United Nations. The United Nations **Office of Legal Affairs** is responsible for the registration, deposit and publication of treaties and conventions. It publishes the *United Nations Treaty Series*, which contains the texts of more than 50,000 treaties and related information. It also issues the volume, *Multilateral Treaties Deposited with the Secretary-General*, which includes more than 500 major treaties deposited by member states (see *http://untreaty.un.org*).

Chapter 7
Decolonization

DECOLONIZATION

More than 80 nations whose peoples were formerly under colonial rule have joined the United Nations as sovereign independent states since the world Organization was founded in 1945. Additionally, many other Territories have achieved self-determination through political association or integration with an independent state. The United Nations has played a crucial role in that historic change by encouraging the aspirations of dependent peoples and by setting goals and standards to accelerate their attainment of independence. United Nations missions have supervised elections leading to independence — in Togoland (1956 and 1968), Western Samoa (1961), Namibia (1989) and, most recently, in Timor-Leste (formerly East Timor).

The decolonization efforts of the United Nations derive from the Charter principle of "equal rights and self-determination of peoples", as well as from three specific chapters in the Charter — XI, XII and XIII — which are devoted to the interests of dependent peoples. Since 1960, the United Nations has also been guided by the General Assembly's *Declaration on the Granting of Independence to Colonial Countries and Peoples*, also known as the Declaration on decolonization, by which member states proclaimed the necessity of bringing colonialism to a speedy end. The United Nations has also been guided by General Assembly resolution 1541 (XV) of 15 December 1960, which defined the three options offering full self-government for Non-Self-Governing Territories.

Despite the great progress made against colonialism, some 2 million people still live under colonial rule, and the United Nations continues its efforts to help achieve self-determination in the remaining Non-Self-Governing Territories.

International trusteeship system

Under Chapter XII of the Charter, the United Nations established the international trusteeship system for the supervision of Trust Territories placed under it by individual agreements with the states administering them.

The system applied to: (a) Territories held under mandates established by the League of Nations after the First World War; (b) Territories detached from "enemy states" as a result of the Second World War; and (c) Territories voluntarily placed under the system by states responsible for their administration. The goal of the system was to promote the political, economic and social advancement of the Territories and their development towards self-government and self-determination.

The **Trusteeship Council** was established under Chapter XIII of the Charter to supervise the administration of Trust Territories and to ensure that governments responsible for their administration took adequate steps to prepare them for the achievement of the Charter goals.

In the early years of the United Nations, 11 Territories were placed under the trusteeship system (*see tables in Part Three*). Over the years, all 11 Territories either became independent states or voluntarily associated themselves with a state.

The last one to do so was the Trust Territory of the Pacific Islands (Palau), administered by the United States. The Security Council in 1994 terminated the United Nations Trusteeship Agreement for that Territory, after it chose free association with the United States in a 1993 plebiscite. Palau became independent in 1994, joining the United Nations as its 185th member state. With no Territories left on its agenda, the trusteeship system had completed its historic task.

Non-Self-Governing Territories

The United Nations Charter also addresses the issue of other Non-Self-Governing Territories not brought into the trusteeship system.

Chapter XI of the Charter — the Declaration regarding Non-Self-Governing Territories — provides that member states administering Territories which have not attained self-government recognize "that the interests of the inhabitants of these Territories is paramount" and accept as a "sacred trust" the obligation to promote their well-being.

To this end, administering powers, in addition to ensuring the political, economic, social and educational advancement of the peoples, undertake to assist them in developing self-government and democratic political institutions. Administering powers have an obligation to transmit regularly to the Secretary-General information on the economic, social and educational conditions in the Territories under their administration.

In 1946, eight member states — Australia, Belgium, Denmark, France, the Netherlands, New Zealand, the United Kingdom and the United States — enumerated the Territories under their administration that they considered to be non-self-governing. In all, 72 Territories were enumerated, of which eight became independent before 1959. In 1963, the Assembly approved a revised list of 64 Territories to which the 1960 Declaration on decolonization applied. By 1990, 53 Territories had attained self-government. As of 2003, there were 16 Non-Self-Governing Territories (*see table on facing page*). The current administering powers are France, New Zealand, the United Kingdom and the United States.

Declaration on the Granting of Independence to Colonial Countries and Peoples

The aspirations of the peoples of the Territories to achieve self-determination, and the international community's perception that Charter principles were being too slowly applied, led the General Assembly to proclaim, on 14 December 1960, the *Declaration on the Granting of Independence to Colonial Countries and Peoples* (resolution 1514 (XV)).

Territories to which the Declaration on the Granting of Independence to Colonial Countries and Peoples continues to apply (as of 2003)

TERRITORY	ADMINISTERING AUTHORITY
Africa:	
Western Sahara[1]	
Asia and the Pacific:	
American Samoa	United States
Guam	United States
New Caledonia[2]	France
Pitcairn	United Kingdom
Tokelau	New Zealand
Atlantic Ocean, Caribbean and Mediterranean:	
Anguilla	United Kingdom
Bermuda	United Kingdom
British Virgin Islands	United Kingdom
Cayman Islands	United Kingdom
Falkland Islands (Malvinas)	United Kingdom
Gibraltar	United Kingdom
Montserrat	United Kingdom
St. Helena	United Kingdom
Turks and Caicos Islands	United Kingdom
United States Virgin Islands	United States

---

[1] On 26 February 1976, Spain informed the Secretary-General that as of that date, it had terminated its presence in the Territory of the Sahara and deemed it necessary to place on record that Spain considered itself thenceforth exempt from any international responsibility in connection with its administration, in view of the cessation of its participation in the temporary administration established for the Territory. In 1990, the General Assembly reaffirmed that the question of Western Sahara was a question of decolonization that remained to be completed by the people of Western Sahara.

[2] On 2 December 1986, the General Assembly determined that New Caledonia was a Non-Self-Governing Territory.

The Declaration states that subjecting peoples to alien subjugation, domination and exploitation constitutes a denial of fundamental human rights, is contrary to the Charter, and is an impediment to the promotion of world peace and cooperation. It adds that "immediate steps shall be taken, in Trust and Non-Self-Governing Territories or all other Territories which have not yet attained independence, to transfer all powers to the peoples of those Territories, without any conditions or reservations, in accordance with their freely expressed will and desire, without any distinction as to race, creed or colour in order to enable them to enjoy complete independence and freedom".

Also in 1960, the Assembly approved resolution 1541 (XV), defining the three legitimate political status options offering full self-government — free association with an independent state, integration into an independent state, or independence. (*For the list of Territories that have become integrated or associated with independent states since the adoption of the Declaration on decolonization, see Part Three.*)

The Assembly, in 1961, established a special committee to examine the application of the Declaration and make recommendations on its implementation. Commonly referred to as the Special Committee of 24 or the **Special Committee on decolonization**, its full title is the Special Committee on the Situation with Regard to the Implementation of the Declaration on the Granting of Independence to Colonial Countries and Peoples.

The Special Committee meets annually, hears petitioners and representatives of the Territories, dispatches visiting missions to the Territories, and organizes annual seminars on the political, social, economic and educational situations in the Territories.

In the years following the adoption of the Declaration, some 60 former colonial Territories, inhabited by more than 80 million people, attained self-determination through independence, and joined the United Nations as sovereign members (*see tables in Part Three*).

The Assembly has called upon the administering powers to take all necessary steps to enable the peoples of the Non-Self-Governing Territories to exercise fully their right to self-determination and independence. It has also called upon the administering powers to complete the withdrawal of remaining military bases from the Territories, and to ensure that no activity of foreign economic and other interests hinders the implementation of the Declaration.

In this respect, New Zealand has extended continuous cooperation to the Special Committee regarding Tokelau. France began cooperating with the Committee in 1999, following the signing of an agreement on the future of New Caledonia. In recent years, two administering powers have not participated formally in the Committee's work. The United States has maintained that it remains conscious of its role as an administering power and will continue to meet its responsibilities under the Charter. The United Kingdom has stated that while most of the Territories under its administration chose independence, a small number have preferred to remain associated with it.

In 2003, the annual decolonization seminar took place for the first time in a Non-Self-Governing Territory — the United Kingdom agreed that it would be held in Anguilla and sent a senior representative to participate in it.

In 2003, the United Kingdom agreed that the annual decolonization seminar could take place in Anguilla — marking the first time the annual seminar had been held in a Non-Self-Governing Territory — and sent a senior representative to participate in it.

At the end of the **International Decade for the Eradication of Colonialism (1991-2000)**, the General Assembly declared the **Second International Decade for the Eradication of Colonialism (2001-2010)**, calling on member states to redouble their effort to achieve complete decolonization.

In the case of certain Territories, such as Western Sahara, the Assembly has entrusted the Secretary-General with specific tasks to facilitate the process of decolonization, in accordance with the UN Charter and the objectives of the Declaration.

Namibia

The United Nations helped bring about the independence of Namibia in 1990 — a case history that reveals the complexity of the efforts required to ensure a peaceful transition.

Formerly known as South West Africa, Namibia was an African Territory once held under the League of Nations mandate system. The General Assembly in 1946 asked South Africa to administer the Territory under the trusteeship system. South Africa refused, and in 1949 informed the United Nations that it would no longer transmit information on the Territory, maintaining that the mandate had ended with the demise of the League.

The General Assembly in 1966, stating that South Africa had not fulfilled its obligations, terminated that mandate and placed the Territory under the responsibility of the United Nations Council for South West Africa, which was renamed the Council for Namibia in 1968.

In 1976, the Security Council demanded that South Africa accept elections for the Territory under United Nations supervision. The General Assembly stated that independence talks must involve the South West Africa People's Organization (SWAPO) — the sole representative of the Namibian people.

In 1978, Canada, France, the Federal Republic of Germany, the United Kingdom and the United States submitted to the Security Council a settlement proposal providing for elections for a constituent assembly under United Nations auspices. The Council endorsed the Secretary-General's recommendations for implementing the proposal, asked him to appoint a special representative for Namibia, and established the **United Nations Transition Assistance Group (UNTAG)**.

Years of negotiations by the Secretary-General and his special representative, as well as United States mediation, led to the 1988 agreements for the achievement of peace in southern Africa, by which South Africa agreed to cooperate with the Secretary-General to ensure Namibia's independence through elections.

The operation that led to Namibia's independence started in April 1989. UNTAG supervised and controlled the entire electoral process, which was conducted by the Namibian authorities; monitored the ceasefire between SWAPO and South Africa and the demobilization of all military forces; and ensured a smooth electoral process, including monitoring of local police.

The elections for the constituent assembly were won by SWAPO and were declared "free and fair" by the Secretary-General's special representative, Mr. Martti Ahtisaari. Following the elections, South Africa withdrew its remaining troops. The constituent assembly drafted a new Constitution, approved in February 1990, and elected SWAPO leader Sam Nujoma as President for a five-year term. In March, Namibia became independent, with the Secretary-General administering the oath of office to Namibia's first President. In April, the country joined the United Nations.

Timor-Leste

A more recent United Nations success story is the process that led to the independence of Timor-Leste — formerly known as East Timor. A major UN operation oversaw its transition towards independence, after the East Timorese people voted in favour of independence in a popular consultation conducted by the UN in 1999.

The island of Timor lies to the north of Australia, in the south-central part of the chain of islands forming the Republic of Indonesia. The western part of the island was a Dutch colony and became part of Indonesia when the country attained independence. East Timor was a Portuguese colony.

The General Assembly in 1960 placed East Timor on the list of Non-Self-Governing Territories. In 1974, recognizing the right to self-determination and independence of its colonies, Portugal sought to establish a provisional government and a popular assembly, which would determine the status of East Timor. But civil war broke out in 1975 between the newly formed political parties. Portugal withdrew, stating that it was unable to control the situation. One East Timorese side declared independence as a separate country, while another proclaimed independence and integration with Indonesia.

In December, Indonesian troops landed in East Timor, and a "provisional government" was formed. Portugal broke off relations with Indonesia and brought the matter before the Security Council. The Council and the General Assembly called on Indonesia to withdraw its forces and urged all states to respect East Timor's territorial integrity, as well as the right of its people to self-determination.

The "provisional government" in 1976 held elections for an assembly, which then called for integration with Indonesia. When Indonesia issued a law supporting that decision, the pro-independence movement started armed resistance and an international campaign of opposition. Portugal maintained that the East Timorese had not exercised their right to self-determination, while Indonesia held that the decolonization process had been completed. The UN recognized neither the legitimacy of the assembly nor the annexation by Indonesia, and continued to recognize Portugal as the legal administering power.

At the request of the General Assembly, the Secretary-General in 1983 started talks with Indonesia and Portugal to promote a just and comprehensive settlement. In May 1999, through his good offices and those of his personal representative (appointed in 1997), agreements were reached that paved the way for a popular consultation — giving the East Timorese people a choice between an autonomous status with Indonesia or a transition to independence under the aegis of the United Nations.

On the basis of the agreements, the **United Nations Mission in East Timor (UNAMET)** organized and conducted voter registration and an official ballot. On 30 August, some 78.5 per cent of 450,000 registered voters rejected the proposed autonomy within Indonesia. When the results were announced, militias opposing independence unleashed a campaign of systematic destruction and violence, killing many and forcing more than 200,000 East Timorese to flee their homes — mostly to West Timor. The UN had to evacuate most of its personnel, but 86 international staff remained in the headquarters compound in Dili, the capital, together with some 1,000 East Timorese who had taken refuge there.

After intensive talks, which included a high-level mission sent by the Security Council to Jakarta and Dili, Indonesia accepted the deployment of a UN-authorized multinational force to restore peace and security. Acting under Chapter VII of the Charter, the Security Council in September 1999 authorized the dispatch of the **International Force in East Timor (INTERFET)**, which helped to restore order.

In October 1999, the Council established the **United Nations Transitional Administration in East Timor (UNTAET)**, with full executive and legislative authority during the country's transition to independence. Mr. Sergio Vieira de Mello was appointed head of UNTAET and special representative of the Secretary-General in East Timor. In February 2000, UNTAET's military component, comprising some 8,800 troops and 1,600 civilian police, took over the task of maintaining peace and security. UNTAET also established a civil administration throughout the Territory, while helping to develop social services, assisting in reconstruction, and building East Timor's capacity towards nationhood.

On 30 August 2001, more than 91 per cent of East Timor's eligible voters went to the polls to elect an 88-member constituent assembly, tasked with writing and adopting a new constitution and establishing the framework for future elections and the transition to full independence. On 22 March 2002, it signed into force the Territory's first Constitution. On 14 April, following presidential elections, Xanana Gusmão was appointed president-elect, having received 82.7 per cent of the vote.

The two preconditions for a handover of power had thus been met, and East Timor attained its independence on 20 May 2002. The constituent assembly was transformed into the national parliament, and the new country adopted the name Timor-Leste. On 27 September, it became the 191st member state of the United Nations.

The UN has continued its support for Timor-Leste after independence through the **United Nations Mission of Support in East Timor (UNMISET)**, established by the Security Council on 17 May 2002. It is mandated to: assist the nascent state in developing core administrative structures critical to its viability and political stability; provide interim law enforcement and security; assist in developing the country's police service; and contribute to the maintenance of its internal and external security.

Western Sahara

The United Nations has been dealing since 1963 with an ongoing dispute concerning Western Sahara — a Territory on the north-west coast of Africa bordering Morocco, Mauritania and Algeria.

Western Sahara became a Spanish colony in 1884. In 1963, both Morocco and Mauritania laid claim to it. The International Court of Justice, in a 1975 opinion requested by the General Assembly, rejected the claims of territorial sovereignty by Morocco or Mauritania.

The United Nations has been seeking a settlement in Western Sahara since the withdrawal of Spain in 1976 and the ensuing fighting between Morocco — which had "reintegrated" the Territory — and the Popular Front for the Liberation of Saguia el-Hamra and Río de Oro (Frente POLISARIO), which was supported by Algeria (*see footnote to table in this chapter*).

In 1979, the Organization of African Unity (OAU) called for a referendum to enable the people of the Territory to exercise their right to self-determination. By 1982, 26 OAU member states had recognized the "Saharawi Arab Democratic Republic (SADR)" proclaimed by POLISARIO in 1976. When SADR was seated at the 1984 OAU summit, Morocco withdrew from the OAU.

In 1983 and again in 1984, the General Assembly reaffirmed that the people of the Territory had yet to exercise their right to self-determination and independence, and that the parties should negotiate a ceasefire allowing for a referendum.

A joint good offices mission by the Secretary-General and the OAU Chairman led to their 1988 settlement proposals, which called for a ceasefire and a referendum to choose between independence and integration with Morocco. Both parties gave their agreement in principle to the proposals, and in June 1990, the Security Council approved the Secretary-General's report in which they were presented.

By its resolution 690 of 29 April 1991, the Security Council created the **United Nations Mission for the Referendum in Western Sahara (MINURSO)** to assist the Secretary-General's special representative in all matters related to the organization and conduct of a referendum of self-determination for the people of Western Sahara. All Western Saharans aged 18 and over counted in the 1974 Spanish census would have the right to vote, whether living in the Territory or outside. An identification commission would update the census list and identify voters. Refugees living outside the Territory would be identified with the assistance of the Office of the United Nations High Commissioner for Refugees.

In addition to the office of the special representative, MINURSO was to consist of civilian, security and military units. On 6 September 1991, the ceasefire came into effect and has been observed ever since by MINURSO's military observers. There have been no major violations.

While both parties reiterated their confidence in the UN and their commitment to the settlement plan, they continued to have different views on many aspects of its implementation — particularly on the question of voter eligibility for the referendum.

The Secretary-General had set out criteria for voter eligibility in a 1991 report to the Security Council. Morocco accepted them, while considering them unduly restrictive. POLISARIO stated that in its view, it had been originally agreed that the sole basis for the electorate would be the list of Saharans counted in the 1974 census, and that the new criteria would unduly expand the electorate beyond the persons included in the census — with the possible inclusion of persons who were not Saharans from the Territory.

In August 1994, the identification commission started to identify potential voters on the basis of a compromise proposed by the Secretary-General. However, the process was impeded throughout the 1990s by successive deadlocks. Despite their agreement to proceed with the identification process, both parties maintained their initial positions with respect to the composition of the electoral body. POLISARIO insisted that under the settlement plan, only those who had been counted in the 1974 Spanish census should take part in the referendum. Morocco held the opposite view — namely, that thousands of additional Saharans were equally qualified to vote, including those who were in the Territory at the time of the census but had not been counted; those who had fled to Morocco in previous years; and those from regions that were formerly part of the Territory but had subsequently been retroceded by Spain to Morocco in the 1950s and 1960s.

In 1997, a compromise known as the Houston Agreements was brokered by the Secretary-General's personal envoy for Western Sahara, Mr. James A. Baker, III. The identification process was completed in December 1999, and the identification commission issued a provisional list of about 86,000 people eligible to vote. Those deemed non-eligible were free to appeal the decision. By the end of 2000, a total of 131,038 applicants had submitted appeals.

Despite several rounds of consultations between the parties and neighbouring countries during 2000 and 2001 under the auspices of the Secretary-General's personal envoy, disagreements persisted between the parties over implementation of the settlement plan.

On 30 July 2002, the Security Council asked the personal envoy to continue his efforts for a political solution that would provide for self-determination. His proposal was presented to the parties and neighbouring countries during a visit to the region in January 2003. Both parties objected to aspects of the peace plan. However, on 6 July, the Frente POLISARIO, wrote to inform the Secretary-General that it had accepted the peace plan. Morocco was expected to present its response to the plan in 2004.

On 31 July 2003, the Security Council, by its resolution 1495, expressed unanimous support for the peace plan, as an optimum political solution on the basis of agreement between the two parties. In August, the Secretary-General appointed Mr. Alvaro de Soto as his special representative for Western Sahara. In September, POLISARIO released 243 Moroccan prisoners of war; two months later, it released 300 more. POLISARIO still held 613 Moroccan prisoners of war.

In November and December, Mr. de Soto travelled to the region to consult with the parties and to address the situation of some 165,000 Western Sahara refugees who have spent nearly three decades in desert camps in western Algeria. Plans were discussed to re-establish personal contacts between the refugees and their relatives across the border. Family visits between Saharans living in the Territory and those in the refugee camps began on 5 March 2004.

On 15 April 2004, during a meeting with the Secretary-General's personal envoy, Morocco delivered its final response to the peace plan, calling for a negotiated solution based on "autonomy within the framework of Moroccan sovereignty". In his subsequent report to the Security Council, the Secretary-General observed that "the issue of sovereignty is, of course, the fundamental issue which has divided the parties for all these years. Morocco does not accept the Settlement Plan to which it had agreed for many years ... and it also now does not accept elements of the Peace Plan."

In the view of the Secretary-General and his envoy, the Council now had to consider whether to "terminate MINURSO and return the issue of Western Sahara to the General Assembly, thereby recognizing and acknowledging that ... the United Nations was not going to solve the problem of Western Sahara without requiring that one or both of the parties do something they would not voluntarily agree to do" — or else "try once again to get the parties to work towards acceptance and implementation" of the peace plan.

On 29 April, the Council reaffirmed its support for the peace plan as "an optimal political solution on the basis of agreement between the two parties" and called on the parties and the states of the region to cooperate fully with the Secretary-General and his personal envoy. It also extended MINURSO's mandate until the end of October.

PART THREE

Appendices

UNITED NATIONS MEMBER STATES

(as of December 2003)

Member State	Date of admission	Scale of assessments for 2004 (per cent)	Population (est.)
Afghanistan	19 November 1946	0.002	22,083,000
Albania	14 December 1955	0.005	3,122,000
Algeria	8 October 1962	0.076	30,836,000
Andorra	28 July 1993	0.005	66,000
Angola	1 December 1976	0.001	12,768,000
Antigua and Barbuda	11 November 1981	0.003	77,000
Argentina	24 October 1945	0.956	36,224,000
Armenia	2 March 1992	0.002	3,458,000
Australia	1 November 1945	1.592	19,387,000
Austria	14 December 1955	0.859	8,066,000
Azerbaijan	2 March 1992	0.005	8,114,000
Bahamas	18 September 1973	0.013	307,000
Bahrain	21 September 1971	0.030	651,000
Bangladesh	17 September 1974	0.010	140,880,000
Barbados	9 December 1966	0.010	268,000
Belarus[a]	24 October 1945	0.018	9,973,000
Belgium	27 December 1945	1.069	10,273,000
Belize	25 September 1981	0.001	257,000
Benin	20 September 1960	0.002	6,417,000
Bhutan	21 September 1971	0.001	2,699,000
Bolivia	14 November 1945	0.009	8,274,000
Bosnia and Herzegovina	22 May 1992	0.003	4,067,000
Botswana	17 October 1966	0.012	1,680,000
Brazil	24 October 1945	1.523	172,386,000
Brunei Darussalam	21 September 1984	0.034	344,000
Bulgaria	14 December 1955	0.017	8,033,000
Burkina Faso	20 September 1960	0.002	12,259,000
Burundi	18 September 1962	0.001	6,412,000
Cambodia	14 December 1955	0.002	13,311,000
Cameroon	20 September 1960	0.008	15,429,000
Canada	9 November 1945	2.813	30,007,000
Cape Verde	16 September 1975	0.001	445,000

Member State	Date of admission	Scale of assessments for 2004 (per cent)	Population (est.)
Central African Republic	20 September 1960	0.001	3,770,000
Chad	20 September 1960	0.001	8,322,000
Chile	24 October 1945	0.223	15,402,000
China	24 October 1945	2.053	1,285,229,000
Colombia	5 November 1945	0.155	43,071,000
Comoros	12 November 1975	0.001	726,000
Congo	20 September 1960	0.001	3,542,000
Costa Rica	2 November 1945	0.030	3,873,000
Côte d'Ivoire	20 September 1960	0.010	16,939,000
Croatia	22 May 1992	0.037	4,445,000
Cuba	24 October 1945	0.043	11,230,000
Cyprus	20 September 1960	0.039	690,000
Czech Republic	19 January 1993	0.183	10,224,000
Democratic People's Republic of Korea	17 September 1991	0.010	22,409,000
Democratic Republic of the Congo[b]	20 September 1960	0.003	49,785,000
Denmark	24 October 1945	0.718	5,337,000
Djibouti	20 September 1977	0.001	681,000
Dominica	18 December 1978	0.001	71,000
Dominican Republic	24 October 1945	0.035	8,528,000
Ecuador	21 December 1945	0.019	12,156,000
Egypt[c]	24 October 1945	0.120	67,886,000
El Salvador	24 October 1945	0.022	6,313,000
Equatorial Guinea	12 November 1968	0.002	468,000
Eritrea	28 May 1993	0.001	3,847,000
Estonia	17 September 1991	0.012	1,353,000
Ethiopia	13 November 1945	0.004	65,374,000
Federated States of Micronesia	17 September 1991	0.001	107,000
Fiji	13 October 1970	0.004	822,000
Finland	14 December 1955	0.533	5,188,000
France	24 October 1945	6.030	59,191,000
Gabon	20 September 1960	0.009	1,237,000
Gambia	21 September 1965	0.001	1,420,000

Member State	Date of admission	Scale of assessments for 2004 (per cent)	Population (est.)
Georgia	31 July 1992	0.003	5,224,000
Germany	18 September 1973	8.662	82,357,000
Ghana	8 March 1957	0.004	20,028,000
Greece	25 October 1945	0.530	10,020,000
Grenada	17 September 1974	0.001	101,000
Guatemala	21 November 1945	0.030	11,683,000
Guinea	12 December 1958	0.003	8,242,000
Guinea-Bissau	17 September 1974	0.001	1,407,000
Guyana	20 September 1966	0.001	762,000
Haiti	24 October 1945	0.003	8,132,000
Honduras	17 December 1945	0.005	6,619,000
Hungary	14 December 1955	0.126	9,968,000
Iceland	19 November 1946	0.034	285,000
India	30 October 1945	0.421	1,017,544,000
Indonesia[d]	28 September 1950	0.142	214,840,000
Iran (Islamic Republic of)	24 October 1945	0.157	64,530,000
Iraq	21 December 1945	0.016	23,860,000
Ireland	14 December 1955	0.350	3,917,000
Israel	11 May 1949	0.467	6,445,000
Italy	14 December 1955	4.885	57,948,000
Jamaica	18 September 1962	0.008	2,621,000
Japan	18 December 1956	19.468	127,130,000
Jordan	14 December 1955	0.011	5,183,000
Kazakhstan	2 March 1992	0.025	14,831,000
Kenya	16 December 1963	0.009	31,065,000
Kiribati	14 September 1999	0.001	85,000
Kuwait	14 May 1963	0.162	2,275,000
Kyrgyzstan	2 March 1992	0.001	4,955,000
Lao People's Democratic Republic	14 December 1955	0.001	5,403,000
Latvia	17 September 1991	0.015	3,539,000
Lebanon	24 October 1945	0.024	3,537,000
Lesotho	17 October 1966	0.001	2,189,000
Liberia	2 November 1945	0.001	3,099,000
Libyan Arab Jamahiriya	14 December 1955	0.132	5,299,000

Member State	Date of admission	Scale of assessments for 2004 (per cent)	Population (est.)
Liechtenstein	18 September 1990	0.005	33,000
Lithuania	17 September 1991	0.024	3,484,000
Luxembourg	24 October 1945	0.077	441,000
Madagascar	20 September 1960	0.003	16,439,000
Malawi	1 December 1964	0.001	11,140,000
Malaysia[e]	17 September 1957	0.203	23,492,000
Maldives	21 September 1965	0.001	276,000
Mali	28 September 1960	0.002	10,400,000
Malta	1 December 1964	0.014	395,000
Marshall Islands	17 September 1991	0.001	57,000
Mauritania	27 October 1961	0.001	2,724,000
Mauritius	24 April 1968	0.011	1,200,000
Mexico	7 November 1945	1.883	101,754,000
Monaco	28 May 1993	0.003	34,000
Mongolia	27 October 1961	0.001	2,442,000
Morocco	12 November 1956	0.047	29,170,000
Mozambique	16 September 1975	0.001	17,656,000
Myanmar	19 April 1948	0.010	48,205,000
Namibia	23 April 1990	0.006	1,930,000
Nauru	14 September 1999	0.001	12,000
Nepal	14 December 1955	0.004	23,152,000
Netherlands	10 December 1945	1.690	16,044,000
New Zealand	October 1945	0.221	3,850,000
Nicaragua	24 October 1945	0.001	5,205,000
Niger	20 September 1960	0.001	11,134,000
Nigeria	7 October 1960	0.042	117,823,000
Norway	27 November 1945	0.679	4,513,000
Oman	7 October 1971	0.070	2,478,000
Pakistan	30 September 1947	0.055	142,280,000
Palau	15 December 1994	0.001	20,000
Panama	13 November 1945	0.019	2,897,000
Papua New Guinea	10 October 1975	0.003	5,460,000
Paraguay	24 October 1945	0.012	5,604,000
Peru	31 October 1945	0.092	26,347,000
Philippines	24 October 1945	0.095	77,151,000

Member State	Date of admission	Scale of assessments for 2004 (per cent)	Population (est.)
Poland	24 October 1945	0.461	38,641,000
Portugal	14 December 1955	0.470	10,024,000
Qatar	21 September 1971	0.064	598,000
Republic of Korea	17 September 1991	1.796	47,343,000
Republic of Moldova	2 March 1992	0.001	4,276,000
Romania	14 December 1955	0.060	22,408,000
Russian Federation[f]	24 October 1945	1.100	144,400,000
Rwanda	18 September 1962	0.001	8,066,000
Saint Kitts and Nevis	23 September 1983	0.001	46,000
Saint Lucia	18 September 1979	0.002	158,000
Saint Vincent and the Grenadines	16 September 1980	0.001	109,000
Samoa	15 December 1976	0.001	175,000
San Marino	2 March 1992	0.003	27,000
Sao Tome and Principe	16 September 1975	0.001	153,000
Saudi Arabia	24 October 1945	0.713	22,829,000
Senegal	28 September 1960	0.005	9,803,000
Serbia and Montenegro[g]	24 October 1945	0.019	10,651,000
Seychelles	21 September 1976	0.002	81,000
Sierra Leone	27 September 1961	0.001	4,573,000
Singapore	21 September 1965	0.388	4,131,000
Slovakia	19 January 1993	0.051	5,380,000
Slovenia	22 May 1992	0.082	1,948,000
Solomon Islands	19 September 1978	0.001	450,000
Somalia	20 September 1960	0.001	9,088,000
South Africa	7 November 1945	0.292	44,328,000
Spain	14 December 1955	2.520	40,847,000
Sri Lanka	14 December 1955	0.017	18,700,000
Sudan	12 November 1956	0.008	31,627,000
Suriname	4 December 1975	0.001	429,000
Swaziland	24 September 1968	0.002	1,058,000
Sweden	19 November 1946	1.998	8,860,000
Switzerland	10 September 2002	1.197	7,231,000
Syrian Arab Republic[h]	24 October 1945	0.038	16,720,000
Tajikistan	2 March 1992	0.001	6,293,000

Member State	Date of admission	Scale of assessments for 2004 (per cent)	Population (est.)
Thailand	16 December 1946	0.209	62,968,000
The former Yugoslav Republic of Macedonia[i]	8 April 1993	0.006	2,035,000
Timor-Leste	27 September 2002	0.001	711,000
Togo	20 September 1960	0.001	4,686,000
Tonga	14 September 1999	0.001	101,000
Trinidad and Tobago	18 September 1962	0.022	1,294,000
Tunisia	12 November 1956	0.032	9,674,000
Turkey	24 October 1945	0.372	68,610,000
Turkmenistan	2 March 1992	0.005	4,720,000
Tuvalu	5 September 2000	0.001	10,000
Uganda	25 October 1962	0.006	22,788,000
Ukraine	24 October 1945	0.039	48,416,000
United Arab Emirates	9 December 1971	0.235	2,879,000
United Kingdom	24 October 1945	6.127	58,789,000
United Republic of Tanzania[j]	14 December 1961	0.006	34,569,000
United States of America	24 October 1945	22.000	284,797,000
Uruguay	18 December 1945	0.048	3,361,000
Uzbekistan	2 March 1992	0.014	25,068,000
Vanuatu	15 September 1981	0.001	202,000
Venezuela	15 November 1945	0.171	24,632,000
Viet Nam	20 September 1977	0.021	79,197,000
Yemen	30 September 1947	0.006	18,863,000
Zambia	1 December 1964	0.002	10,570,000
Zimbabwe	25 August 1980	0.007	12,960,000

States which are not Members of the United Nations but which participate in certain of its activities, shall be called upon to contribute towards the expenses of the Organization on the basis of the following percentage rates:

Holy See   0.001

[a] On 19 September 1991, Byelorussia informed the United Nations that it had changed its name to Belarus.

[b] The Republic of Zaire informed the United Nations that, effective 17 May 1997, it had changed its name to Democratic Republic of the Congo.

[c] Egypt and Syria were original members of the United Nations from 24 October 1945. Following a plebiscite on 21 February 1958, the United Arab Republic was established by a union of Egypt and Syria and continued as a single member. On 13 October 1961, Syria, having resumed its status as an independent state, resumed its separate membership in the United Nations. On 2 September 1971, the United Arab Republic changed its name to the Arab Republic of Egypt.

[d] By letter of 20 January 1965, Indonesia announced its decision to withdraw from the United Nations "at this stage and under the present circumstances". By a telegram of 19 September 1966, it announced its decision "to resume full cooperation with the United Nations and to resume participation in its activities". On 28 September 1966, the General Assembly took note of this decision and the President invited representatives of Indonesia to take seats in the Assembly.

[e] The Federation of Malaya joined the United Nations on 17 September 1957. On 16 September 1963, its name was changed to Malaysia, following the admission to the new federation of Singapore, Sabah (North Borneo) and Sarawak. Singapore became an independent state on 9 August 1965 and a United Nations member on 21 September 1965.

[f] The Union of Soviet Socialist Republics was an original member of the United Nations from 24 October 1945. In a letter dated 24 December 1991, Boris Yeltsin, the President of the Russian Federation, informed the Secretary-General that the membership of the Soviet Union in the Security Council and all other United Nations organs was being continued by the Russian Federation with the support of the 11 member countries of the Commonwealth of Independent States.

[g] On 12 February 2003, the Federal Republic of Yugoslavia informed the United Nations that it had changed its name to Serbia and Montenegro, effective 4 February 2003.

[h] Egypt and Syria were original members of the United Nations from 24 October 1945. Following a plebiscite on 21 January 1958, the United Arab Republic was established by a union of Egypt and Syria and continued as a single member. On 13 October 1961, Syria, having resumed its status as an independent state, resumed its separate membership in the United Nations.

[i] The General Assembly decided on 8 April 1993 to admit to United Nations membership the States being provisionally referred to for all purposes within the United Nations as "the former Yugoslav Republic of Macedonia" pending settlement of the difference that had arisen over its name.

[j] Tanganyika was a United Nations member from 14 December 1961 and Zanzibar was a member from 16 December 1963. Following the ratification on 26 April 1964 of Articles of Union between Tanganyika and Zanzibar, the United Republic of Tanganyika and Zanzibar continued as a single member, changing its name to the United Republic of Tanzania on 1 November 1964.

GROWTH IN UNITED NATIONS MEMBERSHIP, 1945-2003

Year	Number	Member States
1945	Original 51	Argentina, Australia, Belgium, Bolivia, Brazil, Belarus, Canada, Chile, China, Colombia, Costa Rica, Cuba, Czechoslovakia, Denmark, Dominican Republic, Ecuador, Egypt, El Salvador, Ethiopia, France, Greece, Guatemala, Haiti, Honduras, India, Iran, Iraq, Lebanon, Liberia, Luxembourg, Mexico, Netherlands, New Zealand, Nicaragua, Norway, Panama, Paraguay, Peru, Philippines, Poland, Russian Federation, Saudi Arabia, South Africa, Syrian Arab Republic, Turkey, Ukraine, United Kingdom of Great Britain and Northern Ireland, United States of America, Uruguay, Venezuela, Yugoslavia
1946	55	Afghanistan, Iceland, Sweden, Thailand
1947	57	Pakistan, Yemen[1]
1948	58	Myanmar
1949	59	Israel
1950	60	Indonesia
1955	76	Albania, Austria, Bulgaria, Cambodia, Finland, Hungary, Ireland, Italy, Jordan, Lao People's Democratic Republic, Libyan Arab Jamahiriya, Nepal, Portugal, Romania, Spain, Sri Lanka
1956	80	Japan, Morocco, Sudan, Tunisia
1957	82	Ghana, Malaysia
1958	82[2]	Guinea
1960	99	Benin, Burkina Faso, Cameroon, Central African Republic, Chad, Congo, Côte d'Ivoire, Cyprus, Gabon, Madagascar, Mali, Niger, Nigeria, Senegal, Somalia, Togo, Democratic Republic of the Congo
1961	104[3]	Mauritania, Mongolia, Sierra Leone, United Republic of Tanzania
1962	110	Algeria, Burundi, Jamaica, Rwanda, Trinidad and Tobago, Uganda
1963	112	Kenya, Kuwait
1964	115	Malawi, Malta, Zambia
1965	117[4]	Gambia, Maldives, Singapore
1966	122[5]	Barbados, Botswana, Guyana, Lesotho
1967	123	Democratic Yemen[1]

Year	Number	Member States
1968	126	Equatorial Guinea, Mauritius, Swaziland
1970	127	Fiji
1971	132	Bahrain, Bhutan, Oman, Qatar, United Arab Emirates
1973	135	Bahamas, Federal Republic of Germany[6], German Democratic Republic,
1974	138	Bangladesh, Grenada, Guinea-Bissau
1975	144	Cape Verde, Comoros, Mozambique, Papua New Guinea, Sao Tome and Principe, Suriname
1976	147	Angola, Samoa, Seychelles
1977	149	Djibouti, Viet Nam
1978	151	Dominica, Solomon Islands
1979	152	Saint Lucia
1980	154	Saint Vincent and the Grenadines, Zimbabwe
1981	157	Antigua and Barbuda, Belize, Vanuatu
1983	158	Saint Kitts and Nevis
1984	159	Brunei Darussalam
1990	159[1,6]	Liechtenstein, Namibia
1991	166	Democratic People's Republic of Korea, Estonia, Federated States of Micronesia, Latvia, Lithuania, Marshall Islands, Republic of Korea
1992	179	Armenia, Azerbaijan, Bosnia and Herzegovina[7], Croatia[7], Georgia, Kazakhstan, Kyrgyzstan, Moldova, San Marino, Slovenia[7], Tajikistan, Turkmenistan, Uzbekistan
1993	184	Andorra, Czech Republic[8], Eritrea, Monaco, Slovak Republic[8], The former Yugoslav Republic of Macedonia[7]
1994	185	Palau
1999	188	Kiribati, Nauru, Tonga
2000	189	Tuvalu, Serbia and Montenegro[7]
2002	191	Switzerland, Timor-Leste

---

[1] Yemen was admitted to membership in the United Nations on 30 September 1947 and Democratic Yemen on 14 December 1967. On 22 May 1990, the two countries merged and have since been represented as one member with the name "Yemen".

[2] The total remains the same because from 21 January 1958 Syria and Egypt continued as a single member (United Arab Republic)

[3] Syria resumed its status as an independent state.

[4] Indonesia withdrew as of 20 January 1965.

[5] Indonesia resumed its membership as of 28 September 1966.

[6] The Federal Republic of Germany and the German Democratic Republic were admitted to membership in the United Nations on 18 September 1973. Through the accession of the German Democratic Republic to the Federal Republic of Germany, effective from 3 October 1990, the two German states have united to form one sovereign state.

[7] The Socialist Federal Republic of Yugoslavia was an original member of the United Nations, the Charter having been signed on its behalf on 26 June 1945 and ratified 19 October 1945, until its dissolution following the establishment and subsequent admission as new members of Bosnia and Herzegovina, the Republic of Croatia, the Republic of Slovenia, The former Yugoslav Republic of Macedonia, and the Federal Republic of Yugoslavia. The Republic of Bosnia and Herzegovina, the Republic of Croatia and the Republic of Slovenia were admitted as members of the United Nations on 22 May 1992. On 8 April 1993, the General Assembly decided to admit as a member of the United Nations the state being provisionally referred to for all purposes within the United Nations as "The former Yugoslav Republic of Macedonia" pending settlement of the difference that had arisen over its name. The Federal Republic of Yugoslavia was admitted as a member of the United Nations on 1 November 2000. On 12 February 2003, the Federal Republic of Yugoslavia informed the United Nations that it had changed its name to Serbia and Montenegro, effective 4 February 2003.

[8] Czechoslovakia was an original member of the United Nations from 24 October 1945. In a letter dated 10 December 1992, its Permanent Representative informed the Secretary-General that the Czech and Slovak Federal Republic would cease to exist on 31 December 1992 and that the Czech Republic and the Slovak Republic, as successor states, would apply for membership in the United Nations. Following the receipt of such applications, the Security Council, on 8 January 1993, recommended to the General Assembly that the Czech Republic and the Slovak Republic be admitted to United Nations membership. They were thus admitted on 19 January 1993 as member states.

PEACEKEEPING OPERATIONS, PAST AND PRESENT

(As of July 2004)

UNTSO*
United Nations Truce Supervision Organization (Jerusalem)
May 1948

UNMOGIP*
United Nations Military Observer Group in India and Pakistan
January 1949

UNEF I
First United Nations Emergency Force (Gaza)
November 1956–June 1967

UNOGIL
United Nations Observation Group in Lebanon
June–December 1958

ONUC
United Nations Operation in the Congo
July 1960–June 1964

UNSF
United Nations Security Force in West New Guinea (West Irian)
October 1962–April 1963

UNYOM
United Nations Yemen Observation Mission
July 1963–September 1964

UNFICYP*
United Nations Peacekeeping Force in Cyprus
March 1964

DOMREP
Mission of the Special Representative of the Secretary-General in the Dominican
Republic
May 1965–October 1966

UNIPOM
United Nations India-Pakistan Observation Mission
September 1965–March 1966

UNEF II
Second United Nations Emergency Force (Suez Canal and later Sinai peninsula)
October 1973–July 1979

UNDOF*
United Nations Disengagement Observer Force (Syrian Golan Heights)
May 1974

UNIFIL*
United Nations Interim Force in Lebanon
March 1978

UNGOMAP
United Nations Good Offices Mission in Afghanistan and Pakistan
May 1988–March 1990

UNIIMOG
United Nations Iran-Iraq Military Observer Group
August 1988–February 1991

UNAVEM I
United Nations Angola Verification Mission I
December 1988–June 1991

UNTAG
United Nations Transition Assistance Group (Namibia and Angola)
April 1989–March 1990

ONUCA
United Nations Observer Group in Central America
November 1989–January 1992

UNIKOM*
United Nations Iraq-Kuwait Observation Mission
April 1991

UNAVEM II
United Nations Angola Verification Mission II
May 1991–February 1995

ONUSAL
United Nations Observer Mission in El Salvador
July 1991–April 1995

MINURSO*
United Nations Mission for the Referendum in Western Sahara
April 1991

UNAMIC
United Nations Advance Mission in Cambodia
October 1991–March 1992

UNPROFOR
United Nations Protection Force (former Yugoslavia)
February 1992–December 1995

UNTAC
United Nations Transitional Authority in Cambodia
March 1992–September 1993

UNOSOM I
United Nations Operation in Somalia I
April 1992–March 1993

ONUMOZ
United Nations Operation in Mozambique
December 1992–December 1994

UNOSOM II
United Nations Operation in Somalia II
March 1993–March 1995

UNOMUR
United Nations Observer Mission Uganda-Rwanda
June 1993–September 1994

UNOMIG*
United Nations Observer Mission in Georgia
August 1993

UNOMIL
United Nations Observer Mission in Liberia
September 1993–September 1997

UNMIH
United Nations Mission in Haiti
September 1993–June 1996

UNAMIR
United Nations Assistance Mission for Rwanda
October 1993–March 1996

UNASOG
United Nations Aouzou Strip Observer Group (Chad/Lybia)
May–June 1994

UNMOT
United Nations Mission of Observers in Tajikistan
December 1994–May 2000

UNAVEM III
United Nations Angola Verification Mission III
February 1995–June 1997

UNCRO
United Nations Confidence Restoration Operation in Croatia
March 1995–January 1996

UNPREDEP
United Nations Preventive Deployment Force (former Yugoslav Republic of Macedonia)
March 1995–February 1999

UNMIBH
United Nations Mission in Bosnia and Herzegovina
December 1995–December 2002

UNTAES
United Nations Transitional Administration for Eastern Slavonia, Baranja and
Western Sirmium (Croatia)
January 1996–January 1998

UNMOP
United Nations Mission of Observers in Prevlaka
February 1996–December 2002

UNSMIH
United Nations Support Mission in Haiti
July 1996–June 1997

MINUGUA
United Nations Verification Mission in Guatemala
January–May 1997

MONUA
United Nations Observer Mission in Angola
June 1997–February 1999

UNTMIH
United Nations Transition Mission in Haiti
August–November 1997

MIPONUH
United Nations Civilian Police Mission in Haiti
December 1997–March 2000

UNPSG
United Nations Civilian Police Support Group (Croatia)
January–October 1998

MINURCA
United Nations Mission in the Central African Republic
April 1998–February 2000

UNOMSIL
United Nations Observer Mission in Sierra Leone
July 1998–October 1999

UNMIK*
United Nations Interim Administration Mission in Kosovo
June 1999

UNAMSIL*
United Nations Mission in Sierra Leone
October 1999

UNTAET
United Nations Transitional Administration in East Timor
October 1999–May 2002

MONUC*
United Nations Observer Mission in the Democratic Republic of the Congo
December 1999

UNMEE*
United Nations Mission in Ethiopia and Eritrea
July 2000

UNMISET*
United Nations Mission of Support in East Timor
May 2002

UNMIL*
United Nations Mission in Liberia
September 2003

MINUSTAH*
United Nations Stabilization Mission in Haiti
April 2004

ONUB*
United Nations Operation in Burundi
May 2004

---

*Current operation, as of July 2004.

Trust and Non-Self-Governing Territories that have achieved
independence since the adoption of the 1960 Declaration*

State or entity	Date of admission to the United Nations
Africa	
Algeria	8 October 1962
Angola	1 December 1976
Botswana	17 October 1966
Burundi	18 September 1962
Cape Verde	16 September 1975
Comoros	12 November 1975
Djibouti	20 September 1977
Equatorial Guinea	12 November 1968
Gambia	21 September 1965
Guinea-Bissau	17 September 1974
Kenya	16 December 1963
Lesotho	17 October 1966
Malawi	1 December 1964
Mauritius	24 April 1968
Mozambique	16 September 1975
Namibia	23 April 1990
Rwanda	18 September 1962
Sao Tome and Principe	26 September 1975
Seychelles	21 September 1976
Sierra Leone	27 September 1961
Swaziland	24 September 1968
Timor-Leste	27 September 2002
Uganda	25 October 1962
United Republic of Tanzania[1]	14 December 1961
Zambia	1 December 1964
Zimbabwe	18 April 1980

---

* Declaration on the Granting of Independence to Colonial Countries and Peoples, adopted by the General Assembly on 14 December 1960.

State or entity	Date of admission to the United Nations
Asia	
Brunei Darussalam	21 September 1984
Democratic Yemen	14 December 1967
Oman	7 October 1971
Singapore	21 September 1965
Caribbean	
Antigua and Barbuda	11 November 1981
Bahamas	18 September 1973
Barbados	9 December 1966
Belize	25 September 1981
Dominica	18 December 1978
Grenada	17 December 1974
Guyana	20 September 1966
Jamaica	18 September 1962
Saint Christopher and Nevis	23 September 1983
Saint Lucia	18 September 1979
Saint Vincent and the Grenadines	16 September 1980
Suriname[2]	4 December 1975
Trinidad and Tobago	18 September 1962
Europe	
Malta	1 December 1964
Pacific	
Federated States of Micronesia	17 September 1991
Fiji	13 October 1970
Kiribati	14 September 1999
Marshall Islands	17 September 1991
Nauru	14 September 1999
Papua New Guinea	10 October 1975
Palau	15 December 1994
Samoa	15 December 1976
Solomon Islands	19 September 1978
Tuvalu	5 September 2000
Vanuatu	15 September 1981

---

[1] The former Trust Territory of Tanganyika, which became independent in December 1961, and the former Protectorate of Zanzibar, which achieved independence in December 1963, united into a single state in April 1964.

[2] By resolution 945(X), the General Assembly accepted the cessation of the transmission of information regarding Suriname following constitutional changes in the relationship between the Netherlands, Suriname and the Netherlands Antilles.

DECOLONIZATION

Dependent Territories that have become integrated or associated with
independent States since the adoption of the 1960 Declaration*

Territory	Remarks
Cameroons under British administration	The northern part of the Trust Territory joined the Federation of Nigeria on 1 June 1961 and the southern part joined the Republic of Cameroon on 1 October 1961
Cook Islands	Fully self-governing in free association with New Zealand since August 1965
Ifni	Returned to Morocco in June 1969
Niue	Fully self-governing in free association with New Zealand since August 1974
North Borneo	North Borneo and Sarawak joined the Federation of Malaya in 1963 to form the Federation of Malaysia
São Joao Batista de Ajuda	Nationally united with Dahomey (now Benin) in August 1961
Sarawak	Sarawak and North Borneo joined the Federation of Malaya in 1963 to form the Federation of Malaysia
West New Guinea (West Irian)	United with Indonesia in 1963
Cocos (Keeling) Islands	Integrated with Australia in 1984

---

* *Declaration on the Granting of Independence to Colonial Countries and Peoples,* adopted by the
General Assembly on 14 December 1960.

DECOLONIZATION

Trust Territories that have achieved self-determination

Togoland (under British administration)
United with the Gold Coast (Colony and Protectorate), a Non-Self-Governing Territory administered by the United Kingdom, in 1957 to form Ghana

Somaliland (under Italian administration)
United with British Somaliland Protectorate in 1960 to form Somalia

Togoland (under French administration)
Became independent as Togo in 1960

Cameroons (under French administration)
Became independent as Cameroon in 1960

Cameroons (under British administration)
The northern part of the Trust Territory joined the Federation of Nigeria on 1 June 1961 and the southern part joined the Republic of Cameroon on 1 October 1961

Tanganyika (under British administration)
Became independent in 1961 (in 1964, Tanganyika and the former Protectorate of Zanzibar, which had become independent in 1963, united as a single state under the name of the United Republic of Tanzania)

Ruanda-Urundi (under Belgian administration)
Voted to divide into the two sovereign states of Rwanda and Burundi in 1962

Western Samoa (under New Zealand administration)
Became independent as Samoa in 1962

Nauru (administered by Australia on behalf of Australia, New Zealand and the United Kingdom)
Became independent in 1968

New Guinea (administered by Australia)
United with the Non-Self-Governing Territory of Papua, also administered by Australia, to become the independent state of Papua New Guinea in 1975

Trust Territory of the Pacific Islands:

(a) **Federated States of Micronesia**
Became fully self-governing in free Association with the United States in 1990

(b) **Republic of the Marshall Islands**
Became fully self-governing in free Association with the United States in 1990

(c) **Commonwealth of the Northern Mariana Islands**
Became fully self-governing as a Commonwealth of the United States in 1990

(d) **Palau**
Became fully self-governing in free Association with the United States in 1994

BUDGET OF THE UNITED NATIONS

For the 2004-2005 biennium, the appropriation for the regular budget of the United Nations (i.e. excluding the bulk of offices and programmes, as well as the specialized agencies and other associated bodies), as initially approved in 2003, totalled $3,160,860,300, divided into 13 main categories of expenditures, as follows (in United States dollars):

1.	Overall policy-making, direction and coordination	593,884,900
2.	Political affairs	349,252,200
3.	International justice and law	70,245,400
4.	International cooperation for development	336,495,300
5.	Regional cooperation for development	388,613,700
6.	Human rights and humanitarian affairs	170,670,500
7.	Public information	155,969,900
8.	Common support services	516,168,900
9.	Internal oversight	23,227,200
10.	Jointly financed activities and special expenses	102,445,300
11.	Capital expenditures	58,651,300
12.	Staff assessment*	382,270,700
13.	Development account	13,065,000

The main source of funds for the regular budget is the contributions of member states, who are assessed on a scale specified by the Assembly on the recommendation of the 18-member Committee on Contributions. The fundamental criterion on which the scale of assessments is based is the real capacity of member states to pay. The Assembly has fixed a maximum of 22 per cent of the budget for any one contributor and a minimum of 0.001 per cent. (For scale of assessments of member states, see pages 297-303.)

Initial income estimates for the biennium 2004-2005, other than assessments on member states, totalled $415,291,800.

1.	Income from staff assessment*	386,491,700
2.	General income	24,043,200
3.	Services to the public	4,756,900

---

* To equalize the net pay of all United Nations staff members, whatever their national tax obligations, the organization deducts from their salaries a sum of money designated as "staff assessment". The rate of withholding is roughly equivalent to the amount paid by United States citizens for

federal, state and local taxes calculated at the standard rate. The money collected by the United Nations from the staff assessment is then credited towards the United Nations membership "dues" of the staff member's home country.

Most governments excuse nationals who are United Nations employees from further taxation. The United States is the main exception; its citizens who work for the Secretariat must pay the same income taxes as all other United States citizens. To enable them to pay their taxes, the United Nations refunds to United States employees that part of their staff assessment, which is equal to what the national revenue authorities require for taxes. The citizen then pays that amount to those authorities. In this way, United States nationals are not required to pay taxes twice.

The regular programme budget, to which these assessments apply, covers expenses relating to substantive programmes, programme support and administrative activities of the organization, both at Headquarters and around the globe.

UNITED NATIONS SPECIAL OBSERVANCES

INTERNATIONAL DECADES AND YEARS

1994-2004	International Decade of the World's Indigenous People
1995-2004	United Nations Decade for Human Rights Education
1997-2006	United Nations Decade for the Eradication of Poverty
2001-2010	Decade to Roll Back Malaria in Developing Countries, Particularly in Africa
2001-2010	Second International Decade for the Eradication of Colonialism
2001-2010	International Decade for a Culture of Peace and Non-violence for the Children of the World
2003-2012	United Nations Literacy Decade: Education for All
2005-2014	United Nations Decade of Education for Sustainable Development
2005-2015	International Decade for Action, "Water for Life" (from 22 March 2005)
2004	International Year to Commemorate the Struggle against Slavery and Its Abolition
2004	International Year of Rice
2005	International Year of Microcredit
2005	International Year for Sport and Physical Education
2006	International Year of Deserts and Desertification

ANNUAL DAYS AND WEEKS

8 March	United Nations Day for Women's Rights and International Peace
21 March	International Day for the Elimination of Racial Discrimination
Beginning 21 March	Week of Solidarity with the Peoples Struggling against Racism and Racial Discrimination
22 March	World Day for Water
7 April 2004	International Day of Reflection on the 1994 Genocide in Rwanda (ten years later)

3 May	World Press Freedom Day
15 May	International Day of Families
21 May	World Day for Cultural Diversity for Dialogue and Development
22 May	International Day for Biological Diversity
Beginning 25 May	Week of Solidarity with the Peoples of Non-Self-Governing Territories
29 May	International Day of United Nations Peacekeepers
4 June	International Day of Innocent Children Victims of Aggression
5 June	World Environment Day
17 June	World Day to Combat Desertification and Drought
20 June	World Refugee Day
23 June	United Nations Public Service Day
26 June	International Day against Drug Abuse and Illicit Trafficking
26 June	International Day in Support of Victims of Torture
First Saturday of July	International Day of Cooperatives
11 July	World Population Day
9 August	International Day of the World's Indigenous People
12 August	International Youth Day
16 September	International Day for the Preservation of the Ozone Layer
21 September	International Day of Peace
1 October	International Day of Older Persons
First Monday of October	World Habitat Day
Second Wednesday of October	International Day for Natural Disaster Reduction
4-10 October	World Space Week
16 October	World Food Day

17 October	International Day for the Eradication of Poverty
24 October	United Nations Day
24-30 October	Disarmament Week
6 November	International Day for Preventing the Exploitation of the Environment in War and Armed Conflict
16 November	International Day for Tolerance
20 November	Africa Industrialization Day
21 November	World Television Day
25 November	International Day for the Elimination of Violence against Women
29 November	International Day of Solidarity with the Palestinian People
1 December	World AIDS Day
2 December	International Day for the Abolition of Slavery
3 December	International Day of Disabled Persons
10 December	Human Rights Day
11 December	International Mountain Day
18 December	International Migrants Day

OTHER INTERNATIONAL DAYS

Other international days observed throughout the United Nations system include:

21 February	International Mother Language Day
23 March	World Meteorological Day
7 April	World Health Day
23 April	World Book and Copyright Day
17 May	World Telecommunication Day
31 May	World No-Tobacco Day
23 August	International Day for the Remembrance of the Slave Trade and its Abolition
8 September	International Literacy Day

Last week in September	
	World Maritime Day
5 October	World Teachers' Day
9 October	World Post Day
10 October	World Mental Health Day
24 October	World Development Information Day
20 November (suggested)	
	Universal Children's Day
5 December	International Volunteer Day for Economic and Social Development
7 December	International Civil Aviation Day

AFRICA

Accra

United Nations Information Centre, Gamel Abdul Nassar/Liberia Roads
(P.O. Box 2339), Accra, Ghana
Telephone: (233 21) 665 511
Fax: (233 21) 665 578
E-mail: *info@unicar.org.gh*
Services to: Ghana, Sierra Leone

Addis Ababa

United Nations Information Service, Economic Commission for Africa
(P.O. Box 3001), Addis Ababa, Ethiopia
Telephone: (251 1) 515 826,
Fax: (251 1) 510 365
E-mail: *ecainfo@uneca.org*
Services to: Ethiopia, Economic Commission for Africa

Algiers

United Nations Information Centre, 9A, rue Emile Payen, Hydra
(Boite postale 823), Algiers, Algeria
Telephone: (213 21) 48 08 71
Fax: (213 21) 69 23 15
E-mail: *unic.dz@undp.org* (Internet: *www.unic.org.dz*)
Services to: Algeria

Antananarivo

United Nations Information Centre, 22 rue Rainitovo, Antananarivo, Madagascar
Telephone: (261 20) 22 241 15/22 375 06
Fax: (261 20) 22 375 06
E-mail: *unic.ant@dts.mg* (Internet: *www.onu.dts.mg*)
Services to: Madagascar

Brazzaville

United Nations Information Centre, Avenue Foch, Case Ortf 15
(P.O. Box 13210 or 1018), Brazzaville, Congo
Telephone: (242) 81 44 47/81 46 81/61 20 68
Fax: (242) 81 27 44
E-mail: *prosper.mihindou@undp.org*
Services to: Congo

Bujumbura

United Nations Information Centre, 117, Avenue de la Révolution
(P.O. Box 2160), Bujumbura, Burundi
Telephone: (257) 225 018/228 569
Fax: (257) 241 798
E-mail: *unicbuj@cbinf.com*
Services to: Burundi

Cairo

United Nations Information Centre, 1, Osoris St. Garden City
(P.O. Box 262), Cairo, Egypt
Telephone: (20 2) 790-0022
Fax: (20 2) 795-3705
E-mail: *info@unic-eg.org* (Internet: *www.unic-eg.org*)
Services to: Egypt, Saudi Arabia

Dakar

United Nations Information Centre, Rues de Thann x Dagorne
(P.O. Box 154) Dakar, Senegal
Telephone: (221) 889-11-89
Fax: (221) 822 14-06
E-mail: *cinu.dakar@sentoo.sn* (Internet: *cinu-dakar.org*)
Services to: Senegal, Cape Verde, Gambia, Guinea-Bissau, Côte d'Ivoire,
Mauritania, Guinea

Dar es Salaam

United Nations Information Centre, Marogoro Road/Sokoine Drive,
Old Boma Building, Ground Floor (P.O. Box 9224), Dar es Salaam
Telephone: (255 22) 212 6055 (NIO); (255 22) 211 9510 (UNIC)
Fax: (255 22) 211 2923
E-mail: *unic.urt@raha.com* (Internet: *unic.undp.org*)
Services to: United Republic of Tanzania

Harare

United Nations Information Centre, Sanders House, 2nd Floor,
corner First Street/Jason Moyo Avenue
(P.O. Box 4408), Harare, Zimbabwe
Telephone: (263 4) 777 060
Fax: (263 4) 750 476
E-mail: *unic@samara.co.zw* (Internet: *www.samara.co.zw/unic*)
Services to: Zimbabwe

Khartoum

United Nations Information Centre, United Nations Compound, Gamma'a Ave
(P.O. Box 1992), Khartoum, Republic of the Sudan
Telephone: (249 11) 773 772/121/123
Fax: (249 11) 773-128, 783-764
E-mail: *unic.sd@undp.org*
Services to: Sudan, Somalia

Kinshasa

United Nations Information Centre, Immeuble Losonia, Boulevard du 30 Juin
(P.O. Box 7248), Kinshasa, Democratic Republic of the Congo
Telephone: (243) 8845537 (Acting Director)
Fax: (243) 8843675
E-mail : *unic.kinshasa@undp.org*
Services to: Democratic Republic of the Congo

Lagos

United Nations Information Centre, 17 Kingsway Road, Ikoyi
(P.O. Box 1068), Lagos, Nigeria
Telephone: (234 1) 269 4886
Fax: (234 1) 269 1934
E-mail: *uniclag@unicnig.org* (Internet: *unicnig.org*)
Services to: Nigeria

Lomé

United Nations Information Centre, 107 Boulevard du 13 Janvier
(P.O. Box 911) Lomé, Togo
Telephone: (228) 221 2306
Fax: (228) 221 2306 (same as telephone no.)
E-mail: *cinutogo@bibway.com*
Services to: Togo, Benin

Lusaka

United Nations Information Centre, Revenue House, Ground floor, Cairo Road
 (P.O. Box 32905), Lusaka 10101, Republic of Zambia
Telephone: (260 1) 228 487, 228 488,
Fax: (260 1) 222 958
E-mail: *unic@zamtel.zm*
Services to: Zambia, Botswana, Malawi, Swaziland

Maseru

United Nations Information Centre, UN Road, UN House
(P.O. Box 301), Maseru 100, Lesotho
Telephone: (266-22) 312 496
Fax: (266-22) 310 042 (UNDP)
E-mail: *unic.maseru@undp.org*
Services to: Lesotho

Monrovia

United Nations Information Centre, UNDP-Simpson Building,
(P.O.Box 0274), Mamba Point, Monrovia, Liberia; GCS P.O. Box 1608,
New York, NY 10163
Telephone: (231) 226 194/195/211
Fax: (231) 205 407 280 (UNIC direct line)
E-mail: *registry.lr@undp.org*
Services to: Liberia

Nairobi

United Nations Information Centre, United Nations Office, Gigiri
(P.O. Box 30552), Nairobi, Kenya
Telephone: (254 20) 623292/3
Fax: (254 20) 624349
E-mail: *Nairobi.UNIC@unon.org* (Internet: *www.unic.nairobi.org*)
Services to: Kenya, Seychelles, Uganda

Ouagadougou

United Nations Information Centre, 14 Avenue Georges Konseiga, Secteur No. 4
(P.O. Box 135), Ouagadougou 01, Burkina Faso
Telephone: (226) 30 60 76/33 65 03
Fax: (226) 31 13 22
E-mail: *cinu.oui@fasonet.bf* (Internet: *www.cinu-burkina.org*)
Services to: Burkina Faso, Chad, Mali, Niger

Pretoria

United Nations Information Centre, Metro Park Building, 351 Schoeman Street
(P.O. Box 12677), Pretoria, South Africa
Telephone: (27 12) 338 5077, 338 5078
Fax: (27 12) 320 1122
E-mail: *unic@un.org.za*
Services to: South Africa

Rabat

United Nations Information Centre, 6 Angle avenue Tarik Ibnov Ziyad and Ruet
(P.O. Box 601), Rabat, Morocco
Telephone: (212 37) 76 86 33
Fax: (212 37) 76 86 77
E-mail: *unicmor@unicmor.ma* (Internet: *www.cinu.org.ma*)
Services to: Morocco

Tripoli

United Nations Information Centre, Muzzafar Al Aftas St., Hay El-Andalous (2)
(P.O. Box 286), Tripoli, Libyan Arab Jamahiriya
Telephone: (218 21) 477 7885
Fax: (218 21) 477 7343
E-mail: *tripoli@un.org*
Services to: Libyan Arab Jamahiriya

Tunis

United Nations Information Centre, 61 Boulevard Bab-Benat
(P.O. Box 863), Tunis, Tunisia
Telephone: (216 71) 560 203
Fax: (216 71) 568 811
E-mail: *onutunis@planet.net* (Internet: *www.onu.org.tn*)
Services to: Tunisia

Windhoek

United Nations Information Centre, 372 Paratus Building, Independence Avenue
(Private Bag 13351), Windhoek, Namibia
Telephone: (264) 61 233034/5
Fax: (264) 61 233036
E-mail: unic@un.na
Services to: Namibia

Yaounde

United Nations Information Centre, Immeuble Tchinda, Rue 2044, derrière camp
SIC TSINGA
(P.O. Box 836), Yaounde, Republic of Cameroon
Telephone: (237) 221 23 67
Fax: (237) 221 23 68
E-mail: *unic.cm@undp.org* (Internet: *www.un.cm/cinu*)
Services to: Cameroon, Gabon, Central African Republic

THE AMERICAS

Asunción

United Nations Information Centre, Avda. Mariscal López esq. Saraví,
Edificio Naciones Unidas
(Casilla de Correo 1107), Asunción, Paraguay
Telephone: (595 21) 614 443
Fax: (595 21) 611 988
E-mail: *unic.py@undp.org*
Services to: Paraguay

Buenos Aires

United Nations Information Centre, Junín 1940, 1er piso, 1113
Buenos Aires, Argentina
Telephone: (54 11) 4803 7671/7672/0738
Fax: (54 11) 4804 7545
E-mail: *buenosaires@unic.org* (Internet: *www.unic.org.ar*)
Services to: Argentina, Uruguay

La Paz

United Nations Information Centre, Calle 14 esq. S. Bustamante,
Edificio Metrobol 11, Calacoto
(P.O. Box 9072), La Paz, Bolivia
Telephone: (591 2) 279 5544 Ext.511/2
Fax: (591 2) 279 5820
E-mail: *unicbol@un.org.bo* (Internet: *www.nu.org.bo/cinu*)
Services to: Bolivia

Lima

United Nations Information Centre, Lord Cochrane 130, San Isidro (L-27)
(P.O. Box 14 0199), Lima, Perú
Telephone: (511) 441 8745, 422 4149, 422 0879
Fax: (511) 441 8735
E-mail: *informes@uniclima.org.pe* (Internet: *www.uniclima.org.pe*)
Services to: Peru

Managua

United Nations Information Centre, Palacio de la Cultura (temporarily inactive)
(P.O. Box 3260), Managua, Nicaragua
Telephone: (505 2) 66 42 53,
Fax: (505 2) 22 23 62
E-mail: *cedoc@sdnnic.org.ni*
Services to: Nicaragua

Mexico City
United Nations Information Centre, Presidente Masaryk 29-2do. piso
11570 México, D.F.
Telephone: (52) 55 52 63 97 00
Fax: (52) 55 52 03 8638
E-mail: *infounic@un.org.mx* (Internet: *www.nacionesunidas.org.mx*)
Services to: Mexico, Cuba, Dominican Republic

Panama City
United Nations Information Centre, Calle Gerardo Ortega y Ave. Samuel Lewis,
Banco Central Hispano Building, 1st floor (P.O. Box 6-9083 El Dorado),
Panamá, Republic of Panama
Telephone: (507) 223 0557
Fax: (507) 223 2198
E-mail: *cinup@cciglobal.net.pa* (Internet: *www.cinup.org*)
Services to: Panama

Port of Spain
United Nations Information Centre, Bretton Hall, 2nd Floor, 16 Victoria Avenue
(P.O. Box 130), Port of Spain, Trinidad, West Indies
Telephone: (868) 623 4813, 623 8438
Fax: (868) 623 4332
E-mail: *unicpos@unicpos.org.tt* (Internet: *www.unicpos.org.tt*)
Services to: Trinidad and Tobago, Antigua and Barbuda, Bahamas, Barbados,
Belize, Dominica, Saint Kitts and Nevis, Grenada, Guyana, Jamaica, Saint Lucia,
Netherlands Antilles, Saint Vincent and the Grenadines, Suriname

Rio de Janeiro
United Nations Information Centre, Palácio Itamaraty, Av. Marechal Floriano 196,
20080-002 Rio de Janeiro, RJ Brazil
Telephone: (55 21) 2253 2211
Fax: (55 21) 2233 5753
E-mail: *infounic@unicrio.org.br* (Internet: *www.unicrio.org.br*)
Services to: Brazil

San Salvador
United Nations Information Centre (temporarily inactive)
Edificio Escalón, 2o. Piso, Paseo General Escalón y 87 Avenida Norte, Colonia
Escalón (P.O. Box 2157), San Salvador, El Salvador
Telephone: (503) 279 1925 (UNDP)
Fax: (503) 279 1929 (UNDP)
Services to: El Salvador

Bogotá
United Nations Information Centre, Calle 100 No. 8A-55, Piso 10
(P.O. Box 058964), Bogotá 2, Colombia
Telephone: (57 1) 257 6044/257 6244
Fax: (57 1) 257 7936
E-mail: *cinucol@columsat.net.co* (Internet: *www.onucolombia.org*)
Services to: Colombia, Ecuador, Venezuela

Santiago
United Nations Information Service, Edificio Naciones Unidas, Comisión
Económica para América Latina y el Caribe, Avenida Dag Hammarskjöld
Casilla 179-D, Santiago, Chile
Telephone: (56 2) 210 2000
Fax: (56 2) 208 0252 (ECLAC)
E-mail: *dpisantiago@eclac.cl* (Internet: *www.eclac.org/prensa*)
Services to: Chile, Economic Commission for Latin America and the Caribbean

Washington, D.C.
United Nations Information Centre, 1775 K Street, N.W., Suite 400
Washington, D.C. 20006, United States
Telephone: (202) 331 8670 ext. 104
Fax: (202) 331 9191
E-mail: *unicdc@unicwash.org* (Internet: *www.unicwash.org*)
Services to: United States of America

ASIA AND THE PACIFIC

Bangkok
United Nations Information Service, United Nations Economic and Social
Commission for Asia and the Pacific (ESCAP), United Nations Building
Rajdamnern Noq, Avenue Bangkok 10200, Thailand
Telephone: 66 (0) 2 288 1866
Fax: 66 (0) 2 288 1052
E-mail: *unisbkk.unescap@un.org* (Internet: *www.unescap.org/unis*)
Services to: Thailand, Cambodia, Lao People's Democratic Republic, Malaysia,
Singapore, Socialist Republic of Viet Nam, Hong Kong, China, ESCAP

Beirut

United Nations Information Center, United Nations Economic and Social Commission for Western Asia (ESCWA), Riad El Solh Square (P.O. Box No.11-8575-4656), Beirut, Lebanon
Telephone: (961 1) 981 301/311/401
Fax: (961 1) 97 04 24 (UNIC)
E-mail: *unic.beirut@un.org* (Internet: *www.escwa.org.lb*)
Services to: Lebanon, Lebanon, Kuwait, Syrian Arab Republic, ESCWA

Colombo

United Nations Information Centre, 202-204 Bauddhaloka Mawatha (P.O. Box 1505), Colombo 7, Sri Lanka
Telephone: (94 1) 580 691
Fax: (94 1) 581 116 (UNDP)
E-mail: anusha.atukorale@undp.org
Services to: Sri Lanka

Dhaka

United Nations Information Centre, IDB Bhaban (14th floor) Begum Rokeya Sharani, Sher-e-Bangla Nagar, (P.O. Box 3658), Dhaka 1000, Bangladesh
Telephone: (880 2) 8117 868
Fax: (880 2) 8112 343
E-mail: *unic.dhaka@undp.org or info.unic@undp.org*
(Internet: *www.unicdhaka.org*)
Services to: Bangladesh

Islamabad

United Nations Information Centre, House No. 26, 88th Street, G-6/3 (P.O. Box 1107), Islamabad, Pakistan
Telephone: (92 51) 2270 610/2281 012/2123 976
Fax: (92 51) 271 856
E-mail: *unic@isb.comsats.net.pk* (Internet: *www.un.org.pk/unic/unic.htm*)
Services to: Pakistan

Jakarta

United Nations Information Centre, Gedung Surya, 14th floor, Jl. M.H. Thamrin Kavling 9, Jakarta, Indonesia
Telephone: (62 21) 3983-1014
Fax: (62 21) 380 0274
E-mail: *unicjak@cbn.net.id*
Services to: Indonesia

Kabul

United Nations Information Centre (temporarily inactive)
Shah Mahmoud Ghazi Watt (P.O. Box 5), Kabul, Afghanistan
Telephone: 24437/22684
Services to: Afghanistan

Kathmandu

United Nations Information Centre, (P.O. Box 107) Pulchowk,
Patan, Kathmandu, Nepal
Telephone: (977 1) 524 366 (Director); (977 1) 523-200 ext. 1600
Fax: (977 1) 543 723; (977 1) 523 911/986 (UNDP)
E-mail: *registry.np@undp.org*
Services to: Nepal

Manama

United Nations Information Centre, United Nations House, Bldg. 69 Road 1901,
Segaya (P.O. Box 26004), Manama 319, Bahrain
Telephone: (973) 311 676/311 600 (UN House)
Fax: (973) 311 692
E-mail: *unic.bahrain@undp.org*
Services to: Bahrain, Qatar, United Arab Emirates

Manila

United Nations Information Centre, NEDA Building, 106 Amorsolo Street,
Legaspi Village, Makati City (P.O. Box 7285 ADC (DAPO) Pasay City)
Metro Manila, Philippines
Telephone: (63 2) 892 0611 through 25, Exts. 255 258
Fax: (63 2) 816 3011, 817 8539
E-mail: *infocentre@unicmanila.org*
Services to: Philippines, Papua New Guinea, Solomon Islands

New Delhi

United Nations Information Centre, 55 Lodi Estate, New Delhi-110003, India
Telephone: (91 11) 2462 88 77
Fax: (91 11) 2462 0293
E-mail: *feodor@giasdl01.vsnl.net.in* (Internet: *www.unic.org.in*)
Services to: India, Bhutan

Sana'a

United Nations Information Centre, Handhal Street, 5, Al-Boniya Area
(P.O. Box 237), Sana'a, Republic of Yemen
Telephone: (967 1) 274 000/041
Fax: (967 1) 274 043
E-mail: *unicyem@y.net.ye*
Services to: Yemen

Sydney

United Nations Information Centre, 46-48 York Street, 5th Floor
(GPO Box 4045), Sydney, NSW, 2001 Australia
Telephone: (61 2) 9262-5111
Fax: (61 2) 9262 5886
E-mail: *unic@un.org.au* (Internet: *www.un.org.au*)
Services to: Australia, Fiji, Kiribati, Nauru, New Zealand, Tonga, Tuvalu,
Vanuatu, Western Samoa

Tehran

United Nations Information Centre, 185 Ghaem Magham Farahani Ave,
Tehran 15868 (P.O. Box 15875-4557, Tehran), Islamic Republic of Iran
Telephone: (98 21) 873 1534
Fax: (98 21) 204 4523
E-mail: *unic@unic.un.org.ir* (Internet: *www.unic-ir.org*)
Services to: Iran

Tokyo

United Nations Information Centre, UNU Building, 8th Floor,
53-70, Jingumae 5-chome, Shibuya-ku, Tokyo 150, Japan
Telephone: (81 3) 5467 4451
Fax: (81 3) 5467 4455
E-mail: *unic@untokyo.jp* (Internet: *www.unic.or.jp*)
Services to: Japan

Yangon

United Nations Information Centre, 6 Natmauk Road, Yangon, Myanmar
Telephone: (95 1) 292 637
Fax: (95 1) 544 531
E-mail: *unic.myanmar@undp.org*
Services to: Myanmar

EUROPE

Ankara
United Nations Information Centre, 2 Cadde No. 11, (P.K. 407)
06610 Cankaya, Ankara, Turkey
Telephone: (90 312) 454 1051/2/3
Fax: (90 312) 496 14 99
E-mail: *unic@un.org.tr* (Internet: *www.un.org.tr/unic.html*)
Services to: Turkey

Athens
UNIC Athens was closed on 31 December 2003. For service to Greece, contact the Regional United Nations Information Center in Brussels.

Bonn
UNIC Bonn was closed on 31 December 2003. For service to Germany, contact the Regional United Nations Information Center in Brussels.

Brussels
Regional United Nations Information Centre
Résidence Palace, 155, rue de la Loi
1040 Brussels, Belgium
Telephone: (32 2) 289 2890
Fax: (32 2) 502 4061
E-mail: *unic@unbenelux.org*   (Internet: *www.unbenelux.org*)
Services to: Belgium, Cyprus, Denmark, Finland, France, Germany, Greece, Holy See, Iceland, Ireland, Italy, Luxembourg, Malta, the Netherlands, Norway, Portugal, San Marino, Spain, Sweden, United Kingdom, European Union

Bucharest
United Nations Information Centre, c/o UN House,
48A Primaverii Blvd. 011975 1, (P.O.Box 1-701), Bucharest, Romania
Telephone: (40 21) 201-78-77/78/79
Fax: (40 21) 201 78 80
E-mail: *unic@undp.ro*
Services to: Romania

Copenhagen
UNIC Copenhagen was closed on 31 December 2003. For service to Denmark, Finland, Iceland, Norway and Sweden, contact the Regional United Nations Information Center in Brussels.

Geneva

United Nations Information Service, UN Office at Geneva, Palais des Nations, 1211 Geneva 10, Switzerland
Telephone: (41 22) 917 2300
Fax: (41 22) 917 0030 (Director)
E-mail: *presse_geneve@unog.ch* (Internet: *www.unog.ch/frames/unis/unis1.htm*)
Services to: Switzerland, Bulgaria

Lisbon

UNIC Lisbon was closed on 31 December 2003. For service to Portugal, contact the Regional United Nations Information Center in Brussels.

London

UNIC London was closed on 31 December 2003. For service to United Kingdom and Ireland, contact the Regional United Nations Information Center in Brussels.

Madrid

UNIC Madrid was closed on 31 December 2003. For service to Spain, contact the Regional United Nations Information Center in Brussels.

Moscow

United Nations Information Centre, 4/16 Glazovsky Pereulok, Moscow 121002, Russian Federation
Telephone: (7 095) 241 2894, (7 095) 241 2537
Fax: (7 095) 230 2138
E-mail: *dpi-moscow@unic.ru* (Internet: *www.unic.ru*)
Services to: Russian Federation

Paris

UNIC Paris was closed on 31 December 2003. For service to France, contact the Regional United Nations Information Center in Brussels.

Prague

United Nations Information Centre, nam. Kinskych 6, 15000 Prague 5, Czech Republic
Telephone: (420) 257 199 831/32
Fax: (420) 257 31 6761
E-mail: *unicprg@terminal.cz* (Internet: *www.unicprague.cz*)
Services to: Czech Republic

Rome

UNIC Rome was closed on 31 December 2003. For service to Italy, contact the Regional United Nations Information Center in Brussels.

Vienna

United Nations Information Service, Vienna International Centre,
Wagramer Strasse 5, A-1220 Vienna
(UN Office at Vienna, P.O. Box 500, A-1400 Vienna), Austria
Telephone: (43 1) 26060 4666/5676/4677
Fax: (43 1) 26060 5899
E-mail: *unis@unisvienna.org*   (Internet: *www.unis.unvienna.org*)
Services to: Austria, Hungary, Slovakia, Slovenia

Warsaw

United Nations Information Centre, Al. Niepodleglosci 186, 00-608 Warszawa
(P.O. Box 1, 02-514) Warsaw 12, Poland
Telephone: (48 22) 825 57 84
Fax: (48 22) 825 7706
E-mail: *unic.pl@undp.org*   (Internet: *www.unic.un.org.pl*)
Services to: Poland

OFFICES IN THE COMMONWEALTH OF INDEPENDENT STATES AND ERITREA

Almaty

United Nations Office, 67 Tole Bi, 480091 Almaty, Kazakhstan
Telephone: (7 3272) 582 643/695-327
Fax: (7 3272) 582 645
E-mail: *Vladimir.polyakov@undp.org* or *registry.kz@undp.org*
Services to: Kazakhstan

Asmara

United Nations Office, Andinet Street, Zone 4 Admin. 07
Airport Road, (near Expo), Asmara, Eritrea
Telephone: (291 1) 15 18 86
Fax: (291 1) 15 11 66
E-mail: *Michael.araia@undp.org*
Services to: Eritrea

Baku

United Nations Office, 3 UN 50th Anniversary, Baku 1001, Azerbaijan
Telephone: (99412) 98 98 88/92 19 39
Fax: (99412) 98 32 35
E-mail: *dpi@un-az.org*   (Internet: *www.un-az.org/dpi*)
Services to: Azerbaijan

Kiev

United Nations Office, 1 Klovsky Uzviz, 1, Kiev 252021, Ukraine
Telephone: (380 44) 253 93 63
Fax: (380 44) 253 26 07
E-mail: *registry@un.kiev.ua* (Internet: *www.un.kiev.ua*)
Services to: Ukraine

Minsk

United Nations Office, 17 Kirov Street, 6th Floor 220050 Minsk, Belarus
Telephone: (375 17) 227 38 17
Fax: (375 17) 226 03 40
E-mail: *dpi_unit@undp.org* (Internet: *www.un.minsk.by/dpi/dpi_r.html*)
Services to: Belarus

Tashkent

United Nations Office, 4 Taras Shevchenko St., Tashkent 700029, Uzbekistan
Telephone: (998 71) 133 0977/139 4835
Fax: (998 71) 133 6965
E-mail: *registry.uz@undp.org* (Internet: *www.undp.uz*)
Services to: Uzbekistan
Tbilisi

United Nations Office, Eristavi St. 9, Tbilisi 380079, Republic of Georgia
Telephone: (995 32) 99 85 58 25 11 26/28/29/31 ext.132
Fax: (1 995 32) 2502 71 or 72
E-mail: registry.ge@undp.org
Services to: Georgia

Yerevan

United Nations Office, 14 Karl Libknekht Street, 1st floor,
375010 Yerevan, Armenia
Telephone: (374 1) 560 212/580-032
Fax: (374 1) 561 406
E-mail: *dpi@undpi.am* (Internet: *www.undpi.am*)
Services to: Armenia

This selection of United Nations publications and products can be obtained from the Organization, some at no charge and other as sales items. The letters in parentheses at the end of each entry refer to where the publications can be obtained (*see Where to Order, page 342*).

Periodicals

UN Chronicle. UN/DPI. E/A/C/F/R/S. Annual subscription $20 (a)

Quarterly magazine providing coverage of the work of the UN and its agencies.

Africa Recovery. UN/DPI. E/F. Annual subscription: $20 (a)

Quarterly magazine covering issues of economic and social reform in Africa and international cooperation for development.

Development Update. UN/DPI. Free

Bi-monthly newsletter with updates on the development activities of the UN system.

General

Charter of the United Nations. UN/DPI. DPI/511. E/A/C/F/R/S. $3

Yearbook of the United Nations. 1554 pp. Sales No. E.03.I.1. ISBN: 92-1-100857-3. E. $150.00 (a)

The most comprehensive reference book on all aspects of the work of the UN system. Published annually, it provides a detailed account of UN activities in a given calendar year.

Discovering the United Nations. UN/DPI. DPI/2006. E. $5 (a)

Written especially for children, this booklet teaches about the UN through questions and answers, activity proposals and quizzes.

Understanding the United Nations. The Official Guidebook. UN/DPI. 80 pp. Sales No. E.97.I.8. ISBN: 92-1-100536-1. E. $14.95 (a)

A photographic tour of the UN daily working, at Headquarters and all over the world.

"We the Peoples." The Role of the United Nations in the 21st Century, by Secretary-General Kofi Annan. 2000. 80pp. Sales No. 00.I.16. ISBN: 9211008441. E/F. $10.00 (a)

Examines the challenges facing the world community and outlines a vision for the UN in the new century.

The United Nations in Our Daily Lives. 1998. 116 pp. Sales No. E.98.I.11. ISBN: 92-1-1-100654-6. E/F. $5.00 (a)

In a story format designed for a general audience, illustrates the many ways in which the UN is a part of everyone's life and how much we rely on its programmes.

Colouring Book: The United Nations in our Daily Lives. 1999. 64 pp. Sales No. E/F.GV.99.0.9. ISBN: 92-1-000134-6. $7.50 (a)

Through short descriptions and pictures, this book introduces children to the United Nations, its agencies and its programmes, and denotes the part they play in everyone's life. This activity book provides scenes of the issues discussed for children to colour. This is the English/French version of the Coloring Book.

Annual reports

World Economic and Social Survey: Trends and Policies in the World Economy. United Nations E/F/S. $60 (a)

Authoritative and reliable, it offers unique insight and commentary on current trends and policies in the world economy. Issued by the UN Department of Economic and Social Affairs.

Trade and Development Report. UN Conference on Trade and Development. E/F. $45 (a)

It makes compelling reading for those seeking answers to some of the most pressing policy challenges in today's rapidly changing global economy.

World Investment Report. UN Conference on Trade and Development. E. $49 (a)

The most up-to-date and comprehensive source of information as well as analysis regarding foreign direct investment.

The Least Developed Countries Report. UN Conference on Trade and Development. E/F. $45 (a)

The most comprehensive and authoritative source of socio-economic analysis and data on the world's 48 least developed countries.

Human Development Report. UN Development Programme. E/F/S/A/R. $22.95 (a)

A comprehensive guide to global human development: it contains thought-provoking analyses of major issues, updated Human Development Indicators that compare the relative levels of human development of over 175 countries, and agendas to help transform development priorities.

The State of the World's Children. UNICEF. E/F/S/A and other languages. $12.95. Free summary available from UNICEF (a)

Draws international attention to the challenges facing children and presses for action to promote their well-being.

The State of the World Population. UN Population Fund. E/F/S/A and other languages. $12.50 (a)

Annual report on population issues and their impact on world development.

World Health Report. World Health Organization. Geneva. E/F/S/A/C/R. (b)

Takes an expert look at health trends, assesses the global situation and predicts how health conditions, diseases, and the tools for managing them will evolve.

World Development Report. World Bank/Oxford University Press. $25.95. E/F/S. (c)

Produced by the World Bank, it focuses on major development issues facing policy-makers worldwide. Includes selected World Development Indicators.

World Economic Outlook. International Monetary Fund. E/F/S/A. (d)

Global economic survey published twice a year (May and October).

Peace and security

The Blue Helmets. UN/DPI. 1996. 820 pp. DPI/1800. Sales No. E.96.I.14. ISBN: 92-1-100611-2. E/F. $29.95 (a)

A review of UN peacekeeping, with a comprehensive account of peacekeeping operations from their inception in 1948 up to early 1996.

UN Peacekeeping: 50 Years (1948-1998). UN/DPI. 1998. 88 pages. DPI/2004. E/F/S.

An overview of five decades of peacekeeping operations.

United Nations Disarmament Yearbook. E/F/S. $55 (a)

Annual publication reviewing the main developments and negotiations during the year in all areas of disarmament

Economic and Social

The World's Women 2000: Trends and Statistics. 2000. 200 pp. Sales No. E. 00.XVII.14. ISBN: 92-1-161428-7. E/F/S. $16.95. (a)

A unique compilation of the latest data documenting progress for women worldwide in six areas: health, human rights and political decision-making, and families.

Global Environment Outlook 2002. UNEP/Earthscan Publications Ltd. 416 pp. Sales No: E. 02.III.D.19. ISBN: 9280720872. E/F/S. $37.50 (a)

The UN Environment Programme's comprehensive review and analysis of environmental conditions around the world.

The World Conferences - Developing Priorities for the 21st Century. UN/DPI. 1997. 112 pp. Sales No. E.97.I.5. ISBN: 92-1-100631-7. E/F/S. $12.00 (a)

Provides a broad perspective on the recommendations and current actions flowing from the conferences on Children, Human Rights, Social Development, Crime, Environment, Women, Population, Food, Human Settlements, Small Islands, Trade and Natural Disasters.

World Labour Report 2000. Income security and social protection in a changing world. International Labour Office. 2000. 321 pp. ISBN: 92-2-110831-7. E/F/S. $34.95. (e)

Examines the changing context in which women and men are trying to achieve income security for themselves and their families.

Everybody Counts, Every Drop Matters. UN/DPI. 2003. 128pp. DPI/2332 Sales No. E.04.I.3. ISBN: 92-1-100931-6. E. $15. (a)

This classroom resource guide is designed to inform students about the world's water resources and get them involved in preservation. Bibliography and resources for further research are also provided.

Human Rights

Human Rights Today: a United Nations Priority. UN/DPI. 1998. 74 pp. Sales No. E.98.I.22. ISBN: 92-1-100796-6. E/F/S. $10. (a)

Outlines United Nations action in the field to ensure rights for all, and provides a blueprint of the work of the various intergovernmental human rights bodies.

Human Rights: A Compilation of International Instruments. 950 pp. Sales No. 94.XIV.1. ISBN: 92-1-154099-2. E/F/S. $55. (a)

This two-volume set constitutes a comprehensive catalogue of the existing human rights instruments adopted at both universal and regional levels.

WHERE TO ORDER

(a)   For North America, Latin America and the Caribbean and Asia and the Pacific: United Nations Publications, Room DC2-853, 2 UN Plaza, New York, NY 10017, USA. Telephone: (212) 963 8302, Toll Free 1 800 253 9646 (North America only). Fax: (212) 963 3489. E-mail: *publications@un.org*. Internet: *www.un.org/publications*.

For Europe, Africa and the Middle East: United Nations Publications, Sales Office and Bookshop, CH-1211, Geneva 10, Switzerland. Telephone: (41 22) 917 2614, Fax: (41 22) 917 0027, E-mail: *unpubli@unog.ch*. Internet: *www.un.org/publications*.

(b)   World Health Organization (WHO):
       Distribution and Sales, 20 Avenue Appia, CH 1211 Geneva 27, Switzerland.
       Tel.: (41 22) 791 2476. Fax: (41 22) 791 4857. E-mail: *publications@who.ch*
       In the USA: WHO Publications, 49 Sheridan Ave., Albany, NY 12210. Tel:
       (518) 436 9686, E-mail: *QCORP@compuserve.com*.

(c)   World Bank:
       The World Bank, P.O. Box 960, Herndon, VA 20172-0960, USA.
       Tel. (703) 661 1580 or (800) 645 7247. Fax (703) 661 1501.
       E-mail: *books@worldbank.org*

(d)   International Monetary Fund (IMF)
       Publication Services, Catalog Orders, 700 19th Street, NW, Washington, D.C.
       20431, U.S.A. Tel.: (202) 623 7430. Fax: (202) 623 7201. E-mail: *pubweb@imf.org*

(e)   International Labour Office (ILO):
       ILO Publications, 4 route des Morillons, CH-1211 Geneva 22, Switzerland.
       Tel.: (41 22) 799 7301. Fax: (41 22) 798 6358. E-mail: *pubvente@ilo.org*

United Nations Bookshops

United Nations, Concourse Level, First Ave. & 42nd St., New York, NY 10017
Tel.: (212) 963 7680, 1 800 553 3210 (US and Canada), Fax: (212) 963 4910,
E-mail: *bookshop@un.org*

United Nations, Palais des Nations, Door 40 and Door 6, CH-1211 Geneva 10,
Switzerland, Tel.: (41 22) 917 2613/14, Fax: (41 22) 917 0027
E-mail: *unipubli@unog.ch*

INDEX

A

acid rain, 216

administration of justice, 239

Administrative Committee on Coordination, 21

Advisory Board on Disarmament Matters, 125

Advisory Committee on Administrative and Budgetary Questions, 19

ageing, 170, 197

Agenda 21, 184, 207, 208, 209, 208–9, 210

agricultural development, 33, 34, 50, 156, 157, 156–58, 176, 216

AIDS, 17, 19, 39, 41, 42, 82, 141, 147, 148, 149, 150, 170, 174, 175, 177, 178, 180, 182, 185, 189, 190, 193, 194, 195, 200, 204, 258, 259

air transport, 56, 160, 161

apartheid, 81, 82, 241, 242

Arbitration and Media Centre, 167

aviation, international, 160–61

B

Bill and Melinda Gates Foundation, 181

biodiversity, pollution and overfishing, 216–17

biological diversity, 210, 273, 274

biological weapons, 26, 112, 122, 128, 129

BONUCA, 78, 89, 90

Bretton Woods Conference, 52. *See* World Bank Group

budget of the United Nations, 19–20

building peace through development. *See* peace-building

C

carbon dioxide emissions, 213, 214, 222

CEB, 21, 31

Central Emergency Revolving Fund, 255

Centre for International Crime Prevention, 248

chemical weapons, 62, 122, 124, 129

Chief Executives Board for Coordination, 21

children, 42, 43, 77, 108, 110, 123, 130, 131, 133, 144, 171, 174, 175, 177, 179, 180, 184, 185, 189, 195, 196, 197, 207, 208, 227, 232, 234, 237, 239, 240, 248, 256, 257, 277

children in war, 258-9

children, promoting their rights, 192–94

children, special session on, 193

cities, 109, 178, 181, 182, 183, 184

civil aviation, 56, 160, 161

civil society, 11, 13, 15, 18, 19, 26, 28, 29, 32, 36, 37, 45, 49, 90, 101, 122, 130, 136, 142, 146, 150, 154, 173, 174, 181, 183, 184, 188, 201, 202, 205, 208, 211, 258

climate. *See* weather, climate and water

climate change and global warming, 213–14

Commission for Social Development, 12, 172, 195

Commission on Crime Prevention and Criminal Justice, 12, 202, 248

Commission on Human Rights, 12, 45, 233, 234, 235, 237, 238, 243, 245, 246

Commission on Narcotic Drugs, 12, 200

IBRD. *See* World Bank Group

ICAO, 56, 160, 161, 279

ICSID. *See* World Bank Group

IDA. *See* World Bank Group

IFAD, 59, 60, 146, 147, 157, 158, 176, 177, 216, 246

IFC. *See* World Bank Group

ILO, 12, 49, 50, 148, 159, 160, 169, 180, 192, 196, 240, 243, 244, 259

IMF, 52, 53, 150, 151, 152, 203

immunization, 178, 179, 194, 257

IMO, 56, 57, 161, 162, 163, 217, 218, 274, 279

indigenous peoples, 60, 197–98, 207, 208, 238, 246

industrial development, 60, 158–59

infectious diseases, 129, 178, 181

information. *See* communication and information

Information and Communication Technologies Task Force, 205

INSTRAW, 47, 192

intellectual property, 59, 166, 167, 166–67

Inter-Agency Standing Committee, 27, 28, 256

Intergovernmental Panel on Climate Change, 213, 219

interim administrators. *See* peace-building

internally displaced persons, assistance to, 262

International Atomic Energy Agency, 10, 61, 112, 127, 128, 222, 279

International Bank for Reconstruction and Development (IBRD). *See* World Bank Group

International Bill of Rights, 228

International Centre for Settlement of Investment Disputes (ICSID). *See* World Bank Group

International Centre for Theoretical Physics, 223

International Civil Aviation Organization, 56, 160, 279

International Civilian Mission in Haiti (MICIVIH), 100

International Civilian Support Mission in Haiti, 100

International Court of Justice, 6, 7, 9, 13–14, 25, 90, 105, 267, 292

jurisdiction, 14

membership, 14

International Covenant on Civil and Political Rights, 230

International Covenant on Economic, Social and Cultural Rights, 228–30

International Criminal Court, 259, 277, 278, 279

International Criminal Tribunal for Rwanda, 84, 278

International Criminal Tribunal for Rwanda (ICTR), 35

International Criminal Tribunal for the former Yugoslavia, 122

International Criminal Tribunal for the Former Yugoslavia (ICTY), 35

International Development Association (IDA). See World Bank Group

International Finance Corporation (IFC). *See* World Bank Group

International Fund for Agricultural Development, 59, 146, 157, 176

International Institute for Labour Studies, 50, 160

International Labour Conference, 50, 159, 160, 240

International Labour Organization, 3, 49, 159, 240, 244

International Law Commission, 25, 269, 279

international law, overview, 267

Subcommission on Prevention of
Discrimination and Protection of
Minorities, 234
Subcommission on the Promotion and
Protection of Human Rights, 234
sustainable development, 14, 17, 28, 33,
36, 38, 40, 46, 51, 54, 61, 137, 141,
144, 146, 147, 148, 150, 154, 174,
184, 186, 188, 206–11, 215, 216,
221, 222, 264
changing human behaviour, 209
Sustainable Development, World
Summit on, 207, 209–10
sustainable forest management, 215

T

technical assistance, 33, 44, 55, 57, 58,
61, 79, 98, 137, 147, 149, 150, 152,
156, 165, 166, 169, 192, 201, 203,
235, 248
technical cooperation, 36, 37, 47, 50,
52, 61, 134, 154, 155, 156, 158, 159,
160, 161, 163, 202, 221–22, 239,
244
telecommunications, 57, 64, 123, 150,
161, 163–65
terrorism, 10, 37, 38, 48, 67, 73, 106,
199, 200, 202, 203, 267, 279–80
Timor-Leste, 20, 68, 79, 80, 149, 262,
277, 285, 290–92
torture, 88, 229, 230, 231, 232, 234,
237, 238, 246
toxic chemicals, 212
trade and development, 154–56
tribunals, international, 278–79
Trusteeship Council, 6, 7, 13, 285
tuberculosis. See "malaria, SARS and
tuberculosis"
Twenty-twenty (20/20) Initiative, 193

U

UN action for peace in Africa, 81–99
Africa, a UN priority, 82
Angola, 81–83
Burundi, 85–87
Cameroon-Nigeria boundary
dispute, 90–91
Côte d'Ivoire, 91–93
Democratic Republic of the Congo
(DRC), 87–89
Ethiopia and Eritrea, 98–99
Guinea-Bissau, 95–96
Liberia, 93–95
Sierra Leone, 96–98
Southern Africa, 81
West Africa, 90
UN action for peace in Asia and the
Pacific, 101–18
Afghanistan, 105–11
Bougainville/Papua New Guinea,
118
Cambodia, 117
India and Pakistan, 115–16
Iraq, 111–15
Lebanon, 103
Middle East, 101–5
Middle East "Road Map", 104–5
Middle East peace process, 103–5
Tajikistan, 116–17
UN action for peace in Europe, 118–22
Balkans, 120–22
Cyprus, 118–19
Georgia, 119
Kosovo, 121–22
UN action for peace in the Americas,
99–101
Central America, 99
Colombia, 101
El Salvador, 99–100

355